Driving Michigan

Driving Michigan

Mile by Mile on I-75

Leslie Mertz

Arbutus Press, Traverse City, MI

Travel
ISBN   1-933926-08-2
ISBN 13   976-1-933926-08-7

Photo Credits—Page 8: Lewis Cass, Library of Congress Prints and Photographs Online Catalog (PPOC), circa 1850; President James Monroe, Library of Congress PPOC; General George Armstrong Custer, University of Texas Libraries; Sitting Bull, Library of Congress PPOC, D.F. Barry, circa 1885.

Manufactured in the United States of America
First Edition/First Printing

Interior design and layout by Julie Phinney, Richmond, Vermont
   (802-434-6654 – mjphinney@msn.com)

To the army of dedicated state employees who help to make Michigan a truly spectacular state.

And also to my husband who makes every trip on I-75 one to remember.

Contents

Depending on whether you're heading north or south, you are either entering or leaving a unique state. Geographically, Michigan is distinctive for many reasons, but most notably for its two peninsulas which together touch four of the five Great Lakes. This arrangement affects the state's weather, its crops, the distribution of its animals, and its history.

Speaking of history, Michigan has many, many stories to tell, so let's start here at the border of Michigan and Ohio. It may be hard to imagine now, but the people on each side of the border weren't always good neighbors. In 1835, two years before Michigan gained statehood, the Michigan territory went to battle with its neighbor to the south over a stretch of land called the "Toledo strip" which amounted to about 470 square miles in size.

The prize wasn't Toledo, but the mouth of the Maumee River, which runs from Lake Erie southwest

Michigan's first governor.

At the Border

through what is now the city of Toledo, Ohio. Each side wanted to cash in on a proposed canal project that would flow from the Maumee.

Although the fight for the tract of land was an almost completely non-violent one, people called the conflict the Ohio War. It even garnered a few songs. One carried a verse that referred to two Michigan leaders, Territorial Governor Stevens T. Mason and Michigan Brig. Gen. Joseph Brown, as well as the nickname for Michigan residents, the Wolverines:

> "We held a general muster;
> we trained till past sundown.
> At the head of all the Wolverines
> marched Mason and old Brown:
> a valiant-hearted general,
> a governor likewise,
> a set of jovial Wolverines
> to bung* Ohio's eyes."

BRAINBUSTERS

Basic: Before Michigan was a state, it was a territory. What was the territory's first capital city?

Intermediate: Before the Michigan Territory was named, the land was part of the much bigger Northwest Territory. The Northwest Territory included land now in which six states?

Advanced: The first governor of the state of Michigan (see photo) was only in his mid-20s when he took office. What was his name?

See next page for answers.

---

*The phrase "bung Ohio's eyes" in the last line of the song means to shut them. Bung refers to the stopper used to seal beer kegs.

The Ohio War remained mostly a battle of words between the two states' politicians, until a little incident in a tavern. There, an argument escalated into a knife fight, and an Ohio man stabbed a Michigan sheriff. The sheriff survived, but the incident gained minor historical prominence as the only blood-drawing event of the Ohio War. Perhaps the strangest thing about the scuffle was the Ohioan's name: Two Stickney. Two was the second son born to the Stickney family. His older brother was named—what else?—One.

Exit 6

The Ohio War had barely begun when Congress and President Andrew Jackson stepped in to put an end to it. To receive statehood, President Jackson and the Congress insisted that Michigan give up the Toledo Strip in exchange for the western three-quarters of the Upper Peninsula, which was formerly part of the Northwest Territory. A good many people thought Michigan was getting the raw end of the deal, including the state's politicians, who called the U.P. "a sterile region on the shores of Lake Superior, destined by soil and climate to remain forever a wilderness." *The Detroit Free Press* agreed, describing it as a "region of perpetual snows." (While snow does have a way of sticking around in the U.P.—small, melting piles of snow in the woods well into May and early snowfalls in September aren't out of the question—it is hardly perpetual.)

Despite the initial disappointment with the U.P. trade, Michigan soon saw the benefits of the northern wilderness. The region showed its economic worth within a few decades when mining and forestry enterprises swept through the peninsula. On the other hand, the canal venture on the Maumee River—the project that started the skirmish between the Michigan territory and Ohio in the first place—never materialized.

Exit 6

This exit leads to Luna Pier, which sits just east of I-75 on Lake Erie. *Luna* is the Latin word for moon. During the Big Band era of the 1940s,

THE ANSWERS

The Northwest Territory covered the area northwest of the Ohio River, and included land now in *Michigan, Ohio, Wisconsin, Indiana, Illinois,* and part of *Minnesota.* Michigan gained the status of territory in 1805 with *Detroit* named as its capital.

In 1834, 22-year-old *Stevens T. Mason* became the acting governor of the territory, after already serving three years as acting territorial secretary. When Michigan gained statehood in 1837, he became the state's first governor and served from 1837–1839. Michigan was much different then than it is now. Detroit was the only city, and the state's entire population added up to fewer than 175,000 people—just three people per square mile of land. The current population density of the state is about 178 people per square mile as of 2006.

the nights were alive on a dance pier here on the lake. The pier drew many famous bands that performed for large crowds. The dance pier burned in 1954, but the city of Luna Pier remains a small community and resort destination with its own half-mile-long, crescent-moon shaped pier jutting from a sandy shoreline into the blue waters of Lake Erie.

Lake Erie is one of the four Great Lakes surrounding Michigan. In fact, the name Michigan may come from an Ojibwe/Algonquin Indian word for Great Lakes or "big water." or possibly "swimming turtle." The latter presumably arises from a certain offshore vantage point in northern Michigan, where the outline of the land rising out of one of the Great Lakes looks like a swimming turtle.

Although Lake Erie is the smallest of the Great Lakes in volume, it is still a huge freshwater body. The lake holds 116 cubic miles of water. In other words, the lake's water would fill a box 5 miles wide, 5 miles long, and 4.5 miles tall. The far eastern shores of this long, comparatively thin lake flow east beyond the Ohio border, past the northwestern tip of Pennsylvania, and all the way to Buffalo, N.Y.

Michigan has miles of beautiful shoreline along the four Great Lakes within its borders. (Leslie Mertz)

shops legally sell them to buyers—and some of the buyers come from Michigan.

Mile Markers 9–13

Along this stretch of road, southbound travelers will likely see numerous billboards advertising the sale of fireworks in Ohio. While Michigan state law prohibits the general public from using projectile and loud fireworks, including bottle rockets, mortars, and firecrackers, several Ohio

BRAINBUSTERS

Basic: Michigan's borders extend well into the Great Lakes, giving the state a total size of nearly 100,000 square miles (that would cover an area 250 miles long and 400 miles wide!). How much of that 100,000 miles is water surface: 20 percent (one-fifth), 40 percent (two-fifths), or 60 percent (three-fifths)?

Intermediate: Other states include water surface within their boundaries. Name the three states with the most water surface.

Advanced: Considering land mass only, name the five largest states east of the Mississippi.

See page 5 for answers.

3

Michigan's boundaries extend into the Great Lakes.

pal firework displays held each year in communities throughout the state. For example, the International Freedom Festival, hosted by Detroit and Windsor, Ontario, is one of the most spectacular in the nation, and draws hundreds of thousands of onlookers to the cities, which are located across from one another on the Canadian and U.S. sides of the Detroit River. Pyrotechnic experts shoot fireworks from barges anchored in the river while spectators ooh and ahh from vantage spots on blankets and lawn chairs along the shorelines, from the decks of boats, and from parties inside the high-rise office buildings that line the river.

Regardless of where the fireworks originate, Michigan's neighborhoods are filled with sometimes-unlawful explosions come Independence Day. These small, private exhibits, however, pale in comparison to the large munici-

In Michigan, fireworks aren't limited to just the nights around the Fourth of July. Urban and rural communities host festivals throughout the year, and many punctuate the evenings with fireworks. Even

Satellite view of Michigan and the Great Lakes taken March 6, 2000. (NOAA, Great Lakes Environmental Research Laboratory)

in January and February, numerous northern Michigan towns make fireworks displays part of their wintertime festivals. The mid-air explosions in these displays are particularly dazzling against the contrasting background of a jet-black, star-filled sky and soft, white snow drifts.

Exit 13

Just south of this exit, the 100-mile-long River Raisin crosses I-75. Named for the abundance of wild grapes (in French, *raisin*) on its banks, the river is layered with salt, sand, sandstone, limestone, and various minerals, all of which have been used commercially: The sand and sandstone create glass; the salts become road salt and assorted cleansers; and the limestone yields lime for mortar and cement. A chief component of sand is silica, which is now used as the primary material in making the

Great egret, also called common egret. (Dr. Thomas G. Barnes/U.S. Fish and Wildlife Service)

Exit 13

THE ANSWERS

Michigan has 56,800 square miles* of land surface and about 40,000 square miles of water surface, for a total land and water size of about 96,800 square miles. That means about *40 percent, or two-fifths*, of the total size is water surface. With its combined land and water mass, Michigan is the largest state east of the Mississippi River, and the eleventh largest out of all 50 states.

The three states with the largest water surface contained in their boundaries are:

- *Alaska* with 86,000 square miles of water surface;
- *Michigan* with 40,000; and
- *Florida* with almost 12,000.

In land mass only,* the five largest states east of the Mississippi are:

- *Georgia*, about 58,000 square miles;
- *Michigan*, 56,800 square miles
- *Illinois*, 55,600 square miles;
- *Wisconsin*, 54,300 square miles; and
- *Florida*, 53,900 square miles.

---

*According to the U.S. Census Bureau.

Great blue heron. (Steve Hillebrand/U.S. Fish and Wildlife Service)

semiconductor chips found in computers, cars and a wide variety of electronic gadgets.

Just north of Exit 13 on the southbound side of I-75, you can see great egrets (see photo on page 5) in this marsh for much of the year. These large, white, wading birds can grow to more than 3 feet in length from the tips of their bills to the ends of their tail feathers. They have sweeping, curved necks; long, yellow bills; and tall, black legs. During the breeding season, a great egret's bill turns orange, and the bird grows plumes that extend past its rump.

You may also see a great blue heron here. Like the egrets, which are in the same family as the herons, great blue herons hold their necks in an S-shape when they fly, and let their legs and feet hang behind them. These impressive, gray birds are even larger than the great egrets, growing to around 4 feet long from bill tip to tail tip.

Exit 15

This exit leads to downtown Monroe and connects to the historical Dixie Highway.

A good length of Dixie Highway actually runs along a part of the Saginaw Trail, a footpath the Ojibwe, Potawatomi and Ottawa Indians used to travel from what is now Detroit north through Pontiac, Flint and Saginaw. Both the U.S. 10 and U.S. 127 (formerly known as U.S. 27) expressways also follow parts of the trail.

Like many Michigan cities, Monroe may be fairly tame now, but it had a wild past. Begun as a settlement of Potawatomi Indians (pronounced pot-uh-WOTT-oh-mee), it became a French settlement known as Frenchtown in the late 1700s. Frenchtown holds the distinction of being the first place in Michigan where the United States flag flew. That was in 1796, just two decades after the American forefathers signed the Declaration of Independence.

Frenchtown continued to grow until the War of 1812, when it became the site of the Battle of the River Raisin. The War of 1812 pitted the newly formed United States against Great Britain. By 1813, the Americans had suffered several wartime disappointments, including the surrender of Detroit (see page 33). Despite these losses and the general poor condition of many of the troops due to a lack of food and other supplies, the Americans pressed on in hopes of regaining the northern lands that had fallen under British control. Frenchtown was one such area. U.S. Brig. Gen. James Winchester ordered troops from the Maumee River (in what is now northern Ohio) to Frenchtown. American troops arrived on Jan. 18, 1813, to face the British-led force, which was a combination of a Canadian militia plus 200 Potawatomi Indian warriors.

With a three-to-one advantage, the Americans prevailed on the first day of fighting. Gen. Winchester himself and 250 soldiers arrived two days later and joined the 650-man contingent already at Frenchtown. Word of the raid spread rapidly through the British ranks, and a counterattack took form. On Jan. 22, a British force of 500 soldiers and 800 Indians (under the command of Shawnee Indian Chief Tecumseh) pounced on the Americans and quickly captured Frenchtown. The Battle of the River Raisin became known as "The Massacre" when, despite promises of protection from the British, the Indians killed more than 60 of the wounded and captured American soldiers. Stories of the loss at River Raisin struck deep among American patriots, but rather than lose hope, they persevered, soon regaining Frenchtown and other southeastern Michigan lands.

In 1817, just four years after The Massacre, Michigan Territorial Governor Lewis Cass renamed Frenchtown to Monroe in honor of a visit to the settlement by U.S. President James Monroe (see photos on page 8). The entire county was likewise named for the newly elected president.

Exit 15

Over the next few decades, the community of Monroe had time to develop without the threat of war. By the 1860s, however, Monroe residents' thoughts again turned to the military, and particularly George Custer, who over the years has been described as both a great leader who bravely led his troops into battle and an egomaniac who paid for his arrogance with the lives of his men.

Custer (see photo on page 8) was born in Ohio but raised in Monroe. He started his military career after he graduated from West Point in 1861 . . . at the bottom of his class. Although he led successful charges, he lost many men and soon became the Union's military leader with the greatest number of casualties among his soldiers. According to historians, one reason for the high number of casualties was that Custer seldom paid heed to scouting reports and regularly sent his troops on very dangerous mis-

BRAINBUSTERS

Basic: Can you name the state flower?

Intermediate: Name the state fish.

Advanced: Name the state stone. This stone represents a living thing—what?

See next page for answers.

| Lewis Cass | President James Monroe | General George Armstrong Custer | Sitting Bull |

sions. He reportedly survived, in part, by often excusing himself from the battlefield and instead taking a few men elsewhere for hunting excursions.

Despite this less-than-stellar record, he remained popular in the public's eyes, leaving his superiors to struggle over whether to discipline him, remove him from command, or go along with the public praise of him. At one point, the military convicted and sentenced Custer to a year's suspension for abandoning his post and improperly dealing with deserters (Custer had

THE ANSWERS

The state flower is the *apple blossom*, a simple but lovely and fragrant flower that blooms from apple trees every spring.

The *brook trout* is the state fish. It grows to about 11–16 inches long and a pound or two, sometimes bigger, and has a greenish-brown to dark-brown back with lighter-colored sides. It is the state's only native, stream-dwelling trout, although it may venture into Great Lakes bays and estuaries. The fish is favored by anglers for its excellent meat, which ranks up there with such sought-after game species as whitefish and walleye.

The *petoskey stone* is the state stone. It is a fossil coral. Corals are commonly tube-shaped, underwater animals that attach to rocks or other surfaces. A coral's mouth is at the unattached end of the tube. Tentacles fan out from and surround the mouth to help draw in food particles. Back in the Devonian Age about 350 million years ago, warm sea water covered what is now Michigan and provided a perfect habitat for a certain type of coral known as *Hexagonaria percarinata*. A petoskey stone actually represents a whole colony of these corals. Each small hexagon that you can see on the stone's surface encloses a single living coral. The dark spot at the center of each hexagon is the spot where the coral's mouth used to be and the tiny, radiating spokes represent the tentacles. Rock collectors, also called rockhounds, typically search Lake Michigan beaches near the hamlet of Petoskey in northwestern Michigan for the stones, but they can find them in many areas of the state, including inland sites.

them shot dead without a hearing). Custer served 10 months of that sentence before being reinstated.

His military career finally brought him to the American plains to run off Sioux and Cheyenne Indians and open gold-mining operations in the Black Hills of South Dakota. In June 1876, Custer led his 265 men to the fateful Battle of Little Big Horn against a huge Indian force under the command of Indian chiefs Sitting Bull and Crazy Horse.

News in the late 1800s traveled more slowly than it does now. It took nearly two weeks for details of the Battle of Little Big Horn to appear in the press. The July 7, 1876, *New York Times* described the encounter:

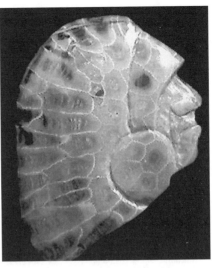

Petoskey stone. On the bottom right, the somewhat hexagon-shaped cells are visible. Each one contained a single living coral.

"So far as an expression in regard to the wisdom of General Custer's attack could be obtained at headquarters, it was to the effect that Custer had been imprudent, to say the least. It is the opinion at headquarters among those who are most familiar with the situation, that Custer struck Sitting Bull's main camp. (Military opinion is) that Sitting Bull began concentrating his forces ... and that no doubt, Custer dropped squarely in the midst of no less than 10,000 (Indians) and was literally torn to pieces . . . ."

The article goes on to say that Custer had earlier refused the offer of four additional companies of soldiers, and when he learned that another U.S. infantry contingent was on its way to assist in the battle, he rushed his men to Little Big Horn to get there first. The article continues:

"Instead of marching from 20–30 miles per day as ordered, Custer made a forced march and reached the point of destination two or three days in advance of the infantry; then finding himself in front of the foe, he foolishly attempted to cut his way through . . . ."

The Indians overwhelmed Custer and his troops. Custer and all of his men, except for one half-Indian scout, perished. Listed among the dead soldiers were Custer's brother, nephew, and brother-in-law.

Although the *New York Times* described the attack as a grave tactical error on Custer's part, public outcry demanded that the army respond quickly and aggressively to avenge the man who the citizens generally viewed as a fallen hero. The army answered the call

9

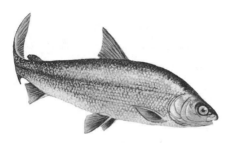

Lake whitefish. (NOAA, Great Lakes Environmental Research Laboratory)

Actual Size 7.8 mm

Amphipod diporeia are tiny shrimp-like creatures that are a major part of the whitefish's diet. (NOAA, Great Lakes Environmental Research Laboratory/M. Quigley, April 2000)

and escalated its attacks on the plains Indians.

Mile Marker 16

Sandy Creek flows under I-75 north of this mile marker. It continues to the east for another approximately 2 miles, and then enters Lake Erie's Brest Bay along the northern border of William C. Sterling State Park. Sterling is the only Michigan state park on Lake Erie. The park has several lagoons for fishing, a mile-long beach for swimming and shore-side Great Lakes fishing, a boat launch, 6 miles of nature trails that afford good bird-watching, and a large campground.

Exit 18

Stony Creek flows from the northwest, runs beneath the freeway just to the north of this exit, and continues a few miles southeast to Lake Erie's Brest Bay. Brest Bay is popular with anglers for two favorite fishes: perch and walleye. In fact, some describe Brest Bay as the "walleye capital of the world." In the past, however, one of the most-prized fish in Brest Bay and Lake Erie was

the lake whitefish, an excellent tasting member of the trout and salmon family. The fish spent most of their time in Lake Erie, but swam into the Detroit River to spawn every fall. Throughout the 1700s and 1800s, fishing operations hauled vast numbers of whitefish from Lake Erie—so many, in fact, that the population started to drop off. The fishery took another hard blow in 1908 when construction began on a shipping channel in the Detroit River not far upstream from Lake Erie (see photo). To widen the channel, workers blasted away the bedrock, and this action destroyed the spawning grounds for the whitefish.

Still, the whitefish held on, although in smaller numbers. In the mid-20th century, pollution also became a problem because it reduced the tiny shrimp-like creatures called *Diporeia* (pronounced die-por-I-uh) that are a major part of the whitefish diet. Things looked bleak, but concerted efforts to improve the habitat have helped the fish to rebound. In 2006, employees of the U.S. Geological Survey found newly hatched

10

Here, work continues on a shipping channel in the Detroit River in the early 1900s. The project temporarily exposed the rocky riverbed (shown in the foreground) and destroyed the spawning ground for whitefish. (U.S. Geological Survey/G.W. Stose)

whitefish in the lower Detroit River. According to the U.S. Environmental Protection Agency, this marked the first confirmed report of "native, reproducing lake whitefish in the Detroit River in approximately 100 years."

Mile Marker 21

Watch for the tiny Swan Creek to cross I-75 in this area. The creek continues northwest for about 15 miles as the crow flies, and another 5 miles southeast to Lake Erie. Before it reaches Lake Erie, it widens considerably. Near the junction between Lake Erie and Swan Creek is the Fermi 2 nuclear power station. For more on the plant, see the Brainbuster.

Mile Marker 26.5

The Huron River crosses in this area. The waterway runs about 80 miles, ending at Lake Erie, and has a smooth, flat, rock riverbed. The town of Flat Rock, located about 2 miles northwest of this location, takes its name from this geological feature. In the past, Flat Rock has gone by other names, including Vreeland for a family who settled there, and Smooth Rock, which also pays homage to the riverbed.

Miles 26–28

Throughout much of Michigan, you will see a variety of tall plants growing alongside I-75 and many other roads.

Some of the most common are the cattails and reeds you can view on both the northbound and southbound sides of the freeway here. These plants grow in marshy areas, which are common alongside I-75 and other freeways. Freeways are typically constructed so the roads lie above the adjacent land. This, combined with sloping road surfaces, allow rainwater to flow off the road and onto the surrounding lower land, either creating or augmenting marshy conditions.

The reeds resemble gigantic grass plants—sometimes up to 15 feet tall—with wispy seed-laden heads that seem to move with every slight shift of the wind. These reeds are also called *Phragmites* (pronounced frag-MI-tees), which is the scientific, or genus (pronounced GEE-nus), name. Scientists around the world use these often-difficult-to-pronounce names to describe very specific groups of plants or animals. No matter where you are in the world and what language you're using, for example, all scientists recognize this particular group of reeds as *Phragmites*. If the scientist wants to be more detailed and talk about just one type of *Phragmites*, he or she would give the full scientific name, which includes both a genus name (which is always capitalized) and a species name (which is always in lower case). In this instance, the giant reed's scientific name is *Phragmites communis*.

Cattails are interesting plants for several reasons. We actually have two species in Michigan (*Typha latifolia* and *Typha augustifolia*), which are quite similar. In the early summer, the cigar-shaped brown seed heads are topped by what looks like a second, much thinner and lighter-colored seed head. This second head is actually the male part of the plant and contains the pollen. The pollen drifts on the breeze to land upon and fertilize the female seed heads. In the summer, only the fuzzy brown seed head remains, and by fall, it becomes an elongated cottony puff of seeds, each seed awaiting dispersal by the wind.

Frequently, you will see cattails that seem to keep their cottony seed heads all year long. When a mat of fuzz remains on top of a cattail through the winter and into the next spring, it is a sign that a moth has infected the plant. Here's what happens: The adult moths, appropriately called cattail moths, lay their eggs, and the young caterpillars hatch out and find a home on the cattails.

BRAINBUSTERS

Basic: Besides its association with Gen. George Custer, Monroe is also known as the home of the Fermi 2 nuclear power plant, which supplies energy to much of the surrounding area. When did the power plant begin to produce commercial power: 1965, 1988, or 2002?

Intermediate: The Fermi 2 plant is named for Enrico Fermi, who won a Nobel Prize in 1938 for being the first person to do what?

Advanced: If this plant is Fermi 2, what happed to Fermi 1?

See page 14 for answers.

The wispy seed head of *Phragmites*. (Robert H. Mohlenbrock, USDA)

Cattails at the edge of a small wetland. (Derek Jensen)

Their association with the cattail continues as they spin silk around the seed head and live inside over the winter. The caterpillars eventually pupate and emerge as moths late in the following spring. By then, the seed head is fluffy and typically drooped to one side. Sometimes, almost every other cattail in a marsh shows signs of being infected.

Cattails also have many edible parts, including the root, which tastes rather like a starchy cucumber, and can be dried and ground into an edible flour-like material, called meal. The immature seed head can also be boiled and eaten like an ear of corn. Before trying a cattail root, however, make sure you've identified it correctly! A very poisonous plant known as blue flag, a type of iris that is common in the same habitat as cattails, has leaves that look very much like a cattail's, but the blue flag iris has purple flowers instead of the cattail's brown seed head. After you have properly identified the cattail, you should also make sure its habitat is clean before nibbling on the root. For instance, marshes and ditches next to busy highways may contain oil, antifreeze or other residues from automotive traffic, and might have tainted nearby plants.

Exit 29

Lake Erie Metropark is nearby, beginning about 2 miles east of the community of Rockwood and continuing east to the Lake Erie shoreline. It is part of the Huron-Clinton Metroparks, a five-county, 13-park system that is one of the largest regional systems in the United States. The Metroparks date back to a 1939 act of the Michigan State Legislature. The first park was Kensington, which opened in 1948 a few dozen miles northwest of here. Kensington is still a popular park.

Lake Erie Metropark covers 1,607 acres. Each fall, the park draws bird-watchers, also known simply as bird-ers, from throughout the country who hope to catch a glimpse of majestic hawks, soaring eagles, and other birds that follow a migration route along the Erie shoreline. Recently, the park added a 1.5-mile trail through the Cherry Island marsh with lookout points where hikers can view Lake

Erie and the Detroit River. The Detroit River is actually the connect-ing waterway between Lake Erie to the south and Lake St. Clair to the north. Farther north, another river, the St. Clair River, connects Lake St. Clair to Lake Huron.

Exit 32

This exit leads to Grosse Ile and to Trenton.

Grosse Ile (pronounced "grose-eel" almost as one word) is an island in the Detroit River, which is a few miles to the east of I-75.

Exit 32

THE ANSWERS

The Fermi 2 nuclear power plant began to produce commercial power in *January 1988*.

Enrico Fermi won the Nobel Prize for his work on nuclear reactions. Although he didn't realize exactly what he had done at the time, *he was the first person to split a uranium atom—a process now known as nuclear fission*. His work paved the way for the atomic bomb, a powerful and destructive weapon used dur-ing World War II, and also for nuclear power plants. The plants use the heat produced by nuclear fission to gener-ate steam that turns the blades on turbines, which are essentially huge fan-like devices. The turning blades power a generator, which produces the electricity used by businesses and residences. According to Detroit

Edison, the energy company that owns and operates Fermi 2, the plant "is one of the largest fossil fuel power plants in the United States" and "gen-erates more than 1,100 megawatts (1.1 million kilowatts), enough elec-tricity to serve a city of about one million people."

The first Fermi reactor, also located in Monroe County, *suffered a partial meltdown* (a dangerous overheating of the reactor fissible material, or core) and a release of radiation on Oct. 5, 1966, during a test run. Engineers were able to intervene and contain the radiation, but some officials' first thoughts were to evacuate portions of southeastern Michigan, includ-ing the city of Detroit. Fermi 1 finally began operating again in 1970, but shut down for good in 1972.

Grosse Ile, about 7–8 miles long and almost 2 miles wide, was a common 17th-century stopping point for French missionaries and a trading place for explorers, who made deals with the local Potawatomi (pronounced pot-uh-WOTT-oh-mee) Indians. Even French explorer and eventual fort commandant Antoine de la Mothe Cadillac stayed on the island in 1701 before building Fort Pontchartrain on the future site of Detroit (see exit 46).

Despite its many visitors, Grosse Ile remained primarily in the hands of the Potawatomi Indians until 1776 when brothers Alexander and William Macomb bought the small island.

Exit 34

The Grosse Ile lighthouse was built in 1906 on the north channel of the island. (NOAA, Great Lakes Environmental Research Laboratory/J. Lefevre)

Trenton sits on the shore of the Detroit River. Before it was called Trenton, the town in 1837 received the name of Truaxton after Major Caleb Truax, a boundary land surveyor. Truaxton gained a reputation as a steamship port and a shipbuilding center. The town's name later changed to Trenton, which is a type of limestone found in the area.

See next page for answers.

BRAINBUSTERS

Basic: What is a peninsula anyway?

Intermediate: Which is longer: the Upper Peninsula from west to east, or the Lower Peninsula from north to south?

Advanced: Minnesota's slogan is "land of 10,000 lakes." Michigan includes parts of four of the Great Lakes. According to the Michigan Department of Natural Resources, how many lakes to the nearest thousand are within the boundaries of Michigan?

Exit 34

Off this exit, you will find the cities of Riverview, Wyandotte, and Ecorse.

Riverview's name comes from its location on the Detroit River, and Wyandotte from the Wyandot (pronounced WHY-en-dot or WINE-dot) Indians who once lived in a village named Maquaqu there. When the French first met these native people for the first time, they named them the Huron Indians, because some of the men had unusual hair styles—shaved heads with only a little clump of hair left to grow—and the French explorers thought the style resembled the hair on a wild boar. In the French language, "hure" is the word for boar. Hure became Huron.

Exit 34

The city of Wyandotte is also known as the place that turned around a severe economic downturn that threatened all of southeastern Michigan in the 19th century. In 1873, numerous companies in the Detroit region fell on tough times, and many believed this entire section of the state was headed for economic disaster. That viewpoint changed when an oil and gas company in Wyandotte struck not oil, but salt. The area underlying Wyandotte and

surrounding communities is a vast salt bed. A salt-mining industry sprang up and brought in much-needed money and employment to this corner of Michigan. Although not as bustling as it once was, the salt industry in Michigan is still active today, primarily mining the road salt that is spread on icy and snowy roads.

The discovery of salt led not only to a booming industry in southeastern Michigan, but also to a delightful fictitious yarn. According to the story, the legendary giant lumberman Paul Bunyan created the salt beds. Paul needed water for his sawmills, so he dug a ditch from the Atlantic Ocean to ponds he excavated in the Midwest. For Paul, everything was on a large scale: The excavated dirt from

THE ANSWERS

A peninsula is *a piece of land that projects into and is nearly surrounded by a body of water*. It differs from an island in that a peninsula is still connected to the mainland. The word "peninsula" comes from two Latin words: paene, which means almost; and insula, which means island. A peninsula is therefore "almost an island."

The Upper Peninsula is longer from west to east than the Lower Peninsula is from north to south. You would have to drive farther to get from Ironwood on the west side of the U.P. to the edge of Drummond Island on the east than

you would to drive from the Straits of Mackinac at the northern tip of the Lower Peninsula to the Ohio border. To get an idea of the overall size of this very large state, consider the flying distance from Detroit in the southeastern Lower Peninsula to Ironwood in the far western Upper Peninsula. If you flew in a straight line from one city to the other, you would rack up more miles than if you flew from Detroit to Washington, D.C., or from Detroit to the northwest corner of South Carolina.

With about *11,000* inland lakes, Michigan tops Minnesota's mark of 10,000.

Many cities along the Detroit River were host to rumrunners illegally bringing liquor across the river from Canada during Prohibition. Here, armed Coast Guard men aboard the *USS Seneca* have caught up with a rummrunner in 1924. (Source: Library of Congress, circa 1924)

the ponds became the Black Hills of the Dakotas, the ditch became the St. Lawrence River, and his ponds are now known as the Great Lakes. As the story goes, the salt beds throughout southeastern Michigan resulted when Paul erected a plant to filter out the salt from the ocean water before filling Lake St. Clair.

In reality, the salt in Michigan's salt beds actually came from an ancient, saltwater sea that covered not only Michigan, but also stretched south to Ohio and West Virginia and east past parts of Ontario to New York more than 400 million years ago. Over many, many years, the water in the sea evaporated, leaving behind the sea's salt. These salt beds are so vast that even decades of mining have hardly made a dent on their size: At the current rate of usage, the salt bed under southeastern Michigan alone will last many millions of years.

A few miles north of Wyandotte, the community of Ecorse (pronounced EE-course) played a large

BRAINBUSTERS

Basic: Besides rumrunning — importing illegal alcohol into the state during Prohibition — gangsters also engaged in bootlegging. What was this type of bootlegging?

Intermediate: What is a blind pig?

Advanced: The Purple Gang was infamous during Prohibition in Detroit for its illegal activities. Even criminals have competition, and this gang's main competitor was a well-known Chicago gangster. Who was it?

See next page for answers.

role in one of the most turbulent eras in Michigan history: Prohibition.

During the Prohibition era of the 1920s and early 1930s, the manufacture, purchase and consumption of alcoholic beverages was illegal. Penny-ante crooks and organized gangsters alike would typically wait until dark and then traverse the Detroit River to pick up the brews from Canada and deliver them illegally to Michigan loca-tions. Called "rumrunning," the illicit activity became such a thriving business in Ecorse that its waterfront earned the nickname Rummer's Row. Rumrunning brought criminal activity to many cities along the Detroit River, but Ecorse was the most notorious. For one thing, it was located near Detroit, but outside its police jurisdiction. In addition, the river crossing to Canada skirted a number of islands, which provided

THE ANSWERS

Exit 34

Instead of buying pre-made alcohol in Canada and smuggling it into Michigan, some people made their own. *Bootlegging is the illegal manufacture of alcohol, sometimes called "moonshine," that occurred during the Prohibition era.* Actually, Michigan had already experienced two liquor-free years before the national ban took effect in 1920. In 1917, the state prohibited liquor, but the state law fell in 1919 when it was deemed unconstitutional.

A blind pig, also known as a speakeasy, is an establishment that serves illegal alcoholic beverages. During Prohibition, Detroit was home to some 25,000 blind pigs. The establishments would spring up almost overnight and remain in business until police shut them down. Sometimes, proprietors would get advance warning and close up shop just ahead of police arrival.

The Purple Gang was a group of violent thugs known not so much for rumrunning or bootlegging as it was for extortion. Members would sell "protection" to business owners in exchange for "protection," usually from the gang itself. Gang members also stole moonshine from other criminals, committed arson, and killed the leaders of other gangs. The Purple Gang competed with famed Chicago gangster *Al Capone* and successfully kept him and his men out of Detroit. The Purple Gang is also remembered for its role in the so-called Cleaners and Dyers War in Detroit, which began when the owners of a group of dry cleaners wanted to triple the rates for cleaning services throughout the city. When some owners refused to participate in the price hike, the group hired the Purple Gang to convince the hold-outs with any means necessary, including murder. Soon, the detractors relented and rates rose. The reign of the Purple Gang was a short one. By the end of the 1930s, the gang's members either had died at the hands of other criminals or were imprisoned for their offenses.

excellent cover for clandestine, night-time transits.

What began as a small-time smuggling operation, with single or small teams of men rowing across the river to Canada to pick up a few cases of liquor at a time, quickly turned into a full-fledged rumrunning operation coordinated by armed gangsters and criminal organizations. By 1929, the illegal liquor operation employed some 50,000 people and was one of the biggest businesses in the state—only the auto industry was more profitable.

Ecorse soon became the country's largest port of entry for illegal Canadian alcohol. It was also home to the Green Lantern Club, one of the most famous blind pigs in the state (check the Brainbusters on this and the next page for the definition of a blind pig). A last-ditch effort to cut off the rum-running traffic was the erection of a wooden fence along the Ecorse waterfront, which remained in place until Prohibition was repealed in 1933. At that point, Michiganians on the whole breathed a sigh of relief. Most people believed that the national repeal would not only bring a reprieve from the crime spree that many blamed on Prohibition, but would also fill the state's coffers with tax dollars to be generated from now-legal liquor sales.

The city of Ecorse wasn't always so boisterous a location, however. The town's name and that of the Ecorse River—*Rivièra aux Ecorces* in French—recall more peaceful times. *Rivièra aux Ecorces* means Bark Creek, so named because local Indians would use bark from shoreline birch trees to craft their canoes and wigwams. For the canoes, they used the sturdy, brown-colored, inner bark, rather than the outer bark, which is thin and white, and would not keep the water out. The city of Ecorse rests on the former campsite and burial ground of the Wyandot Indians.

Mile Marker 37

I-75 passes through the southeastern portion of the city of Taylor. The city got its name from General Zachary Taylor, a famous soldier in the Mexican War who went on to become the 12th president of

BRAINBUSTERS

Basic: On a typical day, more than 1,500 takeoffs and landings occur at Metro Airport—more than one a minute on average. On its busiest days, 100,000 passengers can pass through the airport in a single 24-hour period. What is the airport's busiest day of the year?

Intermediate: Before Metro Airport, Detroit-bound commercial airliners flew into Willow Run Airport, which is now mostly used for cargo planes, and smaller, private or corporate aircraft. Willow Run is perhaps most well-known for its participation in the country's World War II effort. What role did the airport play?

Advanced: Who was Rosie the Riveter?

See page 21 for answers.

General Zachary Taylor (Source: Library of Congress, circa 1848)

the United States. The general was also the second cousin to another president: James Madison. Madison served as the nation's fourth president from 1809–1817 when Taylor was still in his 20s.

Taylor was born in 1784 in Virginia, and spent much of his youth and young adulthood working on his father's plantation. When he was 23, however, he switched careers to become a soldier. He fought in many battles against Indians, and earned celebrity for his efforts in the War of 1812 and the Mexican War. By the mid 1840s, when Taylor was in his early 60s, he had attained national renown as a soldier and gained the nickname "Old Rough and Ready," in part due to his often-haggard dress. He ran for the presidency on the Whig ticket against a formidable opponent: one-time Michigan Governor Lewis Cass. Cass, a Demo-

cratic candidate, may have won the election had not a third party formed. That third party, called the Free Soil Party, nominated Martin Van Buren as an alternative to Cass. With some of his votes now going to Van Buren, Cass lost the 1849 election to Taylor. Taylor's stint in office was a short one, however. About 16 months after he took office, he participated in a ceremony to begin construction of the Washington Monument. After the ceremony, he became ill and died five days later at the age of 65. While the cause of death was listed as gastroenteritis, which is an inflammation of the digestive tract, many felt foul play was involved, and his demise was the result of arsenic poisoning. In 1991—nearly 150 years after his death—scientists exhumed Taylor's body to search for evidence of arsenic poisoning. Using fingernail and hair samples, they found that arsenic was not the culprit, and put to rest the controversy surrounding the president's death.

Exit 37

Allen Road leads to Detroit Metropolitan Airport, one of the largest and busiest airports in the nation. The airport came about over the course of several decades, beginning with the purchase of a square mile of land in 1928, construction of a landing strip in 1929 and the first official airplane landing in 1930. In the 1940s, the U.S. Army used the airport as a staging base for bombers bound for Europe and World War II. In 1950, commercial airlines began to run service to and from the airport, taking business away from the nearby Willow Run Airport. Within a decade, Detroit Metropolitan Airport would become the primary airport for southeastern Michigan.

Growth at the airport has continued. In 2005, its busiest year to date, the airport served some 36.4 million passengers. That is the equivalent of about three-and-a-half times the population in the entire state of Michigan. The airport is one of the busiest anywhere, usually placing in the top dozen in the nation and among the top 20 in the world. (What is the busiest airport in America? The answer is the Hartsfield-Jackson Atlanta International Airport in Georgia.)

The full name of the airport is actually Detroit Metropolitan Wayne County Airport, but locals shorten it to "Metro Airport," or just "Metro." Like all airports, Metro has a three-letter abbreviation, or airport code, that is used by the aviation industry

---

THE ANSWERS

The busiest day of the year at Metro Airport is the Sunday after Thanksgiving, when passengers rush back home after holiday family visits.

Willow Run Airport became famous during WWII when automobile manufacturer Henry Ford and aviator Charles Lindbergh teamed up to build a factory at the airport that would eventually turn out more bombers than any other facility in the world. *Their primary product was B-24 bombers.* Also known by their colorful nickname of "liberators," these aircraft were used for long-range missions over the Pacific, in Europe and in north Africa. Four 1,200-pound engines powered the aircraft, which had a wingspan of 110 feet and fuselage about 66 feet long. With 5,000 pounds of bombs, the B-24 had a range of 2,300 miles—roughly the distance from San Diego, Calif., on the west coast of the United States to Savannah, Georgia, on the east coast. In addition to delivering bombs, B-24s participated in transport, air-sea rescue, and other operations.

When the Willow Run bomber facility was at its busiest, it employed some 42,000 workers, many of them *women whose husbands or boyfriends were fighting in the war. The generic nickname for these women was "Rosie the Riveter."* As part of the nation's effort to encourage women to take on what were then considered to be "men's jobs," a government film team in 1942 prepared to make a short promotional movie about the women. On a visit to Willow Run, the team discovered a woman working on B-24 bombers. She not only was a riveter, but her name was Rose. The 22–year-old Rose Will Monroe, not only appeared in the film, but also became the model behind a war poster campaign. Another well-known poster with the slogan "We can do it!" featured Michigan worker Geraldine Doyal.

21

We Can Do It!

Michigan factory worker Geraldine Doyle served as the model for this famous poster that was used during World War II to encourage women to take on the jobs left vacant by men who had been called to fight overseas. (National Archives and Records Administration)

to identify it. Metro Airport's abbreviation is DTW, which gets the DT from Detroit and the W from Wayne. Willow Run's code is YIP, taken from its location in Ypsilanti.

Exit 40

This exit leads to both Allen Park and Southgate. Southgate got its name from its position at the southern entrance or gateway to Detroit, while Allen Park's name came from the Allen family who settled in the area in the early 1800s.

Like many of the towns of this area, Southgate and Allen Park began to show real growth following the completion of the Erie Canal in 1825,

which finally connected Lake Erie to eastern waterways and ultimately the Atlantic coast. With the opening of the canal, Michigan settlers finally felt connected with the rest of America. Now afforded easy travel and shipping to and from the East Coast, Michigan settlements quickly grew.

The canal ran from the Lake Erie shore in Buffalo, N.Y., through the New York cities of Syracuse, Rome and Troy to the Hudson River. Then-U.S. President James Monroe refused to use federal funds for the project, so the New York State Legislature authorized needed monies with the stipulation that future users would pay tolls to cover the construction costs. New York Governor DeWitt Clinton was such a strong supporter of the canal project that the Erie Canal was often described as "Clinton's Ditch."

Ultimately, the $7-million canal had a series of 85 locks to correct a 500-foot difference in elevation from one side to the other. A lock is basically a giant four-walled box set within a canal so that it completely blocks water movement. When a boat approaches, a gate on one side opens to admit the boat, then closes to surround the vessel. At that point, a person called a lockkeeper either raises or lowers the water level within the lock to match the water level on the far side. Then the gate on that end of the lock opens and the boat continues through. Without lock systems, boaters would face dangerous and possibly unsurpassable rapids.

The Erie Canal continued as the primary transit route from the East

Coast well into the 1800s, but was eventually replaced by ever-expanding railways and then the automobile. The Erie Canal is now part of the New York State Barge Canal Waterway System, which includes several additional canals to Lake Ontario and other destinations. The canal system has since shifted its primary traffic from commercial vessels to recreational boats.

Mile Marker 42

Lincoln Park crosses I-75 in this vicinity. Within the city's current boundaries rests Council Point, which played a part in the struggle for control of Detroit in the 1700s.

Since the late 1600s, French explorers and fur traders had become increasingly common in the Great Lakes area. Relationships formed between the Indians and the Frenchmen, with the Indians trading pelts and other goods and services for hunting guns, ammunition, and other supplies.

In the mid-1700s, however, the British began to move into the Midwest, eventually gaining control of many French-built forts that dotted the land. In 1758, Sir Jeffery Amherst became the British commander-in-chief in North America. Amherst saw no reason to form a working relationship with the Indians, and even disdained the native population. He refused to take up the French tradition of supplying them with goods, and the now-British forts followed suit.

One of these was Fort Pontchartrain (pronounced PONCH-uh-train) in Detroit, which had switched from French to English control in 1760. Rumblings among the Indian tribes escalated to talk of ending the British reign through the Midwest, and an Ottawa Indian chief brought together the leaders of several tribes to discuss their options at Council Point in what is now Lincoln Park. The chief's name was Pontiac, which is actually an English corruption of his real name, Obwandiyag (pronounced more like BWON-dee-ack).

Pontiac and the other chiefs planned a surprise attack of about 400 warriors on the Detroit fort. In the spring of 1763, they sent word to the fort's commander, Major Henry Gladwin, that they wished to perform a dance, and then have a goodwill summit there. Beneath their blankets, however, the Indians concealed knives and guns that they hoped to use to overrun the fort. Somehow, Gladwin received advance warning of their intentions, and the warriors left the fort without drawing their weapons.

Over the next five months, Pontiac led numerous raids on the English at

MM 42

BRAINBUSTERS

Basic: Why was southern Michigan sometimes called New France?

Intermediate: Michigan was the site of a good many English-French battles in the 1700s. What were they fighting over?

Advanced: Did the Indians in Michigan always favor the French over the English?

See page 25 for answers.

Michigan native Preston Tucker created this revolutionary automobile that he named the Tucker. It is shown here at the Blackhawk Museum in California. (Sean O'Flaherty)

Detroit, but all failed. After sustaining extensive casualties, he finally relented and the British retained control. Two years later, Pontiac agreed to end all hostilities with the stipulation that the English did not own the land at Detroit, but were merely leasing it from the Indians. British officials agreed, but the Indians were never to regain the land.

After making the agreement, Pontiac left Michigan to begin a new life on the Mississippi River near St. Louis, Mo. A rival Indian tribe heard of his impending arrival, and in 1769 Pontiac died of stab wounds at the hands of a Peoria brave. The chief's final resting place is unknown, but one legend holds that his body was transported back to Michigan and buried on Apple Island in Oakland County's Orchard Lake.

The importance of Council Point and the 1763 fight for Detroit is still remembered. A 26-acre Council Point Park commemorates the location's historical significance, while both Major Gladwin and Chief Pontiac are remembered in the names of cities in Michigan. Gladwin County is in the middle of the Lower Peninsula, and Pontiac is a large city north of Detroit.

Besides its connection to Council Point, Lincoln Park is known for at least one famous resident: Preston Tucker, the maker of the Tucker automobile. Tucker was born in 1903 in Capac (pronounced KAY-pack), a small town in Michigan's "Thumb," but soon moved with his family to Lincoln Park. As a young man, he held several jobs, including police officer. There, he spent considerable time with the other officers chasing rumrunners across the Detroit River during Prohibition. (See exit 34 for more information on rumrunning.) During his spare time, he tinkered with cars, eventually coming up with the idea for his self-named and revolutionary automobile: an air-cooled, rear engine-powered, fastback vehicle with independent four-wheel suspension. Safety innovations in the car included a padded dashboard, disk brakes, and a headlamp that turned with the front wheels to light the road ahead when rounding a curve. Despite the vehicle's advances, production of the Chicago-made Tucker automobile was short-lived. Financial, bureaucratic and legal problems combined to force the company's closure after building only 51 cars. Today, Tucker automobiles are collector's items. A silver 1948 Tucker Model 48, for instance, fetched $461,500 at an auction in 2005.

Exit 43

The surrounding industrial site includes oil refineries and filling stations. The Rouge River, which flows

Exit 43

THE ANSWERS

Many of the first white men to explore northern North America were French. They even designated the area "New France," which encompassed the eastern half of Canada and the Great Lakes region, including Michigan. As French explorers traveled west from the Atlantic they gave many sites names in their native language.

While the French were moving farther toward the interior of North America, the English were establishing settlements mainly along the eastern seaboard, an area that is still called New England. Soon the English sought to expand throughout North America. The conflict between the French and English arose *because each wanted to claim as much of this new continent as possible for their own country.* One of the primary draws was the very lucrative fur-trapping and -trading industry. Instead of working together to set up friendly boundaries, the countries fought for the land.

The Indians, who lived in North America long before the white men arrived, were neither consistently pro-French nor pro-English. Although different Indian tribes communicated with one another, they seldom acted in a united fashion. Instead, each tribe would make individual decisions on whether to side with or take arms against the French or the English, depending on which action was most beneficial to the tribe. For example, a tribe might side with those who provided guns, food, or other supplies, or against those who were less accommodating.

through this area, is now recovering from years of use as essentially a drain for industrial waste. According to the Michigan Department of Environmental Quality, "The Rouge River has been classified as one of the most polluted rivers in the United States and in 1981 was designated an Area of Concern by the International Joint Commission because of its severely degraded condition and its impact on the Great Lakes." While the description is dire, federal-, state-, and locally funded efforts are well under way to clean up the 126-mile-long river. Many businesses are also contributing to the river's restoration.

Exit 43

One recent sign of success was the discovery in May 2001 of a certain type of insect in the river's tributaries, or offshoot creeks. That insect, a stonefly, occurs only in clean water, and the finding provided an indication that clean-up efforts were paying off.

As adults, stoneflies have long, fairly thin bodies ranging from about a half inch to 2 inches long, depending on which of the dozens of species of stoneflies they are. They have long antennae—usually about as long as the body—and two, thin "tails," called cerci (pronounced SER-see). The adults spend time near water, but not in it. When stoneflies are young, however, they look much different, and actually live underwater. Young stoneflies are flat, wingless insects that cling to underwater stones, logs, and branches. They make a good gauge of water quality because they can't take up oxygen very well. Some breathe through small, feathery gills and others absorb oxygen right through their shell-like, outer body covering, which is called a cuticle. Neither the gills nor the cuticle can draw enough oxygen from polluted water, so they cannot survive there. For this reason, stoneflies are known as "environmental indicators," and their presence is a good sign of a healthy environment.

— — — —

Long before the industrial era, the Rouge River area held a distinction among American Indians. It was the site of some of world's largest Indian Burial Mounds. These mounds, which could spread over hundreds of feet and reach heights of 40 feet, left their marks on the landscape for many years until 19th century pioneers arrived and leveled the land.

Other unusual human-made formations once dotted the landscape in southern and western Michigan. Called garden beds, although their use was unknown, these low mounds covered acres of land with soil formed into geometrical patterns. The garden beds have since been leveled, but their purpose remains one of the great Michigan mysteries.

— — — —

About a half mile east of I-75 is Zug Island, which actually wasn't always an island: It was part of the mainland. The piece of marshy land, which measured only about three-quarters of a mile square, had the Rouge River as its southern boundary and the Detroit River as its eastern edge. In the 1800s, manmade canals around the north and west sides cut off the property from the mainland, and created the tiny island. It later became an industrial site, and its smokestacks are readily visible to boaters on the river. The island's name, which is now pronounced to rhyme with "bug," is named for the German immigrant who built and operated a furniture factory there. Zug in German is actually pronounced "tsoog."

— — —

Zug Island also played a role in the sinking of the freighter *Edmund Fitzgerald* on Nov. 10, 1975. The *Fitzgerald's* story begins in 1958, when the newly built freighter was launched on the Rouge River, and then proceeded into the Detroit River and the Great Lakes beyond. At 729 feet long, she would be the largest ship on the Great Lakes for more than a decade. In 1972, Ernest McSorley became the vessel's third—and last—captain. The *Fitzgerald* spent the next three years plying the Great Lakes with little problem, other than some damaged hatches, which were scheduled to be repaired in the spring of 1976. That repair never occurred. On Nov. 9, 1975, the *"Fitz"* left Superior, Wis., loaded down with 26 tons of iron ore pellets known as taconite, and bound for Zug Island. She headed out into Lake Superior, the largest of the Great Lakes, just 10 minutes ahead of another large freighter, called the *Arthur M. Anderson*, and just 19 minutes ahead of the gale warnings posted by the Weather Service. Both the *Fitzgerald* and the *Anderson* continued on, close enough

together that they could see each other across the water.

At 1 a.m.—less than 11 hours after the two set sail from Wisconsin—the waves were 10 feet tall and winds were at 52 knots (60 miles per hour). Twelve hours later, at 1 p.m. on Nov. 10, the winds had dropped by more than half, but the waves were 12 feet. Within the hour, McSorley reported to the *Anderson* that the *Fitzgerald* was "rolling some," but he would stay to his current heading. By 2:45 that afternoon, the winds had increased to 42 knots (48 mph), and a half hour later, the captain of the *Anderson* noted to his first mate that the *Fitzgerald* appeared to be too close to some shallow shoals, where the waves would be much more fierce. In a few minutes, McSorley called the *Anderson*, reporting some topside damage and a list (a leaning to one

Exit 43

BRAINBUSTERS

Basic: A type of insect called a stonefly has big eyes, called compound eyes, because they are made up of many small segments or facets. When a fly looks at a flower, how many flowers does it see?

a) many flowers, like a human might see a single flower through a kaleidoscope

b) one flower

Intermediate: What is a generic term for a young stonefly?

Advanced: Are stoneflies really a type of fly? Why or why not?

See next page for answers.

side). McSorley asked, "Will you stay by me 'til I get to Whitefish?" The *Anderson* agreed to keep watch as they both proceeded to the protected waters of Whitefish Bay in eastern Lake Superior. Through the rest of the trip, the *Anderson* monitored the *Fitz* by radar and, when possible, visually, although heavy snow was by then making the latter difficult.

Forty minutes later, at 4:10 p.m., McSorley again radioed the *Anderson* that the freighter had lost both of its radars. At 4:30, the *Fitz* was near the eastern end of the Upper Peninsula, and its crew began scanning for the on-shore, navigational radio beacon and light at Whitefish Point, but they found out a half hour later that neither the beacon nor the light

were working. The *Fitz* asked the *Anderson* for a position. By 6 p.m., the Fitz radioed: "Am taking heavy seas over the deck. One of the worst seas I've ever been in." Weather conditions worsened as evening fell. At 7 p.m., the *Anderson* reported winds of 50 knots (58 mph) and waves of 16 feet. The last transmission from the *Fitzgerald* came at 7:10 p.m.: "We are holding our own." Five minutes later, a squall hit the *Fitz*, and its lights and radar blip dropped from the *Anderson's* view. The *Anderson* radioed the *Fitzgerald*, but got no response. After repeated attempts to reach the freighter, the *Anderson* contacted the Coast Guard, which also tried unsuccessfully to hail the *Fitz*. Rescue efforts began, but to no avail.

THE ANSWERS

Although science fiction movies and cartoons often liken insect vision to the view seen through a kaleidoscope, *insects only see one object*. Each tiny segment in their compound eyes "sees" one tiny piece of the view, projects it to the brain, and the brain puts all the views together to form one picture. It's somewhat like the way a TV or computer monitor produces a single picture from many pixels.

A young insect is called a nymph or a naiad (NYE-add). Nymph is used to describe young insects that live on land, and naiad is used for those that live underwater. *A young stonefly, therefore, is a naiad.* In some insects,

like dragonflies, the naiad can live underwater for two to three years before crawling out of the water and transforming into a winged, adult dragonfly.

Stoneflies aren't actually flies at all. Flies have two wings along with two tiny nubs called halteres that help the fly to balance when flying, but stoneflies have four full-fledged wings. Insect scientists, called entomologists, distinguish real flies by using a common name that lists the word "fly" separately: house fly, deer fly, horse fly, etc. Among other insects that only superficially resemble flies, like the stoneflies, there is no space between stone and fly.

The *Fitzgerald*, which was officially identified the following spring: It was torn in two and laid 530 feet down on the bottom of Lake Superior, where it still remains.

All 29 crew aboard the *Edmund Fitzgerald* perished. The men ranged in age from 20 to 63 years old. Singer/songwriter Gordon Lightfoot immortalized the tragedy in his song "The Wreck of the Edmund Fitzgerald," which appeared on his 1976 "Summertime Dream" album. The song provides a stirring account and much historically accurate information about the ship's last days. In the lyrics, however, the *Fitz* "left (Wisconsin) fully loaded for Cleveland." While the *Fitz* was chartered to the Oglebay Norton Co. of Cleveland, she was headed to Zug Island on that fateful voyage.

state's overall population, which totals nearly 10.1 million.

The city has gone through many changes in the last few centuries. From its quiet beginnings as a wooded land inhabited by Indians, the area then spent some time as a fur-trading post, and subsequently the site of a French, then British and finally American fort. Once houses and businesses began to spread in the 1800s, Detroit took on its own personality. Lovely tree-lined streets criss-crossed the growing metropolis, and Detroit became known as the "most beautiful city in America." It held that distinction until the advent of the automobile, when residents clamored for wider streets, even if it meant chopping down the trees that were the town's hallmark. Automobile manufacturing then became

Exit 46

You are either entering (northbound) or leaving (southbound) Detroit, the state's largest city. Because of the city's geographical size, I-75 has more of its length inside Detroit's boundaries than within any other Michigan city.

Detroit spreads out over 138.7 square miles, including a little more than 4 square miles of water. As of 2006 it had 871,121 residents, according to the U.S. Census Bureau. Like many other northern, industrial cities in the United States, Detroit's population has dropped from its peak. Its current population is less than half of its highest mark: 1.85 million in 1950. Currently, Detroit holds a little less than 9 percent of the

BRAINBUSTERS

Basic: The Great Lakes have seen many shipwrecks over the years, including the *Edmund Fitzgerald* in 1975. In the song "The Wreck of the Edmund Fitzgerald," singer Gordon Lightfoot sings about Gitche Gumee. What is Gitche Gumee?

Intermediate: Are most big ships removed from the Great Lakes after they sink, or are they left in the water?

Advanced: What do the following nautical terms mean now, and how did the terms originate: mayday, scuttlebutt, port, and starboard?

See page 31 for answers.

29

Detroit's Motown Museum recalls the successes of Berry Gordy and the Motown Sound. (Mark J. Arpin)

the city's claim to fame, and Detroit was soon known as the "Motor City," which is still used today.

Detroit is also widely recognized as the home of the Motown sound and the launch pad for such internationally known artists as the Jackson Five and Michael Jackson, Stevie Wonder, the Supremes, Gladys Knight and the Pips, and the Commodores.

Motown hails back to 1957 when a 27-year-old upholstery trimmer who worked at an automobile assembly plant in Detroit wrote what would become a pop hit. The songwriter was Berry Gordy, and the song was "Reet Petite," performed by Jackie Wilson. With that success under his belt, Gordy quit the factory and continued writing. By 1959, he had scored with another Top 10 hit, and started up Tamla Record Co. He soon changed the name to Motown Record Corp., set up a recording studio in the basement of a two story house near Exit 54 of I-75, and

began making records. The rhythmic, jazz-meets-gospel-meets-rock music was hard to define in words but unmistakable when heard. In 1961, Motown had its first number-one R&B hit in "Shop Around" by the Miracles. Shortly afterward, the company released its first albums, one by the Miracles and one by Marvin Gaye, and hit number one on the pop charts with "Please Mr. Postman" by the Marveletttes.

In just four years, Gordy had gone from a virtually unknown —songwriter to the owner of the —hottest new music studio in the nation. Over the years since, many big names have recorded under the Motown label, including Martha and the —Vandellas ("Heat Wave"), Mary Wells ("My Guy"), and the Four Tops ("I Can't Help Myself"). Gordy sold Motown Records for $61 million in 1988. Five years later, the company changed hands again— this time for $325 million. In 1990,

Gordy earned a place in the Rock and Roll Hall of Fame.

— — —

Detroit sits on the (now, often-concrete covered) western banks of the Detroit River, which connects with Lake St. Clair to the north. Canada is on the opposite side of the river, less than a mile from downtown Detroit and readily visible across the water. Detroit's location on the river has proven to be an attraction throughout its history. In fact, the city's name comes from the French word détroit, which means straits. The first to see the benefits of the area were the American Indians, who built several villages here.

French explorer and soldier Antoine de la Mothe Cadillac arrived much later to the river banks than the Indians, but he is still considered the city's "founder." Cadillac's voyage to what is now Detroit began in 1701, when he left Quebec in Canada with about 100 soldiers, Canadian traders and craftsmen, along with a number of American Indians and Cadillac's 9-year-old son, also named Antoine.

THE ANSWERS

Lake Superior is also known as Gitche Gumee (pronounced GIT-chee GOOM-ee). Gitche Gumee is an approximation of the Chippewa Indian word for great water or great lake. Lake Superior is the largest of the five Great Lakes. In all, the lake covers 31,700 square miles, more than half the size of the entire land surface of Michigan's Upper and Lower Peninsulas combined.

Unless the wreck occurs in shallow waters and poses a potential threat to lake-faring vessels, *sunken freighters and other large ships are left underwater.* Michigan actually has an underwater preserve system that protects wrecks from any plundering and provides divers with a wealth of ships to explore.

Mayday is a distress call, used by boaters and pilots alike, to indicate a dire need for assistance. The term arose from the French word for help me: "m'aidez." On a ship, if you are facing the front (or stern), *left is port and right is starboard.* The two terms originated in England when sailors noted the directions as starboard for the side from which they steered the vessel, and larboard for the loading side. The two words sounded too much alike, so they switched larboard to port. Cargo and other large vessels always moor to the dock with the port side. *Scuttlebutt is now used as another word for rumors.* The term comes from a wooden vat, or butt, that had a hole, or scuttle, through which a tap delivered drinking water. Sailors would gather around the scuttlebutt and trade tales, and U.S. Navy seamen began calling rumors "scuttlebutt."

General Anthony Wayne (Library of Congress, circa 1878)

remained in command at Detroit for almost a decade.

— — —

The French retained control of the fort from Cadillac's era through 1760 when the British took over. At that time, the French were losing ground to the British in North America, and surrendered Montreal, hundreds of miles away in Canada. The repercussions spread to Michigan. As part of the surrender, the British assumed control of Fort Pontchartrain and other French forts. The British continued their hold on Pontchartrain until 1796—13 years *after* the United States officially won the Revolutionary War, which ended with the Treaty of Paris in 1783.

The road to Detroit's overdue liberation from the British began in 1792 when then-President George Washington selected Revolutionary

The group arrived from the north in a long string of bark canoes after a nearly two-month, 600-mile paddle through lakes and rivers. They first landed farther south on the island of Grosse Ile, but backtracked to what Cadillac viewed as a perfect strategic site to control traffic on the river, which serviced two of the Great Lakes: Erie and Huron. He ordered the construction of Fort Pontchartrain du Détroit (pronounced PONCH-uh-train), that measured about 200 feet square. Cadillac's wife arrived at the fort in the fall. He named the fort after France's minister of the colonies, Jerome Phelypeaux, Compte de Pontchartrain.

The word Pontchartrain refers to a particular bridge (*pont* in French) that was located on the way to the city of Chartres, which is near Paris. Shortly after Fort Pontchartrain was constructed, a small French settlement sprang up around it. Cadillac

BRAINBUSTERS

Basic: What is the significance of the shield-like symbol found on Cadillac cars?

Intermediate: At what other Michigan fort did Cadillac serve as commander?

Advanced: Why did Cadillac eventually leave Fort Pontchartrain in Detroit?

a) a promotion for exemplary service

b) British takeover of the fort

c) charges of improper behavior

See page 34 for answers.

War hero Gen. Anthony Wayne (for whom Detroit's Wayne County is named) to come out of retirement and lead the U.S. Army's efforts to protect settlers from an escalating number and severity of Indian raids. Wayne's personality, which combined bravery with a quick-to-anger temperament, earned him the nickname "Mad Anthony." He led his men through Ohio and what was then mostly Indian territory, erecting several forts and razing Indian villages along the way. In 1794, the Indians prepared to stop Wayne's progress at a spot near what is now Toledo in northern Ohio. Here, a tornado had ravaged the land and downed many trees, providing excellent hiding places for the Indians. Wayne and his men arrived at the site, appropriately named Fallen Timbers, and the fight raged. Wayne lost nearly three dozen men, but was successful in overpowering the opposing force. Within a year, many tribes, including the Delaware, Miami, Wyandot, and Shawnee, signed a treaty that greatly improved the safety of settlers in the Northwest Territory, which included what would become Michigan. With the treaty in hand, General Wayne set his sights on British-held forts, including Fort Pontchartrain in Detroit. Wayne's

Exit 46

The fort at Detroit changed hands more than once. On Aug. 16, 1812, it was the Americans' turn. The American commander at the time was the 59-year-old William Hull, who also happened to be the governor of the Michigan Territory and a one-time Revolutionary War hero. He had taken the post at Detroit reluctantly and only after repeated requests. He had been in Detroit for just a month when he learned of an imminent attack by the British. Apparently believing the British force was much larger than it actually was, he quickly surrendered without consulting any of his officers and without firing a single shot. The image at right is a poster that displayed the terms of surrender. For his action, which many considered cowardly, Hull was court-martialed and sentenced to death. U.S. President James Madison remitted the sentence due to Hull's previously exemplary military service, and Hull moved to Massachusetts where he spent much of the remainder of his life trying to clear his name. The United States recaptured the fort for good in 1813. (Hiram Walker Historical Museum collection, Archives of Ontario)

CAMP at DETROIT 16 August 1812.

CAPITULATION for the Surrender of Fort Detroit, entered into between Major General Brock, commanding His Britannic Majesty's forces, on the one part; & Brigadier General Hull, commanding the North-Western Army of the United-States on the other part.

1st. Fort Detroit, with all the troops, regulars as well as Militia, will be immediately Surrendered to the British forces under the Command of Maj. Gen. Brock, & will be confided prisoners of war, with the exception of such of the Militia of the Michigan Territory who have not joined the Army.

2d. All public Stores, arms & all public documents including every thing else of a public nature will be immediately given up.

3d. Private Persons & property of every description shall be respected.

4th. His excellency Brigadier Gen. Hull having expressed a desire that a detachment from the State of Ohio, on its way to join his Army, as well as one sent from Fort Detroit, under the Command of Colonel McArthur, should be included in the above Capitulation, it is accordingly agreed to. It is however to be understood that such part of the Ohio - Militia, as have not joined the Army, will be permitted to return to their homes, on condition that they will not serve during the war, their arms however will be delivered up, if belonging to the public.

5th. The Garrison will march out at the hour of twelve o'clock, & the British forces will take immediately possession of the Fort,

APPROVED.
(Signed) W. HULL, Brigr.
Genl. Comg. the N.W. Army.

APPROVED.
(Signed) ISAAC BROCK,
Major General.

A true Copy.

(Signed) J. McDONELL Lieut.
Col. Militia. P. A. D. C.
J. B. GLEGG Major A. D. C.
JAMES MILLER Lieut. Col.
5th. U. S. Infantry.
E. BRUSH Col. 1 st. Regt.
Michigan Militia.

ROBERT NICHOL Lieut. Coll.
& Qr. M. Genl. Militia.

advance guard arrived at the fort in July 1796, and the British simply handed it over to the Americans.

Fort Pontchartrain covered a small space, approximately the area within the downtown streets of Washington, Larned (pronounced LAR-ned), Griswold, and Atwater (AT-water). The fort burned down in the great fire of 1805 (see page 49) that destroyed many of Detroit's buildings. Although the fort was rebuilt, it eventually was demolished to make way for the area's expansion as a residential and business community.

This exit leads to the Ambassador Bridge, constructed from 1927–1929 to connect Detroit with the Canadian city of Windsor, Ontario. The four-lane bridge spans nearly 7,500 feet, and its towers are 500 feet tall—386 feet above the surface of the Detroit River, and the remainder below. At the top of each tower are the words "Ambassador Bridge," spelled out in 6-foot letters. It is known as a suspension bridge, which means that the bridge's road deck is

THE ANSWERS

The shield-like symbol on the automobiles is the coat of arms that Antoine de la Mothe Cadillac said belonged to his family. Actually, however, Cadillac made up the coat of arms, along with his family's aristocratic heritage and even his name. He was born Antoine Laumet, a commoner from a small French town, and came to North America in the 1680s almost penniless. He soon saw the benefits that a more noble background could bring, so he changed his name and fashioned a better background for himself. Then, he befriended a powerful man who appointed Cadillac *military commander at Fort de Buade* in the far southern Upper Peninsula. There, Cadillac spent much of his time as a fur merchant, although not necessarily an honorable one. He traded liquor for furs from the Indians, and then sold the pelts at outrageous profits to fur traders.

Jesuits complained fiercely to the French government about his tactics, especially the alcohol distribution, but Cadillac's conduct continued until the French closed Fort de Buade in 1696.

Cadillac compounded his less-than-stellar reputation once he arrived in Detroit and set up Fort Pontchartrain. Repeated charges that he was mean-tempered, greedy, and unfit for command reached the French government, which sent an agent to review and report on activities at the fort. *The agent found that Cadillac had alienated the Indians, engaged in extortion of local tradesmen, and lied to the French government about financial matters.* In response, the government ordered Cadillac transferred from Detroit to a fort in New Orleans.

Exit 47

Sunset image of the Ambassador Bridge between Detroit and Windsor, Canada. (Robert Lawson)

actually hanging from the cables that are visible stringing from one tower to the next and then to the ground at either end.

Although most people assume the Ambassador is government-owned, it is actually is held by a local, private company under the leadership of businessman Manuel "Matty" Moroun, who owns large parcels of land along the Detroit River. Moroun's company is interested in building a new six-lane bridge that would cross the river right next to the Ambassador, but the plan is controversial. Many people feel a future border-crossing bridge should be publicly owned, and government discussions are under way to consider the option.

BRAINBUSTERS

Basic: Before the Lions moved to downtown Detroit's Ford Field in 2002, they played at the Pontiac Silverdome about 25 miles to the northwest. Where did they play before that?

Intermediate: Now to baseball: Until 1907, the Detroit Tigers played their Sunday home baseball games outside of the city limits. Why?

Advanced: Before the team moved to Comerica Park, the Detroit Tigers played at the corner of Michigan Avenue and Trumbull Street for nearly a century. What was at Michigan and Trumbull before the ball park?

See next page for answers.

Exit 48

A careful scan of the horizon beyond the northbound side of I-75 will reveal a pair of spires from Ste. Anne's Church. The church heralds back to the time Antoine de la Mothe Cadillac first set foot in what would become Detroit and began constructing Fort Pontchartrain in 1701.

One of the first buildings he ordered built was a chapel, which was called Sainte Anne's. Although it is no longer housed in the simple structure of Cadillac's day, Sainte Anne's parish in Detroit is still active, making it the nation's second-oldest Catholic parish with a continuous record. Its earliest records date back to 1704. The current church has European-style arches called flying buttresses, and four gargoyles at the entrance. Located a few blocks east of I-75 at the corner of Howard and Ste. Anne streets, the church is open to the public and holds mass throughout the week. Ste. Anne's original cemetery holds the remains of many of Detroit's early settlers.

Exit 49

This is the interchange for U.S. 10, which is known as the Lodge Freeway within metropolitan Detroit. It is named for John C. Lodge, who had the distinction of serving twice as acting mayor of Detroit, and as mayor-elect of the city. His first stint as acting mayor came when Detroit Mayor James Couzens left office in 1922 to become a U.S. senator. He also served as acting mayor from 1922–23 and again in 1924 to take over terms of two mayors who resigned. One of the two was Mayor

Exits
48 & 49

THE ANSWERS

The Detroit Lions and the Detroit Tigers both played in Tiger stadium from 1938–1974. In 1975, they moved out of the city and to the Silverdome in the northern suburb of Pontiac.

All of the Tigers' Sunday games were held on Dix Highway just south of the ballpark—but beyond the Detroit city limits—through 1907. The reason was that *Detroit had so-called "blue" laws that prohibited boisterous activities, like watching a ball game, on Sundays* when residents ought to be in church or at least have more solemn thoughts on their minds.

The corner of Michigan and Trumbull, where Tiger Stadium would eventually stand, was a *dog pound and hay market* when construction of the ballpark began. During building, most of the huge trees on the site were removed … but not all of them. A line of trees remained along the left-field foul line, and five others stood in left-center field. The trees were finally cut down in 1900, a few years before the Tigers became a major-league team. Outfielders were, no doubt, relieved to contend only with the sun in their eyes, rather than a tree trunk in the face.

The Detroit Tigers once played at Bennett Park, shown here during the 1907 World Championship Series between Detroit and Chicago. (Library of Congress, Oct. 12, 1907)

James Couzens, who served as Detroit mayor from 1919–22, but left the office to become a U.S. senator. Lodge temporarily filled in as acting mayor until Frank Doremus was appointed to the position in April 1923. Doremus was elected the following November, but resigned in June 1924 due to ill health. Lodge again filled in temporarily. Finally in 1927, Lodge took the office as elected mayor and held the position through 1929.

— — —

Like many large roadways in Michigan, U.S. 10 has its roots in an Indian route, in this case called the Saginaw Trail. U.S. 10 roughly follows this trail from Detroit to the northern suburb of Pontiac.

Back in the mid-1800s, roads throughout Michigan were little more than wide paths carved through the woods and marshes. Because much of the land in southeastern Michigan was low-lying and prone to flooding or at least saturated conditions, roads here were frequently filled with mud. According to the

book *Michigan* by William F. Dunbar, one legend from the era recounts a person who saw a beaver hat lying in a stretch of muddy road:

> " . . . (W)hen, at the risk of his life, he waded out to it, he found a man under it and yelled for help. But the man under the hat protested: 'Just leave me alone, stranger, I have a good horse under me, and have just found bottom."

Exit 49

BRAIN BUSTERS

Basic: I-75 is an interstate highway. Since interstate literally means "between states," what is an interstate highway?

Intermediate: What can you tell about I-75 simply by reading the number 75?

Advanced: What can you tell about the Upper Peninsula's US-2 by its number?

See next page for answers.

Enterprising folks would lay claim to the most troublesome mudholes along a road and augment their income with the fees they charged to extract stuck wagons from the treacherous pits. According to long-ago tales, the value of some real estate parcels spiked in value if the property contained or had close access to a traffic-stopping mud-hole on a well-traveled road.

On the northbound side of I-75 sits the decades-long home stadium of the Detroit Tigers baseball team—a distinction it held until 1999, when the Tigers moved to a new facility in downtown Detroit. Nostalgic Tiger fans affectionately remember this site at the intersection of Michigan Avenue and Trumbull Street simply as "The Corner." The team joined the American League in 1903 and played its first major-league game on this site at what was then called Bennett Park. The park took its name from Charlie Bennett, a catcher on Detroit's previous professional baseball team,

THE ANSWERS

Although the name "interstate" might give the impression that all such highways cross state lines, some do not. The word "interstate" actually refers to their funding source: The federal government funds these highways with a pool of interstate money, that is, money that is shared by the states. In fact, the very remote and isolated states of Hawaii and Alaska both have interstate highways. Here in Michigan, one interstate highway has a place in the record books. The four-lane I-375 in Detroit is just over a mile long, making it the shortest interstate highway that is fully signed as an interstate highway and meets interstate standards, which include controlled-access (entry and exit via ramps). I-375 is actually left over from an early plan to run I-75 closer to the Detroit riverfront. Today, I-375 connects I-75 to downtown Detroit.

For the most part, odd-numbered interstates like I-75 run north and south, while even-numbered interstates are east-west in direction, although stretches here and there may veer a bit from this rule. In addition, higher numbers among the north-south interstates are farther east: I-75 runs from Michigan to Florida in the United States, while I-5 runs from California to Washington on the U.S. West Coast. Higher numbers among the east-west interstates, on the other hand, are farther north: I-94 in the northern states, including Michigan, versus I-10 in southern states.

Like interstates, north-south U.S. highways have odd numbers, and east-west highways have even numbers. Opposite from the interstates, however, north-south U.S. highways have the lowest numbers in the east, and east-west U.S. highways have the lowest numbers in the north.

called the Wolverines, that played from 1882–88. After the Wolverines' demise, Bennett had a terrible accident, losing both legs when he slipped on some ice and fell under a train. Nevertheless, the tenacious Bennett was on hand at the Tigers' inaugural major-league game to catch the ceremonial opening pitch. The game turned out to be a thriller. The Tigers fell behind by 10 runs, but rallied in the eighth and ninth innings to win the game with a score of 14–13. Bennett Park and its 6,000 wooden seats continued to host fans until 1911, when the park was dismantled to prepare the site for a new ballpark.

On April 12, 1912, a much more substantial stadium opened at "The Corner." Called Navin Field in honor of team owner Frank Navin, the ballpark drew a crowd of 26,000 on its opening day. Spectators filled bleachers that lined the infield, and the crowds spilled over to the outfield, where they stood behind ropes to watch the game. Many also bought seats on so-called "wildcat" bleachers. Set up by some business-minded adjacent landowners, the wildcat bleachers were rickety structures that stood just behind but towered above the ballpark's bleachers to give spectators a view of the field.

In 1938, the name of the ballpark changed to Briggs Stadium for team owner Walter Briggs. Numerous renovations brought the stadium's capacity to more than 50,000 by 1938. When John Fetzer bought the Tigers in 1961, he changed the name to Tiger Stadium. The team stayed at the stadium for nearly four more decades, and despite the cries of many fans who fought the move away from "The Corner," the Tigers relocated to the new Comerica Park in 2000. (For more about Comerica Park, see Exit 50.)

Professional baseball in Michigan has also encompassed female players. The state had two teams in the All-American Girls Professional Baseball League: The Grand Rapids Chicks and the Muskegon Lassies. The league formed in response to World War II, which drew most of the players from the men's major league teams and left behind a public that was hungry for something to take its mind off of the battlefield. The All-American Girls Professional Baseball League started up in 1943 with four teams from Indiana, Illinois, and Wisconsin. By the end of the war, the league had expanded to seven teams, including the two from Michigan and another from Indiana. Three more teams joined the league by 1948. The players' uniforms were one-piece, short dresses, but that didn't stop these talented athletes from playing competitively, sliding with bare legs into base, or diving for line drives. The league gained in popularity and press coverage until the war ended and men's major-league baseball resumed its pre-war quality. The women's league dissolved in 1954.

Exit 50

This exit will take you to the new home of the Detroit Tigers and the stunning Fox Theatre, both located just a few blocks away here in Detroit's downtown.

Construction on the new stadium for the Tigers baseball team began in the fall of 1997, and nearly three years and $300 million later, the ballpark opened to fans in the spring of 2000. It has 40,000-plus seats surrounding a sunken baseball diamond. Fans can see downtown Detroit skyscrapers over the right-field wall. A Detroit-headquartered financial services company called Comerica Inc. paid the Tigers $66 million over a 30-year span for the naming rights, so the stadium is known as Comerica Park. However, many people, including the media, frequently shorten the name to CoPa.

The Fox Theatre has a much longer history than Comerica Park. William Fox had the theater built in the 1920s when the automobile industry was flourishing and the city was one of the nation's rising stars. Fox was the owner of Fox Film Corp., which would later merge with another company to form the major film studio still known today as 20th Century Fox. Detroit's Fox Theatre (see page 43) is an opulent building that has overwhelmed first-time visitors since its opening-night playing of a silent movie on Sept. 21, 1928. At that time, the 5,000-seat theater had a distinctly Asian flare, and was decorated with gold leaf, stained glass, and hand-stenciled ceiling panels. The theater became one of the city's premier destinations, and continued to draw large audiences even during the Great Depression of the 1930s when money was tight. Over the following decades, the theater featured top Broadway plays, Hollywood films, and live performances by major entertainers like Frank Sinatra and Sammy Davis Jr.

A major renovation of the theater in the late 1980s resulted in a grand reopening on Nov. 19, 1988, and a revival of the theater's place as one of North America's most magnificent and highest-grossing entertainment centers. Beyond an 87-foot-long, six-story-tall lobby, the theater's auditorium boasts an enormous, two-ton, stained-glass chandelier that stretches 13 feet in diameter and holds 200 light bulbs. The auditorium pipe organ is the second-largest in the world, and its 2,500-plus pipes

BRAINBUSTERS

Detroit is the hometown of many famous people. Who are the following individuals?

Basic: Marshall Mathers, Robin Williams, and Charles Lindbergh.

Intermediate: Francis Ford Coppola, Aretha Franklin, and Casey Kasem.

Advanced: John N. Mitchell, Elmore Leonard, and Thomas Hearns.

See next page for answers.

fill the theater with sound. Since 2000, entertainment has ranged from world-class plays and dance performances, to musical revues and individual acts like comedians Jerry Seinfeld and Artie Lange, recording artists Enrique Iglesias, Josh Groban, Mary J. Blige, the Smashing Pumpkins, and magician David Copperfield, to name just a few.

Speaking of magicians, a few miles northeast of here is where the famed magician and escape artist Harry Houdini performed one of his most celebrated—and greatly exaggerated—feats. It happened just after the turn of the century in 1906 on the bridge to Belle Isle, a city island park located in the Detroit River. The popular version of the story tells that the 31-year-old Houdini, clad in handcuffs, leg irons and chains, jumped from the Belle Isle bridge and sank through a small hole cut in the solid ice covering the river. By the time he struggled to free himself from the

THE ANSWERS

Marshall Mathers is better known as Eminem, a rap performer who has been releasing albums since 1996. *Robin Williams is a comedian and actor*, who has starred in many films, including "Mrs. Doubtfire" (1993), "Goodwill Hunting" (1997), and "Happy Feet" (2006), as well as the popular 1970s TV show "Mork and Mindy." *Charles Lindbergh was an aviator, and the first person to fly solo across the Atlantic Ocean.* Lindbergh made the historic trip in 1927—flying from a field near New York City to Paris, France in less than 34 hours.

Francis Ford Coppola is an award-winning filmmaker and television producer with such film credits as "American Graffiti" (1973) and "Apocalypse Now" (1979 film). *Aretha Franklin is an internationally known singer*, whose 1967 hit "Respect" still receives considerable air play. *Casey Kasem is a radio personality*, who for many years hosted "America's Top 40." (The current host of the program is Ryan Seacrest.)

John N. Mitchell was attorney general in the administration of President Richard Nixon. Mitchell was convicted of conspiracy, perjury, and obstruction of justice surrounding the break-in of Democratic Party headquarters at the Watergate Hotel. The break-in eventually led to Nixon's resignation. Mitchell served 19 months before being released for medical reasons. He died in 1988. *Elmore Leonard is the author of several best-selling fictional novels.* Some, like *Get Shorty*, have been made into movies. *Thomas "Hit Man" Hearns is a boxer* who holds world-championship titles in numerous weight classes. His latest bout was in 2006, when the nearly 50-year-old Hearns beat Shannon Landberg at a match held north of Detroit in The Palace of Auburn Hills.

Detroit's Fox Theatre is one of North America's most magnificent and highest-grossing entertainment centers. (Balthazar Korab)

Exit 50

shackles, he had drifted underwater some distance from the hole. He survived in the numbingly cold water by breathing the air trapped in pockets between the water and overlying ice, and eventually found his way back to the entry hole. Houdini perpetuated this legend himself, frequently recounting the details of his miraculous escape. In fact, this rendition was dramatically portrayed by actor Tony Curtis in the 1953 movie "Houdini."

The legend has a few flaws: Not only was Houdini secured with a 113-foot-long lifeline during the stunt, but the Detroit River wasn't even frozen over. According to a front-page account of Houdini's exploits in the Nov. 27, 1906, *Detroit News*, the handcuffed magician vaulted from the bridge that afternoon into the cold, but unfrozen, water. After freeing himself from the restraints while beneath the water's

Harry Houdini performed one of his most famous (and exaggerated) escapes in Detroit. He died at Detroit's Grace Hospital 20 years later. (Library of Congress. Chicago : National Pr. & Eng. Co., [1895])

surface, he swam to a lifeboat that was stationed nearby. Apparently, Houdini felt the accomplishment deserved more widespread attention, along with just a bit of embellishment, and he helped to create the more colorful story of his miraculous escape from the icy grips of death.

Houdini's Detroit connection didn't end there. Twenty years later on an October afternoon, he died in the city's Grace Hospital of an abdominal inflammation and gangrene of the appendix, either resulting from or exacerbated by a punch to the stomach he had received 10 days earlier in Montreal, Canada. It happened like this: Houdini often bragged about his great strength and claimed he could sustain even the most severe strikes to his stomach. He accomplished the

feat by first firming his abdominal muscles in preparation for the impact. In Montreal, however, a fan delivered a punch to the gut before Houdini could brace himself, and the magician suffered a serious blow. Houdini continued to perform despite severe abdominal pain, but keeled over two days later following a Detroit show. He died at 1:26 p.m. on Halloween in 1926 at the age of 52.

During his life, Houdini was a vocal skeptic of the supernatural, believing that fortune-telling and contact with the dead were nothing but scams. To prove his point, he worked up a secret code with his wife that he promised to answer beyond the grave, if it were at all possible. If he didn't answer in 10 years—he did not—it would put to rest such claims. The result, however, wasn't quite what Houdini expected. To this day, believers hold a séance each year to try to contact the magician.

Exit 52

Many of the streets in Detroit, as in other cities, carry the names of prominent citizens. Three of them, John R, Mack, and Woodward Avenues, are all accessible from this exit.

John R and Mack refer to former Detroit mayors. John R commemorates John R. Williams, a landowner and bank president who was elected Detroit mayor in 1824. Mack Avenue bears the name of Andrew Mack, who became the mayor of Detroit 10 years later.

Woodward, which like U.S. 10 and other major roads in southeastern Michigan started off as a simple Indian footpath through the woods, carries the name of Augustus B. Woodward, who was appointed by Thomas Jefferson to be a Michigan territorial judge. Woodward arrived in Detroit shortly after the Great Fire in 1805 that leveled much of the city, and devised the city's new road plan to resemble the street design he knew from Washington, D.C. In this plan, major north-south and east-west roads would crisscross the city, and other diagonal thoroughfares would radiate from the downtown area through the grid. When a north-south, an east-west, and a diagonal road intersected, they would form a circular area, called a circus. Although the plan went through a number of changes before the streets were laid, the underpinnings of Woodward's design are still evident. One of the major Detroit streets is Woodward Avenue. Although it has his name, the judge claimed it wasn't chosen as a tribute to him, but rather because it led to the woods.

BRAINBUSTERS

Basic: What is a gnome?

Intermediate: Legend tells tales of the Red Gnome of Detroit. What is the Red Gnome?

Advanced: What famous Detroit-brewed beverage featured a gnome on its bottles?

See next page for answers.

On the southbound side of I-75 lies Wayne State University's medical campus, and about a half mile farther Wayne State's main campus. In fall 2006, the university's enrollment was nearly 33,000 students, and included one of the nation's most diverse student bodies, drawing enrollees from throughout southeastern Michigan and from around the world. The university campus has undergone great change over the last two decades, when most of the last remaining houses-turned-office buildings were removed, numerous new buildings constructed, and many historic buildings renovated. One of the latter is Old Main, which was originally a high school building when it opened its doors in 1896. Numerous legends about Old Main have circulated through the years. One of the most bizarre is that the building has numerous, now-abandoned basement levels, including one that has a full-sized pool. The most extreme rumors put the swimming pool at 13 floors underground and home to alligators.

Wayne State is part of the University Cultural Center Area, which includes the Detroit Institute of Arts, Detroit Historical Museum, the main branch of the Detroit Public Library, and, more recently, the Museum of African-American History and the Detroit Science Center. The art institute is especially notable for its vast collections, including the famous "Detroit Industry" frescoes, painted by artist Diego Rivera of Mexico in 1932-33. The mammoth murals

45

Detroit Institute of Arts (J. Bruce Hubbard)

depict the range of workers and of businesses in the city, and are considered Rivera's finest work.

Mile Marker 53

Henry Ford opened the first of his large automotive plants near here on the corner of Piquette Avenue and John R Street. The Ford Piquette Avenue Plant, which was built in 1904, turned out the first Model T automobile in 1908. This is also where Ford began experimenting with a moving assembly line, a method that would soon revolutionize manufacturing in the United States and far beyond. Ford saw the assembly line as a way to cut the cost of automobile

THE ANSWERS

A gnome is a *small creature, somewhat like a leprechaun, that mainly lives underground where it guards its piles of treasures.*

According to legends that date from the 1700s to current day, *the Red Gnome of Detroit (also known by its French name of Nain Rouge) wanders the city, where it wreaks havoc especially on those who disturb it.* For instance, Detroit founder Antoine de la Mothe Cadillac is said to have tussled with the creature just before he lost of his post as fort commander (see page 34). Numerous gnome sightings also preceded the bloody 1763 battle between British soldiers and Chief Pontiac's American Indian force (see mile marker 42) and

the massive fire of 1805 that burned down much of the city (see page 49). To this day, people claim to see the gnome before calamity strikes.

For many years, *Vernors ginger ale* has featured a gnome on its products. Vernors, first sold in a pharmacy in Detroit back in the 1860s, is a fizzy soda pop that can effervesce right up your nose and cause you to give a little sneeze or cough. According to some Vernors company literature, James Vernor began experimenting with a mix for the unique-tasting drink before leaving to serve in the Civil War. When he returned four years later, he found that the mix had aged perfectly and soon began selling it as a soda pop.

The Model T, shown here at Greenfield Village, helped to turn Detroit into the Motor City. (The Henry Ford)

Exit 53

production, and make the cars afford-able to the average working citizen. Within just two years of producing its first Model T, Ford needed a larger plant, and began plans to construct a much larger facility in nearby High-land Park. He began mass producing Model Ts on assembly lines at the new plant, eventually manufacturing up to 9,000 cars in a single day. The price for a new Model T was $290, and every one of them left the plant the same color: black. The demand for the cars, which were nicknamed Tin Lizzies and Flivvers, skyrocketed. By the time the last Model T rolled off the assembly line in May 1927, Ford's workers had produced 15 mil-lion of the automobiles and put the country on wheels.

The Ford Piquette Avenue Plant, a modest, three-story, brick structure, still stands, although it had fallen into disrepair by the late 1990s and may have faced the wrecking ball were it not for a nonprofit group by the name of the Model T Automotive Heritage Complex Inc. The group acquired the building in 2000 and began renova-tions. Within a few short years, the group began hosting events and invit-ing visitors to see the building's many historical displays and imagine a typi-cal day in the plant a century earlier.

Exit 53

I-94, or the Ford Freeway, as it is known to metropolitan Detroiters, crosses I-75 here. It gets its name from automobile pioneer Henry Ford. The freeway travels from Port Huron on the east side of the state all the way to Kalamazoo on the west side, and then on past Michigan's border through Chicago, up to Wisconsin, northwest through Minnesota, then west to North Dakota and Montana. In Michigan, I-94 roughly follows the old Territorial Road, which served as a stagecoach line for travelers to and from Chicago before becoming a road for automobiles. (Note that Michiganders refer to the local names of highways by preceding them with the word "the," as in "the Ford" for I-94 or "the Lodge" for U.S. 10. However, they never precede the letter/number combinations with the word "the." A Michigander calls I-94 just "I-94." A Californian, on the other hand, would refer to the freeway as "the I-94" or "the 94.")

Like the other even-numbered interstate freeways, I-94 is mainly an east-west highway. As it sweeps from metropolitan Detroit up to its end in Port Huron, however, it has a decidedly north-south orientation. Despite the minor confusion that sometimes results, the road signs continue to designate the freeway as "I-94 east" and "I-94 west" regardless of the direction the road is actually taking. I-94 ends in Michigan at the Blue Water Bridge in Port Huron. The bridge traverses the St. Clair River to Sarnia in Ontario, Canada. To the north, the St. Clair River connects with Lake Huron, the third largest of the Great Lakes by volume. To the south, the river flows into Lake St. Clair, which is quite a large lake, but not one of the Great Lakes. The waterway does not end there. Lake St. Clair connects with the Detroit River to the south, and that river joins

the eastern edge of Lake Erie, which is the smallest Great Lake by volume. Lake Erie continues along to border Ohio, Pennsylvania, and New York.

Exit 54

Until 2005, the Detroit Mounted Police Unit had a stable about a mile west of this exit. The stable, which had been used for 100 years, became horseless in February 2005, when the unit transported its remaining three horses to its one lingering mounted-police stable in downtown Detroit's Rouge Park. The department disbanded its mounted division shortly thereafter. Horseback police can still be seen in the area however. The mounted patrol of the Wayne County Sheriff's Department, which serves the county that includes Detroit, is still active with a human staff of six officers and an animal component of four horses. The county department also maintains a reserve mounted unit comprising eight officers who bring their own horses to work.

The Wayne County mounted patrol is fairly recent, beginning in the 1970s, but the Detroit Mounted Police dates all the way back to 1893 when the mayor at the time felt he had to do something to deal with the escalating calls about livestock wandering off of farms and onto the roads. The mayor, Hazen Pingree, fought fire with fire—or rather, animal with animal—and decreed that officers would patrol the roads on the backs of a half dozen horses. As cows and other farmyard creatures became less common in Detroit, the mounted unit became useful in other ways, particularly crowd control. On horseback, the officers could merge with mobs of people, yet still be high enough above the ground to scan for problems that needed their attention. By 1973, the unit was one of the nation's finest with 60 horses, and it participated in precision drills that thrilled audiences at the Michigan State Fair for many years. In the 1990s, the police force shifted its resources away from mounted patrols, and residents began seeing fewer and fewer of the horseback officers trotting along with the cars on city streets. The Detroit Police Department disbanded the division in 2005 although many long-time residents and city visitors miss the clop of hooves and hope it will make a comeback someday.

— — —

Just south of this exit is West Grand Boulevard, known to locals simply as "The Boulevard." About a mile west of this exit on West Grand Boulevard stands the one-time headquarters of General Motors, and the landmark Fisher Building in the area of Detroit known as the New Center. Architect Albert Kahn was involved heavily in both of these buildings. A German immigrant, Kahn was the darling of the automobile industry. During his career, he had a hand in the design of more than 1,000 auto-related buildings, many of them in the city of Detroit. They include the *Detroit News* building downtown, the Detroit Police headquarters, numerous banks, the Willow Run plant that built bombers for World War II

(see exit 37), and a number of homes for Detroit's high-rolling automobile elite.

The former GM headquarters building, which was constructed in 1922, remains a tour-de-force today. Arched entrances lead into a long lobby with a cavernous, vaulted ceiling. The lobby unites the four, rectangular, 15-story office towers of this nearly 1 million-square-foot building. In the late 1990s, GM moved its headquarters to the Renaissance Center in downtown Detroit, but the GM Building is still a busy business place. Following extensive renovations, the building now houses almost 2,000 state government employees under its new name of Cadillac Place.

The neighboring Fisher Building was built in 1927–28 by seven brothers of the Fisher family. Sons of a carriage maker, the men arrived in Detroit two decades earlier and started the Fisher Body Co. That

Exit 54

BRAINBUSTERS

Basic: People occasionally see mounted police making the rounds in the Detroit area . . . and so do dogs. Sometimes, particularly hostile dogs will run at the horses with teeth bared. How does a mounted police officer typically respond to an aggressive dog?

Intermediate: Where did the term "freeway" come from?

Advanced: Detroit was completely destroyed in the Great Fire of 1805. How did the fire start?

See next page for answers.

venture brought in a considerable profit: They started the company with a $50,000 investment, and in 1926, General Motors bought out the company for more than $200 million. With a considerable fortune in hand, the Fishers hired Albert Kahn as the architect of the Fisher Building and instructed him to build "the most beautiful building in the world." The result was a lavish, $10 million, 10-story work of art with a 25-story central tower that was visible for several miles. The gold-gilded tower became even more noticeable when it was lit at night. Workers removed the gold gilding during World War II over unwarranted fears that enemy bombers would enter Detroit and see the tower as an inviting target.

Inside the Fisher Building, ornate plasterwork, stone carvings, about 430 tons of bronze embellishments, gold leafwork, and even etched elevator doors awe its visitors. In its theater, moviegoers were entertained by films, as well as talking macaws that flitted about the theater and swooped down to patrons holding out treats for the birds. The macaws are long since gone, but the 2,089-seat theater still draws crowds. Nowadays, the still-magnificent theater is known as a premier, live-entertainment venue that frequently presents star-studded Broadway plays.

Here in Detroit, the Fisher name is also remembered as the alternative title for this stretch of I-75: "the Fisher Freeway."

THE ANSWERS

When approached by an aggressive dog, a mounted police officer typically *turns the horse and charges the canine head-on.* In the vast majority of cases, the dog will turn tail and run off.

The Interstate Highway Act of 1956 proposed thousands of miles of free (no-toll) express highways to crisscross the nation. *"Free express highways" was shortened to freeways.*

According to various legends, the fire started in June 1805 when lit tobacco from the pipe of a baker (some blame it on a stablehand instead) blew onto a pile of hay. The day was windy enough to turn the tiny flame into an inferno and engulf the town.

Exit 55

Just east of this exit lies Hamtramck (Ham-TRAM-ick). It was established as a township in 1798, decades before Michigan became a state. Named for Colonel John F. Hamtramck, a Revolutionary War soldier, the town was mostly a farming community until the 1910s when new faces streamed into Hamtramck to earn a living in the bustling auto factories and made the town the fastest growing community in the nation. Many of the new workers were Polish immigrants. Although the population is not as overwhelmingly Polish as it once was,

Hamtramck still boasts many Polish restaurants and establishments. One Polish tradition, in particular, remains alive and well throughout southeastern Michigan today: the paczki (pronounced POONCH-key). Polish Catholics celebrate Fat Tuesday with a snack of paczkis. Fat Tuesday is the day before Ash Wednesday, which begins the 40-day, pre-Easter, Lenten season of fasting. Although paczkis look like jelly doughnuts, they are heavier, more filling, and more fattening. One paczki can contain a whopping 400–450 calories and 25–27 grams of fat. That's more than twice the calories of a standard glazed doughnut, and more than three times the fat. Diet is overlooked on Fat Tuesday, however, and long lines form at Polish bakeries in Hamtramck early in the morning as patrons select paczkis by the dozen. The pastries come with a variety of fillings from custard to jellies, with prune jelly being one of the traditional favorites. Supermarkets and doughnut shops outside of Hamtramck have begun offering their versions of "paczkis" in the weeks leading up to Easter, but purists claim they can taste the difference and will only buy the treats from a real Polish bakery and only on Fat Tuesday.

Other favorite Polish foods include kielbasa, a garlic-laden sausage often served with fresh horse radish (which has an odor that can clear the sinuses); pierogies (pronounced pee-ROH-geez), which are dumplings usually filled with sauerkraut, cheese or potatoes; golabki (guh-wump-key), a combination of meat-and-rice filling rolled inside cabbage leaves; and potato pancakes.

The town of Hamtramck was once next to Detroit, but as the Detroit's population and geographic size increased, the city eventually grew to surround the hamlet.

Exit 56

The Davison Freeway runs rights through a small city, called Highland Park, which was once an outlying suburb of Detroit but like Hamtramck, is now completely surrounded by the larger city. Highland Park's name comes from a ridge, or high land, that was the tallest point north of the Detroit River. Road builders have long since leveled the ridge for easier passage of Woodward Avenue, one of the main roads leading north out of Detroit. In the past, Highland Park has gone by different names, including Cassandra and Whitewood. One of its

BRAINBUSTERS

Basic: At Hazel Park raceway, like most other horse-racing tracks, patrons bet on the horses to win, place or show. What do the three terms mean?

Intermediate: What is a daily double in horse-racing terms?

Advanced: In horse racing, what does it mean when a bettor tells the clerk "$1 trifecta key number 4 on top of 2, 3 and 6"? How much does this bet cost?

See next page for answers.

most well-known native sons is Tim Meadows, who was born in Highland Park in 1961 and went on to land a long-running spot on TV's *Saturday Night Live* from 1991–2000. He has since won roles in movies and makes frequent TV appearances.

Exit 57

The main campus of the University of Detroit–Mercy, located about 3 miles to the west on McNichols Road, is the oldest and largest Catholic university in the state. It is actually a combination of two colleges: Detroit College, which was founded by a group of Jesuits (Roman Catholic clerics) in 1877; and Mercy College, which was established by the also-Catholic Religious Sisters of Mercy in 1941. Detroit College later changed its name to the University of Detroit, or "U of D." The two colleges merged in 1990 to form the University of Detroit–Mercy. Currently, the university has three campuses, including one in downtown Detroit. Its student body numbers about 5,600 undergraduate and graduate students.

Less than a mile past the University of Detroit–Mercy is another Catholic institution of higher learning: Marygrove College. The 53-acre college had its start in 1905 in Monroe, a city south of Detroit, but moved to its current Detroit location 22 years later. Marygrove's student body is about a quarter of the size of U of D-Mercy.

Education is not the only draw to this area. A large attraction is the Detroit Golf Club, a private club that had its start in 1899 in a farmer's field. In addition to the golf course, its members enjoy a large clubhouse,

THE ANSWERS

"Win" means that the bettor is choosing the horse he or she feels will come in first. "Place" is a bet that the horse will come in either first or second, and "show" is a bet that the horse will be first, second or third.

For a daily double, *bettors select the winning horses in back-to-back races.* Most racetracks allow betting on daily doubles in the first two races and the last two races of the day.

In a trifecta, bettors try to pick the top three winning horses in a race in the correct order: the correct first-place horse, the correct second-place horse, and the correct third-place horse. In a trifecta key, the bettor picks the horse he or she thinks will finish first, and then picks two or more horses to finish in either second or third. In "$1 trifecta key number 4 on top of 2, 3 and 6," *the bettor is selecting number 4 as the "key" or winning horse, and two of the three horses numbered 2, 3 and 6 to come in second and third.* The ticket costs $1 per combination—4-2-3, 4-2-6, 4-3-2, 4-3-6, 4-6-2 and 4-6-3—for a total of $6.

swimming pool, and tennis courts. It also has a notable reminder of the city's earlier days. Between the seventh and eighth fairways, golfers can see a tree that was once used by Indians as a trail marker. The Indians bent the tree when it was a sapling to direct the way to the city of Saginaw nearly 100 miles to the north.

Exit 59

Eight Mile Road, immortalized in the 2002 film "Eight Mile" that starred rapper Eminem and female actor Kim Basinger, is the boundary between Detroit and its northern suburbs. It also approximates the base line that was established in 1815 and used by surveyors to plan township boundaries in the state. At the point where I-75 crosses this busy east-west thoroughfare, Eight Mile Road marks the border for Wayne County to the south and Oakland County to the north. Wayne County is named for General Anthony "Mad Anthony" Wayne. He was a hero of the Revolutionary War, and as the American general in command, he accepted the surrender of the Northwest Territory from the English in 1796. He was a hero of the so-called "Indian wars" of southeast Michigan in the 1800s.

Oakland County's name reflects the many oak trees within its boundaries. Technically speaking, Oakland County and much of eastern Michigan didn't become part of the United States until 1819 when American Indians finally signed the Treaty of Saginaw that covered this region.

Today, traffic on Eight Mile Road is particularly heavy around Labor Day when the oldest state fair in the nation sets up at the fairgrounds about a mile east of this exit. The Michigan State Fair dates back to 1849, just 12 years after Michigan gained statehood. For the first few decades, a different city hosted the fair each year, but in 1905, four citizens set out to bring it to Detroit permanently. One of the four was Joseph L. Hudson, who founded Hudson's department store. He purchased 135 acres of what was then farmland and sold it for $1 to the state for use as fairgrounds. The land, plus a few more acres, is still home to the fair. The Michigan State Fair includes many activities, such as the traditional midway of rides and games, and many agricultural displays and livestock showings.

Exit 59 also leads to the suburbs of Ferndale and Hazel Park. Both municipalities take their names from a prominent natural feature. Ferndale was once noted for having a fern-covered understory, and Hazel Park (originally called Hazel Slump) was filled with hazelnut bushes. The busy, little town is now home to the Hazel Park Raceway, a horse track. The track specializes in harness races, in which the horses pull two-wheeled carts, called sulkies or bikes, that carry a highly skilled driver. In harness racing, the horses must trot. If a horse "breaks stride," or shifts from a trot to a gallop, the driver must take the horse to the side and slow it down until it resumes the trotting gait. By the time the horse resumes the race, it is usually much too far behind to be a contender. At Hazel Park, like most other racetracks, visitors come to bet on the races. For more on betting, see the Brainbuster on page 51.

— — —

Although most people assume that I-75 was constructed from Detroit north, the stretch of I-75 here was laid in 1972, after the northern portion of the freeway was already completed. This stretch finally connected the northern portion of I-75, which ran all the way to Sault Ste. Marie in the Upper Peninsula, and the southern portion, which continued down to Ohio.

MM 63

Mile Marker 63

I-75 passes through Royal Oak here. More than one story is associated with the town's name, but they all involve a massive oak tree and Lewis Cass. Cass had a very busy political life. He was governor of the Michigan territory for nearly two decades from 1813–1831, then served as secretary of war under President Andrew Jackson from 1831–1836 and as ambassador to France, and also held the position of U.S senator from Michigan. In addition, he made an unsuccessful bid for the U.S. presidency in 1848 (see exit 37).

One tale of the Royal Oak's city name reports that Cass fell asleep under the enormous oak tree, and awoke to see its large branches spreading above him. The governor remarked, "This is truly a royal oak." Another story relates that the governor likened the tree to the famed Royal Oak in Scotland. There, in the mid-1600s, a disputed king named Charles successfully evaded would-be executioners by cutting his hair, dressing like a woodsman, and hiding in a large oak tree, which was thereafter called the Royal Oak.

Cass, who died in 1866, is buried in one of Detroit's oldest cemeteries, the Elmwood Cemetery. History buffs can find the graves of other famous Michiganders, like the state's first geologist Douglass Houghton and numerous war heroes, at the Elmwood, which is located near downtown Detroit.

— — —

The Detroit Zoological Park, which sits west of the freeway, thrilled crowds when it opened in 1928, because it was the first zoo in the nation to showcase its animals in exhibits that were surrounded by moats rather than fences. In addition, the zoo's landscaping was second to none, and included a well-thought-out plan with sculptures, fountains and flower gardens. As the zoo grew, its exhibits became more natural-looking, providing visitors with not only astounding views of the animals, but an appreciation for how the different species live in the wild. Today, the 125-acre zoo is still one of the world's premier animal parks, housing more than 3,000 animals from 340 species. Some of the zoo's main attractions include an impressive

Great Apes of Harambee exhibit, a Penguinarium with views of the swimming birds above and below the water line, a National Amphibian Conservation Center surrounded by a wetland that looks as if it has always been there, and the largest polar bear exhibit on Earth. The polar bear exhibit, called the Arctic Ring of Life, opened in 2001 and features a 70-foot long tunnel that cuts through the underwater portion of the exhibit. From this clear-walled, round tunnel, visitors can watch the enormous bears swim alongside and over top of them.

Exit 65

A sign on the southbound side of I-75 points out the city of Madison Heights, named for President James Madison. Nearby in 1763, Indians ambushed English soldiers who had come to attack Ottawa Chief Pontiac. The bloody skirmish is recalled in the name of a creek that flows through this area: Red Run.

Oakland Mall, visible on the northbound side of I-75, includes more than 120 shops and eateries. As an idea of its size, a person can walk an entire mile by hiking around the outer perimeter of all three of its levels. Besides foot traffic, the mall can draw thousands of shoppers and during the holidays, traffic to the mall sometimes backs up onto I-75.

Mile Marker 68

White Chapel Memorial Cemetery sprawls along the southbound side of I-75 here. A unique feature of the cemetery is a large marble sculpture of a growling polar bear straddling a helmet and a cross. It is a monument to the members of the 339th Infantry Regiment, the 1st Battalion of the 310th Engineers, the 337th Ambulance Co., and the 337th Field Hospital of the U.S. Army's 85th Division—collectively known as the "Polar Bears." These troops battled the Soviet Bolshevik army in the frigid regions of North Russia from the last months of World War I in 1918 until May 1919.

The United States became involved in the campaign when the French and British governments sought the assistance of President Woodrow Wilson and U.S. troops to assist those fighting for an independent Czechoslovakia, to drive the Soviets from the Eastern Front, and to stop the spread of communism. The battles took place in a barren landscape where temperatures dropped to 40 and 50 degrees below zero. Of the 5,000 U.S. troops deployed to North Russia, nearly 200 lost their lives to battle injuries or to disease. The monument at White Chapel stands amidst 56 graves of the men who served in the conflict.

Exit 69

This road, known here as Big Beaver, is actually 16 Mile Road (16 miles from downtown Detroit). Farther to the east, its name changes to Metropolitan Parkway, and farther to the west, it is called Quarton (QUART-un). The Big Beaver section of this road report-

The nearby 319-acre Cranbrook Educational Community includes schools, as well as other buildings such as the Cranbrook House (shown here) and a science institute. (Courtesy of Cranbrook)

edly got its name from a huge beaver dam that once straddled the nearby Beaver Creek, now known as Sturgis Drain. Several waterways in southeastern Michigan, including the Sturgis Drain, started off as creeks but were excavated and sometimes lined with concrete to facilitate the removal of runoff from the adjacent land.

Big Beaver Road runs through the city of Troy. Like other municipalities throughout Michigan, Troy's name mimics that of a city in the eastern United States, in this case Troy, N.Y. Newly relocated settlers to Michigan often nostalgically named their new cities after their hometowns back East. In the past, Troy was also known as Hastings, after a bank president, and Troy Corners. Troy is currently a bustling city filled with high-rise business centers and corporate headquarters, and is home to more than 81,000 residents.

Just north of Birmingham and about 4 miles to the west of I-75 is the 319-acre Cranbrook Educational Community, which is listed as a National Historic Landmark. The educational community was founded by Ellen Scripps Booth and one-time *Detroit News* president George G. Booth. The Booths purchased the land in Bloomfield Hills in 1904 and began transforming it from a farm into a lovely, gardened retreat for their extended families. They eventually decided to turn the property into an educational complex. Famed architect Albert Kahn designed Cranbrook House, the family's residence, and Finnish architect Eliel Saarinen designed the majority of Cranbrook, which was built in stages from 1926–1943. The Booths chose the name of the educational community to commemorate the family's ancestral home in Cranbrook, England. The

This pool and sculpture are located on the grounds of Cranbrook Educational Community. (Courtesy of Cranbrook)

MM 75 & 77

Cranbrook community is a combination of several buildings, including Cranbrook House, Cranbrook Schools, a church, the Cranbrook Academy of Art, and the Cranbrook Institute of Science. Currently, more than half a million visitors stroll Cranbrook's grounds or attend events on the campus, and 1,620 students from Michigan and around the world attend its lower, middle, and upper schools.

Mile Marker 75

Pontiac, the largest city in Oakland County, is named for Ottawa Indian Chief Pontiac, who lived in the 18th century. Pontiac, who led an unsuccessful attack on the British at Detroit in 1763, spent his summers near here. (Details of Pontiac's attack are listed under mile marker 42.) This area, dotted with small lakes, still draws sportsmen and sportswomen for hunting and fishing trips.

Since Chief Pontiac's time, the city's appearance has changed. In the 1800s, sawmills and flour mills took over the landscape. Later it became a town known for manufacturing carriages and, later yet, for producing automobiles. Now, the city's nightlife is drawing people to its re-energized downtown area, which has been dubbed New Pontiac. Local residents sometimes call the city by its informal nickname "The Yak" referring to the last syllable of Pontiac.

Mile Marker 77

Just south of mile marker 77, a building with the name Foamade Co. looms alongside I-75. According to company literature, its history can be traced back several decades to a father and son reupholstering a chair. The experience provided the son, Morris Rochlin, with a look at the padding and his first glimpse of a piece of synthetic foam rubber, which had been developed less than a decade earlier. The young Morris, who had recently graduated from the University of Michigan with an engineering degree, saw a bright future for foam as a replacement for the springs used in furniture and mattresses. Using money borrowed from his sister, Morris and a friend opened the first Foamade Industries shop in Detroit in 1947. His friend soon bowed out, but Morris persevered. One of his new company's major products was the cushions used to pad the kneelers in Catholic church pews. Through the years, the company has switched from foam rubber to urethane products, and has diversified into producing such items as automotive air filters, gaskets, various packaging materials, seat cushions, and toys. In 1980, the company moved into this building, which still serves as its headquarters and research-and-development facility. The company also now has facilities in Hillsdale, Mich., and Verona, Miss.

In various areas along I-75, including here on the southbound side, signs warn of fog. What is fog? Fog is actually a thick, low-lying cloud of tiny, suspended droplets of water. The cloud hovers along the ground, where it can obscure a driver's line of sight. Fog typically forms in the morning or in the evening when the temperature of the colder ground chills the air

above it. Warmer air can hold more water than cooler air, so as the air cools enough—to what is known as the dew point—water droplets condense out of

BRAINBUSTERS

Basic: Which companies make up the Big Three automotive giants?

Intermediate: Where are the Big Three's world headquarters?

Advanced: Walter Chrysler, who founded Chrysler Corp. in 1925, had already held a position with General Motors as the head of Buick making $6,000 a year. To keep Chrysler at Buick, GM founder Billy Durant in 1916 offered him a three-year contract totaling:

a) $6,000 a year (about $115,000 in today's dollars) with a $5,000 bonus ($96,000) at the end of each year

b) $12,000 a year (about $230,000 today) with a $50,000 ($960,000) bonus at the end of each year

c) $120,000 a year (about $2.3 million in today's dollars) with a $500,000 bonus ($9.6 million) at the end of each year

Advanced: After leaving Buick and before founding Chrysler Corp., Chrysler accepted a position at Willys-Overland Motor Co. for a salary of:

a) $500,000 a year (about $9.6 million in today's dollars)

b) $750,000 a year (about $14.4 million)

c) $1 million a year (about $19.2 million)

See answers on page 60.

the air, and fog forms. In the same way, fog can arise if an area of warm and humid air moves over colder ground and cools to the dew point. Fog often lasts an hour or less, but sometimes persists for many hours, and if conditions are right, even into the middle of the day. Mist is the same thing—tiny water droplets in the air—but the droplets are not as dense so it doesn't obstruct driving like fog can.

Certain areas, like this low-lying section of I-75, are especially prone to fog. As the ground cools in the evening and chills the air above it, the coldest air sinks and the warmest air rises. In areas with even a small valley, the coldest air flows down the hillsides to the valley's bottom and if it reaches its dew point, forms fog here even when other nearby hillsides and hilltops are fog-free.

When driving in fog, experts recommend that drivers resist the temptation to use their high-beam headlights because that will actually reduce visibility. This is because the fog reflects the light, essentially creating a wall of light rather than a better view ahead. Your low-beam lights are the best bet in foggy conditions. In addition, drivers should watch their speed. Because fog can hide the passing scenery and give the illusion that both other cars and your own are moving much more slowly than they really are, you can quickly find that you are speeding.

Walter P. Chrysler (Chrysler Historical Archives)

Exit 78

Exit 78

The massive Chrysler Headquarters and Technology Center rises on the northbound side of I-75. The complex, which exceeds 4 million square feet, includes the readily visible highrise portion that is topped with the star-in-a-pentagon, or "pentastar," logo. Despite its prominence on this headquarters of the Big Three automobile company, the pentastar faded from use for several years. As of 2007, however, it is once again the company logo.

Chrysler has undergone a number of changes over the years. Its roots can be in part traced to the Maxwell Motor Co., an automobile company that produced a number of models in the early 1900s but began experiencing financial problems by 1920. Walter P. Chrysler, who had already held highlevel and extremely lucrative positions at Buick and another car manufacturer called Willys-Overland Motor Co. in the past, became chairman of the board of the Maxwell company in 1921. The company produced its first Chrysler-named car in 1923, and in

1925 the newly named Chrysler Corp. officially took over Maxwell Motor Co. The year 1928 was a busy one for the new corporation. It introduced Plymouth and DeSoto models, and also purchased Dodge Brothers Inc., which had already become a very well-known automobile company.

The changes didn't end there. More recently, in 1987, Chrysler Corp. purchased American Motors Corp., which produced Jeeps among other vehicles. In 1998, German manufacturer Daimler-Benz merged with Chrysler to form Daimler-Chrysler. This name held until 2007, when the now-struggling car giant sold an 80.1 percent stake in the company to a private investment firm called Cerberus Capital Management. DaimlerChrysler's name is now Chrysler LLC, also known as "The New Chrysler."

More information on Walter Chrysler and the company is available in the Walter P. Chrysler Museum, which is located here and is part of the campus of the Chrysler Headquarters and Technology Center.

A short drive east on University Drive will take you to Oakland University, a 17,000- to 18,000-student public institution. The university's roots are actually tied to the Dodge automobile fortune. Here's the story: The Dodge brothers, John and Horace, started a machine company in Detroit in 1902 and first produced parts for stoves, and later for cars. The car parts were mainly transmissions for Oldsmobiles.

After a meeting with Henry Ford, however, they ended their arrangement with the Oldsmobile company and in early 1903 began building Ford's Model A automobiles. Ford and his partners in his venture, however, were short on cash, so they paid the Dodge brothers in company stock. John and Horace Dodge invested well, built up their own company and soon each had enough money to build mansions: John's was in Detroit and Horace's was in Grosse Pointe, a suburb that abuts Detroit along its northeastern boundary. John also began buying farm acreage in the area where Oakland University now stands. The

THE ANSWERS

The Big Three automotive giants are: *Ford Motor Co. (sometimes shortened to FoMoCo); Chrysler LLC; and General Motors Corp. (or GM).* All three have their world headquarters in Michigan: Ford's in Dearborn, a suburb south of Detroit; Chrysler's in Auburn Hills, a suburb north of Detroit; and General Motors' in downtown Detroit.

GM founder Billy Durant offered Walter Chrysler $10,000 a month, or *$120,000 a year* with an annual $500,000 bonus to head Buick for three years. After leaving Buick, Chrysler moved on to Willys-Overland Motor Co., where his salary was *$1 million a year,* an eye-popping amount for the time. These two positions helped make the Kansas-born Chrysler one of the wealthiest men in America.

Dodge brothers' fortune grew and the two started manufacturing Dodge automobiles in 1915. On the home front, John had lost his first wife, Ivy, to tuberculosis in 1901 and remarried his one-time secretary Matilda in 1907. Matilda, it turns out, would be the key to the start of Oakland University, but more on that in a minute.

In the summer of 1919, Horace became a victim of the great 1918 influenza pandemic that killed between 20 million and 40 million people worldwide, and nearly 700,000 of them in the United States alone. John rushed to Horace's bedside. Horace was lucky and recovered, but John was not so fortunate. He caught the flu and died in January 1920. Horace, who like his brother had always been a heavy drinker, took the news hard. Less than a year later, Horace died of cirrhosis of the liver, a condition that is related to alcohol abuse.

The men's two widows held onto the Dodge Brothers Motor Car Co. for five years, finally selling it for $146 million in 1925. Also that year, John's widow Matilda remarried a lumber broker named Alfred Wilson and moved to the Dodge farm property. Matilda did not rest on her laurels: She oversaw the construction of a Tudor revival-style mansion named Meadow Brook Hall (see page 63), served on the governing board of Michigan State University from 1931-1937, and in 1940 accepted an appointment from Michigan Gov. Luren Dickinson to become the state's first female lieutenant governor. Matilda and Alfred also expanded Meadow Brook, eventually amassing more than 2,500 acres and constructing numerous outbuildings, including a retirement home they named Sunset Terrace. In 1957, the pair donated Meadow Brook Hall, 1,500 acres of the surrounding property and a $2 million endowment to begin a branch of Michigan State University there. Matilda was so enthralled with the MSU venture, which was named Michigan State University-Oakland, that she presented each member of its first graduating class with a diamond ring.

Exit 79

BRAINBUSTERS

Basic: What is the job of a lieutenant governor in the state of Michigan?

Intermediate: Michigan Gov. Luren Dickinson took office in 1939 upon the death of then-Gov. Frank Fitzgerald. Unusually, Dickinson's swearing-in ceremony took place not in Lansing, but on a nearby farm not far from the small rural community of Charlotte (pronounced shar-LOT). What was the significance of that farm?

Advanced: Which of the following about Dickinson's stint as governor are true?

a) With his appointment, he became the state's oldest governor.

b) With his appointment, he became the longest-serving Michigan governor.

c) With his appointment, he became the first — and only — lieutenant governor to succeed a Michigan governor who died in office.

See next page for answers.

The branch eventually became the independent institution of Oakland University that is located there today. The 110-room and 88,000-square-foot Meadow Brook Hall is now preserved as a museum and hosts a variety of events, including dinners, lectures, and tours.

This is one of three I-75 exits that lead to The Palace of Auburn Hills (the others are exits 79 and 83), an indoor stadium that hosts musical concerts, various consumer shows, and other entertainment programming through-out the year. It also is home to the Detroit Shock, a team in the Women's National Basketball Association, but perhaps its best known association is with the Detroit Pistons. The Palace, as it is commonly known, is the last in a series of homes for the Pistons. When the team first came to Michigan, it played in Olympia Stadium for four years before moving to Cobo Arena, where it remained for 17 years. Both the Olympia and Cobo were located in Detroit. In 1978, the team moved out of the city and to the Pontiac Sil-verdome, a stadium farther north on I-75, and remained there until moving to The Palace for its 1988–89 season.

The year the Pistons arrived at The Palace also marked their first NBA championship. The team repeated the feat the following year. The Pistons had a few lean years afterward, but again became NBA champs in the 2003-04 season. The team nearly had back-to-back NBA titles once again, but in game seven of the final series in the 2004-05 season, it lost a heart-breaker to the San Antonio Spurs by a score of 74–81.

The Palace notes the three Pistons NBA championships, as well as the two earned by the Detroit Shock

THE ANSWERS

In addition to taking on whatever miscellaneous jobs that the gover-nor asks, the *lieutenant governor in Michigan stands in for and represents the governor in his or her absence; pre-sides over and is the tie-breaking vote in the state Senate; and serves on the State Administrative Board,* which has a supervisory role over state depart-ments and agencies.

Luren Dickinson was a farmer, and maintained his farm near Charlotte even while serving as the state's lieu-tenant governor for 17 years under five different governors (various periods from 1915 -1939). He not only had his swearing-in ceremony for governor on his farm, but also conducted much of his official busi-ness there. When Dickinson took office in 1939, he was the *first and only lieutenant governor to succeed a Michigan governor who died in office.* Dickinson, who was 79 when he was sworn in, was also *the oldest person ever to assume the position of state governor.* He ran for the office of gov-ernor in 1940, but lost, and he died in 1943.

Matilda Dodge Wilson, the widow of automobile mogul John Dodge, oversaw the construction of the impressive Meadow Brook Hall, which is now a museum at Oakland University. (Travel Michigan)

Exit 81

women's team, in its address. With every championship win, it adds to its street number, which as of 2007 was 5 Championship Drive. Mail will also, however, reach The Palace at the building's original address of 3777 Lapeer Road.

Besides being one of 30 teams in the National Basketball Association, the Pistons also played a key part in the formation of the NBA back in 1949. Then-Pistons owner Fred Zollner wanted to combine the two currently existing basketball leagues—the National Basketball League and the Basketball Association of America—into one bigger and better association. He took the bull by the horns and invited the leaders of both organizations to his house. There, at his kitchen table, they hammered out an agreement to combine the two into the NBA we know

today. His role in basketball history is remembered in part through the NBA Western Conference championship trophy, which is named the Zollner Trophy.

If you took this exit and continued north on Lapeer Road, which is also

BRAINBUSTERS

Beginner: The Detroit Pistons' roots are in not only another city, but another state. In what state did the Pistons organization begin?

Intermediate: How did the team get its name of Pistons?

Advanced: When did the Pistons come to Detroit, and why?

See next page for answers.

known as the highway M-24, for about 26 miles, you would reach the city of Lapeer. It is located in the similarly named Lapeer County. The name Lapeer is probably an adaptation of the French words *la Pierre*, which means "the stone," and is a tribute to the rocky bed of the major river through the area: the south branch of the Flint River. Some people believe the name Lapeer may instead be derived from *la Pere*, which means "the father" and may have been used for its religious meaning by French missionaries in the area. Yet another hypothesis is that Lapeer was copied from a similarly named town elsewhere that was a previous home of one of the early settlers.

The first settlers in the Lapeer area, Alvin Hart and his family, arrived in 1831. Twelve years later, Hart became a state senator, representing an area that now covers the entire Upper Peninsula and six counties of the Lower Peninsula. He was instrumental in moving the

Exit 83

state capital from its then-location in Detroit's Capitol Park to Lansing in 1847. Lansing, where the capital is still located today, is about 90 miles west northwest of Detroit, and about 75 miles west of here. After the move, the old Detroit capitol building's first floor became a city library, and the second story became a high school.

Exit 83

About 3 miles to the north is the Olde World Canterbury Village, a collection of ornate buildings that house specialty shops and a banquet center. The village sits on a small part of the farm estate of William Scripps, who was the publisher of the *Detroit Evening News*, the forerunner of the *Detroit News*, from 1929–1952. Scripps spent a great deal of time at the estate, which was known as Wildwood Farm, and in 1931, he began using an aircraft to aid his travel to and from Detroit. His commute no doubt turned more

THE ANSWERS

The *Pistons organization started out in 1941 as part of the National Basketball League in Indiana.* Known as the Fort Wayne Zollner Pistons, the team played in a high school gymnasium. *The team's owner was Fred Zollner, a Minnesota native who ran an Indiana plant that manufactured pistons* for automobile, boat and other engines. (A piston is a cylindrical device that slides up and down inside a larger, hollow cylinder located in the engine, and plays a role in converting burning fuel into power.) *The team remained in Indiana until 1957*, when Zollner felt it should be associated with a larger city. Since Detroit's previous basketball team, the Detroit Falcons, had recently folded, he moved his Pistons to Detroit. The city was the automotive capital of the world, so the team's name didn't even have to change, and the Detroit Pistons was born.

than a few heads, because the aircraft he used was one of the world's first helicopters.

Only a small part of Scripps' estate falls within the confines of Olde World Canterbury Village. Much of the remainder is preserved within the boundaries of several parks in the area, including the beautiful Bald Mountain State Recreation Area.

Bald Mountain offers more than 4,600 acres of hilly terrain, small lakes, and streams. Many mountain bikers visit the park to ride its 15 miles of trails in the summer, while cross-country skiers take advantage of some of these paths in the winter. The park also has access for boaters to no less than eight lakes. Anglers often fish one of the park's lakes or the two designated trout streams, and swimmers enjoy the beach on Lower Trout Lake. Besides its appeal to human visitors, the park's rugged landscape and considerable forests make it a good home for many species of animals, including deer, mink, muskrat, and beaver, among others.

Exit 89

Sashabaw Road (pronounced SASH-uh-baw) is named for an American Indian chief who lived in this area of Oakland County. During Chief Sashabaw's day in the early 1800s, his tribe hunted and farmed here. In 1818, the families of Detroiter Oliver Williams, a major, and his brother-in-law arrived in the area to verify earlier reports of undesirable conditions in the lands north of Detroit. One from U.S. Surveyor General Edward

Tiffin was especially influential. He wrote, "Taking the country altogether so far as it has been explored and … together with information received concerning the balance, (the land) is so bad, there would not be more than one acre out of 100, if there would be one out of 1,000, that would in any case admit of cultivation." The Williams families found that his description was way off the mark, and returned to Detroit with their own testimonials of a beautiful and fertile land that would be excellent for farming and was also filled with a multitude of sparkling lakes. Major Williams was so impressed that his family built a 1,000-square-foot home on the shores of one of the lakes, which they named Silver Lake, and moved there.

With the acres upon acres of pristine woodlands and lakes came a very healthy animal population, and that of course, included some less-desirable species like pesky mosquitoes and snakes. One snake in particular caught Williams' attention. It was the blue racer, a native—and non-venomous—Michigan reptile that has a lovely slate-blue back and can grow to 5 or 6 feet long. These beautiful reptiles are still located in this area and much of the southern half of the Lower Peninsula today. Major Williams eventually captured and killed a few and sent them to museums for their collections.

Besides the wildlife, the major also encountered an Indian tribe that called the area home, and he formed an especially strong friendship with the tribe leader, Chief Sashabaw. The feeling was mutual and the chief even gave Indian names to the members of the Williams' clan.

Chief Sashabaw died in 1834, and was buried on the edge of Silver Lake not far from the Williams family home. The tribe members continued their lives there for a while longer, but the landscape was changing. In fact, Alexis De Tocqueville, a visitor to the area in 1831, wrote: "Already, indeed, the white man is approaching through the surrounding woods; in a few years he will have felled the trees now reflected in the limpid waters of the lake, and will have driven to other wilds the animals that feed on its banks." Eventually this Indian community, like many others in Michigan, headed southwest beyond the state's borders and to the central plains.

BRAINBUSTERS

Drivers who take Dixie Highway north from exit 93 will travel through Springfield Township.

Basic: Residents here overturned the township's original name of Painsville, and instead named it after the numerous natural springs within its boundaries. What is a natural spring?

Intermediate: The headwaters for three rivers and 25 lakes fall within the township's borders. What are headwaters?

Advanced: Name the three rivers that have headwaters within Springfield Township's borders.

See page 68 for answers.

One Indian from western Michigan summed up his feelings and no doubt those of many of his peers in a small booklet he wrote and distributed in Chicago in 1893. The Indian was Simon Pokagon, son of Potawatomi Chief Leopold Pokagon. He wrote of the white man, "And while you ... bring the offerings of the handiwork of your own lands, and your hearts in admiration rejoice over the beauty and grandeur of this young republic, and you say, 'Behold the wonders brought by our children in this foreign land,' do not forget that this success has been at the sacrifice of *our* homes and a once-happy race .... The cyclone of civilization spread westward; the forests of untold centuries were swept away; streams dried up; lakes fell back from their ancient bounds; and all our fathers once loved to gaze upon was destroyed, defaced or marred, except the sun, moon and starry skies above, which the Great Spirit in his wisdom hung beyond (your) reach."

Exit 91

The city of Clarkston sits off Exit 91. Its name comes from Nelson Clark, who with his brother Jeremiah constructed a dam and grist mill building in town in 1839. A grist mill processes grain. Nelson opened a general store three years later, and other businesses sprang up shortly thereafter. Nowadays, Clarkston is a busy little town with a small, about two-block-long downtown area that residents simply call "the village."

Not far from the downtown is the multi-acre property of rock singer Robert James Ritchee, better known as Kid Rock. He has made many of his often-raunchy and sometimes quite explicit recordings there in a studio that he named the Clarkston Chophouse. For some star-watchers, his biggest claim to fame is not his music, but his marriage to actress Pamela Anderson. The pair wed—and divorced—in 2006. Kid Rock was born in Romeo, Mich., a small village about 25 miles east of Clarkston.

———

Exit 93 also brings northbound travelers up state highway M-15 to Davison, a town that was named for a man who never lived there. Here's what happened. The town was originally supposed to be called Middlebury, but another town already had that name. At about the same time in a nearby little town called Atlas, another quandary developed. That little town's original name was Davisonville and referred to Norman Davison, an early settler and mill owner there, but was switched to Atlas to reflect its location within Atlas Township. The state legislature grasped the opportunity to give a new name to Middlebury while appeasing the mill owner, and renamed Millbury to Davison, even though Norman Davison actually lived someplace else. Nowadays, the town of Davison has the slogan "City of Flags," and in its municipal courtyard hangs a flag from each of the 50 states. Residents and business people also join in the fun, and often display flags at different times throughout the year.

On the northbound side of I-75 is a residential development called Bridge Valley that contains more than 50 acres of preserved land, including a rare type of wetland known as a fen. A fen is a marshy area fed by groundwater that is rich in certain minerals, including calcium and magnesium. The homeowners association owns the land in the preserve, but a local conservation organization, called the North Oakland Headwaters Land Conservancy, has an easement for it. The result is a joint stewardship arrangement that protects the site into the future. The homes in the development are arranged around the fen preserve in a so-called "clustered" style. In a typical development, the land is divided up among all of the residents. In a clustered development, the residential lots are a bit smaller and grouped together in patches, while the remaining land is set aside as shared or, in this case, natural space. This particular development is often used as an example of good environmental design. As a testament to its ecological benefits, a variety of animals and plants—some of them very rare—inhabit its 50-acre preserve ... despite its location next to a major interstate freeway!

Just north of Exit 93 on the northbound side is a billboard carrying the likeness of Jesus Christ and the words: " Are you on the right road?" For many travelers, the billboard, which has greeted drivers for decades, marks the passage from southeastern Michigan to places "Up North." The billboard belongs to the adjacent Dixie Baptist Church. As of 2007, church administrators were considering selling the land to a development company, but they insist that the billboard will either remain at this site or at the location of a new church facility they are planning farther north along I-75.

— — —

This exit empties onto to Dixie Highway, which is the predecessor to I-75. Before the freeway was constructed, Dixie handled the majority of the north-south traffic in this part of the state. Remnants of old buildings, including a long-closed drive-in restaurant a few miles north, still dot the sides of the road.

— — —

Drivers heading south on Dixie reach Waterford a few miles down the road. Waterford, along with a string of other Michigan communities, were sites of stations along the Underground Railroad, a trail rather than an actual railroad that was used by runaway slaves to escape from their "masters" in southern states to freedom in Canada. Beginning in about 1830, slaves would seek their freedom by traveling the route during the night and staying by day in a station, which was often just the home of a sympathetic farming family who provided shelter, food, and warm or dry clothing if necessary. Occasionally, especially dangerous conditions would force the slaves to remain at a station for more than a day. Many of these brave farming families would hide the often-frightened but determined runaways in secret rooms and cellars, believing that the fight for freedom was more important than the threat of fines and imprisonment for harboring a fugitive.

THE ANSWERS

Exit 93

A spring is water that flows to the surface from a natural underground source. When you buy a bottle of spring water, you are getting water collected either right at the spring or from the underground formation that feeds the spring.

The headwaters for numerous waterways lie within Springfield Township. *Headwaters are the smallest of creeks and streams that feed larger water systems, like rivers and lakes. The three rivers arising within Springfield Township are the Huron, Shiawassee (shy-uh-WAH-see) and Clinton.* The Huron and Shiawassee rivers begin near Big Lake, which is just west of exit 93. The Huron runs south all the way to Lake Erie, while the Shiawassee flows in a mainly northerly direction to Lake Huron. The Clinton River starts a few miles northeast of here and drains southeast into Lake St. Clair. In addition, some of the headwater streams for the Flint River are also in the extreme northern edge of Springfield Township. The Flint River flows through the city of Flint to the north and eventually over to Lake Huron.

Many Americans fought for slavery to end, and state by state, it did. In 1862 and 1863 President Abraham Lincoln signed the two parts of the emancipation proclamation that abolished slavery in much of the United States, and many of the remaining states took action themselves to end it within their borders, too. With its job done, the Underground Railroad dissolved one state at a time, and the participating farming families returned to concentrating on their fields. By 1865, all states had ended slavery except Kentucky and Delaware. The 13th amendment to the U.S. Constitution, signed in that year, abolished slavery in the United States for good.

Exit 98

A few miles to the west of this exit is the village of Holly, a quaint little town containing dozens of businesses and homes that are listed on the National Historic Register. The town began to make its mark when one of its early settlers, Ira Alger, constructed a dam on the Shiawassee River that runs through the area, and used the now-controlled water flow from it to power a lumber mill and later a grist (grain) mill. This attracted a rail line, and the first train came to town in 1855. With the advent of the locomotive traffic and later a second railway line, the town quickly grew. It did, however, have a setback in 1875 when a massive fire raced through many of the earliest structures, which were made of wood, and destroyed much of the downtown area. The replacement brick buildings, however, have stood the test of time and still stand on Holly streets to this day.

Besides its collection of grand old homes and buildings, Holly attracts visitors with two rather unusual festivals, one honoring traditional Christmas book, and the other a hatchet-wielding religious zealot.

The first is the Dickens Olde Fashioned Christmas Festival, during which the town turns back the hands of time to the era of Charles Dickens' book *A Christmas Carol*, which was set in 19th-century England. Actors stroll around town playing the roles of Ebenezer Scrooge, Tiny Tim, Jacob Marley, the Ghost of Christmas Past, and others from the book. Vendors sell various true-to-the-period treats, such as roasted chestnuts, while describing their goods with cockney accents, and numerous activities also lend themselves to the theme. These may include strolling singers, marching chimney sweeps, or rides in a horse-drawn carriage. Admission is free. The festival runs consecutive weekends from late November through mid-December.

The second festival, which is held on the weekend after Labor Day, is the Carry Nation Festival. It is named for a woman who was a member of the anti-alcohol Temperance Movement and, according to some accounts, once came to Holly to take on drinkers there. During the U.S. Temperance Movement's early days in the late 1700s, members promoted temperance, or drinking in moderation, but by the 1830s and 1840s, many members took a harder line

Carry Nation was not only vocal in her abolitionist beliefs, she often wielded rocks and a hatchet to destroy bottles and barrels of alcohol. (Library of Congress. Bain News Service, circa early 1900s)

and began to favor abstinence. Carry Nation took the latter route . . . by force. A large woman at 6 feet tall, she gained a reputation from 1899-1910 for striding into saloons and using rocks that she nicknamed "smashers," and later a hatchet, to destroy bottles and barrels of alcohol, along with the equipment used to dispense it. Sometimes, other women would accompany her on the raids, singing hymns and shouting prayers while the rocks and/or hatchets flew. Between her bar-bashing escapades, Nation was very vocal, even praising the 1901 assassination of President William McKinley, whom she believed was a heavy drinker. In the 10 years she spent walloping saloons, Nation was arrested nearly three dozen times, but always managed bail, which she paid from money earned by giving lectures or by selling souvenirs. These were no ordinary souvenirs; they were souvenir hatchets.

Nation's zest for fighting alcohol consumption apparently came in some part from her failed first marriage to a raging alcoholic, but mainly from what she described as a heavenly vision that instructed her to hurl rocks inside saloons in the Kansas town of Kiowa. She soon added the hatchet to her arsenal and expanded her activities far beyond Kiowa. Reports indicate that Nation arrived in Holly on Aug. 29, 1908, to promote her views against alcohol and against smoking, which she considered another great evil. At the time, Holly had become known for a number of saloons, which received a great deal of business situated as they were near the busy railroad station.

Nation died in 1911 at the age of 64, but her stop in Holly is still remembered during the Carry Nation Festival that has been an annual event here since 1973. The 2007 festival, for instance, included reenactments of Nation's 1908 stopover along with a barroom brawl. Visitors who were gluttons for punishment needed only take out a cigarette or carry a brown paper bag while at the festival, because it also included a Carry Nation impersonator who walked the streets and was not shy about hurling choice words at anyone she thought was taking a smoke or, worse yet, a drink.

Exit 101

This road, Grange Hall Road, is named for a nearby grange hall. A grange hall is a local meeting place usually used by farmers to talk about agriculture.

Speaking of roads, back in the 1800s when this area was changing from forests to farms and lumbering towns, roads were in high demand by settlers and business owners alike. One of the noted road builders of the era was a man named William Gage. Due to his impressive build, which he carried on a 6-foot-2-inch frame, he became known as "Big Bill." Gage came to the area with his wife Sarah Ayers Ingraham from their native New Hampshire. The two were wed in the early 1830s and traveled by covered wagon to Michigan where they became two of the first settlers to move to the area near Holly. There, they started a farm and the highly religious Bill began preaching his views during various meetings with his neighbors. Big Bill also spent several years in the 1840s and 1850s constructing many of what were called plank roads between various nearby communities in the region. These roads were basically planks of wood laid boardwalk-style over the ground. The roads made possible horse-drawn transportation over what would otherwise be muddy and frequently impassable pathways. His contributions to the region did not end there. He also won election to the Michigan Legislature in 1842.

An interesting side note to the lives of Big Bill and Sarah was an odd run-in they had with a local Indian chief. As the story goes, the chief took a fancy to Sarah, and challenged Big Bill to a wrestling match: If he could beat Bill, he would win his wife Sarah. Fortunately for the couple, Bill quickly pinned the chief. The chief was determined, however, and continued to confront Bill. Apparently unable to refuse the bets, Bill fought the chief four more times and won each match. Finally on the sixth challenge, a rather-perturbed Bill slammed the chief to the ground with such force that the chief abandoned his desire for Sarah and thereafter left the couple alone.

Big Bill died on Feb. 25, 1856 while he was building a yet another plank road between the towns of Fenton, situated to the west, and Flint, which is located farther up I-75. According to reports, a limb from a large tree crashed to the ground and killed him during the road construction. The body of William "Big Bill" Gage lies buried in a cemetery nearby.

Mile Markers 101–102

Watch for a downhill skiing site known as Mount Holly on the northbound side. The hill has something for skiers of many levels, and boasts a total of 18 slopes, the longest with a vertical drop of about 350 feet. It also has a special "terrain park," which is an area filled with fun obstacles for snowboarders to ride or jump. Night

**Exit 101
MM
101–102**

71

Snowboarding in Michigan. (Vito Palmisano)

lighting permits late-hour skiing and snowboarding, and snow-making equipment extends the season when the snow here stops falling.

Although not visible from I-75, a large piece of property sits just north of Mount Holly where visitors can return to the days of the Renaissance and listen to the thundering hooves of armor-clad horses as the knights on their backs hurl toward one another in full-contact jousting matches. This is just one of the great variety of events that are part of the annual Renaissance Festival, held here every August and September. Thousands of visitors—some of them who come dressed in elaborate period costumes—enjoy the entertainment and foods of the time, and pick up an unusual, hand-crafted item or two at the festival marketplace. A huge troupe of performers, including sword swallowers, magicians, sword fighters, dancers and comedians, provide a bustling and exciting atmosphere against a backdrop of castle walls, the smells of freshly cooked turkey drumsticks and Scottish eggs (hard-boiled eggs, each surrounded with breakfast sausage and deep fried), and a cacophony of children playing, people laughing and musicians playing at every turn.

Exit 106

This marks the border between Genesee County to the north and Oakland County to the south. Genesee (pronounced jen-eh-SEE) was named by settlers to reflect their previous home in a similarly named county in New York. The word Genesee is actually a Senaca Indian word for beautiful valley. Oakland

County has simpler roots: It was named for the many oak trees within its boundaries.

This exit leads to the city of Grand Blanc (pronounced locally as grand blank) and to Warwick Hills Country Club, the home of the annual Buick Open golf tournament that brings in top PGA golfers, including the likes of Tiger Woods, Vijay Singh, Jim Furyk and John Daly.

Grand Blanc is a city of about 8,000 residents. Its name means "great white" in French, and was apparently named for a large trader, known only as Fisher, who came through the area in the 1700s and earned the nickname of Grand Blanc from area Indians.

Mile Marker 108

Just south of mile marker 108 runs the railroad tracks of CSX Transportation, a corporation that provides train services for much of the eastern United States, including southern Michigan. The company's locomotives are emblazoned with a large blue CSX logo and a smaller number toward the front. The number identifies each individual locomotive. Some CSX locomotives, however, may still bear the paint and logos of the companies that have since merged into CSX. These include the Chesapeake and Ohio Railway, and the Seaboard System Railroad, among others. The tracks here are part of 800 miles of rail that CSX maintains in Michigan. According to CSX, trains can move a ton of freight "three times as far as a truck on a gallon of fuel."

In all, the company operates a 21,000-mile rail network (as of 2007) that connects dozens of ports on lakes, rivers and the Atlantic ocean. According to CSX, the company has nearly 4,000 locomotives and more than 100,000 freight cars. Each day, 1,200 of the locomotives are rolling, transporting a total of 20,000 freight car loads.

A hospital called Genesys Regional Medical Center is visible north of this mile marker on the southbound side of I-75. It has 410 beds, about 75 percent of which are usually filled, delivers some 3,000 babies a year, and handles more than 100,000 emergency visits annually. One of its more unusual services is a free mini-medical school that teaches members of the general public about all sorts of medical subjects, like genetics and anatomy, as well as more general topics such as obesity and nutrition, and how to be a healthy traveler.

BRAINBUSTERS

Downhill skiing has been a popular sport in Michigan for decades, and snowboarding has become increasingly common in recent years. What do the following snowboarding terms mean?

Basic: Bonk.

Intermediate: Corduroy and chatter.

Advanced: Duck-footed and goofy-footed.

See next page for answers.

M-54, also known as Dort Highway here, runs north for about 30 miles where it connects up to I-75 again. Like other roads in Michigan that are designated as state highways, M-54 is posted with a sign having a white diamond containing a black letter M and a number. Wisconsin was the first state to number and post its state highways, and in 1918–19, Michigan became the second. Shortly after these two states instituted the system, other states did the same. Now all states, as well as the provinces of Canada and indeed most developed countries the world over, have similar numbered and marked highways.

I-75 is not a state highway. Instead, it is an interstate highway and is posted with a red and blue shield with "interstate" across the top in a red band, and the number prominently displayed in the lower blue portion of the shield. In all, the United States has more than 46,000 miles of interstate highways. These highways almost always have no traffic lights or stop signs, and have no cross traffic. Instead, crossroads go over the highway, or the highway goes over the crossroad. Parts of 14 different interstate highways are located within the state of Michigan. That accounts for more than 1,200 miles inside this state's boundaries.

Another type of highway in Michigan is the U.S. highway. These are major thoroughfares that are designated with a number. If you travel these roads, however, you will find that significant stretches are not freeway but are roads that travel through the middle of towns. In other words, they have intersecting crossroads and in many cases, their traffic must stop periodically for streetlights. These roads are designated with a white shield on a black background. The number is displayed in black within the shield. Michigan contains about 2,400 miles and at least some part of 19 separate U.S. highways.

Many drivers in Michigan are familiar with US-27, a highway that ran north and south along a lengthy stretch of the Lower Peninsula.

THE ANSWERS

A snowboarder *bonks* when he or she hits something that isn't snow, like a tree or another snowboarder. *Corduroy* is the pattern that results when a tracked vehicle (often a Sno-Cat) grooms, or smooths out, a trail. For snowboarders who want to make sharp turns, corduroy is a great surface to do it. *Chatter*, on the other hand, occurs when the snowboard vibrates as it rides over an icy or otherwise uneven surface. *Duck-footed* snowboarders stand on their boards with their toes pointing outward, duck-style. A *goofy-footed* snowboarder rides in a "left-handed" way with his or her right foot toward the front of the snowboard rather than the left. Riding with the left foot forward is called regular-footed.

Michigan's US-27 is no more. The Michigan Department of Transportation changed its name from US-27 to US-127, and in 2002 switched all of the signs to reflect the new number. The switch gives this stretch of the highway the same number as the highway has in its southern reaches. In all, U.S. 127 runs from Michigan and through both Ohio and Kentucky to Tennessee.

Along I-75, you will see numerous offshoots, like 475 here that veers away from I-75 for a few miles and then reconnects with I-75 farther north at exit 125. Each of these offshoots, known as business loops, are named with an even number (here, it's a 4) that precedes the number of the interstate (75). Like other business loops, 475 takes travelers through a downtown area, which in this case is Flint.

Many people know the city of Flint best from the 1989 movie "Roger & Me," a documentary of sorts from filmmaker Michael Moore, who is a native of Flint. In the movie, Moore chronicles his attempts to track down Roger Smith, then-chairman of General Motors, and confront him about the effect that the downsizing of GM had on the city of Flint and its residents. The movie alternates from comical to satirical and often has a dark undercurrent as it shows how the city has changed and its residents have had to cope with the loss of jobs. The film brought atten-

tion not only to Moore, who is the son of a Flint autoworker, but also to the city of Flint. The city is now undergoing numerous redevelopment efforts to attract new businesses and diversify its economy, and to promote the area's institutions of higher education, which include the University of Michigan-Flint and Mott College.

Since the film "Roger & Me," Michael Moore has made several additional films. His 2002 "Bowling for Columbine" again used satire and humor, this time to tackle violence and guns in American society. "Bowling" won an Academy Award for Documentary Feature. Another film "Fahrenheit 9/11" was Moore's portrayal of the George W. Bush presidency and life in the United States since the Sept. 11, 2001, terrorist attacks. In 2005, "Fahrenheit" became the first documentary ever to win the People's Choice Award for Best Movie of the Year. Frequently political and always controversial, Moore's films have staunch supporters and equally-staunch detractors. Love him or hate him, most people applaud his pro-Michigan efforts. Recently, Moore spearheaded a Film Festival in the

BRAINBUSTERS

Basic: What is a Humvee?

Intermediate: How did the Humvee get its name?

Advanced: Which of the following are products of General Motors: Buick, Chevrolet, Chrysler, Dodge, Jeep, Lincoln, Mercury, Pontiac, Saturn?

See next page for answers.

northwestern Lower Peninsula community of Traverse City. Although it only began in 2005, the summer festival already attracts thousands of film buffs from around the country and even around the world who can select from a sweeping array of both independent and classic films.

— — —

The city of Flint took a place in the record books in 1966 when the city commission elected Commissioner Floyd McCree as the city mayor. The action was momentous because the country at the time was still embroiled in civil rights issues, and McCree was a black man. The election made him the first black person ever to serve as mayor of a major U.S. city. By comparison, the residents of Detroit would not elect their first black mayor, Coleman Young, until seven years later in 1973.

Mile Marker 112

Fenton Road crosses here. It leads to the city of Fenton about 10 miles to the south. The city got its name in a rather unusual way. Apparently two of the early settlers there had different ideas of what their town should be called and resolved their dispute with a card game. The winner was Col. William Fenton, who would later become the lieutenant governor of Michigan, and the town took the name of Fenton. The loser was Robert LeRoy, who owned a hotel in town. He did not leave empty-handed, however: The town's main thoroughfare became LeRoy Street.

Mile Marker 116

If you hear an airplane that sounds too close for comfort, it is likely either taking off from or landing at

THE ANSWERS

The *Humvee began as a truck made by AM General*, a one-time subsidiary of the Jeep Corp., for the U.S. Army. The truck's original name was rather ungainly: *High Mobility Multi-Purpose Wheeled Vehicle, or HMMWV. That was quickly shortened to Humvee.* AM General began the initial design of the vehicle in 1979 and by 1983 had an order for 55,000 of the trucks from the U.S. Army. The public heard about and became enthralled with the Humvee mainly through its performance in the Gulf War during the early 1990s. AM General saw a potential market, and in 1992 the company began making a version of the Humvee for civilians. This was the Hummer H1. General Motors got involved in the product line in 1999, and now does all marketing and distributing of Hummers, which currently come in several other models.

The *GM products in the list are Buick, Chevrolet, Pontiac and Saturn.* Lincoln and Mercury are Ford Motor Co. products. Chrysler, Dodge and Jeep are products of Chrysler.

President Gerald Ford. (Library of Congress, Feb. 6, 1975)

1987 and is now drawing about five times that number each year, is the state's third-busiest airport. Detroit Metropolitan Airport is the busiest, followed by the Gerald R. Ford International Airport, located in Grand Rapids in southwestern Michigan.

On the northbound side of I-75 is the 1.9-million-square-foot General Motors metal fabrication plant. Its 1,400 workers (as of 2007) here help stamp and assemble panels of sheet metal for use in trucks and vans, and also make other parts for other vehicles, including passenger cars.

Bishop International Airport, which is visible on the southbound side of the freeway. The rather small airport has become increasingly attractive to people who want a full-service passenger airport, but not the crowds that go with a major hub like Detroit Metropolitan Airport (see exit 37). The lines inside Bishop Airport are usually extremely short, and parking is typically available a short walk from the terminal entrance during all but the busiest travel seasons. As an added bonus, passengers often find that many of the flights from Bishop Airport are actually cheaper than similar flights out of Metro Airport, in spite of the fact that they often connect through Metro.

Currently, Bishop Airport is one of the fastest growing airports in the nation. The airport, which served around 223,000 passengers in

Exit 118

This exit leads to Owosso, a town of less than 20,000 residents and located about 25 miles to the west. Owosso is named for Wosso (sometimes spelled Wassa or Wossa), the chief of an Ojibwe (also known as

BRAINBUSTERS

Basic: Michigan's Gerald Ford was U.S. president from 1974–1977. Who was president before him?

Intermediate: Ford was a star athlete at Grand Rapids High School in Michigan and at the University of Michigan. Both the Detroit Lions and Green Bay Packers asked him to play for them professionally. Where did he go after U-M?

Advanced: What was Gerald Ford's birth name?

See next page for answers.

77

Chippewa) Indian tribe. According to legend, Wosso's mother died when she threw herself into the path of a poison arrow that was meant for her husband. The motto for the city of Owosso is "the bright spot that's a shade better," and refers both to the meaning of Chief Wosso's name, which is "the bright spot," and the abundance of shade trees in the area.

Exit 118

While you are driving along this stretch of the freeway, keep your eyes out for a cougar. Over the years, many residents have reported seeing the large cat prowling through fields and forests in this and other parts of the state. In the spring of 1995, numerous residents called the police with sightings of a large brown to tan, 5- to 6-foot-long cat in the neighborhood of Corunna and Linden roads, which

is less than a mile from the southbound side of I-75 here.

Cougars, also known as pumas, mountain lions or panthers, are normally associated with the western United States or with Florida. They did once live in Michigan, but became scarce by the mid-1800s and disappeared about a century ago. The question now is: Are they making a comeback? Wildlife experts have generally discounted recent reports as misidentifications of dogs or perhaps bobcats, which are smaller wild cats that do live in Michigan, but the tide is turning. A DNA analysis of a tuft of hair that was pulled from a car bumper in 2004 positively identified it as belonging to a cougar. The driver reported hitting the cat while driving in Menominee County in the Upper Peninsula, and a state trooper collected the hair sample. Another

THE ANSWERS

Gerald Ford became vice president of the United States under *President Richard Nixon* when then-V.P. Spiro Agnew resigned in 1973. When Nixon himself resigned in 1974, Ford became president. He is the only person in U.S. history to serve as vice president and president, but never to have won an election for either post.

After helping the U-M Wolverines win back-to-back undefeated seasons and national titles in 1932 and 1933, Ford turned down the overtures from the Lions and Packers, and instead took an assistant coaching job at *Yale*

University where he hoped to get into law school. He held the job for two years before he was finally admitted to Yale's law school program.

Ford was born *Leslie Lynch King Jr.* in 1913 and was named for his father. His parents, however, soon divorced. His mother remarried Gerald Rudolff Ford a little more than two years later and began calling her son by her new husband's name. The switch did not become official, however, until Ford finally and legally changed his own name when he was 22 years old.

positively identified hair sample came the next year from a car in Iron County, which is also in the U.P. The Lower Peninsula now has some compelling evidence, according to the Michigan Wildlife Conservancy. The conservancy notes, for instance, that a 1,200-pound Arabian show horse died after a mauling in Jackson County in southern Michigan in 2005. By analyzing the bite marks, its scientists and animal control officers determined that the attacker was indeed a cougar. They also found tracks, and the township supervisor reported seeing a cougar the following day less than a mile from the site of the horse mauling. Still, some doubt exists. After receiving numerous reports from the public about cougar sightings in the Sleeping Bear Dune National Lakeshore in northwestern lower Michigan, the U.S. Fish and Wildlife Service surveyed the area in 2004 and 2005, and even set up motion-sensing cameras in an area where 15 reports had been made, but they found nothing. Nonetheless, FWS staff did install signs warning visitors about the sightings and instructing them to take precautions.

The Michigan Department of Natural Resources (DNR) suggests on its website that these cougars may have arrived in Michigan either through people who kept them as pets and released them to the wild on purpose or accidentally, or by traveling to Michigan from North or South Dakota, which have breeding populations of the big cats. The Michigan Wildlife Conservancy, however, believes the cougars in Michigan may

MM 119

Cougars (top, USDA National Wildlife Research Center) lived in Michigan but disappeared about a century ago, while bobcats (bottom, USFWS/Conrad Fijetland) are still living in Michigan. Recent reports, however, indicate that cougars may once again be prowling the state.

have always been here, and that their small number and reclusive habits only made it appear that they had disappeared from the state a century ago.

Anyone who sees a cougar or has physical evidence of one should contact the DNR or other authorities immediately.

Mile Marker 119

About 3 miles the east of this exit is a National Historic Landmark. The site, which is located near downtown Flint, was the office of the Durant-Dort Carriage Co. from 1895–1913. This site is where William Crapo "Billy" Durant not only built his carriage company into the country's

Billy Durant was the founder of General Motors Co.

GM, however, he worked with an early race car driver by the name of Louis Chevrolet to set up the Chevrolet Motor Co. in Flint. Billy Durant did so well with Chevrolet from 1911–1916 that he was able to regain control of General Motors in 1916. His hold was short-lived. Heavy debt forced Durant to leave GM once and for all in 1920.

Nonetheless, Durant bounced back and within two months of leaving GM, started up yet another automobile company, this one called Durant Motors. He did very well through the 1920s and soon was a multimillionaire once again. The stock market crash of 1929, which left people across the country without money or jobs, also battered the wealthy, including Durant. He scrambled for a few years, and finally filed for bankruptcy in 1936 with assets of just $250 and debts of nearly $1 million. Although he was now in his 70s, Durant persevered. Switching from automobiles to recreational pursuits, he opened up a bowling alley in Flint in 1940, and then set his sights on opening dozens more and also on possibly becoming involved in a mining operation out West. His grand plans ended when he had a massive stroke in 1942 that essentially concluded his business career, although he did keep operating the bowling alley in Flint. He lived his last years in New York on a small pension provided by General Motors, the company he had begun nearly four decades earlier.

largest producer of such horse-drawn vehicles—it built 150,000 of the vehicles a year, but also saw the wave of the future and struck out into the fledgling automobile industry.

Durant first got into the auto business in 1904 when the owner of the fledgling and nearly bankrupt Buick Motor Co. approached him to take the reins and save the company. He did. Soon afterward, he started a new company called General Motors and in 1908 bought Buick and made it a part of General Motors. Within a year, he also added other automotive manufacturers like Oldsmobile, Cadillac and Pontiac (then called Oakland) to his new company. Just two years later, Durant lost GM in a financial squeeze that was made possible in part because not all of Durant's company acquisitions were successful ones. Instead of giving up on the auto industry when he lost

Mile Marker 120

Scan the sides of the expressway for the Flint River, just north of the River Forest Golf Course on the northbound side of I-75. The city of Flint is named for this river, which meanders about 100 miles from east to west, eventually meeting up with the Shiawassee River and forming the Saginaw River. The river's name reflects the rocky riverbed, which is made of a hard stone called flint.

The town's name wasn't always Flint. In 1819, it went by the name of Grand Traverse, and in 1830 became Todd's Crossing after a nearby landowner. The town name switched to Flint River in 1833, and finally just to Flint three years later. The town became especially busy in 1856 when Massachusetts businessman Henry Crapo (CRAY-poe) moved here. Crapo built sawmills along the river to take in pine logged from other areas of Michigan and floated by waterways to his mills. His sights soon went beyond logging and to politics, first becoming Flint's mayor and later a state senator before winning election to Michigan governor for two terms.

Mile Marker 122

This part of Michigan saw great changes in its landscape from 1800 to 1900, but one event altered it almost overnight. It all began in the summer of 1880, when a severe drought stretched through much of the central Lower Peninsula, including this area. At this time, people were already living throughout the region, some in lumbering towns and others on small farms. As the drought continued, crops withered. In the forests, trees that had not yet fallen to the axes and saws of the lumbering industry stood in brush that had turned so dry as to be crunchy from the lack of rain. The worst, however, was yet to come.

On Sept. 5, what is now known as the Great Fire of 1881 began on the eastern side of the state. Fed by strong winds and dry underbrush, the firestorm raced through the forests there, sending immense billows of thick, black smoke into the sky. The fire moved so quickly that buildings burned to the ground in minutes and residents literally had to run for the lives. Many were not fast enough and perished where they fell. By the next day, fires had spread toward central Michigan, including this part of the state. Newspapers across the state were filled with dire reports of entire towns that were presumably lost to the inferno. An idea of the Great Fire's fury comes from this report, which was reprinted as part of a commemoration of the fire in the 1981 *Tuscola County Advertiser*: "Everybody is moving to the lakes. The fire west of us is coming, but we hope to keep it down and save the town. But God help us if it doesn't rain soon." To make matters worse, the fires burned through the telegraph wires, leaving people on either side of the fire with no means of communication.

Finally on the night of Sept.8, after more than three days of full-scale blazes, the rains came and the fires subsided. They did not come

Drawn by nearly century-old locomotives, the Huckleberry Railroad takes passengers on an 8-mile, 40-minute ride. (Travel Michigan)

soon enough. In just that short time, nearly 300 people died, many more had severe injuries, and 15,000 people were homeless and left with nothing but the clothes they were wearing when they made their mad dashes toward safety.

With about 2,000 acres burned, many of them in the Thumb area to the east, the Great Fire had essentially put an end to the lumbering industry there. It had, however, left the land ready for what would become the next major industry: farming. That industry continues in central Michigan to this day.

Exit 126

To get an idea of what life was like a hundred or more years ago, take this exit to Crossroads Village and Huckleberry Railroad, which are both part of the Genesee (pronounced jen-eh-SEE) County park system. Crossroads Village is a 51-acre recreation of nearly three dozen homes, shops, lumber and grain mills, and other structures, complete with live "residents" who dress as and play the parts of the people who would have worked and dwelled in such a village during the period. Highlights of the park are a paddlewheel riverboat named the Genesee Belle, and the Huckleberry Railroad, which features locomotives that are nearly a century old. The railroad's name comes from the dark berries known as huckleberries. Huckleberries are blueberry-like fruits, but are typically much darker—almost black—in color, and have larger seeds. The railroad takes customers on a slow 40-minute ride along 8 miles of track that surround Mott Lake. The train is so slow, according to the park's literature, that "passengers could jump off the train, pick huckleberries, and jump back on with minimum effort." As a result, it was called the Huckleberry Railroad.

Berry picking is a common pastime for many Michiganders, who ignore the summer heat and spend hours picking the typically very small blueberries from fields of the short, low-bush variety of the plant. Pickers here sometimes, although erroneously, call any darkly colored blueberry a "huckleberry." The state also has high-bush blueberries that grow in wetter areas than the low-bush form and are usually much larger in berry size. As their name suggests, high-bush blueberries are also taller plants, and allow pickers to stand while filling their buckets. The big blueberries available for sale at major grocery stores are related to high-bush blueberries. The next time you buy a quart, check where they came from. Chances are, it was Michigan, which produces more high-bush blueberries than any other state in the nation. Most of these commercial blueberries come from southwestern Michigan, which has a high water table (and therefore lots of water to feed the plants) and the sandy, slightly acidic soils that high-bush blueberries love.

Mile Marker 129

The rest areas on either side of the expressway here are typical on Michigan state roads. The Michigan Department of Transportation (MDOT, which Michiganders pronounce EM-dot) maintains 81 such facilities, each having "modern" restrooms (meaning running water and flush toilets—not "pit" toilets), picnic areas, and dog runs. Some of them, like the rest area on the northbound side, are very nicely landscaped and receive care from Master Gardener programs.

Many of the rest areas in Michigan are named for an honoree. The rest area on the southbound side, for instance, carries the name John S. Kelsch. Kelsch was an MDOT engineer who spent nearly a decade of his career in this part of Michigan.

BRAINBUSTERS

Besides being a major producer of blueberries, Michigan is tops in a number of other categories.

Basic: Michigan grows more tart cherries than any other state. How many tart cherries does it take to make an average cherry pie: 50, 150, or 250?

Intermediate: The people of southeastern Michigan eat more potato chips per person per year than any other place in the world. What huge potato chip company had its start in Detroit and is still located there?

Advanced: Michigan produces more pickling cucumbers than any other state in the nation. Sometimes, cucumbers are described as burpless. What does that mean?

See next page for answers.

According to the MDOT press release that announced his retirement in 1997 and the naming of the rest area, one of his primary contributions was "MDOT's first-ever construction contract that holds road builders financially accountable for assuring their pavements last. The innovation provides contractors the freedom to design their own road projects according to MDOT specifications, but requires they make repairs should any problems develop later."

Mile Marker 130

The Elf Khurafeh Circus Park, which is noted on the northbound side of I-75, is run by the local chapter of the Shriners of North America.

THE ANSWERS

The typical cherry pie contains about *250* tart cherries, and the average tart cherry tree will produce enough cherries in a year to make 28 pies.

Better Made Potato Chips have been a part of Michigan since the first plant opened in Detroit in 1928. The company still makes its chips in Detroit, using Michigan potatoes eight months a year and potatoes from other states for the remaining four months. In all, it uses 40 million pounds of potatoes a year.

Burpless cucumbers are easier on the digestive system than other cukes and make it less likely that a person who eats one will burp.

Most people know the Shriners as men who wear maroon, cup-like hats and drive tiny cars in parades—and they do that! Beyond the fun stunts, however, the Shriners have a serious mission. Members, who number several hundred thousand in nearly 200 chapters throughout North America, fund medical care for children, especially those with difficult orthopedic conditions and children who have serious burns.

Exit 131

Clio (pronounced CLIE-oh) is a small, 1.1-square-mile city with a population of about 2,500. The name Clio comes not from a person's surname or previous hometown, but from—strangely enough—Greek mythology.

The story of the city begins in the mid-1830s when a settler built a sawmill here. It didn't change much for the next three decades or so until the Pere Marquette Railroad reached the area. The train's station was located on a farm owned by the Varney family, so it and the town that sprang up around it took the name Varney. One of the town's citizens was a bit of a romantic and thought the town ought to have a name from Greek mythology. The citizen, a hotel owner, proposed Clio, who was one of the nine daughters of Zeus, the king of the gods, and Mnemosyne, the goddess of memory. The nine daughters were known as muses. Muses are Greek goddesses who inspire some form of creativity such as music, dance, poetry, and even astronomy. Clio was "the glorious one" and the muse of history. The Greek name rang a chord with the town's other residents, and Varney became Clio in 1864.

The other city near this exit is Montrose. At less than 1 square mile in size and with barely 1,600 residents, it's a little smaller than Clio. This town started out with the unwieldy name of Pewonagowink, which to this day is remembered in the name of a local private airport, called Pewanogowink-Banks Airport. The name changed to one that was much simpler to pronounce: Brent, for a local landowner. In fact, just south of this exit, a stream called Brent Run crosses I-75. By the mid-1800s, however, one of the town's residents had a different idea. He was a Scot and wanted to reflect his heritage—and apparently amaze his friends—by renaming the town Montrose. Montrose was the name of a port-side castle in Scotland that once hosted English monarch Edward I in the 13th century. Since the Michigan town of Montrose had no seaport or castle, it is not clear whether his friends were sufficiently impressed.

Mile Markers 133–134

The border between Saginaw County to the north and Genesee (pronounced jen-eh-SEE) County to the south lies between these mile markers. Genesee was named by settlers to reflect their previous home in a similarly named county in New York. Saginaw (pronounced SAG-ih-naw) is a variation of an Ojibwe (pronounced oh-JIB-wuh) Indian word better pronounced SOK-oh-nung that probably means place of the Sauk (pronounced SOK) for a local Indian tribe. Some people, however, say it is actually an Ojibwe Indian word meaning "at the mouth" to reflect the three major rivers—the Shiawassee, Saginaw, and Flint—in the area.

Indian words proved difficult for arriving Europeans. For example, for many years, they spelled and pronounced Ojibwe as Chippewa, dropping the "o" at the beginning, but adding a syllable in the middle. In fact, Central Michigan University sports teams are still called Chippewas, or the Chips. Now, however, Ojibwe (sometimes spelled Ojibway or Ojibwa) is becoming increasingly common in general usage. According to linguists, the word *ojibwe* means puckered, probably in reference to the puckered top of the moccasins that the tribe made and wore.

Exit 136

This exit usually has a good deal of traffic, because it leads to a huge outlet shopping center—supposedly the largest in the Midwest—and a restaurant that is known for its eye-popping portions. Both are on the southbound side of I-75.

The shopping center, Prime Outlets at Birch Run, draws customers who may drive miles and miles from all over Michigan and beyond to look for deals in the center's 150-odd stores. Some of the big-name factory stores are Ann Taylor, Banana Republic, Calvin

Pictured are two common sights in Michigan in the late 1800s: men loading logs onto a waiting rail car (above) and a typical logging camp. Circa 1892. (Library of Congress)

Klein, Coach, Eddie Bauer, Gap, J. Crew, Old Navy, and Pottery Barn. Many of the shops are visible from I-75 just south of this exit.

Besides the shopping center, a restaurant off this exit is a destination in itself. Families frequently plan their trips "up north" around a stop

to the restaurant they know simply as Tony's, although the full name is Tony's I-75 Restaurant. Over its many years of operation, its claim to fame has been the enormous size of its portions: the *eight-piece* French toast breakfast, the omelet made with at least *six* eggs, the BLT with a *pound* of bacon, and the banana split made with a *half gallon* of ice cream! For people who love to eat (or to take home leftovers), this very casual restaurant never disappoints.

Mile Marker 138

Keep an eye out for Birch Run Creek, which crosses here. It got its name from the forests filled with white-barked trees, known as birches, in the area. A nearby town, named Birch Run after the creek, started up as many of the time did: as a new station on the railroad. The railroad put the station at the site because it was halfway between Saginaw to the north and Flint to the south. Birch Run was just within the border of Saginaw County. In the 1800s, the county to the south was "dry" and prohibited alcohol, but Saginaw County did not. Apparently, word got around, and lumberjacks and others from Genesee County soon made it a very popular spot to down a few drinks after long days in the woods or at the mill.

Mile Marker 142

Look along the northbound side of I-75 for the trees with the stark-white bark. These are white birch trees (also called paper birches). White birches are a northern tree, and are uncommon much farther south in Michigan. They grow quite fast in sunny conditions, but they don't live very long . . . for a tree anyway. The typical birch grows to about 70 or 80 feet high and lives less than 150 years. In comparison, the mighty white oak tree of Michigan,

Henry Wadsworth Longfellow (Library of Congress, circa 1880)

MM 138 & 142

grows to about 100 feet tall or so, but can live five or six centuries.

Many of Michigan's American Indian tribes used birch to construct long-lasting, lightweight canoes. The outer, white bark of a birch tree peels off quite easily and is very pliable, but it alone would not be strong enough to construct a canoe. Instead, the Indians made the hull of the canoe from on the inner, yellow-colored bark of the birch, which is much thicker and lies beneath the white, papery skin. For the vessel's cross bracing, they typically used wood from another type of tree, such as a cedar, that also grows along river banks.

Henry Wadsworth Longfellow, a noted poet of the 18th century, brought attention to the Indians' use of birch trees to make their canoes in a famous, epic poem of 1855 called "The Song of Hiawatha" that pays tribute to the Ojibwe (or Chippewa) Indians who lived in Michigan. The poem is set in the Upper Peninsula and includes this passage about the canoes, the Ojibwe word for which is *cheemaun*:

> *"Give me of your bark, O Birch-tree!*
> *Of your yellow bark, O Birch-tree!*
> *Growing by the rushing river,*
> *Tall and stately in the valley!*
> *I a light canoe will build me,*
> *Build a swift Cheemaun for sailing,*
> *That shall float upon the river,*
> *Like a yellow leaf in Autumn,*
> *Like a yellow water-lily!"*

People who camp often have another use for the white, peeling, outer bark of a birch tree: They use is as a fire starter. A small pile of the dry peels topped with a couple of pine cones and a few dry sticks ignites easily. Removing only the outer, white bark from a birch tree trunk does not kill it, but peeling away the inner bark does. For this reason, naturalists recommend that visitors to Michigan woods leave living trees alone. Campers who need a bit of bark for a fire starter can usually find plenty of birch peelings on the ground or on fallen trees. This is easy to do, because most birch forests contain an abundance of fallen trees.

Exit 144

Repeat travelers to this area know they are close to the "Christmas town" of Frankenmuth when they see the sign for Freeway Fritz on the north-bound side of I-75. Freeway Fritz is a roadside restaurant that has a chicken in lederhosen for a mascot.

The restaurant is an offshoot of the much larger Bavarian Inn, one of two enormous restaurants in the city of Frankenmuth (pronounced FRANK-en-mooth), which is located about 6.5 miles to the northeast. The main tourist attraction in Frankenmuth is the downtown area that is rife with Bavarian architecture and design, including big, steeply pitched roofs and lots of wood trim. In fact, the city is sometimes called "Michigan's Little Bavaria." There, tourists find dozens of shops specializing in German sausages, German clocks, German arts, and, well, all things German.

One of the biggest attractions is Bronner's CHRISTmas Wonderland. This huge store, filled with its more than 6,000 styles of ornaments and hundreds of decorated trees, claims to be the world's largest Christmas store and visitors do not disagree. It draws

BRAINBUSTERS

Besides chicken dinners, Frankenmuth's two big restaurants have different German specialties, like Sauerbraten, Weiner Schnitzel, and Rouladen.

Basic: What is Weiner Schnitzel?

Intermediate: What is Rouladen, and what is Sauerbraten?

Advanced: What is Jäger Schnitzel, another Frankenmuth restaurant specialty, and what do the two little dots over the "a" in Jäger do to the pronunciation of the word?

See page 90 for the answers.

The town of Frankenmuth has a 239-foot-long covered bridge that takes both pedestrians and drivers across the Cass River (Travel Michigan)

people all year long—even in the heat of summer.

Shoppers who get a case of holiday overload after a stop inside often decompress with the famous chicken dinners at one of the town's two main restaurants: the Bavarian Inn or Zehnder's (pronounced ZEN-derz) of Frankenmuth. They are huge. The Bavarian Inn has 12 dining rooms that seat 1,200 guests; and Zehnder's has 10 dining rooms and can seat more than 1,500. The restaurants are located across the street from one another, and are both owned by members of the Zehnder family. According to Northwood University, the two restaurants together represent the largest independent restaurant operation in the United States. Both are known for their all-you-can-eat fried chicken dinners served "family style." In other words, servers bring big bowls of soup, and plates of chicken, stuffing, breads, potatoes, vegetables, noodles, and other side dishes to each table so the guests can pass them among themselves. If a plate or bowl empties, the server brings a replacement. Besides the fried chicken dinners, the menu of each of the two restaurants is quite different. Zehnder's has a considerable fish menu, for instance, while the Bavarian Inn has a wider range of German specialties.

89

Another attraction in town is the Glockenspiel, a 50-foot bell tower outside the Bavarian Inn restaurant that has not only a German-imported, 35-bell carillon, but also huge figurines that rotate out of the tower seven times a day to "dance" to the chimes of the carillon and delight the crowds below.

The German style of the city has its origins in the first settlers to the area, a group of men and women from Bavaria, Germany, who arrived in 1845 to teach their religion—they were Lutheran—to the American Indians. The name Frankenmuth comes from Franconia, which was their home district in Bavaria, and the word *Muth*, which means courage in German. (You may have noticed that many of the German words are capitalized. In German, all nouns are written in upper case.) One of

the early buildings was the Exchange Hotel that was constructed in 1856 and rebuilt in 1900. That building now houses Zehnder's restaurant. The Bavarian Inn dates back to 1888, when it was originally Fischer's Hotel. Another early building in Frankenmuth was a brewery that was built in 1862 and remained one of the state's largest for many decades. The brewery stood for more than 130 years until Mother Nature had her way with it. A tornado in 1996 destroyed the old building, but the brewery's memory did not die there. A new brewery now stands in its place and offers a 30-minute program that describes the history of the old building, leads customers on a tour of the beer-bottling operation, and finishes up with a stop in its tasting room for samples of its hand-crafted brews.

THE ANSWERS

Weiner Schnitzel is *breaded veal steak*. For those who aren't attuned to the types of meat, veal is calf meat, and is typically very tender and lean. *Rouladen is a beef roll*, which in Frankenmuth is beef rolled around bacon, celery, onions and a pickle. *Sauerbraten is marinated (sour) roast beef. Jäger Schnitzel, also known as Hunter's Schnitzel, is breaded pork loin.* The two little dots over the "a" in Jäger is an *umlaut (pronounced OOM-laut) and makes the "a" have an "ay" sound.* In addition the "j" in German sounds like an English "y," so Jäger is correctly pronounced YAY-ger.

Although Frankenmuth is a huge draw, this exit also leads to the much less tourist-y community of Bridgeport. The town was originally known as Cass Bend and also as Cass River in reference to the main waterway in the area, but changed to Bridgeport in 1880 to make note of the considerable number of bridges that spanned the river here at that time. One of the largest, wooden, covered bridges in the country stands nearby, but not in Bridgeport. Frankenmuth is home to a 239-foot-long covered bridge that crosses the Cass River. The bridge takes both car traffic and foot traffic.

Archaeologists are interested in Bridgeport for another reason. It

The DeZwaan Windmill, located in Holland, Mich., came from the Netherlands. Every spring the area hosts the Tulip Time Festival and shows off its six million tulips. (Travel Michigan)

holds a registered historic place called the Schmidt site that was used by early Indian people about 4,000 years ago—that's 2000 BCE. (For those who aren't familiar with the BCE designation, it stands for "before the current era" and means the same thing as BC.) The site's evidence for its long-ago human habitants includes arrow points that to the untrained eye look more like flat, chipped pieces of rock than artifacts.

Mile Marker 149

The large building on the northbound side of I-75 is Delphi Saginaw Steering Systems. This is one of several facilities owned by Delphi, which is a major supplier to automobile manufacturers. This particular factory, which covers more than 4 million square feet, makes components for wheel axles and steering systems.

Exit 149

The street at this exit may be called East Holland Road, but the city of Holland in Michigan is actually on the far west side of the state, about 150 miles away and on the shores of Lake Michigan. That part of the state was once inhabited mainly by Ottawa (pronounced OT-uh-wah or oh-DAH-wuh and sometimes spelled Odawa) Indians who lived primarily on the western side of the Lower Peninsula, and the Potawatomi (pot-a-WAH-tuh-mee) Indians, who lived mainly in the southern part of the Lower Peninsula. These tribes, along with the Ojibwe (also known as Chippewa) tribe that lived in the eastern Lower Peninsula and much of the Upper Peninsula, together made up an alliance called the Council of Three Fires. Through much of the state's early history when the British and French were fighting over control

Visitors enjoy the activities at the Japanese Cultural Center in Saginaw during Japan Festival 2007. (Japanese Cultural Center)

of the two peninsulas, the three tribes would sometimes, but not always, side with the French. In fact, it was an Ottawa chief, named Pontiac, who planned a famous surprise attack against a British-held Detroit fort back in 1763. (See mile marker 42 for the details of that planned attack.)

Now, back to Holland, Mich. Dutch immigrants arrived there in the 1840s, created a settlement, and named the town after their previous home in Europe: Holland. To this day, the city still has a decidedly Dutch flavor. That includes an operating, 240-year-old Dutch windmill that came to the city from the country of Holland in the mid-20th century; a park complete with dikes; and the nation's largest tulip festival, which is held every spring. Called the Tulip Time Festival, it is appropriately named because the town has more than *six million* tulips. Besides the waves of colorful flowers, the festival also has three parades, fireworks, and thousands dancers who take to the streets in traditional costumes and kick up their heels in wooden shoes, or clogs. Klompen is the Dutch word for clogs, so the performers are called klompen dancers. Wood may not seem a good material for footwear, but the dancers claim they are actually quite comfortable. Although most people associate the wooden shoes

only with Holland, they were actually once common in England, France, and other European countries. In France the clog is called a sabot. When French loom workers in the 18th and early 19th century got upset with working conditions, they are said to have jammed up the machinery by throwing their shoes—the sabots—into the machinery. And that is where the word sabotage comes from.

Back on this side of the state, this I-75 exit leads to Celebration Square, a couple of miles to the west in the large city of Saginaw (population 62,000). The city is the county seat. A children's zoo, Japanese Cultural Center and Tea House, park, and conference center are located in Celebration Square. For a very short time in history, the United States government set up a fort here. The fort was supposed to help control the Indian population once settlers came to the area in the early 1800s. Fort Saginaw didn't last long. Troops came to the fort in 1822, but after facing a bitter winter, followed by flooding in the spring and a typhoid fever epidemic in the summer, they pulled out in 1823, never to return. The commanding officer offered this summary of the area: "Nothing but Indians, muskrats and bullfrogs could possibly exist (here)."

Exit 149

Mile Marker 154

This large bridge, called the Zilwaukee (zill-WAH-kee) Bridge, crosses the Saginaw River. When some Michiganders hear "Zilwaukee Bridge," the first thing that crosses their minds is either the old drawbridge that it replaced or the major construction accident that added years to the bridge's eventual opening.

Let's start with the old drawbridge. That's right, a drawbridge once existed on I-75. In fact, it was the only drawbridge ever placed on I-75 not only in the state of Michigan but also anywhere on the entire length of the interstate highway, which runs from Florida to Canada. Plans for the drawbridge started in the 1950s at the same time as plans were under way to extend I-75 from southern Michigan through this area. Engineers estimated how much traffic would use the new interstate then and in the future, and decided that a drawbridge wouldn't cause any undue inconvenience, even if traffic did have to stop every time it had to open to let a freighter pass through.

The four-lane bridge opened to traffic in 1960. The drawbridge section was 150 feet long and centered over the 200-foot-wide shipping channel in the river. A few major problems soon arose. First, ships kept running into the pilings that protect the bridge, and occasionally into the bridge itself. For the most part, the accidents resulted because the ships were unable to maneuver through the rather narrow drawbridge opening which was situated near a tight bend in the river. Some of these collisions were severe enough to completely close the bridge while repairs were made. Second, shipping traffic took an unforeseen jump. When the bridge opened, the drawbridge had to rise about 150 times a year to let ships pass, but by its peak year in 1978, the bridge was rising nearly

MM 154

BRAINBUSTERS

During the height of the logging era at the end of the 19th century, the Saginaw River was a busy place, especially in the spring when logs would begin floating in from lumber operations in Michigan's interior to the many mills that lined the river here.

Basic: Lumberjacks in Michigan did most of their work cutting down trees and moving them through the forest in the winter. Why?

Intermediate: The mills processed the incoming logs as fast as they could, but frequently, the logs would stack up on the river, sometimes for long distances. On one occasion, a particularly big log jam occurred on the Tittabawassee (tit-uh-buh-WAH-see) River, which flows into the Saginaw River. How many miles did the logjam stretch on the Tittabawassee: 3 miles, 13 miles, 23 miles, or 33 miles?

Advanced: What is a river driver and a peavey?

See next page for answers.

1,000 times a year. Traffic on I-75, therefore, was stopping an average of two to three times a day. The increase in interstate stoppages coincided with a great deal more automotive traffic than the engineers predicted. This resulted in traffic tie-ups that stretched for miles, not to mention a considerable number of rear-end accidents when drivers who were not expecting traffic to come to a dead stop had to jump on their brakes, causing everyone behind them to screech to a halt, too, and sometimes not quite quickly enough.

By 1975, everyone agreed that the drawbridge wasn't such a great idea, especially since the Michigan Department of Transportation (MDOT, which is pronounced EM-dot) had just expanded I-75 in that area from four lanes to six lanes, which caused a bottleneck at the four-lane bridge even when the drawbridge was

---

THE ANSWERS

In Michigan, lumberjacks did the bulk of the tree cutting and land transportation of the logs in the winter. *Carting logs over frozen ground was much, much easier* than dragging them over muddy trails or deep sand. They would even pack the snow with equipment called snow rollers, and water it down to help create an icy base. During the winter, the lumberjacks would pile up the logs at the edge of the rivers (which they called rollways). If no large waterway was in the area, they would instead bring the logs to railroads for transport by train.

When spring arrived and the rains had swollen the rivers to their deepest and widest, loggers would start dumping the logs into the river. To keep track of which logs belonged to what logging outfit, loggers would mark the end of each log with the logging company's brand. The logs rode the river to the mills, many of which were along the Saginaw River

here. Often the logs would come in faster than the mills could take them, and logjams would form. The jam on the Tittabawassee, for instance, stretched an amazing *33 miles!* Distance-wise, that's as far as it is from here to Standish (to the north) or to Flint (to the south) — at 70 miles an hour, that's almost a half-hour ride! During the log drives on the rivers, certain men would dangerously walk out onto the floating masses of logs. *These men, called river drivers, maneuvered the logs away from obstructions or the river banks with spike-tipped poles, called peaveys (PEE-veez).* The work demanded a great deal of strength, balance and skill, and was extremely hazardous, especially when the river flow was fast, or when its surface was completely covered with layers of logs. The peavey is named for its inventor, Joseph Peavey, who was a blacksmith from Maine. He came up with the idea after watching river drivers working along a waterway near his shop.

down. After considering ideas such as replacing the drawbridge with an underwater tunnel, or rerouting the interstate, MDOT engineers recommended building a much taller bridge that ships could pass under while cars zipped along on top.

In 1979, construction had begun on the bridge you are driving on now: a mile-and-a-half-long structure that reaches about 120 feet high and has twin decks, one for northbound traffic and one for southbound traffic. The bridge's design called for the installation of 52 tall piers, followed by the placement of the decks, which would be a series of massive concrete segments connected to one another by steel cables. All did not go smoothly. In 1982, a major accident occurred. At that point, construction workers had installed all of the tall piers and were beginning to place the concrete segments—one at a time from the north side of the bridge to the south. When they got to the 14th concrete deck segment, something went wrong a few segments back. The 11th segment, which like the others was about 300 feet long, began to tip so that it was several feet higher on one end than on the other. This tipping damaged the pier underneath as well as the footing below that supports the pier. Construction ground to a halt. Repairs started in 1983, and after a change in construction companies, the bridge finally opened to traffic in 1987, four years late and well over budget. Now, veteran I-75 travelers can look back with fond memory on the days of the drawbridge, but only if they can forget about all of the time they spent waiting in a traffic jam for a bridge to raise and lower!

— — —

The bridge has the name Zilwaukee, because it is located in the city of the same name. If Zilwaukee has a familiar ring to it, consider how much it sounds like the much larger city of Milwaukee. Milwaukee is in Wisconsin. Do Zilwaukee and Milwaukee have any connection? It turns out they do . . . sort of. Two brothers named Daniel and Solomon Johnson came to the area from New York in 1848 and started a sawmill. They wanted immigrants, who had

MM 154

BRAINBUSTERS

Saginaw was the birthplace of several famous people, including those in the questions below.

Basic: In what sport does Serena Williams play? Her sister also plays in this sport. What is her name?

Intermediate: Well-known singer/songwriter Stevie Wonder was born in Saginaw in 1950. Stevie is a shortened version of his real first name. What is it?

Advanced: Saginaw native Tim McCoy was a well-known movie and later TV star from the 1920s to the 1950s. What types of movies did he make? Before he married his second wife, she was dating both Adolf Hitler and a future U.S. president at the same time. Who was the future U.S. president?

See next page for answers.

a reputation for working hard and also cheaply, and they set their sights on the Germans. Instead of attracting them with a few extra pennies, they tried something else. They knew that many German immigrants were already crossing the country to move to Milwaukee, so they thought that naming the town Zilwaukee might just sound close enough to Milwaukee to confuse the immigrants to come here instead. Did it work? About 20 percent of the early residents here were in fact German, but whether they were actually duped by the town name is unknown.

Mile Markers 154–155

Kochville Road, which crosses between these two mile markers, is named for Kochville Township, which in turn is named after one of its settlers who had the last name of Koch. The township, which was established in 1855, got a little smaller in 1881 when the state legislature cut out a chunk measuring 3 miles wide and 6 miles long, and created a new township called Frankenlust. The move also cut into the size of Saginaw County, because the state law at the time mandated that every part of a

THE ANSWERS

Sisters Serena and Venus Williams are champion tennis players. Venus was born in California, but Serena, who is a year younger, was born in Saginaw. The two sisters have won numerous tennis tournaments, including four U.S. Open singles events. Serena won the U.S. Open title in 1999, Venus won it in 2000 and 2001, and Serena again came in first in 2002.

Stevie Wonder's full first name is *Steveland*. He had amazing musical skills even as a young boy, and when he was 12, he drew the attention of Ronnie White of the very popular musical group The Miracles, as well as Detroit's Motown record company, which signed on the boy and started marketing him as "Little Stevie Wonder." He had his first big hit with a 1963 song called "Fingertips." The number featured

future Motown star Marvin Gaye on drums.

Tim McCoy was a well-known movie star who made many *western movies* from the 1920s to the 1940s. In the early 1950s, he hosted a live television show in which he told true stories of the American West, and then started working in a traveling show where he displayed his shooting and bullwhip skills. Notably, his second wife, Inga Arvad, was not only Miss Europe before McCoy had met her but she also had dated Adolf Hitler in the mid-1930s. Even more surprising, she was not only married at the time, but was also seeing someone else on the side. This "someone else" was a young ensign in the U.S. Office of Naval Intelligence. Who was the ensign? He was none other than *John F. Kennedy*. Their relationship caught the attention of the FBI and soon ended.

county had to be within a one-day buggy ride from the county seat. Frankenlust was located north of Kochville and outside the one-day limit. It was, however, close enough to the county seat in the adjacent Bay County, so it became part of that county instead.

Exit 155

This exit takes drivers through the large and heavily developed city of Saginaw on a business loop numbered 675. The city is also the county seat of the surrounding Saginaw County. With Bay County to the north and Midland County to the northwest, Saginaw County is part of an area collectively called Saginaw Valley. The valley drains into one of Lake Huron's bays, which is called Saginaw Bay. If you look at your right hand (palm up) as an approximation of the Lower Peninsula's shape, the bay would be located in the crook between your thumb and palm. In reality, Michigan's Thumb is short, fat and stubby compared to a typical person's hand, but the hand-map is still a useful tool.

Michiganders frequently use this style of hand-map to describe locations in the Lower Peninsula, and sometimes add the left hand (palm down) with thumb and little finger extended to depict the Upper Peninsula. For instance, a person living in the northwestern lower Michigan community of Northport might say he or she is from the top of the little finger, while someone living in Mackinaw City at the top of the Lower Peninsula might say he or she is from the tip of the mitt (as in

mitten). Occasionally, some Michiganders will use hand-related terms to make unflattering comments about communities in certain geographic locations, such as calling a town "the hangnail of the Thumb."

As you ride along this stretch of freeway, scan the skies for large flying birds, especially in the spring and fall. The Shiawassee National Wildlife Refuge, which is located a few miles to the southwest is a stopover point for tens of thousands of Canada geese and ducks as they migrate through Michigan. The Canada geese are fairly easy to spot. They have a beige belly with a darker brown back, and black neck and head with a usually noticeable bright white patch or band that runs from one side of the head under the chin and up to the other side of the head. Like many other waterfowl, they often fly in a V-formation, sometimes with more than a dozen birds on each arm of the "V." Why the V? Some scientists think it has to do with flight efficiency: If one bird is following another just right, it can take advantage of the air flow created by the bird in front of it, and won't have to work as hard to fly. Other scientists, however, say the birds don't stay close enough together to get any flight benefit from the V formation, and they instead think the formation is just a way for the birds to communicate with each other better, or to fly as a group without running into each other.

People who want to see the geese and other birds up close have plenty of opportunity at the wildlife refuge,

Peregrine falcon. (Joe Kosack/PGC Photo)

which covers more than 9,500 acres. The Shiawassee National Wildlife Refuge is a combination of forests, fields, marshes, rivers, and crop land that provides excellent wildlife habitat for more than 200 species of migratory birds as well as other animals. The list of all birds seen at the refuge stands at 277 species as of 2007. The Canada geese that come through the refuge in the fall are migrating from James Bay, which is on the southern end of the massive Hudson Bay in Canada. The northward spring migration takes them back to James Bay.

Besides the geese, which are quite common in Michigan, bird-watchers at the refuge also catch a glimpse of several endangered species. These include:

+ the peregrine falcon (also known as a duck hawk)—a crow-sized hook-beaked bird that is one of the fastest animals on Earth. When it is hunting, it flies to great heights in the air and then dives at speeds of 200-plus mph to nab its preferred food: doves and other similarly sized birds. To appreciate the speed of the bird, consider that the velocity of a NASCAR race car is also around 200 mph!

+ the king rail—a long-legged, long-beaked, brown waterfowl that is the size of a small chicken. The king rail spends most of its time in marshes and swamps. The males put on an interesting display before the breeding season. The male sets up a territory and defends it from other male rails by crouching down, pulling in its neck, fluffing up its feathers, and then running at the intruders. If the trespasser doesn't leave immediately, the two birds may scrimmage a bit, but the intruder typically soon flies off, sometimes with the territorial male flying after him as if to say, "And stay out!"

+ the short-eared owl—a medium-sized owl with short feather tufts rising above its eyes. Birders often see this 13–17 inch owl flying during the day. Like the king rail, short-eared owls have interesting breeding-related behaviors. In this case, it is the courtship behavior of the male. To show off his worthiness to a female, he flies up sharply into the air, rising to 700–1,000 feet or more, then hovers for few seconds before gliding back down, and he does it again and again. Sometimes another male appears, and the two will lock talons for a short mid-air battle.

‧ the Kirtland's warbler—a songbird with a black-streaked, bluish-gray back and a yellow underside. The Kirtland's warbler is set apart from similar looking warblers by the way it constantly jerks its tail up and down. For more about this bird, see exit 239.

Mile Marker 157

The border between Bay County to the north and Saginaw County to the south falls along this section of I-75. Bay County's name reflects its location, which is on the western shore of Lake Huron's Saginaw Bay. Saginaw (pronounced SAG-ih-naw) appears to be a variation of a Sauk

BRAINBUSTERS

The nearby Saginaw Valley State is one of Michigan's 15 public universities. It is more or less tied with Northern Michigan University for 10th largest in terms of enrollment. Northern Michigan University is located in Marquette in the Upper Peninsula.

Basic: Name Michigan's three largest public universities.

Intermediate: Universities typically have two colors that they use for their logos and for their sports teams' uniforms. What are the colors of the three largest public universities?

Advanced: What are the names of the three largest public universities' football teams?

See next page for answers.

(pronounced SOK) Indian word that means "place of the Sauk" for the local Indian tribe. Some people, however, claim it means "at the mouth," referring to the three major rivers in the area.

Exit 160

Saginaw Valley State University sits about 5 miles to the southwest. Founded in 1963, the approximately 9,000-student institution is the newest of the 15 public universities in the state of Michigan.

A community college, called Delta College, is also nearby. Outside of courses, one of its major draws is the Delta College Planetarium and Learning Center. The planetarium, funded by NASA and opened in 1997, has a 50-foot-tall domed screen where it shows astronomy-related programs, many of them produced by NASA.

Short-eared owl. (USDA Forest Service/Dave Herr)

This exit connects with M-84, a state highway that links the city of Saginaw to the south and Bay City to the east.

From here north for about 30 miles, I-75 parallels the shore of Lake Huron's Saginaw Bay, which is located about 5 miles to the east. Bay City, located off this exit, lies between here and the bay. If you are heading north on I-75, it is the last city of its size that you will pass along the freeway. Bay City has a population of about 37,000. The next-largest city heading north won't come until you reach the 14,300-resident city of Sault Ste. Marie (pronounced Soo Saint Marie) at the northernmost end of I-75 in the Upper Peninsula. Although Bay City's name suggests that it is located right on the bay, it isn't. Rather, it straddles the Saginaw River, which empties into the bay just outside of the city limits. Bay City takes advantage of its location on the shore of this wide river with a number of water's-edge parks. One of them is the 97-acre Veterans Memorial Park that includes a public marina, historical house that dates back to 1837, and a scenic riverwalk.

The city's connection to the river goes back in history, too. French explorers came to the area first in the 1600s, but instead of setting up housekeeping, they continued by boat down the shore of Lake Huron. The first settlers came in the 1830s, and a couple of decades later, loggers arrived. Bay City was perfect for logging operations, situated as it was on a large river with access to Lake Huron's Saginaw Bay. The river could power the lumber mills, and the bay served as an excellent port for shipping lumber to both U.S. and Canadian buyers. Soon, Bay City became a booming mill town with three dozen

Exit 162

THE ANSWERS

Michigan's three largest public universities are *Michigan State University* in Lansing, which has enrollment topping 45,000, the *University of Michigan-Ann Arbor* with around 40,000, and *Wayne State University* in Detroit with around 33,000. Other universities with an enrollment of more than 20,000 students include (in descending order): Western Michigan, Central Michigan, Eastern Michigan and Grand Valley State.

The University of Michigan's colors are *maize (yellow) and blue*, MSU's colors are *green and white*, and Wayne State's are *green and gold*. Members of U-M's football team are *Wolverines*. Strangely, however, the wolverine is an animal that is not even found in Michigan (see exit 301). MSU's football players are *Spartans*. The name refers to soldiers from Sparta, which is an ancient Greek city. WSU's football players became *Warriors* in 2000, after spending more than 70 years as Tartars. And, no, Tartar doesn't signify tooth plaque. It refers to a Mongolian soldier.

mills, including a few of the largest mills in the nation. Some reports claim that the air was so constantly filled with the smell of freshly sawn lumber that the odor even flavored the food. The mills weren't the only ones making money. This thriving mill town also had quite a collection of saloons, particularly along the city's Water Street, a section of which was called "Hell's Half Mile." It got the name for a reason. Come spring when the lumbering operations were winding up for the season, thousands of lumberjacks would descend on the town, looking for a way to blow off steam and spend their hard-earned money. As the alcohol flowed, fights erupted. According to stories from the day, the saloons had many brawls, some of them quite vicious, and were also the scene of more than a few crimes, including the drugging and robbing of lumberjacks. One saloon had a particularly nasty reputation for the way it ridded itself of crime victims—through a trapdoor built into the floor. The trapdoor dropped into an underground tunnel that led to the river. According to stories from the day, the bodies of victimized lumbermen would be dragged over to the trapdoor and dropped through for their eventual "burial at sea," as it were. The river would conveniently dispense with the victim, and business could continue with minimal disruption . . . and without any pesky questions from the authorities.

Along with the logging industry, Bay City became a large center for making various wood products. Two large wood-product establishments were Bousfield & Co. and the Michigan Pipe Co. The Bay City Bousfield factory was the largest maker of woodenware in the world in the late 1800s. Co. products included pails and washboards, and other household items. The Michigan Pipe Co. was the nation's largest producer of wooden pipes These pipes were basically hollowed out logs that were machined smooth on the outside. Many cities around the country used the pipes for their water and sewer lines. Excavations today are still turning up the old wooden pipes under cities in Michigan. Workers in the state capital of Lansing, for instance, found some of the buried wooden pipe under the downtown streets just a few years ago.

Exit 162

Even after the logging industry started to die out at the end of the 1800s, Bay City found it could carry on very successfully. One of the ways it did was by building ships. An especially long-lasting shipbuilder was Defoe Boat and Motor Works, which started up in Bay City in 1905. It changed its name to Defoe Shipbuilding Co. in 1941, and remained in operation until 1975. During its long history, the company constructed many types of watercraft, including destroyer escorts, minesweepers and guided missile destroyers for the U.S. Navy. The company also built private yachts. One of those yachts in particular has a place in political history. It was the presidential yacht of three

Typical saw mill scene in Michigan's early lumber days. (Library of Congress, N.Y. : The Albertype Co., circa 1889)

U.S. presidents: Dwight Eisenhower, John F. Kennedy and Richard Nixon.

Bay City was also busy as a shipping port both because of its location on Saginaw Bay and because of the many rail lines that led into and out of the city. The brisk traffic on Saginaw Bay spawned more than a few water-related legends, some of them quite fantastic. One of these legends involved a denizen of the deep called a tigerfish that was said to swim beneath the surface of Saginaw Bay. Old salts would describe the ferocious fish to sailors who were new to the bay, explaining that hungry tigerfish would routinely charge and begin to tear apart vessels on the bay until a seaman fell overboard, at which time the tigerfish would switch their attention to the flailing sailor. Another legend covered all of Lake Huron rather than just the bay. Veteran sailors would keep greenhorns busy by telling them to scan the horizon for whales and report any sightings, because a ship-to-whale collision with the largest ones, which could reach more than 100 feet long, could tear the ship asunder. Of course, none of the sailors ever saw a whale in the Great Lakes. For information on the days when the Great Lakes did, in fact, have whales, see the Brainbuster on page 127.

These types of tales, along with a variety of ghost stories, were rampant in the 1800s and early 1900s, but sailors hardly needed any added incentive to use caution on the big waters. More than 10,000 shipwrecks have occurred on the Great Lakes over the years. That number takes into account the *Griffon*, which in 1679 became the first European-owned sailing vessel to ply the waters of the Great Lakes, and the first to disappear there. The *Griffon* was a 30-man boat somewhere between 30 and 60 feet long, that legendary French explorer Rene-Robert Sieur de La Salle ordered built to investigate the largely unknown Great Lakes region. LaSalle and his *Griffon* sailed across Lake Erie to what would become Detroit, up north through lake Huron to the top of the Lower Peninsula, and then headed west through Lake Michigan to Green Bay near Wisconsin. There, his crew loaded the ship with furs and other goods. LaSalle sent a six-man crew to take the vessel back the way it had come. The ship set sail . . . and was never heard from again. No one knows what happened to the *Griffon*, but many suspect it sank in a fierce storm that struck a day after it set sail. A number of shipwreck enthusiasts have searched for the vessel over the years, but to date, its fate still remains a mystery.

Exit 164

Watch for the large American flag on the southbound side of I-75 just north of this exit. This one won't flap in the breeze however, and you'll know why when you see it. The flag has been in this spot alongside the freeway for many years.

— — —

This area of Michigan has a large number of farms. Two major crops along I-75 are corn and sugar beets. Few people look carefully at corn, but it is quite an interesting plant. Corn was one of the first crops that European settlers tried to grow in America, but it is not a native plant. Although scientists aren't certain, they think it probably came from Mexico, Central America, and/or South America originally. Have you ever thought about how corn grows? It is considerably different from most other vegetables. When it comes up from a seed, it looks a lot like a blade of grass but it grows fast and tall. An old farmer's saying is that corn should be "knee high by the Fourth of July" and that's a good approximation here

Exit 164

BRAINBUSTERS

The city of Midland is located about 12 miles to the west of I-75 here. It is home to the nation's largest chemical company, one that makes thousands of products, including plastics.

Basic: What is the name of the chemical company? (Hint: Its logo is a black diamond.)

Intermediate: During World War I, the company began producing mustard gas. Why is it called mustard gas, and what is it?

Advanced: This chemical company's roots date back to 1890, when a chemist came to Midland because it had an abundance of salt brine. He was interested a certain chemical found in salt brine. The chemical was important because it was used to make many medicines of the day. What was the chemical, and what exactly is salt brine?

See next page for answers.

in Michigan. Soon after, it grows a tassel on top and a small ear at the base of one of more of its leaves. The tassel is the male part of the plant that will shed millions of grains of pollen, and the ear is the female part that will make the seeds, or kernels. As the ear grows, it develops thin strands, called silk, from the top of the ear. Each individual silk is related to a single kernel. The strands of silk are actually pollen tubes that will catch pollen raining down from the tassels and transport it down into the ear to help produce the kernel. If pollen doesn't make it down the tube, that kernel will never develop. Backyard gardeners are often disappointed when they plant a dozen corn plants because the ears have so few kernels in them. This is because insects don't transport the pollen; the wind does. With a too-small crop, the pollen may miss most of the silks altogether. In contrast, the plants in farm fields, like those often seen along I-75, don't have that problem. The corn harvest in Michigan starts up in late summer.

Exit 164

What's so interesting about sugar beets? For many people in the United States, their sugar comes from the stalks of a type of grass called sugar cane. Much of this "cane sugar" ships to the United States from Brazil, the world's largest producer. In Michigan, however, the sugar in the stores likely comes from sugar beets, a plant that was introduced to the U.S. from Germany. If you scan the farm fields here, you will likely see some short plants with lush, bright-green, almost spinach-like leaves. These are sugar beet plants. The beet itself grows underground and is an oblong, sometimes rather round, vegetable that reaches about 8–10 inches in length.

Once the beets are harvested in the fall, trucks take them to processing plants, many of which are located in Michigan's Thumb. (If you happen to be driving here in the fall, keep an eye out for wayward sugar beets on the side of the freeway!) At the processing plant, machines wash, cut, and extract the sugar from the beets as a juice, which is then evaporated and crystallized into sugar. Michigan is one of the

THE ANSWERS

The huge chemical business in Midland is *Dow Chemical Co.*, and its first products centered around medicines. During World War I, however, the company shifted its work to primarily support the war effort. Besides producing chemicals for explosives and tear gas, the company began manufacturing another weapon called mustard gas, a *dangerous poison* that can cause blisters, lung damage and death. Mustard gas got its name because it has a *yellow, mustard-like color and reportedly sometimes smells like mustard.*

Chemist Herbert Dow came to Midland to work on a better—and cheaper—way to extract the chemical, called *bromine*, from salt brine, which is *salt-laden water*. He found one. A few years later, he started Dow Chemical Co., which has since become an industry giant.

largest producers of beet sugar in the United States.

Mile Marker 167

An oil pump sits on the northbound side of I-75 (just south of Mackinaw Road). If you look closely, you will likely see many more pumps like this one along the freeway. Some of the pumps may be working and others may not, depending on whether the oil company wants to get oil from that particular location at that particular time. Each pump has a horizontal piece across the top that, when working, tips up and down in see-saw fashion. One side is connected to a motor that powers the tipping motion. The other side is equipped with what looks like a big hammer head, and from that head, a relatively thin "polish bar" reaches down to ground level, through a wellhead, and attaches to another rod underground. The underground rod, called a sucker rod, then connects to a pump, which may be many feet underground. As the sucker rods moves up and down, it creates suction in the underground pump and that suction draws up the oil. The oil then travels down pipelines, and eventually reaches refineries where it is separated into fuel oil, kerosene, gasoline, and many other products.

Oil wells are common sights here because Michigan is the United States' 17th largest oil-producing state.

Exit 168

About 5 miles to the east is the 2,100-acre Bay City Recreation Area, which includes a full mile of sandy beach on the shore of Lake Huron's Saginaw Bay plus one of the largest coastal wetlands on the Great Lakes. Called the Tobico Marsh, the wetlands are home to a great variety of animals, including beaver, muskrat, mink, deer, and many birds, some of them quite rare.

One of the rare birds that nests in the marsh is the ruddy duck. The male ruddy duck is a strange-looking bird. During breeding season, he has a brick-red body, half-black and half-white head, and a very blue bill. In addition to the striking appearance, a male will make his presence known by performing an odd song and doing a strange little display called "bubbling." The song is a series of "chk" sounds that get faster and faster until he finally

BRAINBUSTERS

The Great Lakes have been very busy shipping lanes for hundreds of years, and have generated volumes of harrowing tales. Part of the flavor of sailing here and elsewhere comes from the sailors' superstitions and legends.

Basic: One superstition holds that whistling during a storm brings . . . what?

Intermediate: What is a hoodoo ship?

Advanced: Why did sailors sometimes toss carrots, potatoes or other food to rats on their boats before they left shore?

See next page for answers.

Ruddy duck. (USDA Forest Service/Dave Herr)

makes a soft, ascending quacking noise. During his bubbling display, the male will swim through the water holding his tail stiff and straight up from the body, and then slap his bill against his breast—a movement that creates bubbles in the water.

Besides the male's appearance and his breeding behavior, ruddy ducks are unusual for a couple of other reasons. They are small and only grow to about a foot or so in length, but the female's eggs are 2 inches long, which is the size of eggs seen in much larger ducks. People sometimes observe a male accompanying a female and her youngsters as they paddle through the marsh. Peculiarly, however, the male is usually not the female's partner or the father of the brood. The male actually abandons his mate either before or shortly after she lays her eggs, and then hangs around any other females in the area, even if they already have young in tow.

Exit 171

I-75 crosses the Kawkawlin River just south of this exit. The Indians originally called the river Ogan-conning (oh-GUH-kuh-ning),

but somewhere along the way, it changed to Kawkawlin. The origin of Kawkawlin isn't entirely clear, but some people think Kawkawlin is the very rough English pronunciation of Kishkaukou. Kishkaukou was an Ojibwe (or Chippewa) Indian chief, whose name appears on a treaty that gave the Indians 640 acres along the Saginaw River. Others believe that kawkawlin means "place of the pike fish" or possibly "place of the walleye," which is also a type of fish.

Walleye and northern pike are two very different kinds of food fish. Walleye are the smaller of the two. The state record for a caught walleye is 35 inches, but most people catch them at 20 inches long or less. They have cloudy eyes that appear to stare blankly, and this feature gives them the name walleye. Many

THE ANSWERS

Sailors discouraged whistling during a storm, because they believed that it brought about *more wind.*

A hoodoo ship is *one that has an aura of bad luck,* often evidenced in an always-changing crew. Many seamen and -women will refuse to join a crew on a hoodoo ship.

Sailors would sometimes refuse to board a ship if they saw a rat leaving, because it was a sign that the ship would sink. *To make sure the rats stayed put,* the sailors would sometimes tempt them by tossing them carrots or potatoes.

Northern pike (left) and walleye. (NOAA, Great Lakes Environmental Research Laboratory)

people feel walleye, which are in the perch family, are the best-tasting of Michigan's fish.

Northern pike are considerably larger than walleye. The state record for a caught northern pike is 51.5 inches long, more than a foot longer than the record-holding walleye. Most people catch them at 30 inches or less. Northern pike, also simply called northerns, have only one fin along the back, while walleye have two. Pike have flat, almost bill-shaped jaws that open very wide to show off a mouth full of sharp teeth. Northerns have a slimier body than walleye and many more bones in their filets, but they are excellent-tasting fish, especially when they are skinned.

Exit 173

You are now close to the town that proudly holds the annual August festival honoring . . . the pickle. Linwood is a small community about 3 miles to the east and near the shoreline of Saginaw Bay. It is located on the

BRAINBUSTERS

People frequently see beavers and muskrats gliding through Michigan marshes. They are quite easy to tell apart. Muskrats are in the same family as rats, and actually look a lot like them. They are bigger, though, reaching about 1.5–2 feet long, including a long and thin tail. Beavers aren't closely related to rats, and instead are in their own separate family.

Basic: From the tip of the snout to the end of the tail, how big can beavers grow? How much do they weigh?

Intermediate: Beavers were hunted very heavily in Michigan. For what reason were they hunted? What is *castor gras*, also known as greasy beaver?

Advanced: Scientists have found that if they play a tape recording of something, they can tempt beavers into building a dam in a certain location. What "something" is on the recording?

See next page for answers.

109

border, or line, between two townships, so "lin" comes from line. It was a thickly forested area when it was named in 1882, so the "wood" half of the name came from that feature. The community actually had its start a decade earlier as a station on the tracks of the Michigan Central Railroad. At that time, it was called Terry's Station after the man, James Terry, who ran the local lumber operation.

If you are wondering what happens at the Linwood National Pickle Festival (and who doesn't?), it is a combination of a carnival, pickle-themed parades, chicken dinner, various types of entertainment, and the always-popular pickle giveaway. Of course, it also has the Michigan-festival staple of a beer tent, which is an actual tent where thirsty festival-goers can tip a glass of brew.

The Pickle Festival isn't the only rather unusual festival in Michigan. Other festivals are:

- the Munger Potato Festival, which includes a potato toss, potato-sack race, a parade, rides, potato giveaways, and the crowning of a potato king and queen. A favorite food at the festival is potato bratwurst. Munger also hosts auto races/demolition derbies that are run on a track shaped like a figure eight. According to a press release

Exit 173

THE ANSWERS

Beavers are the largest rodent in the state, with some reaching *4 feet long*, including a foot-long, paddle-shaped tail. They can weigh up to *60 pounds*! Beavers have been trapped for their fur by Europeans since the 1600s, and also hunted by the American Indians before that. (As early as the end of the 17th century, their numbers near the Straits of Mackinac had noticeably declined.) One of the most prized types of pelt was *castor gras* or greasy beaver. This was a beaver pelt that had been broken in by human beings, including both American Indians and European traders. *As a person wore or slept on the pelt, his or her skin oil would soak into the hide and make it supple ... and greasy.* In contrast, dry beaver was a pelt that had been stretched and dried out.

Many of the greasy pelts were made into beaver hats, a very fashionable men's accessory in Europe and in New England.

Beavers chew through trees at a very fast pace, chopping down a 5-inch tree in as little as three minutes! Once the tree falls, they then strip branches off the fallen tree to make dams, sometimes in places where people would prefer they didn't. For example, they often construct dams in locations that block water drains, which can back up water over roads or into backyards. Scientists have been able to convince beavers to build dams in more preferable locations by playing tape recordings of *running water*. Beavers respond to the sound and start a new dam there.

for one such event, "This type of competition blends the thrill of two potential intersection crashes per lap and the motorized mayhem of an all-out derby." Munger is located a short drive southeast of Bay City. Other communities, including Posen in the northeastern Lower Peninsula and Edmore in about the center of the Lower Peninsula, also host potato festivals.

+ the Bologna Festival in Yale, which is home to a long-time bologna-making company. Yale's chamber of commerce describes the festival as "a three-day weekend event that closes the streets and transforms this small community of just under 2,000 to a gathering of over 20,000 Bologna-starved party-goers!" One of the festival's big draws is the Outhouse Race: Entrants build outhouses, put them on wheels, and race them down the town's main street. Yale is located in the eastern Lower Peninsula.

+ the Gizzard Fest in Potterville. One of the big events is the gizzard-eating contest. For those who are unfamiliar with a gizzard, it is an organ found in birds. The gizzard is a muscular, stomach-like pouch that helps birds grind up their food before sending it on to the stomach for additional digestion. Festival-goers who want to avoid the spot-light can have their own plates of gizzard heaven, in such specialties as gizzard fajitas, gizzard burritos, gizzard omelets, and gizzard-laced gravy over biscuits. Deep-fried giz-zards are also available for folks who prefer simpler fare. Potterville is located in southern lower Michigan near the state capital of Lansing.

+ the National Baby Food Festival, held in Fremont. Fremont is the home of baby-food giant Gerber Products Co. One of its signature events is the baby crawl that pits baby against baby in a race to the finish line. Onlookers split their time between watching the ador-able racers and observing their overly excited parents who will do almost anything to cajole their babies to the finish line. Fremont is located on the west side of central lower Michigan.

+ the Wolverine Lumberjack Festival, held in Wolverine in the northern Lower Peninsula. Competitors

BRAINBUSTERS

One of Michigan's many festivals throughout the year is in the community of Mesick (MEE-sik) in northern lower Michigan. It centers around the morel (mor-EL). In fact, morel picking is an extremely popular activity every spring throughout much of Michigan. Many people consider morels to have a wonderful taste. Nonetheless, some people are allergic to them and/or have become sick by eating them.

Basic: What is a morel?

Intermediate: Morels only appear for a short time. What happens to them for the rest of the year?

Advanced: What is a false morel?

See next page for answers.

Spongy-looking morels poke up from the ground under the large white flower of a trillium. (Travel Michigan)

come from miles around to test their abilities in different contests of lumberjack skills, including log rolling (staying upright on a floating log while rotating it with your feet), cross-cut sawing, and axe throwing. Amateurs can also see if they have what it takes to last more than a few seconds log rolling before falling into the drink. Other Michigan communities, such as Newago and Luther, have logging festivals, too.

+ the Bay Port Fish Sandwich Festival, held in the upper Thumb. The main attraction is the food: huge fish sandwiches, of course!

+ the Woodtick Festival, held in the west-central U.P. community of

THE ANSWERS

A morel is a *mushroom*, which is a type of fungus. A morel has an unusual look: Its oblong cap is covered with indentations, making it appear to have been cut out of a sponge. A morel mushroom is actually just the part of the fungus that appears above the ground every spring. The underground part of a morel, and indeed any mushroom, is a much larger mat of hairlike fibers, known as a mycelium (my-SEE-lee-um). Sometimes, the mycelium isn't underground, but instead fans out through the decaying wood of a fallen tree. *When the above-ground morels are gone, the mycelium survives and grows until the next spring when it sends up more mushrooms.* The mushroom part of the morel is involved in reproduction. It makes and releases millions of tiny spores that blow on the slightest air current, land, and if conditions are just right, will develop into new morels.

A false morel, also known as a beefsteak mushroom or lorchel, is another type of fungus that has a wrinkly, pitted surface much like that of a morel. The false morel is an extremely poisonous, even deadly, mushroom if eaten raw. Some people do eat them, but only after properly cooking them—and of course, ensuring that they are not allergic to them. Cooking typically involves boiling the false morels in a precise manner, but even inhaling the steam from the cooking mushrooms can cause dangerous health problems.

Iron Mountain. It's a music festival that started in 1994 as what was supposed to be a small gathering of friends to pluck out a few songs on their guitars and to watch the Green Bay Packers on TV—many folks in the U.P. consider the Packers to be their home team rather than the Detroit Lions. Word of a jam session spread, and a local saloon owner dubbed the garage get-together the U.P. version of Woodstock, jokingly calling it Woodtick. It is now a full-fledged festival that draws regional and nationally known bands, and spreads over four days.

Mile Marker 175

You are now in Michigan's so-called tension zone. The tension zone is a narrow band that stretches across the Lower Peninsula from about Bay City west to Muskegon, and marks a transition area between trees that are more common farther north and those that are more common farther south. Northbound travelers will begin to see more and more needle-leaved species like white, red, and jack pine, black and white spruce, and balsam fir, mixed with broad-leaved species like yellow birch, sugar maple and beech. Southbound travelers will begin to see a higher percentage of broad-leaved trees like oak, hickory, black walnut, and red maple.

Why do the forests change? Part of the reason is the annual temperature pattern—obviously warmer to the south for a longer growing season—but the soil also plays a big part. Southern Michigan has loamy soil that is a blend of clay and sand, and holds water quite well. Northern Michigan soil is extremely sandy, often very dry, and more acidic. Michigan's state soil—that's right, Michigan has a state soil—is of the sandy variety. Called Kalkaska (kal-KASS-kuh) soil, it is orange- to rust-colored and found in about 33 of the state's 83 counties. All 33 of them are in the northern Lower Peninsula or the Upper Peninsula. The soil got its name from the county where it was found. Kalkaska County is in the northwestern Lower Peninsula.

As you drive through the tension zone and to the forests beyond, watch for the rather dramatic change in naturally growing stands of trees along the sides of the freeway.

BRAINBUSTERS

Agriculture is a big business in Michigan. The leading crop is corn, which covered about 2.25 million acres of state farmlands in 2005. The second leading crop is soybeans at 2 million acres.

Basic: Soybeans are not native to Michigan. Where did soybeans come from originally?

Intermediate: Most of the soybeans grown here are not eaten as beans, but used primarily for making something else. What?

Advanced: What are soy milk, tofu and edamame (eh-duh-MAH-may)?

See next page for answers.

Mile Marker 177

Agriculture is a big business in this part of Michigan and in many areas of the state. A common site on many farms is the tower silo, which is typically used to store either grain or livestock feed. Before the silo was developed more than a century ago by a Wisconsin scientist, farmers often used a square or rectangular structure for storage, but had trouble with the corners where feed and grain would collect and get moldy. The silo's cylindrical shape eliminated the corners. In addition, the height of silos makes an easy job of packing the grain and feed inside: The weight of the material itself automatically compresses the grain and feed below. Many of the silos in Michigan contain corn, which is the state's largest crop, and much of it is in the form of silage, or animal feed. To make silage, corn (leaves and all) go

into the silo where it ferments. Silage can also include other plants, such as oats, alfalfa, other grasses and even sunflowers. Farmers ferment rather than dry the plants because the fermentation process preserves more of the plants' nutrition than drying does.

Mile Marker 179

Just to the north of mile marker 179 along the southbound side of the freeway is a small, rectangular pond. Indeed, such small, rectangular ponds appear next to I-75 from one end to the other. The rectangular shape suggests that they were not made by natural forces, and they weren't. When a major road like I-75 or another highway is built, engineers design it so that the road surface is not only as level as possible, but also set slightly higher than the surrounding terrain. This allows rain to drain

THE ANSWERS

Soybeans are native to *eastern Asia* and are a food staple in Japan, China and other countries of that region. Most soybeans grown in the United States are crushed and pressed to remove their *oil*. The oil is used to make cooking oil, margarine and other items at the grocery store, and also to make non-food products such as ink, cosmetics, paint and plastics. Soy milk is a *mixture of mainly water, sweetener and protein collected from soy beans*. Tofu is *curdled soy milk*, which means that the liquid soy milk is turned into a semisolid clump. The clump is tofu. Although the state

grows so many soybeans and the beans are very tasty, Michigan shoppers rarely see the whole beans for sale in the fresh-produce section. Restaurants, however, do sometimes offer them on the menu as a side dish called edamame. Edamame is *soybeans that are picked at the peak of their flavor, placed—pod and all—into boiling water for cooking, and served with a little salt*. Diners pop the beans out of the pod and into their mouths. Now that word of the healthy benefits of soybeans has gotten around, some grocery stores now carry frozen, whole soybeans.

114

off the road. One way they accomplish this is by using "borrow pits." A borrow pit is just what it sounds like: a place where workers borrow sand, gravel, or other material for another purpose, in this case building up the road base. Eventually, these pits fill with rain or groundwater and become small ponds. Over time, plants start to invade the edges, slowly making the ponds smaller and smaller as the years pass.

Exit 181

Pinconning (pronounced pin-CONN-ing) is the name of both a river and town located a few miles to the east. Pinconning is an Ojibwe Indian word meaning "place of the potato." "Potato" in this case probably refers to native root vegetables and not the potato we now find on sale in the grocery aisle. Numerous root vegetables grow in Michigan, and one in particular is called the Jerusalem artichoke. Also known as sunchoke, Jerusalem artichoke is actually a type of sunflower. The perennial plant grows to 3–9 feet tall and is topped with several large daisy-style flowers that can each be 4 inches wide. Both the petals and the centers of the flowers are yellow. Indians grew the plant for its brown root, which looks rather like a ginger root, but a bit more gnarly. Strangely, the Jerusalem artichoke is not an artichoke nor does it have any connection to Jerusalem. The artichoke terminology came from Samuel de Champlain, a French explorer who came to North America, tasted the root, and sent a sample back to Europe

with a description that it tasted like an artichoke. The name stuck. Where did Jerusalem come from? Europeans called the plant *girasole*, which is an Italian word for sunflower, and somewhere down the line, non-Italians misheard the word as the similarly sounding word Jerusalem, and the name Jerusalem artichoke was born.

— — —

Most Michiganders have heard of Pinconning because of its famous

BRAINBUSTERS

You know you're a Michigander if you have eaten a wedge of Pinconning Cheese, or ordered a ginger ale and expected Vernors. You also know you're a Michigander if you can answer these questions.

Basic: Michiganders often make a trip to a party store, but not necessarily for party supplies. What is a party store in Michigan? Also, Michigan youngsters learn the mnemonic HOMES very early in school. What does HOMES stand for?

Intermediate: People from metropolitan Detroit, in particular, use the word "viaduct" to describe a certain feature on a freeway. What is it?

Advanced: Folks who live in the Upper Peninsula are called Yoopers, which arose as a variation of "U.P.ers," and those in the Lower Peninsula are sometimes called Lopers. Yoopers also frequently refer to Lopers as trolls. Why?

See next page for answers.

cheese. Pinconning cheese is sold at deli counters all over the state. This semi-hard, Colby-style cheese has become a home-state favorite. Pinconning cheese had its start when a settler came to the area in 1915 and developed the formula. The Pinconning Cheese Co. still makes the cheese, and the town of Pinconning is now known as the cheese capital of Michigan.

Mile Markers 184–185

Look for Whitefeather Road about halfway between mile markers 184 and 185. It is named for an old station on a logging railroad. The station's was known as White Feather because of its proximity to White Feather River. White Feather refers to a prominent Indian chief in the area. Until the loggers came, local Indians came to the river and surrounding forests to hunt and fish.

Mile Markers 185–186

I-75 crosses the Saganing River about halfway between these two mile markers. The river is also just south of the border between Bay County to the south and Arenac (AIR-eh-nak) County to the north.

Saganing looks and sounds a good deal like Saginaw (a major city and river to the south), and that is no coincidence. Frequently, white settlers had a difficult time pronouncing and attempting to spell the Indian-derived names of rivers, towns and other places. Here, for example, Saganing is probably just a variation of Saginaw.

If you look back through the records for many towns in Michigan, you will see that the spelling and pronunciation of a town's name may have changed several times in the early years as its citizens, its postmaster, employees of the railroad that may have had a station there, and perhaps the lumberjacks or the trappers, alternately and sometimes simultaneously named the towns. The state government, however, had the last word in any naming conflicts and decided on the ultimate spellings.

Bay County's name reflects its location, which is on the western shore of Lake Huron's Saginaw Bay. Arenac County isn't so simple. It is one of the many counties named by Henry Rowe Schoolcraft, a geographer who lived from 1793–1864. Schoolcraft traveled around the middle of the United States and throughout much of Michigan when the country was still new and largely unexplored. He married a half-Ojibwe (Chippewa) woman whom he had met in Sault Ste. Marie (now at the northernmost end of I-75 in Michigan), and from her, he learned

THE ANSWERS

In this state, a party store is another term for a *convenience store*. The mnemonic HOMES is an easy way for school children to remember all five of the Great Lakes: *Huron, Ontario, Michigan, Erie and Superior*. A viaduct is a *freeway overpass*. Yoopers refer to Lopers as trolls because *they live south of the Mackinac Bridge, or "under the bridge."*

the Ojibwe language. He soon became a noted expert in Indian cultures. As a geographer with considerable clout, he also named a number of Michigan's counties, and Arenac was one of them. For many of the names, he combined an Indian word or syllable with another from the Greek or Latin language. This is what he did with Arenac. The first part of the name comes from the Latin word *arena*, which refers to a sandy area where the gladiators fight. Apparently, a sandy surface was perfect for soaking up any spilt blood that resulted from the gladiator competitions. The second part, the "ac," is part of the Algonquin Indian word *akee*, which means "land of" or "place of." Arenac, therefore, is "a sandy place."

Exit 188

This exit connects to US-23, a snaky highway that travels to the east a

---

BRAINBUSTERS

The Au Gres area is now known to anglers as a great spot for catching a variety of fish, especially smelt. Smelt only grow to 6 or 7 inches long.

Basic: What is smelt dipping?

Intermediate: Why is smelt dipping especially popular in the spring?

Advanced: Michigan's smelt are known as rainbow smelt, but a bucket full of the fish reveal only silver-white fish. Where does the "rainbow" come from?

See next page for answers.

Rainbow smelt. (NOAA, Great Lakes Environmental Research Laboratory)

short distance before shifting to the north and then to the northeast until it reaches Lake Huron, at which point it hugs the lakeshore all the way until it reaches the northern tip of the Lower Peninsula. There, traffic from US-23 can merge right back onto I-75. Along its route up the length of the Lake Huron shoreline, US-23 passes through a number of towns with unusual names. Some of them are Au Gres (locally pronounced almost as one word aw-GRAY), Tawas (TAH-wuss) City, and Oscoda (oss-COE-duh):

Exit 188

+ French explorers gave Au Gres its name, which means "gritty stone," after that characteristic of the area.
+ Tawas City is one of a small percentage of cities in Michigan that actually have the word "city" as part of their official names. Many people believed Tawas was named for the Indian tribe Ottawas but with the first syllable missing. According to several sources, however, the name actually pays tribute to local Indian chief Ottawas, also known as Ottawonce or Ottawaus, which means Little Trader. The chief traded with white settlers in Michigan in the early to mid-1800s.
+ Oscoda got its name from geologist Henry Schoolcraft, who

combined two Indian words: *ossin*, which means stone; and *muscoda* or *mushcoda*, which means prairie or meadow.

M-61 is an east-west highway that leads to two county seats. The first large town to the east on M-61 is Standish, about 3 miles from I-75. The first large town to the west is Gladwin about 23 miles from here.

Standish is named for John Standish, a former Detroiter who built a sawmill here in 1871. It was Standish who had the town platted and successfully petitioned to give the community his name. Today, Standish is the Arenac County seat and has about 1,600 residents. Besides the county government, a major area employer is the Standish Maximum Correctional Facility. The facility houses male inmates, particularly those who are "difficult,

hard-to-manage prisoners," according to the Michigan Department of Corrections. To ensure that the inmates don't escape, the facility is ringed with two, tall fences that are armed with razor wire on top, scanned with electronic surveillance systems, and monitored by guards in five gun towers and a patrol vehicle. The facility is one of four maximum correctional facilities in the state. The other three are in Alger (AL-jur), Baraga (BARE-uh-guh) and Ionia (i-O-nya). Alger and Baraga are in the Upper Peninsula. Ionia is in the southern part of the Lower Peninsula.

With 3,000 residents, Gladwin is about twice as big as Standish and is the county seat in Gladwin County. The city and county names honor Major Henry Gladwin, who was stationed for a time in Detroit. To understand Gladwin's place in history, picture his era: the mid-1700s when France and England were both fighting for control of as much land

THE ANSWERS

In the spring, more than a quarter million people head to streams especially in the northern Lower Peninsula and the Upper Peninsula to go smelt dipping, which involves *scooping the schooling fish out of the water with a net.* Anglers typically head out to a stream at night, wade in, and start netting the fish. The best time to go smelt dipping is in the spring, right after the water temperature rises a little above 40°F. This is because *smelt leave the bigger lakes and head*

into gravel-bottomed streams and rivers to spawn. A good smelt-dipper can end up with a big bucket of the silver fish. *When they are underwater in the streams, however, their backs shimmer with a pale green, and their sides shine in shades of purple, pink and blue.* To prepare the tasty fish for eating, anglers simply cut off the head and tail, remove the entrails, and cook them bones and all. In all but the biggest smelt, the bones soften enough to be chewed right up.

here as possible. The French had built a fort in Detroit, but by 1760, the British had gained control of it. The Indians were none too happy with the change. The French had always helped the Indians by providing them with ample ammunition for winter hunting, but the British did not carry on the tradition. By the time that Major Gladwin arrived in 1762 to assume the command of the Detroit fort, tensions were at a fever pitch. An Indian chief named Pontiac called a meeting of hundreds of Indian chiefs and warriors and planned a surprise attack on the Detroit fort for May 1763. Gladwin got wind of Pontiac's plans—some say from an Indian woman who was smitten with the major—and Pontiac called off the attack. Pontiac was not through, however. He instructed the warriors to assault any Brit who ventured outside the fort. Gladwin left Detroit in 1764 and returned to his native England but the Indian aggression in Detroit continued for nearly two years until Pontiac finally relented (For more on the Pontiac rebellion, see mile marker 42.)

Canoeing and kayaking are popular activities in Michigan. Here, canoeists float along the Au Sable River in northern Michigan. (Terry W. Phipps)

Mile Marker 193

In this area, two small creeks run under I-75 within a mile of one another. One is the north branch of the Pine River, and the other is an even smaller branch off that north branch. Many kayak and canoe enthusiasts come to this part of the state to paddle the Pine River, the bulk of which is to the east of I-75. That's because the Pine is one of the

BRAINBUSTERS

Not so long ago, kayaks were seldom seen on Michigan's waterways. Now, they're everywhere. People who use them have certain terms for the parts of their kayaks, and for certain maneuvers.

Basic: Like other boats, a kayak has a bow and a stern. What are they? Also, what is the name of the opening where a kayaker sits?

Intermediate: Novice paddlers may notice that their kayaks will weathercock. What does this mean?

Advanced: What is Cleopatra's needle?

See next page for answers.

119

fastest flowing rivers in the Lower Peninsula and has fairly large rapids, especially in the spring when the water is high. While these rapids may not compare with the white-water rapids of western states, the combination of the current's speed and the tricky passages around underwater boulders and stony ledges can make the Pine a dangerous place first-time paddlers or small children. For experienced canoeists and kayakers, however, the river presents a surprisingly exhilarating challenge.

— — —

Exit 195

If you are heading north on I-75, take note of the increasing number of pine trees in the forests along the freeway. Pines are a hallmark of northern forests in Michigan. For more information on how the forests change from southern to northern Michigan, see mile marker 175.

Exit 195

For many roads throughout Michigan, the name often reveals the name of the nearby town. Here Sterling Road passes through the community of Sterling, which sits just to the east. The village started off in 1871 with a sawmill, and with the same name as its first postmaster: Perkins. A year later, the name changed to Sterling for local lumberman William Sterling. Nowadays, Sterling is a small village with about 500 residents that draws many a summer visitor for canoeing, kayaking and tubing on the Rifle River, which flows just beyond the north end of town. The Rifle flows fairly quickly and has many shallow spots, as well as various logs and boulders that provide a good deal of excitement, especially for inexperienced canoeists. Tubing, which is floating downriver in an inflatable tube, requires no skill and it moves at a much slower pace than canoeing— although new canoeists might give the tubers a run for the money.

— — —

About 20 miles to the west of this exit is a community called Meredith where, at one time, a person could

THE ANSWERS

The bow of a kayak, as in other boats, is its *front end*. The stern is the *rear end*. The center of a kayak where the paddler sits is the *cockpit*. Weathercock refers to *the condition in which a kayak turns into the wind*. This is a particular problem for novice paddlers who do not know how to anticipate it nor correct for it, and find themselves repeatedly off-course. Cleopatra's needle is a bad thing in kayaking. This is the position in which *one end of the kayak fills with water and therefore sinks under the surface of the water, while the other end pops up into the air like a bobber*. Often, the kayak soon completely sinks. This was once all too common, but now with proper floatation and bulkheads built into kayaks, it happens only rarely.

120

earn property by saving up chewing-tobacco packages. Here's the story: The town sprang up in 1885 around the logging industry, but its heyday was short-lived. Lumber ran out by 1890 and the town population plummeted. In spite of this, two new subdivisions were platted in 1892 with nearly 4,000 tiny 25-by-100-foot lots. Why? A tobacco company from Ohio decided to run a promotion in which a person who bought enough of their chewing tobacco would get one of these lots. By the end of the promotion, the company had issued 2,000 lot deeds to people across the country. Apparently, none of the deed owners ever came to Meredith to take possession of their property, and the town became deserted by the end of the 19th century. Currently, Meredith still has a place on the map and has a small population.

Mile Marker 198

The land on either side of the freeway along this section of I-75 is part of the huge Au Sable (aw SAH-bul) State Forest, which stretches eastward all the way to Lake Huron, and in a general northwesterly fashion for many miles. In fact, I-75 cuts through the Au Sable State Forest for much of the next 60 miles to the north. The Au Sable State Forest is not a continuous forest. In other words, private property and even entire communities—some of them fairly large cities—dot the landscape within otherwise state forest lands.

Michigan has a number of state forests, and they all came about as a result of the logging era. In the 1830s, surveyors discovered the huge stands of pines in Michigan, and word quickly spread to timber speculators. They laid claim to much of the land in the state, and by the 1850s the logging boom was on. Over the next five decades, lumberjacks had cut nearly all of the valuable trees. According to the Department of Natural Resources, "By 1897 it was estimated that more that 160 billion board-feet of pine had been cut, with only about six billion board-feet of standing timber remaining, mostly in the Upper Peninsula. In a mere 70 years most of the original pine and hardwood forests of Michigan were gone."

BRAINBUSTERS

Forestry in Michigan is still a thriving industry.

Basic: To the nearest 10 percent, what percentage of the state of Michigan is covered by forests? In the U.P. alone, what percentage of land is covered by forests?

Intermediate: Scientists estimate that Michigan has about 11.5 billion trees. Is that number increasing or decreasing?

Advanced: Trees use water, carbon dioxide and sunlight for photosynthesis, and in the process produce the oxygen that we breathe. Oxygen, however, is just a byproduct. What is main purpose of photosynthesis from the tree's standpoint?

See next page for answers.

The land left behind looked nothing like it had before the logging rush. Where thick forests once stood, only discarded branches remained. With no more use for the land, the logging companies simply stopped paying taxes on it and moved on to other states that still had untouched, so-called virgin forests. As a result, millions of acres reverted to the state for nonpayment of taxes. The state was successful in selling some of the land to farmers, who made use of the fertile soil to grow crops, or to private citizens for other uses, but much remained in the state's hands.

Policy makers struggled over the future of these many acres, and in the early 1900s, decided that recreation and tourism might be a golden opportunity. In 1903, the Michigan Forest Reserve Act established a State Forest Reserve on about 34,000 acres in the center of the northern Lower Peninsula. That land is part of the Au Sable State Forest that still remains today and attracts visitors from all over the state and far beyond. After setting aside that initial land, the state established other reserves, and now has the largest state forest system in the United States. Its state forests include the Pere Marquette (peer mar-KET), Pigeon River Country, and Mackinaw state forests in the Lower Peninsula; and the Copper Country, Escanaba (es-cuh-NOB-uh) River, and Lake Superior state forests in the Upper Peninsula. Together, the state forests cover nearly 3.9 million acres! The Michigan Department of Natural Resources oversees all of these lands, and makes the decisions about managing them for use by people, as well as by the animals and plants that make their homes there.

Besides setting aside the state forests, Michigan also sold millions of acres to the U.S. government to create national forests in the state. The U.S. Department of Agriculture's Forestry Service manages the national forests, which include the Huron and Manistee located in the Lower Peninsula, and the Hiawatha and Ottawa located in the Upper Peninsula.

THE ANSWERS

More than *50 percent* of Michigan's land is covered by forests. In just the U.P., more than *80 percent* of the land is forested. Although 150,000–200,000 people work in the lumber industry in Michigan, *the number of trees in the state is increasing*. According to the Upper Michigan Tree Improvement Center, the state gains about 19 trees per thousand every year. This amounts to eight trees of the thousand dying from natural causes and 12 falling to harvesters, but 39 new trees growing. Trees and plants get energy from the sun to drive photosynthesis, which transforms water and carbon dioxide into *sugar* called glucose. The glucose is then either used by the tree or plant cells, or stored as starch. The process gives off oxygen, which is released into the air.

Mile Marker 201

At about mile marker 201, just north of the rest area that sits on the southbound side of I-75, the freeway crosses over Wells Creek. Back in the 1870s during the lumbering era, Wells was a station on the Michigan Central Railroad, and had enough people living there for a school and a post office. Like many a small logging town, its residents pulled up stakes when the logging company moved on and abandoned the town. Eventually, even the rail tracks disappeared, too.

For professional and amateur historians, Wells and other Michigan ghost towns are wonderful places to explore. They are typically secluded, and either never had a road or had only a small, now long-gone, wagon trail leading to them. Their link to the outside world was the railroad line. Hikers, off-road bicyclists and hunters sometimes come across the remains of these ghost towns: perhaps an old foundation or nearly hidden concrete sidewalk, an aged and overgrown lilac bush or other ornamental shrub in the middle of a wild meadow, a few parallel rows of planted pines, or even a tombstone with its letters nearly worn away. Usually, no building walls or roofs remain. Part of the reason for the lack of remnants is that the logging companies frequently dismantled the buildings, transported the pieces by train to the next up-and-coming boom town, and reused them.

The residences in a typical logging town were simple, small structures just large enough for a single family. Single men stayed in a company-

MM 201

Loggers photographed after dinner at their camp. (Library of Congress, Wm. Morrell Harmer, circa 1892)

owned boarding house (or logging camp), which frequently was done up dorm-style with bunk beds for the men. (For more on lumberjack life, see exit 259 among others.) Railroad stations, like Wells near here, sometimes also had housing—little more than shacks—for the usually poor immigrant men who worked on the railroad. These shacks were often constructed across the tracks from the lumber town. A common saying of the era was that people who lived in the shacks were from "the wrong side of the tracks."

Exit 202

Just off this exit on the north-bound side of the freeway is at least one gas-station store that sells jerky, strips of dried meat that for some reason seem to be especially appealing to persons of the male gender. The jerky here has not just included the traditional plain or smoked beef varieties, but also a number of different flavors and even meats, such as elk and venison, all of which have been sold from tubs that line the counter. Over the years, the store has advertised its wares with a large sign that claims it has the "world's largest selection of beef jerky". When pressed (by the author) a few years back about whether the assertion was true, an employee responded that the selection was indeed "the world's largest . . . for around here."

This exit leads to the community of Alger, which is just south of M-33,

and to Rose City, which is about 20 miles north on M-33. Alger takes its name from Russell Alger, who had a busy life. He was a lawyer-turned-timber businessman, then Civil War soldier and officer. He attained the rank of colonel and then general, and led troops in several major battles. After his army days, he settled in Detroit to focus on his lumber business. He built a solid reputation and in 1885, he became governor of the state of Michigan. He declined offers to nominate him again in 1886, but stayed in politics. In the late 1890s, he accepted the position of Secretary of War under U.S. President William McKinley and became embroiled in the Spanish-American War. He followed that up by becoming a U.S. senator from Michigan in 1902. Besides his name on this small community of Alger, he is also remembered in the name of Alger County, which is located in the Upper Peninsula.

The small burg of Rose City does not take after the flower, as many think, but is named for Allen Rose, an early storekeeper and co-owner of a lumber company. In the late 1800s and early 1900s, Rose City became one of many small towns in Michigan that had a number of homesteaders among its ranks. Homesteading became common here and throughout the nation after the U.S. Congress in 1862 passed a federal act to provide up to 40 acres of land to settlers in a sort of sweat-equity arrangement. The settler had five years to make improvements to the land. If the land was sufficiently improved—for instance, it had become a working farm or had a house built on it—the homesteader would receive the title to the property.

Nowadays, some people know of Rose City as the site of a rather bizarre optical illusion called a "mystery hill" (sometimes known as a gravity hill). A mystery hill is a place where a car that is put in neutral at a certain point on a road will appear to roll uphill. Here in Rose City, a car stopped on its mystery hill will seemingly roll uphill for more than 10 yards. Although the spot is unmarked, word about its location has gotten around. People often head to the mystery hill, situated on Reasner Road just north of Heath Road, to see the quite-convincing optical illusion for themselves.

— — —

Thrill-seekers may want to head about 16 miles north of Rose City to the small community of Mio (MY-o), which has a mystery of its own. This town has had several reported sightings of a 7- to 8-foot-tall, hairy, two-legged beast. That's right, a Bigfoot! And Mio isn't the only place in Michigan where people have claimed to see a Bigfoot. In July 2007, for example, a California group called the Bigfoot Field Researchers Organization arranged (and charged participants for) a four-day, Bigfoot-hunting expedition to Michigan's Upper Peninsula. About 50 people signed up,

Exit 202

BRAINBUSTERS

Legends in Michigan have been around long before the Europeans set foot here. American Indians had their legends, too, and many of the Ojibwe legends center around Manabozho (also called Winabijou), a supernatural being—some describe him as a deity—with great power.

Basic: In one story, Manabozho lived with a wolf that was taken by other supernatural beings called Ogema and then killed. Manabozho went after the Ogema, and on his way, came across a belted kingfisher. What type of animal is a belted kingfisher?

Intermediate: The kingfisher told Manabozho where the Ogema had the wolf, but also admitted that it had eaten some of the wolf's dead body. Manabozho was torn over whether to thank the kingfisher for the information or to hurt the kingfisher for eating his friend, so he did both. He thanked the kingfisher with a necklace made of shells, but then tried to strangle it, shaking its head back and forth. According to this particular legend (and there are several others), the necklace and the head-shaking caused two features that are seen on present-day kingfishers. What are the two features?

Advanced: The many Ojibwe stories surrounding Manabozho provided the inspiration for a noted author to write a very well-known poem about a fictitious American Indian hero. Who was the author and what was the hero's name?

See next page for answers.

and the group members spent their time trudging through forests in the central U.P. looking for any sign of the creature. One night, according to the group, the participants heard a loud and eerie call. They were unable to identify it as anything else, so they declared that it must have been a Bigfoot.

Some Michigan folks have become so enthralled with Bigfoot and other weird phenomena that they get together periodically to discuss them at meetings of the Michigan chapter of MUFON (Mutual UFO Network). Topics in 2006 and 2007 have included, "Proving the Existence of the Unseen," and perhaps more tellingly, "What to do if you uncover evidence of crop formations and/or Bigfoot in your UFO investigation."

Mile Marker 205

The border between Arenac (AIR-eh-nak) County to the south and Ogemaw (OH-guh-maw) County to the north passes through here. The name Arenac is the combination of two words: *arena*, which is Latin for sandy area, and "ac," is which part of the Algonquin Indian word *akee*, and means "land of" or "place." For more on the Arenac name, see mile marker 185.5. Ogemaw, on the other hand, is the Ojibwe (Chippewa) Indian word for chief, but the county was actually named for one particular local chief by the name of Ogema-kega. As frequently occurs with American Indian names, his is listed in various places with several different spellings, all of which have the same general pronunciation, give or take a syllable or two. One of them, Ogemakegate, is how it is written on his tombstone, which still remains in Bay City, Mich. Other documents spell it Ogemawkeketo or Ogemaw-ki-keto.

THE ANSWERS

A belted kingfisher is a *bird* that is common near water, where it uses its long beak to capture and eat small fishes, a primary component of its diet. The belted kingfisher is a dark bluish-gray bird with a white belly. The male has a gray band around its chest, while the female had a rust-colored chest band. According to the legend, the shell necklace became the *white collar band* that all kingfishers have today, and the head-shaking caused a *tuft of feathers* to stick up on the bird's head, another feature that is still evident now.

The legends about Manabozho serve as the basis for *Henry Wadsworth Longfellow's* epic poem "The Song of Hiawatha." The hero of the poem is *Hiawatha*. Longfellow learned about Manabozho from Henry Rowe Schoolcraft, who was known at the time as an expert on the Indian culture. Schoolcraft was also a geographer, who was responsible for many of the county names in Michigan. For more on Schoolcraft, see mile markers 185–186. For more on "The Song of Hiawatha, see mile marker 142.

Ogema-kega has an important part in Michigan history, because he was a key player in the historic Treaty of 1819 that essentially exchanged some six million areas of Indian-occupied land—more than a quarter of the land in the entire Lower Peninsula—for a few reservations and little more than a pocketful of silver. The meeting arose when Lewis Cass, who was then the governor of the Northwest Territories, received orders to make a treaty with the American Indians. He set up a meeting (the Indians called it a council fire) in Saginaw, which is located to the south along I-75. Cass arrived with a company of soldiers and interpreters. The Indians, mostly from the Ojibwe nation, came by the thousands, and their primary speaker was Ogema-kega.

Early in the negotiations, the chief said, "We are here to smoke the pipe of peace, but not to sell our lands... The warm wave of the white man rolls in upon us and melts us away. Our women reproach us. Our children want homes. Shall we sell from under them the spot where they spread their blankets?" Cass responded by saying that the U.S. army had beaten the English army, along with the Indians who had sided with them, and therefore essentially had already won the land. Nonetheless, he said, the U.S. government wanted to provide sufficient acreage for the American Indians to live in peace.

The talks, at times very contentious, proceeded over the next two weeks. In the end, with urging from a number of at least half-Indian men who were essentially government

agents, Ogema-kega and the other chiefs agreed to sign the treaty. It provided payment to the Ojibwe nation in the amount of $1,000 in silver every year forever, and it created 15 reserves totaling 100,000 acres for use by the Ojibwe nation of Indians. It also designated separate 640-acre parcels for certain individuals who had a hand in the treaty negotiations. Three of these individuals were the half-Ojibwe, half-white brothers John, Peter and James Riley. Their father, James Riley Sr., had helped convince the Indians to sign, and two of the brothers had also served as interpreters during the treaty meeting. Besides the Riley brothers, several well-known Indian or part-Indian traders were among those who received tracts of land as part of the deal. In addition, the Indians requested that the treaty compensate certain white men whom they considered friends. These included a doctor who had for years cared for the Indians at no charge,

MM 205

BRAINBUSTERS

Basic: How did glaciers form: from freezing rain or from falling snow?

Intermediate: How far can a glacier move in a month: a couple of inches, a couple of feet, or a couple of miles?

Advanced: People sometimes find the bones of long-dead animals buried in the ground here in Michigan, including the bones of the large elephant-like mastodons and, perhaps most oddly, whales! How did whales get into the Great Lakes?

See next page for answers.

and a few white men whom the tribe had adopted to live among them.

Besides the land provisions, the treaty permitted the Indians to hunt on the ceded lands. Although the treaty was signed in 1819, Indian use of the lands and waters of Michigan was hardly resolved. In fact, it was nearly two centuries later in the year 2000 before a pact settled decades of litigation over whether the state could limit Indian fishing in Michigan Great Lakes waters. In the pact, the Indians agreed to cut back on using large-mesh gill nets, which not only entrap and kill non-target fishes, but also sometimes became tangled with passing boats, and also to do their fishing in areas away from the recreational boaters who were involved in most of the tangling incidents. In turn, the state government bought the Indians new boats equipped with replacement trap nets that cause less tangling prob-

THE ANSWERS

Thousands of years ago, the weather became a little colder (scientists still haven't agreed on why). The *falling snow* began to accumulate and freeze together to form giant ice sheets. The summers were too short and too cold to melt the ice sheets, so each year they grew and eventually formed into glaciers. When the glaciers became very thick and heavy, their weight caused them to move, or flow, very slowly—usually about an inch a day. When the pressure of the ice builds up, however, a glacier can surge forward as much as *2 miles* in a single month.

The immense weight of the glaciers may have been responsible for bringing the whales to Michigan. Fossilized whale bones have turned up near Flint and Tecumseh in southern Michigan, but also in Oscoda in northern Michigan. According to many scholars, the Great Lakes connected more directly to the Atlantic Ocean off the east coast of North America right after the glacier finally receded from the state 11,000–13,000 years ago. The weight of the glacier depressed the land under it and left it lower than sea level. *Until the land rebounded back above sea level, ocean water flowed all the way to the Great Lakes*, which introduced some rather unusual animals to the Great Lakes: namely whales and walruses!

As the glacier retreated, large land animals began to move back into Michigan. One of the most noteworthy species was the mastodon. These elephant-like animals, now extinct, were shorter but heavier than the elephants of today, weighing about 4–6 tons. (For comparison, a typical car weighs 1–2 tons.) Their tusks were different, too. Instead of one pair of tusks coming from the upper jaw, like modern-day elephants, most mastodons had another set growing from the lower jaw, and their massive upper tusks curled upward.

128

lems and can avoid non-target fishes, and the federal government paid more than $8 million to five tribes to compensate those small Indian fishing operations, often just individuals, that would not get the new trap-net boats but would still be restricted from using large-mesh gill nets.

Other lawsuits over Indian fishing and hunting rights Michigan and other parts of the United States are still pending.

Mile Marker 209

As you look out the window, you will probably notice that Michigan has a rolling landscape, sometimes with small hills and valleys, and other times with much more rugged terrain. The rolling nature of the landscape is due to glacier movements. Back one or two billion years ago, this land was downright tropical, and Michigan was covered with a warm sea. Things had changed considerably by about one or two million years ago. The climate had become cool enough for a glacier to advance out of Canada and cover what is now Michigan with a layer of ice that was tens of thousands of feet—at least 2 miles—thick. In other words, Michigan looked a lot like Antarctica!

Over the following millennia, the glacier retreated and advanced many times, and each time the movements changed the appearance of Michigan's landscape by gouging out depressions, leveling hills, carrying in soil and rocks from Canada and transplanting them here, and even making new soil by grinding up rocks

in its path. When the glacier finally retreated from Michigan once and for all about 11,000–13,000 years ago, the landscape took the general shape it has today. Melting ice from the glacier filled the largest depressions to make the Great Lakes of Erie, Huron, Michigan and Superior.

At that time, the Great Lakes were bigger than they are now, in part because the sheer weight of the glacier had compacted, or depressed, the land underneath. The lakes were also much deeper because of the huge volume of water that flowed into them from the melting glaciers. The land bounced back slowly to its current level, and the water level finally dropped by about 50 feet when a pathway opened and allowed it to

BRAINBUSTERS

Although they are not as common as the red-tailed hawks that often sit in branches of trees along the side of the freeway, owls do indeed perch there, too.

Basic: Michigan's largest owl is the great horned owl. What are its two "horns?"

Intermediate: What is unusual about the size of the young great horned owls, called owlets, when they leave the nest?

Advanced: What makes the position of an owl's ears—one higher than the other—important to its hearing, and what makes its wings so perfect for nighttime hunting?

See page 131 for answers.

129

Bald eagle (USFWS/Steve Maslowski) and red-tailed hawk (USDA Forest Service/Dave Herr).

drain out of the lakes and off to the north. Besides its impact on the Great Lakes, the melting glacier also filled the smaller, inland depressions to create the state's 11,000-plus lakes, not to mention its river systems, and many, many other water bodies.

Mile Marker 210

A scan along the treetops on the side of the highway or in the median here sometimes provides a good view of two of Michigan's large birds of prey, the bald eagle and the red-tailed hawk. An adult bald eagle is easily identifiable with its brilliant white head and tail feathers, dark brown body feathers, big, yellow, hooked beak and yellow feet. Immature bald

eagles—those up to about 4 or 5 years old—are all brown except for patches of white here and there on the undersides of the tail and wings. Bald eagles are impressive birds, having a wingspan of 7–8 feet, and weighing 12–16 pounds. They often stick to areas near a river, marsh or lake, which is where they find their favorite prey: fish. Although they are quite capable of catching fish themselves, bald eagles are not above letting another bird of prey do the work and then swooping in to steal it, or even eating a dead fish they find washed up on shore. They will also hunt and eat various mammals, as well as turtles and ducks, and will sometimes peck at roadkill.

One of their most interesting behaviors, though, is their courtship display. Once a male and female have preliminarily selected one another for mates, they fly together high up into the sky and perform a truly death-defying stunt. They lock their 2-inch-long talons and plummet. Their bodies cartwheel as they hurtle down, and just moments before they crash into the swiftly approaching ground, the pair separates and flies back up to the heights.

The red-tailed hawk is smaller than the bald eagle, having a wingspan of about 4 feet compared to nearly twice that size for a bald eagle. It is, however, much more common than the bald eagle, and frequently sits in trees alongside I-75 throughout the state. Observers viewing a red-tailed hawk that is soaring above may have a tough time distinguishing it from other Michigan hawks. That's because soaring hawks usually only display their undersides, and without binoculars, they can look quite similar. When the bird is sitting in a tree with its back toward the observer, however, the rust-red tail feathers on the red-tailed hawk are a sure giveaway even to the unaided eye. Besides the red tail feathers, the bird's back and head are brown, and the leg feathers that peek out are white mottled with brown. Like bald eagles, females are larger than males, but otherwise the two sexes look alike. Red-tailed hawks are predators, too, but instead of a mainly fish diet, they usually fill up on mice and other small rodents.

For some people, the closest they ever get to the actual city of West Branch is the Tanger Outlet Center, located along the freeway's northbound side. The center has about two dozen stores, including Eddie Bauer, Gap and Reebok outlet shops. The small city of West Branch itself—population about 1,900—sits approximately

THE ANSWERS

The great horned owl is an impressive bird for its stocky build, huge eyes, 4-foot wingspan, and its "horns." The horns are actually *tufts of feathers that sit atop its head and look almost like ears.* Baby great horned owls hatch in the middle of winter in Michigan. With ample food from their mother, they grow very quickly. In fact, by the time they leave the nest at about 10 weeks old, *they may actually be bigger than their mother!*

Adult owls are excellent hunters for many reasons. One is their keen sense of hearing. Their ear openings sit on each side of the head, below and behind the eyes. In most birds the ear openings are positioned symmetrically on either side of the head, but in owls, they aren't. This *allows them to judge better the distance and direction from which sound is coming, so they can pinpoint the exact location of their prey*, even a tiny field mouse that's buried under a foot of snow. In comparison, a person must tilt or turn the head to determine the location of a sound, while an owl doesn't have to move. An owl's wings are also well-suited to hunting, especially at night, because *they allow the owl to fly in silence*. The quiet flight is the result of three features: each wing's leading edge is serrated in the fashion of a very short-toothed comb; each wing's trailing feathers have a frayed look; and each wing as well as the bird's legs are coated with down feathers. The combination allows the birds to stealthily cut through the air without making a sound. One way to experience the owl's silent flight yourself is to head out into the woods on a winter's night and lure in an owl by playing a recording of their species' call. If an owl responds, you may see it swoop above your head, but you won't hear it.

a mile and a half to the east. By northern Michigan standards, it is a fairly large city, and even serves as the county seat. West Branch got its name from its position on the west branch of the Rifle River.

— — — —

From here north, the terrain is quite a bit more hilly than it is to the south. To accommodate vehicles that slow down when climbing the hills, I-75 has periodic added lanes accompanied by signs instructing slower traffic to keep to the right. Drivers of big rigs, or semis, almost always take the right lane. In Michigan, you may see trucks, called road tractors, hauling a semi-trailer. A semi-trailer, which is a trailer without a front axle, perches on the back of the road tractor. The road tractor-trailer combination is called a tractor trailer. The arrangement works well for switching the trailers quickly, but means the vehicle can fold, or jackknife, if it starts to slide on snow- or ice-covered roads. Most tractor-trailer drivers have the skills and experience to correct a slide before it causes a jackknife, but they do use extra caution when the trailer is empty and therefore light enough to skid more easily. In Michigan, tractor trailers can also haul a second trailer behind the first. This second so-called "full trailer" has a front axle.

Tractor trailers can appear very tall, and almost look as if they cannot squeeze below overpasses on the freeway. Michigan law limits the height of all tractor trailers to 13-and-a-half feet, and the I-75 overpasses are

higher than that. A driver can obtain an exception to the 13.5-foot rule by applying for and receiving a special permit, and then carefully mapping out a route that takes into account the height of the any overlying obstacles. On surface roads, obstacles may run the gamut from electrical wires to traffic signals, but along I-75, the driver's primary concern is the clearance height of the overpasses. Once in a while, a news report will note an accident involving a truck that hits an overpass. In most cases, the truck was hauling a piece of equipment, such as a bridge section or a construction vehicle, on a flatbed trailer, and it was this equipment that actually clipped the overpass. Frequently, the culprit is a construction vehicle's shovel arm that was mistakenly left in a raised position.

Mile Marker 213

The big smiley face hovering over the treetops on the northbound side of the freeway is the water tower for the city of West Branch. The smiley face has been cheerily welcoming visiting to the nearly 2,000-resident city for decades. At one point, however, the smile was in jeopardy by the costs of repainting the eyes and huge grin, so local booster Ralph Steinhauser took up a collection drive to save the smiley face. His nickname became Mr. Smiley, of course. The initiative to save the water tower prompted such community good will that West Branch now hosts an annual July festival called Smiley Days, as well as a Smiley Hall of Fame. And of course, the city's slogan is "City with a Smile." The town even has a police car with a smiley face prominently displayed on the door. Apparently, the police car started off as an April Fool's Day joke: The city council announced to the local newspaper that it had plans to put the smiley face on all of its police cars, and the newspaper bought the ruse and printed the story. The paper was a bit red-faced when the truth came out, so to ease any tension, the city turned its hoax into reality and duly painted up one of its police cars, albeit it a retired one. The city now puts the car in parades and other promotional events, and also honored the passing of Mr. Smiley in 2003 by using the car to head up the funeral procession.

Water towers like the one in West Branch are actually very common,

BRAINBUSTERS

At one time, the most common bird in North America was the passenger pigeon, and it made up 25–40 percent of the entire bird population in America. The bird also lived in Michigan, where numerous reports in the early to mid-1800s described huge flocks, some covering 5 square miles or more, and so dense that the birds actually blocked out the Sun and cast the land below in darkness.

Basic: In the mid-1800s, people in Michigan reported finding broken branches and hundreds of broken eggs littering the ground under the trees where the birds nested. What caused the branches to break?

Intermediate: The number of passenger pigeons plunged at the end of the 19th century. What caused the decline in Michigan?

Advanced: One of the last large nesting sites—and large harvests—of passenger pigeons in Michigan was in northwestern Michigan, around the community of Petoskey, in 1878. The nesting site was an estimated 3–10 miles wide and 40 miles long, and included some one billion birds. No other bird in Michigan today can even vaguely compare with numbers like that! The harvest from that nesting site totaled at least 1.1 million birds, but it didn't stop there. The hunters also followed the surviving birds, and killed them where they landed. As the massive harvest continued in Petoskey, however, passenger pigeons were already gone or were in very low numbers in other parts of the state. Places that once had millions of birds now reported a few dozen or none at all. By 1897, the Michigan legislature introduced a bill that would stop the hunting of passenger pigeons. Conservationists hoped that the effort would save the few remaining flocks of a dozen or so birds that still lingered in the state. It did not. The birds not only disappeared completely from Michigan, but from everywhere else. In what year was the last documented passenger pigeon seen in the wild? In what year did the last captive passenger pigeon—the sole remaining member of the species—die?

See next page for answers.

low-tech methods of maintaining a town's water pressure. They have a very simple design. In fact, a water tower is really just a water tank that sits high above the average ground level. The tank can either sit well above the ground on tall legs, as it does here, or if a hill is high enough, it can rest right on the ground. The purpose of the height is to provide pressure for the water flowing out of the tank. The water-storage tanks are usually situated 40 or 50 feet above average ground level, and produce a high-pressure water supply that routes to homes and businesses through pipes. For the technically minded, such water supplies usually

---

THE ANSWERS

Passengers pigeons not only traveled together, but nested together. People reported seeing six dozen nests, and sometimes more, in a single tree. *The weight of the nests and the birds* was occasionally enough to break the branches right off the tree, hurtling the nest and the eggs to the ground.

Through the mid 1800s, the woods in Michigan were overflowing with passenger pigeons, and residents here saw a seemingly endless supply of good-tasting meat. The birds traveled so closely together, that they were easy targets for anyone with a gun. A person could often kill 10 pigeons or more with a single shotgun shot. One account, for instance, brags that one shot brought down 42 birds! Certain newspapers posted the birds' locations, and commercial hunters would come by train from many miles away to kill the pigeons, often by netting the birds and then crushing their skulls. They then sold the meat, which was shipped elsewhere. As the uncontrolled hunting continued, the birds faced another threat: habitat destruction due to logging. As loggers leveled the forests in Michigan, the birds no longer had trees for nesting. The demise of the passenger pigeon in Michigan, like in many eastern states, was therefore due to *overhunting and habitat destruction*.

A few small groups of passenger pigeons persisted in the northern Lower Peninsula and in the eastern Upper Peninsula into the latter half of the 1890s. The last documented wild passenger pigeon was seen, and killed, in southern Ohio in March 22, *1900*. Other captive pigeons survived in zoos, but no attempts at mating were successful. The last member of the passenger pigeon species died in a Cincinnati Zoo on Sept. 1, *1914*. The extinction was not in vain: It served as a catalyst for the conservation effort in the United States by providing an all-too-real example of how human actions could cause irreparable damage over such a short time and even to an animal that was once the most common bird in North America.

run at 50–100 pounds per square inch of pressure, which is more than enough to meet the demands of even major appliances. What do people do if they don't live in town and are nowhere near such a water system? They buy their own individual pumps that draw water from some other source, usually from groundwater that has collected in naturally occurring underground pools (called aquifers), and into a storage tank in the home.

Mile Marker 216

Ski Park Road, which crosses here, does indeed go to a skiing area. Called the Ogemaw Hills Pathway, it has 13.6 miles of cross-country, or Nordic, ski trails that carve through Au Sable (aw SAH-bul) State Forest lands. Trails range from novice, which means flat or very gently rolling, to advanced, which includes higher hills sometimes with turns at the bottoms.

A turn at the bottom of a hill may not seem difficult to downhill, or alpine, skiers, but it can be a real challenge to a cross-country skier for a couple of reasons. For people who do so-called "diagonal" cross-country skiing, which is mainly striding with the skis facing forward, a pair of shoe-like boots connect to the skis only at the toe, so that the skier lifts the heel with every stride. The skis are very thin—usually narrower than the skiers foot—and longer than the skier is tall. In comparison, downhill skiers wear tall, stiff, shin-high boots that connect heel and toe to the skis, which are themselves both shorter and wider than cross-country skis.

This cross-country skier uses the "diagonal" skiing method to cross the snow in the Seney National Wildlife Refuge in the Upper Peninsula. (Stephen Zaglaniczny)

The design of downhill skis and boots allow the downhill skier to lean to one side and make sharp turns while moving very fast, and even provide the option of stopping quickly. Leaning on cross-country skis, on the other hand, does little to make any fast and quick changes in direction. To turn, a cross-country skier instead continues gliding forward while picking up one ski at a time and setting it down in the direction of the turn. Even a mild turn can require the skier to pick up and set down each ski several times, a difficult maneuver for a novice who is traveling at a good clip down a hill. If the skier is going too fast to negotiate the turn, he or she either purposely falls to avoid skiing off-course, or does in fact

135

zip off the trail, all the while hoping to glide to a stop without the aid of a shrub, stream, or tree along the way.

Besides diagonal cross-country skiing, another form of cross-country skiing is becoming increasingly popular. That is skate skiing. In this type of cross-country skiing, the skis typically don't come to as sharp a point in the front, and the boots are taller and stiffer. Instead of gliding straight forward, the skier slants each glide outward, using the same overall motion as a hockey player or an inline skater. Skate skiing allows very fast speeds and considerable maneuverability.

Diagonal skiers either make their own trails over an untraveled, snowy countryside, or head to a groomed trail, while skate skiers usually focus only on the groomed routes. On the groomed trails, equipment smoothes the snow, leaving a wide flat track for the skate skiers and two close-sitting grooves on the edge that are a perfect fit for a pair of gliding diagonal skis. Skate skiing is a terrific workout, but diagonal skiing is no slouch either. Diagonal and skate skiers usually find themselves sweating even while wearing minimal outerwear and skiing in temperatures in the 20s or lower.

Mile Marker 218

The golf course on the southbound side of the freeway is "The Dream," and it was literally the dream of the two brothers who built it and opened

BRAINBUSTERS

Hunting is a big industry in Michigan, so much so that the opening day of firearm deer season is considered an unofficial holiday.

Basic: Some schools in the northern Lower Peninsula and many in the Upper Peninsula do something on Nov. 15 every year to observe the opening day of firearm deer season. What do they do?

Intermediate: Each year, about 725,000 people buy at least one Michigan deer-hunting license each. What percentage of firearm- and bow-hunters actually harvest a deer: less than half, two-thirds, three-quarters, or more than 90 percent? Besides the license fees that go toward wildlife and habitat-conservation projects, how much money do the hunters contribute to the Michigan economy during a single deer season: $5 million, $50 million, $500 million, $5 billion?

Advanced: At one time, some hunters in Michigan would dump truckloads of bait, such as corn or sugar beets, onto the ground to attract deer. That is no longer allowed. Instead those hunting in seven northern Michigan counties cannot bait deer at all, and everyone else can only scatter two gallons of bait over the ground. Similar regulations hold true for people who want to feed deer in their yards. Why did the state set restrictions on baiting?

See page 138 for answers.

it for its first season in 1997. The brothers, Dan and Tom Courtemanche, already had a good introduction to the golf business through a course their father owned in Pinconning, Mich., about a 40-minute drive to the southwest. They selected the site for its rolling hills and its location near the city of West Branch. The nearly 7,000-yard, 72-par, 18-hole "The Dream" now has a sister championship course called "The Nightmare." Also 18 holes and 72 par, "The Nightmare," opened in 2003, and features more than 7,000 yards of play, including a number of challenging water hazards to test golfers' skills.

"The Dream" and "The Nightmare" are two of Michigan's more than 700 public golf courses—more than California and indeed more than any other state in the country. In public and private golf courses combined, Michigan's total grows to 850. *Golf Digest* took note of the spectacular variety of courses in Michigan when it named the state the 12th best golf destination in the world.

Mile Marker 220

Watch for signs marking the boundary between Ogemaw (OH-guh-maw) County to the south and Roscommon (rahss-COMM-un) County to the north. Ogemaw's name honors a local Ojibwe chief who played an important role in the 1819 treaty that ceded about a quarter of the land in the Lower Peninsula to the U.S. government. (For details, see mile marker 205.) In stark contrast, Roscommon County got its name from the other

side of the Atlantic Ocean. Some of the early settlers here were Irish immigrants, and they selected Roscommon as a tip of the hat to their home county in Ireland. Before it was named Roscommon, however, this area went by Mikenauk, which was the name of a local Ottawa Indian chief who participated in another treaty, this one in 1836, that yielded land in both the Lower and Upper Peninsulas to the U.S. government. The Indians kept hunting, fishing and gathering rights on those lands until they were "required for settlement." Legal challenges about the scope of those rights have continued since 1973, but a preliminary agreement in September 2007 (still awaiting final approval at the time of publication) set various restrictions. Some of these restrictions prohibited the tribes from:

+ using privately owned lands unless they had the property owner's permission or unless the lands were open to the general public;
+ using certain fishing methods (gill netting and fish snagging) on inland lakes and streams; and
+ engaging in commercial harvesting of game species beyond what is already allowed by the state.

Roscommon County is a very popular vacation destination, primarily because of the three major lakes within its borders: Houghton Lake, Higgins Lake and Lake St. Helen, all of which are described elsewhere in this book. One area that receives less attention, but is nonetheless remarkable is the

25,000-acre Dead Stream Swamp. The swamp is one the largest examples of a northern-white-cedar swamp in the United States. Gardeners may be more familiar with the tree through the smaller cultivated shrubs called arborvitae. In the wild, though, white cedars are evergreen trees that reach 40–50 feet tall. Instead of needle-covered branches like many other pine trees, cedars have green, scaly leaves on their branches. The wood is soft and light, but is extremely resistant to insects. This makes it an especially good choice for outdoor uses, like fences, posts, log cabins, and canoes.

Visitors to Dead Stream Swamp, however, mainly come for the thou-sands of acres of water backed up above the Reedsburg Dam. In and around this mainly wilderness flooding, people in canoes, kayaks or other non-motorized boats can spend hours watching the abundant wildlife. The spring is an especially good time to view the waterfowl because the males are decked out in their mating colors. Male buffleheads and goldeneyes have their strikingly gorgeous patterns of black-and-white plumage, but perhaps the most beautiful is the colorful wood duck. A male wood duck has butter-colored sides; a deep reddish-brown breast; a black back with a glimmering, metallic sheen; an iridescent green and purple head with

THE ANSWERS

So many people, including students, participate in hunting on the Nov. 15 opener that many schools in northern Michigan and the Upper Peninsula *close for the day*. Some businesses also shut their doors on opening day so their employees can get out into the woods.

Less than half of Michigan hunters typically harvest a deer in a given year. In 2006, for instance, the number was 46 percent. In all, the hunters collectively spend more than 10 million days in the field in their pursuits of the deer, which can become amazingly elusive once opening day begins. During the three months of deer-hunting season (bow and firearm) in Michigan, hunters contribute a substantial amount to the state's economy. For food, lodging, transportation, and equipment, the outlay for a single season is about *$500 million*.

The state instituted the restrictions on baiting to help *control and eliminate any outbreaks of bovine tuberculosis*, or bovine TB. This disease, which is caused by bacteria, leads to breathing difficulties among various other health problems. Bovine TB is very rare in deer, but it has shown up in a few individuals mainly in the northeastern Lower Peninsula. Biologists have also discovered it in some elk, black bear and a few other mammals. It spreads from one animal to another through close contact, like that occurring when animals are nose to nose feeding from a bait pile.

A flock of common Michigan ducks called buffleheads. (USDA Forest Service/Dave Herr)

a long crest, red bill and red eyes; and various touches of white and yellow highlighting the head, neck, sides and reddish-purple-bottomed tail. People are frequently surprised to see these ducks peeking out of holes in tree trunks. Wood ducks nest there, sometimes dozens of feet above the water. After the eggs hatch and the ducklings are ready to leave the nest, they

BRAINBUSTERS

Dead Stream Swamp , and indeed many marshy locations and small lakes, are good places to see some of Michigan's 10 different turtle species. Two are especially common. One is the painted turtle and the other is the snapping turtle.

Basic: The painted turtle and snapping turtle look quite different. For one thing, the painted turtle has a lower shell, called the plastron, that covers up the whole belly of the animal. The snapping turtle's plastron is much smaller and only covers the center of the belly. Since the snapping turtle cannot rely on the plastron to protect its nether regions from a predator, how does it defend itself?

Intermediate: People often see painted turtles basking on logs just above the water's surface. One of the reasons they do it is because they are cold-blooded animals, and they use the Sun's warmth to help warm them up. Scientists don't use the term "cold-blooded." What's wrong with it?

Advanced: If a snapping turtle or a painted turtle nest is kept on the warm side, something happens to the young turtles that eventually hatch out of the eggs. What?

See page 141 for answers.

From left to right: Wood ducks, osprey, and common goldeneye. (USFWS/Dr. Thomas G. Barnes)

toddle to the edge of the hole and, although they are still unable to fly, their mother calls to them and they take a big leap of faith, falling through the air to the ground or water below. Surprisingly, the little ducklings can usually survive even if they have to drop 200 feet or more!

Besides waterfowl, the swamp is home to other animals, including mink and river otters. (For more on mink and river otter, see mile marker 327.) One of the often-seen large birds of prey in the swamp are ospreys. Ospreys have a white head, as do the bald eagles that also live in Dead Stream Swamp, but the white of an osprey's head is broken by a wide, dark brown stripe that extends from its beak to the rear of its head, and then continues down toward the back. In addition, its tail is also dark brown rather than the gleaming white of a bald eagle, and an osprey is a smaller bird with a wingspan of 5–6 feet compared to a bald eagle's 7–8 feet. Wildlife officers have placed platforms out on the water of the Dead Stream flooding for the ospreys. The birds build their nests on the platforms. Wildlife officers encourage people to keep their distance from these and other nesting birds, and view them through binoculars. Even at a distance, though, ospreys are fun to watch. When they are hunting, they will hover above the water surface with their feet dangling and eyes intently staring at their prey. Then with a flourish, they will lunge downward, diving feet-first into and often completely under the water surface, before reappearing. With the feet-first position, they

140

clamp onto their prey and then haul it up and out of the water, where they fly off with a fish firmly gripped in their talons.

For people who don't have a boat, a good spot to see the various birds at Dead Stream Swamp is at Michelson's Landing, which is about a mile and a half north of the dam. In the early 1900s, the area was a very busy community set up around the N.

Michelson Lumber Co. The town, long abandoned, has disappeared into the surrounding forests, but for many years, one-time residents held reunions there to reminisce about the old mill town.

About 3 miles north of I-75 is the community of St. Helen, which

---

THE ANSWERS

While the painted turtle will pull its head and legs into the shell to protect its body parts from an attacker, a snapping turtle is vulnerable on its underside. To defend itself, the snapping turtle has *powerful, sheering jaws* that can snap shut with enough force to cause serious damage to a predator. As anyone who has approached a snapping turtle can attest, they are not shy about snapping at people either!

The body temperature of reptiles is indeed cold sometimes, but not always. In other words, *they are only cold-blooded some of the time.* This is because their internal body temperature goes up and down based on the outside temperature. While they may be cold on a chilly morning, their body temperature may rise to become quite warm on a summer afternoon. For this reason, scientists use the term ectothermic. *Ecto-* means outside, and *-thermic* means temperature, so ectothermic means temperature based on an outside source.

Both snapping and painted turtles, along with many other (but not all) Michigan turtles, exhibit something called temperature-dependent sex determination, which means that the sex of the hatchlings is determined by the temperature of the nest. In painted turtles, for example, a nest that is kept at around 72–80°F produces mostly male hatchlings, while a nest that is kept at around 86 degrees produces mostly females. Scientists have learned that the key time frame for temperature to have an impact is during the middle third of the incubation period. Unfortunately, many turtle eggs never hatch. This has nothing to do with temperature, but is due to predation. In Michigan and many other parts of the United States, raccoons and other predators dig up the vast majority of turtle nests and eat the eggs long before they develop.

Bluegill (NOAA, Great Lakes Environmental Research Library)

Exit 222

sits on the shore of Lake St. Helen. Although it is the smallest of the three major lakes in this county, it is still quite large at 2,400 acres. The lake is well-known for its bluegill fishing. Bluegill are tall, somewhat flat fish with a small mouth, dark vertical banding on the sides of the body, and a powdery blue color on the edge of the gillcover (behind the "cheek"). Males and females look the same all year long, except during the breeding season when the males take on a slightly brighter coloration. Anglers are typically hoping to catch bluegill in the 6- to 8-inch range, but these fish can grow considerably larger. The state record is 13.75 inches. A lucky angler who has found just the right spot on Lake St. Helen can sometimes catch bluegill almost nonstop, barely dropping in a freshly baited line before another fish grabs hold. Bluegill fishing is so popular in Lake St. Helen that the community holds a Bluegill Festival every summer. Its 50th Bluegill Festival was in 1999, and it is still going strong.

While diners love the fish for their mild-flavored, flaky meat, scientists have become interested in the bluegill for their bizarre mating behavior. During breeding season, a male will swim into shallow water and swish his tail to make a small depression in the often-sandy bottom. This is the nest. A female swims into the nest and ejects a stream of eggs while the male squirts a liquid called milt over the eggs to fertilize them. The female leaves, but the male stays there to watch over the eggs until they hatch. The male may fertilize the eggs from many females, and sometimes more than one female enters his nest at the same time. As a result, he may have 60,000 eggs to watch over. Strangely, however, not all males mate this way.

Some male bluegill, called sneaker males, don't build nests themselves, but rather hang around in the vegetation near another male's nest. When one or more females enter the nest and start to lay their eggs, and the sneaker males pop out of their hiding places, and make a mad dash through the nest, spraying milt as they go. The sneaker males aren't the only ones the nesting males have to worry about. Other males, called satellite males, never take on the slightly brighter coloration of the other breeding males, which leaves them looking enough like the females to tag along with them as they enter a nest. When the females start laying their eggs, the satellite males spray their milt over them and then make a quick exit before the nesting male gets wise.

The nesting males aren't completely out of luck. Scientists studying the fish found that the nesting

142

dads are able to do a smell test to determine if they did indeed father the bulk of the developing eggs. If he finds that a high percentage of the young are the offspring of sneaker or satellite males, he will still defend his nest but nowhere near as ferociously as he normally would. After all, they're not his kids!

The next time you are at an inland lake in the spring or early summer, scan the shoreline for nesting bluegills. You will often see one depression after another, each with a diligent nesting male inside. If another male approaches too closely, the nesting male may charge the intruder and chase him for several feet before rushing back to his nest.

— — —

One of St. Helen's most famous former residents is film star Charlton Heston. He was born in Evanston, Ill., in 1924, but he spent his boyhood years here in St. Helen, which at the time had only around a hundred residents. His family returned to Illinois by the time Heston entered high school. From there, he did some performing on Chicago radio, then moved to New York where he took odd jobs as a model while starting up his acting career. He was in his mid-20s when he got a role in his first Hollywood movie, and shortly thereafter he started working with the famous director Cecil B. DeMille: first making "The Greatest Show on Earth" in 1953, and then "The Ten Commandments" in 1956. In 1959, Heston won the Oscar for best actor in "Ben Hur."

After the lumbering era ended in Michigan, efforts began to reforest the state, often by planting acres of red pine. One of the earlier reforestation plantations was located here, near the spot where US-127 and I-75 meet. (US-127 merges into northbound I-75 on the left, and exits from southbound I-75 on the right.) The trees have already grown large enough to harvest, and some may have become utility poles in your neighborhood. Other uses for red pine include lumber for general construction and pulpwood for paper production.

The red pine does very well in the sandy soils of northern Michigan and it grows fast, two qualities that have made it the most commonly planted tree species in Michigan. Plantations are easy to distinguish from naturally

MM 225

BRAINBUSTERS

Houghton Lake is the site of a well-known winter festival called Tip-Up Town every January.

Basic: A number of snowmobilers come to the festival to ride the lake or the nearby trails, but many people come up to use their tip-ups in another activity. What activity?

Intermediate: What is the difference between a regular fishing rod and a typical ice-fishing rod? What is a tip-up?

Advanced: What is a Swedish Pimple®?

See next page for answers.

occurring forests because the trees are in parallel rows. When they are first planted, the trees are generally set very close together, which helps decrease the size of the knots, which are remnants of the connection points of branches. This reduction in knot size happens because close-growing trees quickly create shade, and the shade causes the lower branches to die and fall off when they are still small, leaving only a tiny knot. Foresters call red pines "self-pruning" trees because of this feature. As the trees grow taller, foresters remove some of them to encourage the trunks of the remaining trees to maintain their girth even as they get taller, rather than tapering too quickly. A bigger-diameter trunk means more usable wood. This type of forestry management leaves behind the side-by-side rows that are so common in Michigan's pine landscape.

About 8 miles to the west is Houghton (HO-tun) Lake, which at more than 31 square miles is not only the largest lake in Roscommon County, but the largest inland lake in the entire state. Like many thousands of inland lakes, Houghton was formed by the scooping action of a long-ago glacier. (For more on glaciers, see mile marker 209, among others.)

Houghton Lake was long known to American Indians of the region, but it was only in 1849 that state legislator-turned-U.S. surveyor

THE ANSWERS

Historically, Tip-Up Town has primarily been an *ice-fishing* festival. Anglers dig holes through the ice, which can be up to 18 inches thick at that time of year, and fish in one of two ways. In one, an angler uses a tip-up, which is basically *a reel mounted on a platform that straddles a hole in the ice.* The angler baits a hook with a minnow, drops in the line, and sets a flag-tipped rod across the top. When a fish takes the minnow, the rod trips. Anglers, who are usually sitting at another hole fishing with a rod, will race over to the tip-up, grasp the line and give it a firm jerk to set the hook, and then hopefully pull in the fish. Another ice-fishing method is with a more traditional rod, but *ice-fishing rods are only about a third of the size (or smaller) of a normal fishing rod.* The reels are typically simple spooling devices that are more for storing line than for reeling in fish. Since Houghton Lake is quite shallow — averaging about 7.5 feet — anglers simply lift the line out of the water rather than reeling. One of the lures of choice for ice fishing on the lake is a Swedish Pimple®. Pimples are *long, flat, oval-shaped lures*, the style of which has been popular in Sweden for more than a century. Since the Upper Peninsula still has a large population of people of Swedish ancestry, it is no surprise that the pimple is a product of the Bay de Noc Lure Co., located in the south-central U.P. community of Gladstone.

William Burt gave a description of its huge size. He named it Muskegon (muss-KEE-gun) Lake after the Muskegon River that has its start at the lake's north end. Muskegon (listen carefully!) is actually the English interpretation of the French version of an Ottawa Indian word that means "plenty of fish." The French had a strong influence along the Muskegon River because the French traveled the 190-mile river to prime fur-trapping areas back in the pre-logging days. The river runs from Houghton Lake west to Lake Michigan.

Within three years of Burt naming the lake after the Muskegon river, however, it became known as Houghton in honor of the recently deceased Douglass Houghton. Houghton was a state geologist primarily known for his work in the Keweenaw Peninsula in the northwestern Upper Peninsula. Before becoming a geologist, Houghton was a medical doctor with a practice in Detroit. At the request of the city governing officers, he also became a science lecturer and soon caught the attention of noted geographer Henry Schoolcraft. (For more on Schoolcraft, see mile markers 185–186.) Schoolcraft signed him on as joint physician and naturalist on his travels to the Upper Peninsula and beyond. Houghton spent about two years studying the countryside, especially its plants and mineral deposits, and then returned to his practice in Detroit. He remained there for five years, but when Michigan attained statehood in 1837, he set aside his role as doctor and became Michigan's first state geologist.

It was in that position that Houghton would bring about a change in attitude about the Upper Peninsula. At that time in the state's history, many of its residents were extremely disappointed that the U.S. government forced Michigan to give up a strip of land near Toledo in order to obtain statehood in 1837. Even though the U.S. government tried to sweeten the deal by giving Michigan the Upper Peninsula, many still thought the state got the short end of the stick. The disappointment was short-lived, because in 1841, Houghton published an account of the rich copper deposits in the Upper Peninsula and set off a copper rush and mining on a scale that had never

Exit 227

BRAINBUSTERS

Michigan's first state geologist, Douglass Houghton, announced in 1841 that he had seen abundant copper in the Upper Peninsula. This announcement along with another event at about the same time helped spur the copper mining boom in the Upper Peninsula. The other event was hullabaloo surrounding the Ontonagon (on-tuh-NAH-gen) Boulder.

Basic: The boulder was a massive chunk of nearly pure copper. How much did it weigh: 37 pounds, 370 pounds, 3,700 pounds?

Intermediate: The boulder remained in the U.P. until 1843 when it was transported to Detroit. Why?

Advanced: Does the boulder still exist, and if so, where is it?

See next page for answers.

before been seen in the United States. Houghton continued to make other discoveries, including the large salt beds in the center of the Lower Peninsula that would later play a role in the evolution of the Dow Chemical Co. (For more on Dow, see the Brain-buster near exit 162.)

Houghton Lake remained a secluded lake for many decades after Burt first described it in 1849. Much of the reason was accessibility. The lake was surrounded by marshlands, and the best over-land route to the lake even in into the early 20th century was an old and rutted Indian trail that was barely wide enough for a single car. Then, as now, the lake was a draw to anglers, who marveled at the huge northern pike that fought so hard and had such sharp teeth that they could easily cut through anything but wire fishing line. In 1921, the area was growing

Exit 227

enough for the local community, called Prudenville, to open its post office. Word of the lake's great fishing spread quickly and soon rustic rental cabins began springing up. Houghton Lake now has a busy business district on its south shore, but even current residents remember the days a few decades ago when certain areas along the lakeshore still were accessible by little more than two-track roads.

— — —

The marsh that once encompassed Houghton Lake is still present on the northwestern side of the lake. Called the Houghton Lake Flats, it is a 710-acre marsh that is teeming with wildlife-viewing opportunities. Osprey and bald eagles are some of the commonly seen birds of prey, and many species of waterfowl paddle among the marsh vegetation. One of the highlights is a great blue heron rookery,

THE ANSWERS

Although it's hard to believe, the Ontonagon Boulder weighs *3,700 pounds!* The American Indians were the first to see the metal of the boulder, and they told legend-filled stories about it to fur traders and missionaries in the 1600s. They even showed it to a French missionary in 1667. Although stories of the boulder had circulated far and wide, the boulder remained where it was on the bank of the Ontonagon River in the western Upper Peninsula for nearly two centuries longer. Finally in 1843, workers excavated the boulder.

A promoter named Julius Eldred bought it for $150 and transported it to Detroit where *he put it on exhibition and charged people to see it.* The U.S. government quickly determined that it was actually U.S. property, and seized the boulder. It is now *on display at the National Museum of Natural History in Washington, D.C.* The publicity surrounding the boulder exhibition in Detroit helped spur the copper mining boom in the U.P., which made Michigan the largest producer of copper during the period of 1847 to 1887.

This ice fisherman uses a typical small pole to fish for walleye and perch on Houghton Lake. An unused tip-up is seen resting against the wheel of the all-terrain vehicle. (Leslie Mertz)

which is a grouping of heron nests. In the spring, the huge, crook-necked birds nest in a stand of trees in the middle of the marsh. The birds, which reach 4 feet long and have a 5.5- to 6.5-foot wingspan, build their massive nests on the tree branches, often take up a position perching alongside. During breeding season, even passersby without binoculars can easily see dozens of herons in the rookery.

Mile Marker 232

Between the white-barked birches here on the sides of the freeway are other gray-barked trees with leaves that flicker in the slightest breeze. These gray-barked trees are commonly and collectively known as "popples." Michigan has seven species of these trees, and they are all part of the poplar (*Populas*) genus. They include:

+ swamp cottonwood, found only in a couple of small locations in southern Michigan
+ eastern cottonwood, which is more common in the southern half of the Lower Peninsula
+ Lombardy poplar, a long-ago import from Europe that has been a popular ornamental tree in Michigan for more than a century
+ European white poplar, another import that was popular among settlers and is still used occasionally as an ornamental tree
+ bigtooth aspen, found throughout the state, but more common in the southern half of the Lower Peninsula
+ quaking aspen (also known as trembling aspen), seen throughout the state, but does especially well in areas with wet, fertile soil
+ balsam poplar, a tree that is more common in the northern half of the

147

Lower Peninsula and the U.P. than it is in the southern half of the L.P.

In this area of Michigan, quaking aspens, bigtooth aspens and balsam poplars are frequent forest residents. Like all popples, they have leaves that quiver in the wind. The reason they respond this way—even shimmying in minor breezes—is the shape and orientation of the leaf stem, which is also called a petiole (PET-ee-ole). The petioles of most trees are round, but in all of Michigan popples except the balsam poplar, they are flat. In addition, each petiole is attached to its leaf in such a way that the flatness of the leaf is 90 degrees off of the flatness of the petiole. When the wind blows, it catches the leaf, which flips to one side, but then catches the petiole, which flips it back. This back and forth play gives the tree leaves their flickering appearance. The near-constant movement of the leaves makes a beautiful shimmering whisper, allowing a person to identify it as a popple even with the eyes closed!

Another interesting feature of the bigtooth aspen, quaking aspen and balsam poplar is that entire patches of them may be made of clones from just one tree. In these species, many of the new sprouts come not from seeds, but as suckers that grow up from the roots of one "parent tree." Even if a forest fire lays waste to a small forest and kills the parent, the roots not only survive but also send up new suckers. The suckers are exceptionally fast-growing, sometimes soaring to 6 feet tall in a single season. The suckers are called clones, because they have the identical genetic makeup of the original parent tree. The roots and clones can extend an impressive distance from the parent tree, and forests of clones from a single tree can easily cover an acre—that's 209 feet long and 209 feet wide.

BRAINBUSTERS

Travelers sometimes see turkey vultures pecking at roadkill on the sides of I-75. These are large birds. They stand a couple of feet tall, but are most impressive when they spread their wings. Their wingspan reaches 5.5–6 feet.

Basic: Unlike most birds that are feathered everywhere except their feet, the turkey vulture has a red and mainly bare-skinned head. What would be the advantage of a featherless face for a vulture?

Intermediate: Vultures and a few other types of birds, like storks, purposely defecate on their own legs. Why in the world would they do that?

Advanced: People often see these big black birds soaring high overhead, but hardly ever flapping their wings. They even appear to soar in a lazy spiral while actually gaining altitude. How does such a big bird stay aloft without doing much flapping?

See page 150 for answers.

Mile Marker 235

A fact of life, or death, on the freeway is roadkill. A deer may get spooked and run across the express-

Turkey vulture (Jacob Dingel/PGC Photo)

Skunks and raccoon. (Jacob Dingel/PGC Photo)

way, a raccoon or opossum may amble onto the road at night, or a bird may take a low swoop and come into the path of an approaching vehicle. A motorist's gut reaction may be to try to veer out of the way, but traffic experts recommend against it because swerving off of the road is more dangerous to the life and limb of the driver and passengers than hitting the animal.

One of the roadkill animals you might see here but would not see in the southern Lower Peninsula is the porcupine. It looks unlike any other Michigan mammal. Skunks and raccoons, which are also common lying on the side of the freeway, have their own distinctive appearance: the skunk is black with a double white stripe on its back (and often an attention-getting smell), and the raccoon has an obvious series of rings down the length of its tail. A porcupine's most noticeable features are its long fur and spiny quills, and its hefty body. Despite popular opinion fed by countless inaccurate cartoons, porcupines cannot throw their quills. If it is threatened, this normally very reclusive animal will round its back, which makes the quills stand up. If a preda-

tor, such as a coyote, attacks a porcupine, the needle-sharp quills not only puncture the skin, but then detach from the porcupine. Each quill has a barbed tip, which makes it nearly impossible to pull out. To make matters worse, even tiny movements of the predator's muscles draw the quill ever farther and more painfully into the body. If the quill penetrates a vital organ or an artery, as it often does, it can end in death.

With such dangerous quills on their bodies, people often wonder how they mate. Just as the old joke says, they do it very carefully. The female lays down her quills so they don't accidentally impale her mate. More interesting, however, is how they court one

149

another. In one of the weirdest enticements in the animal world, a male porcupine will sometimes approach a female, rise up on his hind limbs with its belly forward, and spray her with urine. Scientists still have no idea what this is supposed to accomplish. This is not the only courtship behavior. The pair rear up on their hind legs and embrace one another, their un-quilled bellies touching, and proceed to make a variety of grunting and whining noises. Occasionally they add a nose rub or a playful head punch to the mix before getting to the business of actually mating.

— — — —

Any roadkill found on the side of I-75 is usually a fairly recently deceased animal. This is because dead animals are routinely removed by employees of the Michigan Department of Transportation, the agency that oversees this and other state roads, and other highway workers. Even if the workers did not remove the roadkill, however, it would still disappear eventually. Carcass-eating birds and mammals would feast on the meat, and any leftover bones or skin slowly succumb to other natural decomposers.

— — —

One of the animals that frequently dines on the dead on I-75 is the American crow. Occasionally, another all-black bird makes an appearance here in the northern Lower Peninsula.

THE ANSWERS

Vultures eat carrion, which can be loaded with bacteria. For another bird with a feathery face, this might present a problem because its feathers would not only become covered with blood and assorted other messes, but would also become a haven for the bacteria. *On a vulture's bare face, however, the bacteria don't stick.* Their rather bizarre behavior of defecating on their own legs has a reason, too. They do it to help them *stay cool.*
The waste, which is actually a mixture of feces and urine, dribbles onto the legs where it evaporates, providing cooling in the same way that a spritz of water might cool a sunbather at the beach.

While its eating and defecating habits may not be that palatable, the vulture's soaring ability is a beauty to behold. This big bird *is capable of sensing where heat is rising from the ground and using these rotating thermal currents to soar up into the sky without having to flap its wings.* It enters a rising current of warm air often fairly close to the ground, and glides up with the upward coil of air, often reaching hundreds of feet in altitude before the air starts to cool. At that point, the vulture soars down to catch an adjacent thermal current, and rides that one up into the sky. A vulture can repeat this again and again, and in so doing, it can stay aloft without beating a wing.

This is the common raven (also known as the northern raven). The two are very similar in appearance, but the raven is much larger. While the crow ranges from 17-21 inches long and has a 3-foot wingspan, the raven can grow to 27 inches long and have a 4.5-foot wingspan. Besides their size, ravens also have a bit of a scruffier appearance than crows, almost looking like they have a short shaggy beard sprouting from the throat. The "beard" is especially noticeable when they are calling.

Here are a few interesting facts about crows and ravens:

+ American crows are family-oriented birds. While the young of many bird species strike out on their own almost as soon as they can fly, most crows stay with both of their parents for up to four years, and sometimes more. They aren't a drain on their parents: They actually help with the raising of their parents' subsequent broods. Sometimes, the families can number 15 crows. When they finally leave their parents and siblings, the young crows start their own families.
+ If you watch a raven for any length of time, you might be treated to a display of its acrobatic flying abilities. This bird can do a roll in mid-air, execute a flying somersault, and even fly upside down for a quarter to a half mile or more.
+ Both ravens and crows don't limit their diets to roadkill. In fact, it's a small part of their diets. A typical diet of a crow or a raven may include small rodents, insects, fruit, seeds, and eggs stolen from other birds' nests.

Exit 239

A couple of miles from this exit, just south of the town of Roscommon, is a touching tribute to firefighters. There, set on the side of a hill, is a 12-foot-tall, bronze statue of a firefighter holding up a lantern in one outstretched hand while carrying a small child close to his chest in the other. This is the Michigan State Firemen's Memorial, dedicated in 1980 to honor the firefighters who risk their own safety to save the lives and the property of people they usually don't even know. Every year

BRAINBUSTERS

Lumberjacks worked hard and played hard, and the latter includes drinking hard. Like many lumbering towns in the last half of the 18th century, Roscommon had more than its fair share of saloons. In fact, at one point the town boasted one hotel . . . and 14 saloons!

Basic: The job of a lumberjack in Michigan didn't just involve cutting down trees. They also served as swampers. What did a swamper do?

Intermediate: In a saloon, lumberjacks would sometimes call a man a "Dick Smith" and make him buy a drink for the house. What is a Dick Smith?

Advanced: What was a saloon's snakeroom?

See next page for answers.

at the site, a Michigan Firemen's Memorial Festival draws firefighters from all over the state for a full schedule of activities. One of the favorites is the waterball competition where two opposing teams of firefighters try to slide a hanging ball along a cable by blasting it with the high-pressure water from a fire hose. For many, however, the most memorable event at the festival is the memorial service and placing of wreaths at the statue site to call to mind the fallen firefighters.

Exit 239

The community of Roscommon is also the home of the Great Au Sable Duck Race, which is held every summer. For this event, people buy tickets and exchange them for rubber duckies on the day of the race. They then toss the numbered rubber duckies into the Au Sable River from a bridge and follow them as they bob along to a nearby park. The race organizers conduct a number of heats, and finally announce the prize winners. Proceeds from the race go to various community projects.

Another big event in the area is the Kirtland's Warbler Festival, which is held on the campus of Kirtland Community College a few miles outside of Roscommon. The main attraction of this festival is the small, bluish-gray

THE ANSWERS

Felling trees was a big part of a lumberjack's job, but so was swamping. Swampers *cleared the trails to and from the logging site.* A less glamorous job to be sure, but removing brush on the trails was critical to transporting the logs out of the woods.

Lumberjacks in Michigan had their own unwritten creed, a strange mix of all-for-one-and-one-for-all combined with tooth-and-nail fighting at the drop of a hat. One of the rules was that a lumberjack with money had to buy drinks for his campmates. *If he bought a drink only for himself,* his so-called friends would pronounce him a "Dick Smith," and with brute force, would insist he keep up the tradition. Smart lumberjacks who had money would sometimes cash in their bills for nickels before they got to the saloon, so they could pay with the coins instead of flashing around something as big as a $5 bill. That way, they could purchase a few drinks and avoid having to buy a drink for the entire house.

Some of the lumberjacks could hold their liquor better than others, and with the amount of drinking that occurred at the saloons, some of the men would simply pass out. Rather than toss them into the street, however, saloon owners typically had a snakeroom in the bar, which was *a place where the intoxicated loggers could sleep it off.* Snakerooms were nothing fancy, but in the frigid winter months, they were far better than a night spent in a snow drift.

and yellow bird, which nests almost solely in northern Michigan and nowhere else on Earth. For a while, the warblers were becoming more and more rare, and birders feared that they would disappear altogether. The bird's low numbers could be traced to two main factors: 1) the unusual habitat it prefers, and 2) another, bigger bird that "cons" adult warblers into raising its young often at the expense of their own.

Let's start with the unusual habitat. The Kirtland's warbler makes small nests on the ground under the low-hanging branches of a certain young trees. These trees, called jack pines, reseed themselves best after a fire. The fire causes their pine cones, which are normally closed up tight, to open up and release the seeds inside. As people became better at preventing and fighting forest fires, however, fewer and fewer of the trees reseeded and this reduced the number of small jack pines, and at the same time, the favored nesting habitat of the warblers. Now, however, prescribed burns of jack pine forests are again providing good reseeding conditions, and the warbler' numbers are responding.

The other threat to the warblers isn't as easy to fix. It comes from another bird, called the cowbird. This bird, considerably larger than the warbler, is what is known as a brood parasite because it lays its eggs in the nests of other birds, like the Kirtland's warbler, and leaves them there for the smaller birds to raise. Unfortunately, these smaller birds do not recognize the eggs as imposters

Kirtland's warbler (USDA Forest Service/TES Photography, Ron Austing)

and care for them as they would their own. Once the cowbird egg hatches, the hatchling is larger than the warbler babies and can easily push them aside—sometimes right out of the nest—as it vies for food from the mother warbler. The cowbird doesn't only target Kirtland's warblers, but many other songbirds, and has caused declines in the numbers of these other species, too.

Despite the bad news about the cowbirds, Kirtland's warbler is doing quite well. In 2007, for instance, wildlife biologists and birders alike were thrilled when the U.S. Fish and Wildlife Service announced evidence of a few of the endangered warblers nesting in Wisconsin.

Exit 239

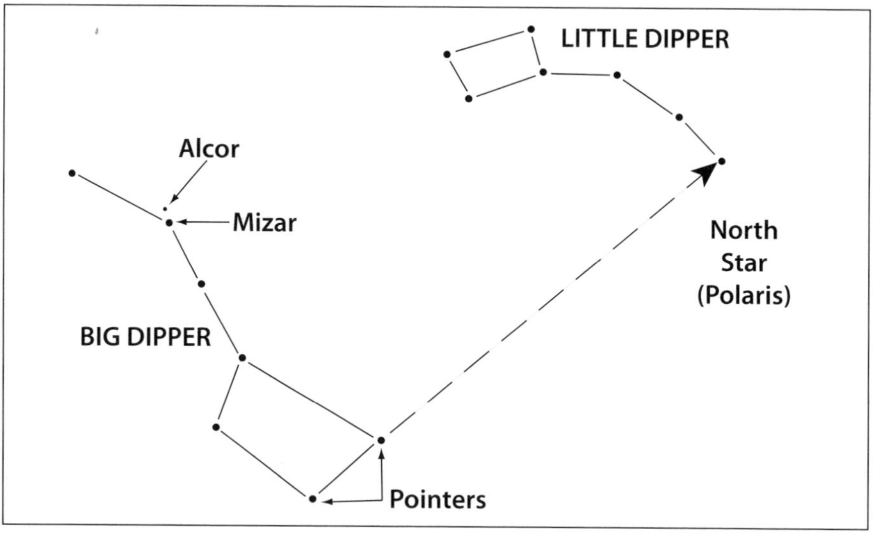

LITTLE DIPPER

Alcor

Mizar

North
Star
(Polaris)

BIG DIPPER

Pointers

Stargazers can find the North Star, the only star that remains in the same place all night long and year-round, by following an imaginary line from the two pointer stars of the Big Dipper.

For those people who want their own view of the little birds, they can find numerous warbler-sighting tours in the area, including several during Kirtland's Warbler Festival.

Mile Marker 241

Stargazing is a common night-time activity in northern Michigan. Although car headlights can be a bit distracting and take away from night vision, car passengers can usually make out several bright constellations. A favorite is the Little Dipper because it contains the North Star, the only visible star in the night sky that stays in the same place at any hour and on any night. From our vantage point here in the Northern Hemisphere, all of the other stars in the sky move during the course of the night. In fact, even the Little Dipper itself rotates around the North Star.

Because the North Star is stationary, however, it is an excellent directional cue. Since it is always located toward the north, anyone who can find it can determine the direction of north, south, east and west even at night.

To find the Little Dipper and the North Star, which is also known as Polaris, first locate the Big Dipper (see the illustration). Pick out the two stars that make up the far side of the "ladel." These are called the pointer stars. Next, draw an imaginary line from the bottom pointer star to the top one and continue upward to the next fairly bright star. It's about five times the distance between the two pointer stars. This fairly bright star is the North Star.

The Big Dipper is even mentioned in a coded folk song used by the slaves to find their way north after escaping from captivity in southern states. The song, "Follow the Drinking Gourd," told them to use the Big Dipper, or the Drinking Gourd, as a guide to set a course to freedom.

Besides finding the way north, the Big Dipper can help you check your eyesight in the same way that people checked theirs in ancient times. The second star in the handle of the Big Dipper is called Mizar, and it has another faint star, called Alcor, just above and to one side of it. The two are also known as the "horse and rider." Almost anyone can see Mizar, but only those with good vision can make out Alcor.

Humans are not the only animals on Earth that can tell direction from the stars. In the fall, hundreds of thousands of birds migrate south for the winter, and often do some of their flying at night. Scientists wondered whether they used the stars to navigate, so they came up with an idea. They knew that birds that were preparing to migrate will point their bodies toward the direction they intend to travel, so the scientists gathered some soon-to-migrate birds and brought them to a planetarium where they could move the stars on the ceiling into new positions. Lo and behold, the birds oriented their bodies to the new position of the stars, and provided good evidence that they use the twinkling lights in the darkness to navigate at night.

Exit 244

North Higgins Lake State Park and the Civilian Conservation Corps Museum are about 5 miles to the west. The state park sits on the northwest shore of Higgins Lake, the second largest lake in Roscommon County. Although it is very close to Houghton Lake just to the south, the two lakes are quite different. Houghton Lake is a shallow lake with an average depth of 7.5 feet, and only a few holes more than 20 feet. It has good weed cover for fish like northern pike and bass. In comparison, Higgins Lake has an average depth of 44 feet, nearly six times that of Houghton, and has deep areas of up to 135 feet. Unlike Houghton, Higgins Lake is spring-fed, which makes its water cold even in the middle of summer. Its chilly, crystal clear water is well-suited a wide range of fishes, including some that Houghton Lake doesn't have, such as smelt, whitefish, lake trout, brown trout and rainbow

MM 244

BRAINBUSTERS

People driving through areas with dark skies often see shooting stars, or meteors.

Basic: A shooting star is not a star at all. What is it?

Intermediate: What causes a meteor shower?

Advanced: Occasionally, northern lights appear even this far south. These are glowing streaks and shapes sometimes in white and sometimes in shades of pinks, reds, blues and greens—that slowly bounce through the sky. They are most common in this part of the country when something happens on the Sun. What is it?

See next page for answers.

155

trout. The trout are not native to Higgins Lake, but were put there by the Michigan Department of Natural Resources. The DNR also stocks trout in many other Michigan inland lakes that have the right conditions for them to survive.

Higgins Lake is named for Sylvester Higgins, a topographer who became chief of the topographical department of the Michigan Geological Survey in the late 1830s. He did considerable surveying work in Michigan, and one of his major jobs was to draw the initial section lines in the Upper Peninsula. After he had already left his post with the Geological Survey, his good reputation suffered a serious blow. According to *Michigan History* magazine, other surveyors in 1849 discovered glaring mistakes in his work, leading to the conclusion that Higgins had shirked on his responsibilities in the central Upper Peninsula and basically made up his surveys without doing the necessary field work. Other surveyors had to go back and do the job right. Despite the fall from grace, a survey that was done in 1852 by U.S.

Exit 244

THE ANSWERS

A shooting star *is the path of light created when a piece of dust or tiny fragment of rock falls toward the Earth and burns in the atmosphere.* Most of the time, the dust and fragments burn up long before they reach the ground. Although shooting stars can appear at any time, they are especially common during meteor showers. A meteor shower occurs *when the Earth passes through the orbit of a comet, which is basically a big icy ball that circles the Sun in a strongly elliptical orbit.* As the comet travels, it leaves debris in its path. This debris includes an abundance of little rock fragments. When the Earth passes through the comet's orbital path, many fragments enter the atmosphere and burn up, causing a meteor shower. In some cases, observers can see more than a meteor a minute during one of the annual meteor showers.

Northern lights don't appear on a schedule like the meteor showers do. Rather, they are based on solar activity. The Sun is continually emitting positively charged particles, or ions, that flow out from its surface. The flow is called the solar wind. When the wind nears the Earth, the Earth's magnetic field draws the ions toward the north and south poles. As the ions enter the atmosphere, a reaction between the ions and other particles occurs, and the result is light. Because of the increased magnetic pull at the poles, northern lights and southern lights are more common there. To reach this far south, the solar wind has to be particularly strong. Scientists are able to monitor the Sun for *increased periods of activity, including sun spots (magnetic explosions on the Sun),* and can predict when northern lights are more likely to occur here.

surveyor William Burt listed Higgins' name on the lake here, and it has remained Higgins Lake ever since.

— — —

This state park also is home to the Michigan Civilian Conservation Corps (CCC) Museum, an excellent source of information about a long-ago program that put 103,000 young men, most of them from Michigan, to work on an assortment of construction, conservation and reforestation projects around the state. According to the Michigan Historical Center, the CCC "planted 484 million trees, spent 140,000 days fighting forest fires, and constructed 7,000 miles of truck trails, 504 bridges and 222 buildings" during the Depression and post-Depression years of 1933 to 1942. The CCC was part of a sweeping effort by U.S. President Franklin Roosevelt to create jobs for Americans during the particularly lean years of the Great Depression when jobs were very scarce. In proposing the idea to Congress, Roosevelt explained,

During the Depression and post-Depression years of 1933 to 1942, the Civilian Conservation Corps in Michigan planted 484 million trees to reforest the state following the logging boom. Here, unidentified CCC workers put seedlings into the ground. (Franklin D. Roosevelt Presidential Library and Museum, Hyde Park, N.Y.)

"(W)e can take a vast army of the unemployed out into healthful surroundings. We can eliminate to some extent at least the threat that enforced idleness brings to spiritual and moral stability."

The Michigan CCC started up almost immediately. Applicants flooded in, but the CCC didn't take just anybody. Qualified applicants had to be in need of a job and in good physical shape, standing between 5 and 6.5 feet tall, and weighing at least 107 pounds. But that wasn't all. They also had to have "three serviceable, natural, masticating teeth above and below." That's right: The CCC drew the line at accepting young men who couldn't chew. The vast majority of the men who made the grade and joined the CCC were in their late teens to early 20s.

The young men in the corps lived in tents at first, but later in simple barracks at about 120 camps all over the state. Each man signed on for a six-month stint, making $30 a month, all but $8 of which they had to send to their dependents back home. During the first four years of the program, the men spent their off-hours pretty much as they chose, often going into a local town to pass the time. By 1937, however, the CCC made a minimum of 10 hours of educational pursuits mandatory, a demand that helped many of the men finally to earn their eighth-grade diplomas, and others to go on to take high school or college correspondence courses

The CCC continued in Michigan until 1942 when the United States became involved in World War II and focused its financial resources there. The museum here in Michigan contains a huge collection of photographs and artifacts, most of them gathered from the CCC alumni themselves, that provide a unique view of the life and times of the men in Civilian Conservation Corps in Michigan.

MM 244

Mile Marker 244

This is the boundary between Roscommon County to the south and Crawford County to the north. The name Roscommon comes

BRAINBUSTERS

"Bridge may be icy" signs are a common sight on the overpasses along I-75.

Basic: Roads that sit on the ground do not get icy as fast as roads on bridges. Why not?

Intermediate: What is black ice?

Advanced: Here's an icy riddle. The city of Cadillac in the northern Lower Peninsula has two lakes (Lake Mitchell and Lake Cadillac) that are connected by a canal. In the winter, the shallow canal freezes before the lakes, but when the lakes finally freeze, the canal thaws out and stays open for the rest of the winter. Why?

See page 160 for answers.

from its early Irish immigrants who selected it to recall their home county in Ireland. (For more on Roscommon County, see mile marker 220.) Crawford County, on the other hand, has an American background. It is one of at least two other counties in the United States that are named for Revolutionary War soldier William Crawford. Crawford was part of the 2,400-soldier contingent who with George Washington famously crossed the Delaware on Christmas night 1776 to wage the Battle of Trenton the following day. The battle was a key win for the fledgling United States.

The Battle of Trenton wasn't the first meeting between Washington and Crawford. The two men had known each other since they were in their late teens. They met while working as surveyors, and later served in the British forces during the French and Indian War. This war in the mid-1700s pitted the British against the French and their American Indian allies, with the source of contention being the wide swath of land from the Great Lakes all the way down to the Gulf of Mexico and stretching from the Mississippi River to the west and the Appalachian Mountains to the east. Both countries wanted the land for expansion, but also for its lucrative fur trade. During the war, Washington was promoted to colonel to head up the British Virginia Regiment, and Crawford served in that regiment under Washington for several years, mainly defending the settlers and themselves from American Indian raids. After the war was over, Craw-

William Crawford, whose name is on a Michigan county, joined George Washington during the famous crossing of the Delaware, which is depicted here. (National Archives and Records Administration)

ford made a life for himself in Pennsylvania as a farmer and fur trader, but continued to do surveying work, some of it again with George Washington. By 1774, however, Crawford was back in the battle fray as a major at a fort in the colony of Virginia, again battling with groups of area American Indians.

When the American Revolution erupted and the colonies formed an army, Washington became its commander-in-chief and Crawford accepted an appointment as colonel of a Virginia Regiment. It was in that role that he joined Washington at the crossing of the Delaware. Crawford stayed in the Continental Army, as it was called, until 1781 when he retired. It was a short retirement. The following year, a general convinced him to take a post as commander of a 500-member volunteer regiment to fight Indians along Sandusky River in northern Ohio. At the time, the American Indians were extremely agitated about Ohio's so-called Moravian massacre in which American forces had killed nearly a hundred Indians, mainly women and children. The American Indians in collaboration with British soldiers got advance warning of Crawford's approach and swiftly surrounded his regiment. Surprised, Crawford's men scattered. The Indians were able to capture many of the soldiers, including Crawford, whom they tortured and burned at the stake. A historical marker and a monument to the colonel recall the events of that skirmish near the banks of the Tymochtee Creek in Ohio where Crawford died.

Before this Michigan county was called Crawford, its name was Shawano as a reference to the chief of the

Ojibwe band of Indians known as the Shawano or Shawnee.

Mile Marker 249

Old 27 crosses south of this mile marker. This road was the predecessor to the U.S. 127 freeway in this part of the state. For much of its length, Old 27 parallels U.S. 127 (onced known as U.S. 27). To the north, U.S. 127 merges into I-75. (For more on

US-127, see exit 109.) A number of other "old" roads appear across Michigan. For example, a state highway called M-76 was built to serve as a temporary connector between stretches of I-75 to the south and north. As soon as M-76 was completed in 1973, it officially became part of I-75, and the name M-76 was decommissioned. Not all of M-76 became part of I-75, however. Some sections still exist as Old 76 in parts of Roscommon County.

THE ANSWERS

Roads sit on the ground, and the ground provides some insulation from cold air, as well as at least some amount of heat from the soil below. Conversely, *bridges are exposed above and below. Without that added insulation and heat from the soil, a wet road on a bridge can start to freeze as soon as the air temperature drops to 32°F.* A road may not start to freeze until the air temperature dips another 5 or 6 degrees. Of course, a road that is already at 32°F can become and remain icy even if the air temperature is a few degrees warmer.

Another concern for drivers is black ice. Black ice is not really black at all, but is just *clear ice that shows the color of the road beneath.* If the road is black asphalt, as many roads are, the ice appears to be black. Black ice is a very thin and smooth coating of ice that results when mist, fog, or cold rain land and freeze on a winter road. It is very dangerous for a few

reasons. First, it can look the same as wet pavement, and can even alternate between wet areas of road depending on the road's terrain or on the winds. Second, black ice sometimes isn't even shiny, which makes it almost impossible to see. Third, black ice is usually not associated with falling sleet or snow, so drivers aren't expecting it. In addition, black ice is very slick.

The mystery of the early freeze and then quick thaw of the canal between Lakes Mitchell and Cadillac has stumped a lot of people, but it simply has to do with the density of ice. The canal freezes first because it is shallower. The water cools down faster and therefore freezes faster. *When the lakes finally freeze, the ice on top puts pressure on the warmer water down below and that water flows into the canal.* The slightly warmer water combined with the current that develops from the moving water is enough to melt the ice in the canal.

Exit 251

Four Mile Road is approximately 4 miles south of the city of Grayling. Appropriately, Five Mile Road is a mile farther south, and Seven Mile Road is another two miles south. No One, Two, Three or Six Mile roads exist.

— — —

Just off this exit, less than a mile to the east, is the Grayling Generating Station, a wood-burning power station that opened in 1992 and produces energy for the region. According to company literature, it burns about 400,000 tons of wood every year, most of it in the form of sawdust, wood chips and wood waste collected from nearby mills, leftover limbs and other debris remaining from logging operations, and waste wood recovered from landfills. All of the wood comes from within a 50-mile radius of the plant. Some of it, for instance, originates in the nearby Weyerhaeuser (WIE-er-how-zer) Co.-Grayling OSB, which makes a product called oriented strand board, or OSB, that is a commonly used material for outside walls and beneath flooring in homes and other buildings. This plant, which is one of the largest OSB facilities in North America, sends any leftover scraps of wood resulting from its operations to the power plant, which burns them to produce energy. Another nearby plant that contributes to the power plant is the AJD Forest Products, which is

located next door to the plant. This company is the largest sawmill in the state, and produces a considerable amount of sawdust and other waste wood that go to the power plant. The Grayling Generating Station sells the electricity it produces to Consumers Power Co., which then distributes it to homes and businesses throughout the region.

Mile Marker 251

The rest area on the northbound side of I-75 carries the name of a retired Michigan Department of Transportation engineer named Monte Endres. In the four years before he retired in 1997, he was chief administrator for highway construction, maintenance, and traffic and safety operations in six counties of the eastern Upper Peninsula, and at the same time, he was chief operating officer for the Mackinac Bridge. One of the many projects he supervised while at the bridge was a toll-plaza makeover that, in part, allowed cars to pass through faster. Over the span of his career, he spent nearly four decades working for the Michigan Department of Transportation.

Exit 254

Immediately to the west of the freeway is downtown Grayling, a community situated on a highly celebrated trout stream called the Au Sable (aw SAH-bul) River. (For information about the river, see mile

Exit 251
MM 251
Exit 254

marker 255). The name of the city comes from a type of fish that was once very plentiful in the Au Sable River, but disappeared not only from the river, but also from the entire state, by the 1930s. Fortunately, the grayling fish still survives in western Canada and in Alaska, along with a few small areas in the western United States, and in Russia and Siberia. (For more on the grayling and the Au Sable River, see mile marker 255.)

This city wasn't always called Grayling. Over the years, it has gone by the names of Au Sable for the river, Forest, Crawford for its place in Crawford County, Crawford Station since it was a station on the railroad, Milltown as it was called by lumberjacks, and Jackson, thanks to the people of the Jackson, Lansing and Saginaw Railroad company who originally platted the then-40 acre town.

The first settler in the new village was a man named Michael Sloat Hartwick, who built a hotel next to the railroad tracks. For those familiar with downtown Grayling, the three-story, log hotel was located on the same site where Shoppenagon's Inn now stands. The name Hartwick is well-known to Michigan travelers because of the nearby Hartwick Pines State Park that was named for Michael Hartwick's son Edward (see exit 259). Soon after the Hartwick hotel opened its doors, people began flooding into the new community, and at its height, the town had about 2,500 residents. By comparison, today's population is about 2,000. Grayling was a bustling town in the late 1800s and at one point had 12 north- and southbound passenger trains, not to mention numerous freight trains, running into and through Grayling every single day. The once-hectic railroad depot in downtown Grayling is now the home of the Crawford County Historical Museum, which recalls the past in photographs, lumberjack tools, and other memorabilia from the era.

BRAINBUSTERS

Exit 254

Grayling counts among its own the famed bow hunter Fred Bear. Bear moved to Grayling from the Detroit area after quitting his job in the auto industry to start building bows full-time.

Basic: Fred Bear was the subject of a well-known song by a Detroit-born hard-rock musician who went by many nicknames, including Terrible Ted and the Motor City Madman. Who is the musician?

Intermediate: At one time, people made their own simple bows. Bear started a company called Bear Archery that became one of the first companies, if not the first company, to mass produce bows, including so-called compound bows that have a pulley and cable system. What does the system do and why is it important to a hunter?

Advanced: When hunters use a bow in the pursuit of a deer, they often add a clump of cloth strips or rubber whiskers, or a puff of wool or fur to the bow string. What is the purpose of this add-on?

See page 165 for answers.

Like other lumber towns, Grayling's population dropped off after the loggers moved on. It has since become a destination for vacationers, especially anglers who come to fish for trout in the Au Sable, and paddlers who come to take a canoe or kayak down the scenic river.

When driving along this part of I-75, your chances are quite good of seeing military vehicles on the highway. This is because the headquarters of one of the nation's largest National Guard training facilities are located just outside Grayling at the appropriately named Camp Grayling. In all, the camp covers nearly 150,000 acres (234 square miles) in this county and two neighboring counties. The camp is always busy training soldiers in National Guard units from the Midwest, as well as active and reserve soldiers in all five branches of the U.S. military, and even units of armed forces from Canada, the United Kingdom and other countries. If you roll down your window, you might even hear a jet screaming overhead or catch the sound of military personnel training on 105 mm and 155 mm artillery, heavy mortars and air-to-ground bombs. Most of this activity is confined to a 7,400-acre (11.5-square mile) site, called Range 40, a distance from the freeway, but the thunder of the explosions can carry a considerable distance.

This is also the exit for M-72, which leads to the 14,500-resident Traverse City about 50 miles to the west. The number of residents may not seem all that great, but the city is the major commercial and cultural center for the seven-county northwestern Michigan area. While it has most of the big-box stores, its quaint but busy downtown and charming, historic residential streets help to maintain its small-town flavor. Traverse City is famous for its cherries (even going by the nickname "Cherry Capital of the World"), its long and sandy beaches on two bays of Lake Michigan, its vineyards that produce award-winning wines, and the nearby Sleeping Bear Dunes National Lakeshore. These, however, are only a few of its attractions. The summers showcase the area's championship golf courses, excellent fishing and boating in the bays and inland lakes, and hiking and biking trails, while the very snowy winters highlight downhill ski slopes, countless ice fishing opportunities, and numerous cross-country skiing and snowshoeing trails. For these reasons—and many others—the region is a favorite Michigan vacation spot.

Mile Marker 255

Watch for the crossing of the Au Sable River just south of North Down River Road. The Au Sable— French for sandy—flows for nearly 150 miles from a few miles northwest of the city of Grayling all the way across the state to Lake Huron. Much of the Au Sable passes through the expansive Huron National Forest, which covers more than 400,000 acres (625 square miles) in the northern

Rainbow trout. (USDA Forest Service)

Arctic grayling. (NOAA/The Fishes of Alaska, Bulletin of the Bureau of Fishes, Vol. XXVI, 1906)

Lower Peninsula. A mainly shallow, but swift river, the Au Sable is the site of the "longest, nonstop canoe race in North America." Called the Au Sable River Canoe Marathon, it pits canoeists against one another in a grueling, 120-mile race that is made even more challenging because much of it occurs in the dead of night. Many of the canoeists train on the river before the race so they can learn how to navigate the river's snaky path and avoid seemingly unending series of obstacles in the current. During the race, some hardy spectators follow their favorite canoeists on land, driving from one bridge or viewing spot to the next to cheer them on as they pass by. Winners generally finish the race in 14–15 hours. The annual canoe race began in 1947, and now entices racers from far beyond the United States.

— — —

The Au Sable River is now a world-renowned trout river, famous for its brown, rainbow and brook trout. One length of the river, called the Holy Waters, is held in special reverence by anglers. Along this 9-mile stretch of the river, fishing is limited to flies-only and to catch-and-release. Fly fishing is a method that uses artificial, usually insect-mimicking lures, called flies, to hook the fish. Catch-and-release rules mandate that all caught fish be set free back in the water.

Although trout draw the anglers today, the fish that caught everyone's attention in the past in the Au Sable River was the grayling. The grayling is a beautiful fish that has a long, sleek, blue-gray or sometimes deep bluish-purple body with a pink sheen on the sides, a tall fin along the top of the back, and scattered dark-colored, often reddish-orange spots and stripes on the fins. The males, which are slightly larger than the females, can grow to nearly 30 inches long.

Until the late 1800s, people could catch their fill of grayling in the Au Sable. In fact, some sources say the grayling was the only game fish in the Au Sable in those days. According to the Michigan Department of Natural Resources, "(L)ore has it that anglers from that time could sometimes catch three fish with one cast. Early historical accounts tell of grayling that 'lay like cordwood in the Au Sable.'" Strangely, however, anglers didn't know the actual name of the fish they were reeling in. They only learned what they were in 1874 when a local guide sent two or three of the long-finned animals to another fish enthusiast named James Fitzhugh, who then forwarded them on to Washington, D.C., for identification. Once the local residents learned the fish's name, they started calling their community Grayling. By then, however, the grayling's days were already numbered, and soon they would disappear not only from this river, but also from waters throughout the entire state.

What happened to the grayling? A major contributing factor was a practice of the lumbering operations. They sent thousands of logs into the Au Sable and other rivers where they floated downstream to mills. Often, the logs completely covered the water surface. In shallow areas, they even bounced along and gouged stream and river bottoms. The jostling and sheer force of the logs killed many grayling outright. It also tore up their spawning grounds. In addition, logging operations cleared acres of land, including the banks, which caused erosion and allowed silt to cloud the waters. The grayling could not survive in those conditions. These factors combined with a growing fishing pressure were too much for the fish.

By 1914, local sportsmen established the Grayling Fish Hatchery Club, and soon opened the hatchery to try to raise grayling and restock the river. Their efforts were unsuccessful, but they did find they could effectively plant brook and brown trout in the Au Sable, and they did. In 10 years, the group sold the hatchery to the state, which ran it until the late 1960s. It was idle until 1983 when local citizens took the reins. Now, the Grayling Recreation Authority runs the hatchery. The hatchery is located just off I-75 on North Down River

---

THE ANSWERS

Rock star *Ted Nugent* performed "Fred Bear" on his 1995 Spirit of the Wild album. Nugent shared many a joint hunting trip with Bear, who was more than 40 years his senior.

In traditional bows, including longbow and recurve styles, the string attaches directly to either end of the bow. The harder it is to pull back (or draw) the string, the faster and farther the arrow will fly. With the pulley and cable system of a compound bow, *the string is much easier to hold at full extension.* When a person draws the string on a compound bow, the system allows the weight of the draw (the force needed to pull it back) to lessen up after the archer has drawn it about halfway back. Instead of the archer holding the full draw weight, it is transferred into the arms of the bow itself. *The drop in draw weight, usually by 65–80 percent, takes the strain off of the archer, allowing him or her to hold the fully-extended bow both steadier and for a longer time than would be possible with a traditional bow.* Hunters usually add strips of cloth and puffs of fur, among other items, to the string of their bow to *dampen the sound* as the string zings through the air when they release it. These add-ons are called silencers.

Road, and to this day still raises tens of thousands of brook, brown and rainbow trout.

Mile Markers 255–257

Many of the trees along both the northbound and southbound sides of I-75 here are jack pines. Rather than the neat appearance of the red pines with their tall, straight, mostly branchless trunks, jack pines have a scraggly guise with branches sprouting willy nilly along its entire length. Some of the branches are long and some are short, and parts of the trunk may have patches without any branches at all. Jack pines are rather small trees, typically only growing to 30-40 feet tall. The tree's small stature

Jack pine. (USDA-NRCS PLANTS Database, D.E. Herman, et al., North Dakota Tree Handbook, 1996)

combined with the lack of symmetry give it its mangy, almost shrubby look.

On close inspection, other characteristics set this tree apart from different Michigan species. One of them is its pine cone. Most pine trees make annual pine cones that open up in their second autumn to release their seeds and then fall to the ground soon after. Jack pine cones are different. The tree generates the cones, but only some of them open up and drop in the second autumn. Many of the cones instead stay on the tree even after they have opened, or remain closed and on the tree for years, sometimes decades. The only thing that will open these closed cones, which are sealed shut with sticky resin, is a forest fire. The fire also clears away other trees to make openings in the forest. This is vital for jack pines, since they do not grow well in shade. Here in Michigan, foresters start so-called "prescribed burns" that both open the cones and clear the forests to help the jack pines regenerate. These prescribed burns aren't just for the sake of the jack pines. They are also important for certain endangered birds, called Kirtland warblers, that nest almost solely in northern Michigan and under the branches of young jack pines. (For more information on the warblers, see exit 239.) Another characteristic of the jack pine is the shape of its closed pine comes. Many of them are shaped rather like a plump teardrop, but with the tapered end slightly curled. The cones are often described as looking like a "J." Finally, the needles of the jack pine come in clusters of two. The pair of needles, which are an inch to an inch-and-a-half long, are separated slightly to form a V.

The jack pine is one of the trees that are much more common in northern Michigan than in the southern part of the state. The main reason is the soil. Southern Michigan soil has more clay and is richer, but jack pines prefer the sandy, dry and more sterile soil typical to northern Michigan areas. The wood of the jack pine does not make premium lumber. Rather, it is often used as pulpwood for making paper, or sometimes as wood for posts.

Exit 259

The beautiful Hartwick Pines State Park is just off this exit. At 9,672 acres

BRAINBUSTERS

When Hartwick Pines State Park first opened, it had 85 acres of old-growth white pine forest.

Basic: Although none of the trees were ever cut, the old-growth forest is now only 49 acres. What happened to decrease the size of the stand?

Intermediate: Bright Lake in Hartwick Pines State Park is named for an animal that was used in the logging industry. Bright was what kind of an animal?

Advanced: What do the following old-time lumberjack terms mean: cootie cage, kill dad and alibi day?

See next page for answers.

(more than 15 square miles), Hartwick Pines is the largest state park in the northern Lower Peninsula, but it is mainly known as a treasure trove of information about Michigan's forests and the history of logging. Points of particular interest are:

Exit 259

+ a reproduction logging camp from the 1800s;
+ a wide-ranging collection of logging equipment and tools from the era;
+ a logging museum that provides a good view of not only the lumbering era, but also about present-day and future forestry in the state; and
+ the extremely rare sight of a 49-acre stand of virgin pine forest, the largest area of never-logged, or "old growth," white pine forest in the Lower Peninsula.

The park itself came from a gift made by Karen Hartwick, who in 1927 bought 8,320 acres (13 square miles) from a Grayling logging company that was partly owned by her father, and then donated the land to the state of Michigan. She wanted to create a park that would chronicle the lumbering era in Michigan and also would be a memorial to her husband Edward, a lumberman who died while serving in World War I. The state quickly designated the park, and from 1934–35, the men of the Civilian Conservation Corps (see exit 244) built a two-building replica of a logging camp, which is still open today. The camp is complete with bunks, a mess hall and a blacksmith shop that give the flavor of lumberjack life the late 1800s.

An actual camp of the day would have had about a half dozen buildings, including a separate mess hall, a stand-alone camp office and several bunkhouses to house up to 100 lumberjacks, or shanty boys as they were called. The bunkhouses were typically crammed with dozens of close-sitting bunks. Until the mid-1870s, most of the felling of trees occurred in the winter when the ground was frozen and therefore more suited to transporting logs, which were dragged along the ground by various means. When the men would return from a day in the field, their clothes were not only wet with sweat but with melted snow and ice. To dry them for the next morning, they hung their clothes from lines strung around the bunkhouse, getting them as near as possible to the wood stove that heated the building. The aroma in the bunkhouse from the drying and fermenting wool overclothes and undergarments was no doubt a memorable one!

Logging became a year-round operation beginning in 1875 when a company in Manistee, Mich., started making a piece of equipment called a logging wheel or big wheel that could transport logs out of the woods even when the roads weren't iced

THE ANSWERS

The size of stand of the old-growth white pines in Hartwick Pines State Park dropped from 85 acres to 49 when a huge storm in November 1940 brought *extreme winds that toppled at least half of the trees*. The remaining trees are in a 49-acre area.

When Karen Hartwick donated the land to create the park, she requested that two of the lakes in the park be named for an *oxen* team used by her father to drag, or skid, newly cut logs out of the forest and to a loading site. The oxen were named Bright and Star. The state Board of Geographic Names approved Bright Lake, but decided the state already had its share of lakes named Star, so it substituted Glory. As a result, the park pays tribute to oxen through the names of Bright Lake and Glory Lake.

Lumberjacks had a number of colorful words to describe their situation in life. In a typical camp, the mattresses on the bunks were stuffed with straw. While they provided a little comfort and warmth to the lumberjacks, they were also well-suited to a number of biting insects that the lumberjacks collectively called cooties. *The bunk was, therefore, the cootie cage. A kill dad was a bucket of community chewing or smoking tobacco.* Set in the bunk house, jacks would toss in any extra they had, and pull out a wad as needed. *Alibi day was payday.* After putting in many hard days in the woods, the jacks would take their money and try to come up with excuses, or alibis, to get them out of work and into town for a little R&R.

The Big Wheel, shown here at Hartwick Pines State Park, was used during the logging era to pull logs from the woods. (Travel Michigan)

over. The big wheel was a simple iron and wood contraption with a pair of huge, 10-foot-diameter wheels set on a wide axle. A cross bar stretched forward from the axle and hitched to a team of horses that provided the power. To load it, lumberjacks tipped up the big wheel and hung logs from beneath the axle and crossbar. Horses or sometimes oxen dragged the big wheel from the forest to a railroad track or other loading point. The development of the big wheel allowed the logging season to extend into spring and summer. This, however, only served to deplete Michigan's forests even faster.

No matter the season, lumberjacks put in a very full and tiring day. To help keep up morale and the health of the crew, most camps offered their men excellent food and a lot of it. Meals would typically include such hearty fare as fried potatoes and either steak, pork chops or ham for breakfast; stew, beans, potatoes, biscuits and pie for lunch; and a selection of a couple of meats, along with soup, potatoes, corn bread, vegetables, pudding, cake and often fresh fruit for dinner. If the men were in the field at lunchtime, the cooks and assistant cooks would bring the food to the men. Complaints about the food were few and far between, in part because the food was good, but also because the cooking staff were often the wives or other family members of the lumberjacks themselves. Occasionally, however, a camp would get a reputation for serving poor food, which was epitomized by a cheap, dry bread called hardtack that had the consistency of a piece of wood and had to be dunked to become soft enough to eat. Lumber-

169

jacks called camps that served such pitiable chow "hardtack outfits."

— — —

By the time the Hartwick Pines park opened, the logging era in Michigan was already done. Its heyday here was from about 1870 to 1890, when the state was the top producer of lumber in the country. The primary logged species in Michigan was the white pine, which is the state tree. This tree, which can grow to at least 90 feet tall and more than 3 feet in diameter, was and still is used for building homes, barns, fences, all manner of cabinetry, doors, and even matches. One of the biggest white-pine customers in the mid- to late-1800s was the railroad, which needed the lumber to build tracks. According information provided by the Hartwick Pines State Park, Michigan loggers had cut 160 billion board feet of pine by 1897. That means loggers had cut the equivalent of 160 billion one-foot-long, one-foot-wide and one-inch-thick boards, "a quantity sufficient to build 10 million six-room houses or to floor the entire land area of Michigan with 1-inch pine boards, with enough remaining to cover the state of Rhode Island."

— — —

Hartwick Pines is also an interesting site for its numerous trails, which take visitors by lakes and rivers, but also past evidence of the glacier that retreated from Michigan about 11,000–13,000 years ago. As the glacier fell back to the north, it deposited gravel

and other rocky materials that it had picked up elsewhere. The boulder-sized pieces of material are called erratics, and some exist within the park. Hartwick Pines State Park also has numerous ridges, called moraines, that are deposits of sandy gravel. Moraines formed mainly because the glacier retreated in spurts. Each time it paused, it laid down more soil, which became the moraines. Besides moraines, Hartwick Pines contains a number of glacier-associated lakes, which are known as kettle lakes. A kettle lake forms when a large chunk of glacier ice breaks off and is buried. As it melts, the water fills the depression where the ice chunk once sat and forms a small lake.

Mile Markers 262–263

The median between the northbound and southbound sides of I-75 contains a large number of maple trees. The most common maple trees here in the northern Lower Peninsula are sugar maples and red maples. Both have lobed leaves and the main veins of each lobe all fan out from the same place at the base of the leaf. This vein pattern is called palmate. Both of these trees also produce their seeds in pairs and with flat wings on them. Children sometimes call these seeds "helicopters" for the whirling way they float to the ground. Both of these trees put on a beautifully vibrant show in the fall with leaves that turn yellow, orange or red. Only one of them, however, is the primary

The buckets in place on this maple tree are collecting sap that will eventually be made into maple syrup. (Travel Michigan)

source of maple sugar and maple syrup, and that, of course, is the sugar maple tree.

Both maple sugar and maple syrup originate in the tree's sap. Sap is a watery substance that runs throughout the tree and brings nutrients to the tree's tissues. Other trees have sap, too, but the sugar maple's sap is the sweetest. Its sap has a sugar concentration in its sap of about 3 percent. The sap flows when the tree isn't growing. In other words, sap in Michigan maples flows from late summer through the beginning of spring the following year. The sap only becomes sweet, however, in the late winter when the temperature of the wood finally warms up to 40°F. That temperature triggers enzymes in certain tree cells to convert stored starch in the tree into something else, and that something else is sugar The sugar passes into the sap.

When the wood's temperature rises to 45°F, the enzymes stop working and the sugar surge shuts off. In northern Michigan, that means that people who want to get the sweetest sap have to be outside and tapping trees in late February to early March. Tapping involves selecting a tree with a diameter of 10–20 inches, drilling a 1.5- to 2-inch-deep hole into its side and inserting a spout, called a tap, that drains the tree's sap into a waiting bucket below. Usually one tap will yield about 10 gallons of sap, enough to make about a quart of syrup. Depending on the sweetness of the sap in the individual tree and the wood temperature, though it can take as little as seven gallons of sap—or as many as 20 gallons—to make a quart of syrup. Concentrating the sap into syrup requires lots of boiling to reach just the right sugar content, which is a very sweet 66 percent.

If you are driving a Michigan side road in March and see a family huddled around a big, steaming vat bubbling away over an open fire, chances are good they are making maple syrup. Maple sugar is made by heating the syrup further and then cooling it down until sugar crystals form.

According to the Michigan Maple Syrup Association, Michigan is the sixth largest producer of maple syrup in the United States, making about 90,000 gallons a year.

Exit 264

Maple syrup originated with American Indians, who introduced it to early European explorers. According one of many Indian legends about the invention of maple syrup, a great hunter named Woksis first tasted maple syrup because of a cooking mishap. His wife Moqua was stewing him some moose meat, but the water boiled off. She didn't have any water handy and didn't want the meat to burn, so she poured in some maple sap and let the meat continue cooking. By the time Woksis returned from hunting and tasted the meat, it was covered with sweet maple syrup.

BRAINBUSTERS

American black bears are resident mammals of the northern Lower Peninsula and the Upper Peninsula.

Basic: In what season of the year do female black bears give birth to their cubs?

Intermediate: Although most people would describe black bears as hibernators, scientists do not consider them true hibernators. Why?

Advanced: An American black bear is an impressive animal. Adults average 150–350 pounds, although a large one can near 1,000 pounds after it has packed on the weight for hibernation. Still, another wild Michigan animal is bigger both in length (a bear is about 6 feet long) and weight. Name the animal.

See page 175 for answers.

Exit 264

The tiny town of Frederic is about 2 miles to the west. Previously known as Frederickville and Forest, the town was ultimately named after early settler Frederic Barker in 1886 after starting out as a railroad station during the logging era. Times have changed, and Frederic is now the self-proclaimed "Snowmobile Capital of Northern Michigan." Frederic has become a very popular stop for snowmobilers, also known as sledders, since major east-west and north-south trails intersect at the town.

Snowmobiling is a huge recreational activity in Michigan. The state has more registered snowmobiles—390,000—than any other state in the nation. Michigan has more than 6,100 miles of interconnected designated snowmobile trails that form a vast web throughout the Lower and Upper Peninsulas. Thanks to local snowmobile clubs and the Department of Natural Resources, along with registration fees and snowmobile

This snowmobiler tackles one of Michigan's 6,100 miles of designated trails. (Vito Palmisano)

permit fees, the trails are maintained and groomed for the snow season, which usually runs from December through March, depending on the weather of a particular year. Snowmobilers can even cross the Mackinac Bridge that rises over the Straits of Mackinac to connect the Upper and Lower Peninsulas. Snowmobilers cannot drive the span themselves, but the Mackinac Bridge Authority will transport them across the structure for a small fee from 8 a.m. to 8 p.m. every day. Sledders just call the bridge authority to arrange a pick-up.

The road into Frederic is County Road 612, which is known just as "six-twelve." It's a winding, hilly, two-lane road that mainly carves through woods west of Frederic. Drivers sometimes see black bears making a

quick dash from one side of the road to the other. Black bears are the only species of bear living in Michigan. They have a short-haired coat that is usually black or very dark brown, but sometimes is reddish and, although rare, occasionally white in color. Many of them have a little patch of white fur on their chest, and most have a tan-colored snout. Black bears are large mammals, and a typical adult can stand about 5 feet tall when it rears up on its hind legs. When on all fours, its shoulder height is 2–3 feet tall. An average adult female weighs 150–175 pounds, while an average adult male can tip the scales at 250–350 pounds. Some males can grow much bigger, however, and may reach as much as 800–900 pounds when they are at their heaviest just before they enter hibernation (see the Brainbuster.

American black bear. (Hal Korber/PGC Photo)

animals that prefer to keep their distance from humans. Young cubs are usually not as observant as adults, however, and they do sometimes wind up fairly close to people. This can be perilous, because a mother black bear is very protective of her youngsters and may perceive the person as a threat. Some wildlife experts recommend that a person who has a close encounter with a menacing bear should raise his or her arms over the head to appear bigger, forcefully speak to the bear and slowly back away. The best bet, however, is simply to avoid any up-close-and-personal meetings by remaining alert and by making noise when walking through deep woods where bears are known to live.

Mile Marker 267

Like many mammals of Michigan, including deer, bears are crepuscular (creh-PUSS-kyoo-ler), which means that they are especially active at dawn and dusk. Most of the time, they plod along in an unhurried fashion, but they can run at speeds of 30 mph over short distances. And yes, that *is* faster than a human being can run. The average person can run at a speed of 15-17 mph, and even the fastest runners in the world are hard-pressed to top 23 mph. In addition, black bears have long, curved claws that make easy work of climbing trees, and they are quite good swimmers. So, if black bears can chase down humans, can swim and can even climb trees after them, are black bears dangerous? The answer is: Usually no. Like most other mammals, black bears are timid

I-75 passes through some beautiful scenic areas in this part of the state, and many are especially gorgeous in the fall when the leaves turn shades of scarlet, orange, gold and brown. Set off against the vibrant green of pines, the color show can be truly breathtaking.

Why do the leaves change color? Both cooler temperatures and a drop in day length are responsible. As long as the trees are growing, they are making chlorophyll, a green-colored chemical that allows the leaves to turn sunlight into energy. The chlorophyll breaks down, so the tree has to keep making more, and this keeps the leaves green through the spring and summer. When day length becomes shorter and temperatures start to drop, the tree slows its growth and also makes less and less chlorophyll. Without new chlorophyll, the underlying "real" color of the leaves starts to show through. For birch, aspen and some maples, the leaves become yellow, orange and brown. That's because the leaves have the same pigments, called carotene (CAIR-oh-teen) and xanthophyll (ZAN-tho-fill), that make carrots orange and bananas yellow. Some oak and maple trees have a high concentration of another kind of pigment: anthocyanin (an-tho-SY-uh-nins). Anthocyanins are also found in such fruits as cherries and blueberries. Trees with lots of anthocyanins have the particularly vivid reds and oranges that really pop in an autumn scene.

Fall color can vary from one year to the next because the weather plays a role especially in the red/purple anthocyanin pigments. Trees make carotene and xanthophyll all summer long, but they only start to make anthocyanin in the fall. Anthocyanin forms in the leaves from sugar, and the leaves make the most sugar when the temperatures are warm. The best color results from a combination of warm, sunny days to make lots of sugars in the leaves, and then chilly but not freezing nights so the leaves hang onto to the sugar rather than releasing it into the tree. Less-intense color results from cloudy, rainy days that cut into sugar production, or from an early hard frost that kills the

THE ANSWERS

Female black bears give birth to their cubs in the dead of *winter*. A typical female has one or two cubs, although they sometimes have three, four or even five in one litter. The tiny, blind and furless cubs glom onto one of their mother's nipples and continue to nurse, even after the mother has dropped back into her winter sleep. When the mother awakens for good in the spring, the family leaves the den. The young continue to nurse at least until the end of the summer while the mother looks for her own food. Bears will eat almost anything from berries, honey and nuts to salmon, rodents and even ants. The family stays together for a year or two before the cubs head out on their own. The young are ready to start their own new families once they reach about 3–6 years old.

Most people think of black bears as hibernators, but scientists don't consider them true hibernators because *the bears are able to wake from their winter deep sleep*, although they do it only rarely. The bears can not only rouse themselves, but may also take a stroll outside their dens.

The only wild animal in Michigan that is larger than the American black bear is the *moose*. An adult moose can reach 9 feet long and weigh 1,100 pounds or more. No wild moose live in the Lower Peninsula, but they are fairly common in parts of the Upper Peninsula.

Staghorn sumac is a common roadside shrub throughout Michigan. It has deep red leaves in the fall, but even when the leaves have already dropped, as they have here, its clusters of rust-red, fuzzy fruit give it away. (Leslie Mertz)

leaves and turns them from green straight to a dull, dead brown.

Once in a while, you'll see a tree that bucks the trend and puts on its fall show weeks long before autumn arrives. This usually happens because of drought, poor soil, an insect infestation or some other stressful event.

South of Mile Marker 269

This is the boundary between Crawford County to the south and Otsego (ott-SEE-go) County to the north. Crawford County was named for Revolutionary War soldier William Crawford who crossed the Delaware on Christmas night in 1776 with George Washington, and six years later died a grisly death while fighting a joint Indian-British force in the battle that has come to be known

as the Moravian massacre. A plaque and memorial commemorate the Ohio battle site and Crawford's contributions. (For more on Crawford County, see mile marker 244.)

Otsego County is named for a county in New York that was the previous home of some Michigan settlers. Otsego means "place of the rock" or "clear water," but Indian experts aren't certain of its origin. The original name of the county was Okkuddo, a word that some contend means sickly or sickly waters, but that name only held from 1840 to 1843, when it was switched to Otsego.

South of Mile Marker 270

Fall and winter are the best times to see Lake Marjory, which sits just behind the trees on the southbound

Smallmouth (left) and largemouth bass. (NOAA/Great Lakes Environmental Research Laboratory)

side of the freeway. If it is summertime, chances are good that people are camping on the north shore of the lake as you whiz past on I-75. Lake Marjory is an approximately 50-acre lake—about the size of 45 football fields, not counting the end zones—that is the site of one of the Michigan's 145 state forest campgrounds, all of which are situated on a river or a lake. With no electricity, hand pumps for drinking water and the only facilities being vault toilets, the state forest campgrounds are rustic but have wide appeal for hardy campers who really want to rough it. Some of the campgrounds are only accessible down foot trails or by canoe, but Lake Marjory here is a drive-up campground.

Campers who stay in one of the Lake Marjory campground's 12 sites can enjoy fishing on the lake for small panfish and for bass. Anglers generally catch the panfish to put into a frying pan or broil for a tasty dinner, but go after the bass for the thrill of catching them. Michigan's inland lakes are home to both smallmouth and largemouth bass. Both of them actually have big mouths, but the

largemouth has the bigger gape. The record for a caught smallmouth and largemouth in Michigan are 27.25 and 27 inches, respectively, but most anglers reel in bass that are well below 20 inches long. What makes them so fun to catch is that, once they are hooked, they are scrappy fighters that frequently break water to leap a foot or so into the air. Although bass are edible and some people really enjoy them, a good number of anglers think they taste a little strong and will

BRAINBUSTERS

SCUBA diving is a popular sport in many of Michigan's inland lakes and in the Great Lakes.

Basic: What does SCUBA stand for?

Intermediate: Name one of the two people, both from France, who first invented the SCUBA-style of equipment most used today, and name the decade in which they invented it.

Advanced: What are the two main functions of the regulator?

See next page for answers.

release the fish back to the water to fight again another day.

When campers at Lake Marjory aren't relaxing on the lake, they often hike or bike on one of the several nearby state forest trails

The village of Waters is just to the west. The town sits on the north shore of Big Bradford Lake.

Big Bradford Lake is an oblong lake that is about a mile and a half long, covers more than 225 acres (about a third of a square mile), and has an average depth of 65 feet with spots that reach 100-plus feet. This spring-fed lake is also very clear, which makes it a good spot for SCUBA diving.

Like countless other lakes in Michigan, Big Bradford Lake has a public-access launch where anyone can pull up a trailer and drop off a boat for a day on the water. Some people, however, stop at a launch not to unload a boat, but to watch the launch activities almost as a spectator sport. On sunny, summer weekends, some launches can become extremely busy, making the ballet of boat loading and unloading seem almost choreographed. That choreography, however, is not always clean. While boating is extremely popular in Michigan, not everyone who owns a boat is an expert at backing up a trailer so it lines up right next to the dock. The problem is that the a turn of the steering wheel in the towing vehicle sends the trailer in the opposite direction, and many people cannot get the hang of it, especially if they only trailer a boat a few times a year. Pulling a boat off the lake and into the dock can also be a challenge, and if the wind is up and waves are high, it can be near-impossible. Together, the loading and unloading

THE ANSWERS

SCUBA stands for *self-contained underwater breathing apparatus*. In 1943, famous oceanographer and filmmaker *Jacques Cousteau* worked with engineer *Émile Gagnan* to develop a device that was soon known as SCUBA. It allowed divers to carry on their backs everything they need to breathe underwater, and to remain underwater for extended periods of time. At the time, a similar device was also available for diving. Called a rebreather, it differed from Cousteau and Gagnon's apparatus because divers exhaled into a tank rather than into the water. The rebreather treated the exhaled air so that the divers could breathe it again, or "rebreathe" it.

An important part of SCUBA is the regulator. *It supplies air—a mix of oxygen and nitrogen—on demand, and also lowers the pressure of the air coming from the tank.* If not for the pressure-lowering action, the air would rush down the diver's windpipe with such high pressure that it would damage the lungs.

can present some good betting opportunities for onlookers: How many tries will it take this person to get his trailer in position? Will that person lose her cool? Will anyone fall in the water? Spectators are wise to remain discreet, however, because already-stressed-out boaters do not necessarily appreciate the extra attention.

At the southern end of Big Bradford Lake near the boat launch is a dam that regulates how much water empties from the lake and into a creek. That creek feeds a major river, the Au Sable, that flows across the eastern half of the state. (For more on the Au Sable River, see mile marker 255.)

SCUBA diving is popular in the Great Lakes and some of the inland lakes. Here, a diver inspects an old shipwreck in the U.P.'s Alger Underwater Preserve. (Tom Buchkoe)

Exit 270

The town's name of Waters comes from the numerous nearby lakes. Eight lakes sit within 2 miles of town, and Waters actually sits between two of them: Big Bradford Lake to the south and Little Bradford Lake to the north. Little Bradford Lake is 21 acres (19 football fields) in size, which is about a tenth of the size of Big Bradford Lake. When the town started out in the 1870s, it was built around a sawmill and its name was Bradford Lake. The name became Waters in 1885.

One of its noteworthy early residents was a man named Henry Stephans, who remained in Waters even after the lumbering industry had stripped the forests. In 1914, he decided to pay tribute to the lumberjacks who emptied many a bottle of alcohol during their time in northern Michigan, by constructing a fence made from old glass bottles and layered with concrete. He paid local children for every bottle they could find, and hired someone to do the masonry. Stephans was a jolly sort of man, and would sometimes take the newly purchased bottles and hide them nearby so the children could find them and sell them to him once again. By the end of the project, the fence included some 15,000 bottles. It was about 5 feet tall and stretched at least 200 feet down two blocks of the town's main street.

The fence stood for many years, even after Stephans had left Waters and someone else had purchased the property. The bottle fence drew the attention of people across the country when it won a place in Ripley's "Believe It or Not" newspaper column and got some additional publicity. This had an unforeseen consequence: Some visitors began taking home

179

Fly fishing is a common sight on Michigan waters. This fisherman tries his luck on Newton Creek in central Michigan. (Travel Michigan)

souvenirs from the fence, and it started to vanish bottle by bottle. Only a few portions of the fence still stand today. Otsego Lake Township now has a historical display at the township hall to remember the story of the old bottle fence.

North of Mile Marker 271

Hatch Lake is visible through the trees on the southbound side of the freeway. The slightly larger Heart Lake is just to the south of Hatch Lake. Heart Lake has a rudimentary public boat launch for people who want to hand-carry their boats into the water. The effort may be worth it, because the Michigan Department of Natural Resources (DNR) periodically stocks Heart Lake with both

rainbow trout and splake. Splake are hybrids that are a cross between male brook trout, also sometimes called speckled trout, and female lake trout. The name splake comes from a combination of speckled and lake.

Brook trout and lake trout are two separate species that only very rarely mate with each other in the wild, but they will mate in the artificial surrounding of a fish hatchery. Because they don't reproduce in the wild, the DNR has to continue stocking them to maintain a population. The DNR here and in other states make the effort with splake for several reasons:

+ Splake grow fast, up to an inch a month in the first year they're stocked, which is faster than either full-blooded brook trout or lake trout.
+ They survive very well, and sometimes better than their parent species, in cold ponds and lakes.
+ Anglers typically find them less difficult to catch than other species of trout, especially in the winter, so the DNR actually gets a good bang for its buck: A successful harvest and happy anglers are the payback for the DNR's investment of stocked fish.

Besides the good fishing in Heart Lake, it is also interesting from a geological standpoint because it is one of Michigan's many kettle lakes. Like the kettle lakes in Hartwick Pines (see exit 259), Heart Lake originated with the glacier that once covered the state. As the glacier retreated, big chunks of ice broke off. Soil and other

Lake trout (top) and brook trout. (NOAA/Great Lakes Environmental Research Laboratory)

debris from the glacier then buried the chunks, and the chunks took their sweet time melting. When they finally did, they left deep depressions that filled with meltwater and with rainwater, forming the lakes. Some of the kettle lakes have since drained and dried up in the thousands of years since, but hundreds of them—like Heart Lake—still remain.

Mile Marker 273

Old State Road crosses I-75 here. This road is also known as county-designated highway F18, usually just called F18. Depending on your location in the state, these county-designated highways are preceded by an A, B, C, D, F, G or H, which refer to particular zones. Zones A through F are in the Lower Peninsula, and G and H are in the Upper Penin-

BRAINBUSTERS

The first settlers arrived at Otsego Lake in the 1860s, but the buzz about the area started when a school teacher-turned-lumber baron named David Ward discovered a vast stand of cork pine here and bought a huge tract of land extending far to the west. Some claimed it was the largest stand of cork pine in the state. Ward built a sawmill about 5 miles west of the lake on a major river, called the Manistee (man-ih-STEE), and then added a railroad to haul the lumber to Lake Michigan, where it was transferred to ships for the journey to Chicago and beyond. He called his operation the D. E. Ward Lumber Co., and the community there soon had the name Deward. The operation was extremely profit-able for Ward, and he made millions before the trees were gone. The town of Deward is gone now though, and is another of Michigan's many logging ghost towns.

Basic: Cork pine is a nickname for a very common tree here in Michigan. In fact, it is the state tree. Name it.

Intermediate: Why was it nicknamed a cork pine?

Advanced: The first settlers on Otsego Lake set up housekeeping on the south shore of lake, and in 1872 their community also had the name Otsego Lake. The town received the title of county seat in 1875, but another town took the title away shortly thereafter. What town?

See next page for answers.

sula. Sometimes, county-designated highways cross zones, and usually their number remains the same, but the letter switches to reflect the proper zone. F18 lies completely within zone F, but other highways, like F38 farther north along I-75 becomes C-38 on the other side of I-75 when it enters the C zone.

— — —

Just a half mile to the northwest is the south shore of Otsego Lake, which at 5 miles long and a mile wide in spots, is the largest lake in the county. It's a rather shallow lake with most spots less than 15 feet. The deepest area is 23 feet. Fishing is a primary activity, and anglers go after panfish, like bluegills and rock bass, as well as larger fish like smallmouth and largemouth bass, and northern pike. Thousands of people visit for swimming and sunbathing in the summer along the half-mile of sandy beach that is part of the popular Otsego Lake State Park, which is

**MM
274–276**

THE ANSWERS

During the lumber era, cork pine was another name for premium *white pine* trees. They were called cork pine because *their logs floated in the water like corks.*

Otsego Lake was only the county seat for two years. At that time, the residents of Gaylord executed a power play and yanked the county seat out from under Otsego Lake. (For details, see exit 279.)

on the southern end of the lake. The 62-acre park has a large day-use area and two campgrounds for a total of 155 campsites, so it can become quite busy in July and August. With lots of trees and rather large campsites, however, campers don't feel overly crowded.

This land became a state park in 1920 after the state bought it on the cheap from a logging company that had already stripped off the trees and had no more use for it. It remained pretty much as it was until 1935 when the young men of the Civilian Conservation Corps arrived to build facilities and set up the park for visitors. (For more about the Civilian Conservation Corps, see exit 244.) Two of those buildings still remain: One is a restroom and the other is a pavilion.

Mile Markers 274–276

In the summer, a great many ferns are visible blanketing the ground along the sides of the freeway here. Depending on the species, some Michigan ferns can grow up to 5 feet tall. When they first sprout in the spring, though, they look little like they do later in the year. They sprout with the top curled into a spiral like the head on the neck of some violins, and consequently, they are known as fiddleheads. Many people search out and eat certain fiddleheads. Not all fiddleheads are safe to eat, however, and some can cause cancer.

Ferns are unusual plants because they don't reproduce like the typical rose, tomato or other flowering

The limestone oak fern (right) is one of the many types of ferns found in Michigan. Like other ferns, it reproduces via spores . The spores of many ferns are grouped into small, round clusters (left), called sori, on the bottoms of the fern fronds. (USDA Forest Service, Ian Shackleford)

MM 274–276

Oak fern. (*The Ferns of Great Britain and Ireland*, 1857, Thomas Moore)

plant. Instead, the ferns have dust-like spores that appear usually in small round capsules on the underside of the leaves, or fronds. As the fern gets larger and its spores become ripe, the capsules rupture to release the spores, which are so light and tiny that they can float many feet from the frond. When a spore lands in a spot that is moist, it germinates into a tiny leaf-like structure called a prothallus. This prothallus then grows the fern's male and female parts. The male part of the fern makes sperm, the counterpart to a flowering plant's pollen. These sperm actually have to swim through the moisture on the ground to reach the female part, which has the egg. The sperm from one prothallus usually fertilizes the egg from different prothallus. Like the sperm, the fertilized egg must remain moist, too, and it eventually starts to grow into the plant that we see here on the sides of the road.

Reproduction in ferns, therefore, requires water. Without it, the sperm can't swim to the egg, the fertilized egg would shrivel up, and the ferns would eventually die out. This dependence on water is an indication of just how primitive the ferns are.

Flowers, pine trees and many other plants have gotten around the dependence on water by making seeds and pollen. Seeds are basically water-tight containers for the eggs inside, and pollen are non-drying sperm. In a flower, for instance, a bee or fly can visit, pick up some pollen on its legs, and fly off to another flower to deposit it. All the while, the pollen remains completely viable. Once it fertilizes an egg, the egg is sealed inside a seed that can keep it just a little bit moist so it can survive until the time comes for it to germinate, or start to sprout. At that point, Mother Nature takes over to provide the moisture.

183

Charles Brink Road crosses I-75 here. It is named for early pioneer Charles Brink. He came from Pennsylvania to southern Michigan first, but then made the move to this area of Otsego County in the spring of 1869 to start a logging operation. At the time, this part of the state was largely unexplored because it didn't have any railroads or other easy access. Brink brought 14 men along and together they cleared 25 acres, which they promptly planted with crops to help sustain them in the winter. An early frost ruined their harvest, but the little camp persevered. Brink's wife made the journey to meet her husband at the camp in November, reportedly becoming the first white woman to set foot in the county. By that time, the men were already hard at work preparing to fell trees for their fledgling logging company.

Another logging operation came to the region about the same time (see mile marker 284), and with the subsequent arrival of a state road and railroads, people started to arrive to set up homes.

By 1875, just six years after Brink and his men set foot in this wilderness, the county already had its own newspaper, called the *Otsego County Herald*. Brink would ultimately have an unusual connection to the man who started up the paper. That man was Charles Fuller, who hailed from another Michigan town called Owosso. Fuller quickly became a

pillar of the community and took positions as both postmaster and county treasurer. The treasurer job would prove to be his downfall. While he held that position, he took $9,000 of county money and lost it while trading wheat options in Chicago. Rather than face up to the consequences of his actions, Fuller headed for the border . . . the Canadian border, that is. When Fuller disappeared, Brink stepped in as treasurer and discovered the depth of Fuller's embezzlement. Brink helped the county recover from the loss, and soon earned a reputation as a honest and hard-working public servant.

When Fuller took flight, he didn't only owe the county. He also left behind a debt to a resident named Henry C. "Mack" McKinley. McKinley made up for the debt by taking control of the newspaper, which he ran for many years. Since then, the paper has changed hands and names a few times, but it is still in operation today as the *Gaylord Herald Times*.

I-75 is flanked on both sides by golf courses here. Marsh Ridge Golf Course is on the southbound side of the freeway, and Loon Golf Club is on the northbound side. Golfers and golf carts are usually visible here and there through the trees. Both courses afford beautiful views of the rolling countryside and marshlands. The 10th hole at Marsh Ridge is especially breathtaking with the sweeping scenery from its elevated tee.

MM 277

Exit 279

This is one of two main exits that lead to the city of Gaylord. This exit takes travelers up a road (Old 27) that runs parallel to I-75 and enters the city from the south. Gaylord is large as northern Michigan cities go, and has about 3,700 residents today. It is also the county seat, but that title did not come easily. Back in 1875, another town called Otsego Lake had that designation. To become the county seat, businessmen in Gaylord traveled out to the northwestern Michigan community of Petoskey. There, they hired lumberjacks to clear some land near Gaylord, but an ulterior motive was to use the men's presence to beef up the population numbers. A vote of county residents, the majority of whom now lived in and around Gaylord, made the city the new county seat in 1878.

Another change in Gaylord about that time was its name. When it was first settled, the community was called Barnes, the last name of the man who originally platted the village. The name changed to Gaylord in 1874 in honor of a man who never even lived in the town. Augustine Gaylord was an attorney from the community of Saginaw, which is more than 100 miles to the southeast. His connection to Gaylord was through his law firm, Gaylord and Hanchett, which owned 40 acres near town (in what is now Hayes Township). He was also an attorney for the Jackson, Lansing and Saginaw Railroad that passed through town.

Between this Gaylord exit and the other to the north, a new freeway crossover is in the works. The crossover will provide an additional travel route to get from one side of the freeway to the other, and hopefully alleviate some of the congestion that sometimes occurs on the current crossovers.

For more on Gaylord, see exit 282.

South of Mile Marker 280

Watch for signs on both the northbound and southbound sides of I-75 that point out where it crosses the 45th parallel, which is the imaginary line of latitude that circles the globe at 45 degrees north of the Equator. Although this is often described as the halfway marker between the North Pole and the Equator, the actual halfway point is a few miles to the north. This is because the Earth is not perfectly round, but rather is just a bit flattened at the North and South Poles, and a bit wider in the middle at the Equator. As a result, the 45th parallel here is about 3,117 miles from the North Pole and 3,105 miles from the equator.

If you were to follow the 45th parallel around the world, it would pass through approximately the northern border of Vermont, northern Italy and southern France, northeastern China, then cross the Pacific Ocean to Oregon, and continue on through the twin cities of Minneapolis and St. Paul in Minnesota before reentering Michigan north of the Sleeping Bear Dunes National Lakeshore.

For those people who are star gazers, the parallel is interesting for another reason. The North Star appears directly above the North Pole, so from this point at the 45th parallel, it shines in the sky at an angle of 45 degrees above the horizon. (For more on the North Star and how to find it, see mile marker 241.)

see mile marker 241.

Mile Marker 281

One of the large buildings on the northbound side of I-75 is the Call of the Wild. This is not a tribute to the famous Jack London book, but a museum. It contains dioramas of dozens of animals mounted in lifelike poses, some of which are accompanied by recordings of their calls. Most of the displayed animals are Michigan natives, but the museum also has a few additions, including an 11-foot polar bear. The family-run museum has stood in the same spot for decades and holds fond memories for many a Michigan traveler who spent an afternoon there as a child.

Exit 282

This exit empties onto M-32, or Main Street, as it is known in the city of Gaylord. Main Street runs right through the downtown, which is done up with a Swiss alpine flair. The Otsego Club resort claims it set the precedent for the alpine-inspired architecture decades ago, and the town followed suit in the 1960s. This city of 3,700 goes beyond the architecture and holds an annual Alpenfest in July. The weeklong festival revs

up with the Burning of the Boogg. This is a tradition that is fashioned after part of a Swiss holiday in which residents say goodbye to winter by loading explosives into a Böögg (that's the traditional spelling), which is a model of a snowman, and then proceeding to light it up. Here in Gaylord, festival goers write down their troubles on a piece of paper, slip them

BRAINBUSTERS

The city of Alpena, which is the Ojibwe (Chippewa) word for partridge country, sits on the shore of Lake Huron about 70 miles east of Gaylord. Alpena is known for its diving, swimming and fishing. It is also known for a big construction industry: cement manufacturing.

Basic: People often say that streets and sidewalks are made of cement, but they're actually made of concrete. What's the difference between cement and concrete?

Intermediate: An hour or two after concrete is first poured, water sprinkled on the concrete will evaporate very quickly. Why?

Advanced: The Huron Portland Cement Co. started up operations just after the turn of the 20th century, and soon helped Alpena become the largest cement-producing center in the world. The presence of what resource made Alpena a good place to have a cement operation?

See page 188 for answers.

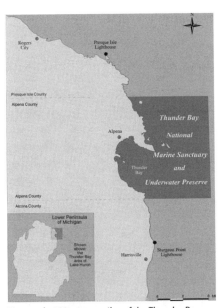

The nearly 450 square miles of the Thunder Bay National Marine Sanctuary and Underwater Preserve holds dozens of shipwrecks. (Map courtesy of the Thunder Bay National Marine Sanctuary and Underwater Preserve)

world's largest coffee break: Coffee, doughnuts and milk for everyone.

Besides the Alpenfest, Gaylord is home to the state's oldest triathlon, the Mark Mellon Memorial Triathlon, as well as the Starker -Mann Biathlon. The triathlon has been an annual summer event since 1981 and has swimming, biking and running components. The biathlon—Starker Mann means strong man— includes a 5k run, followed by a 30k road-bike or 20k mountain-bike ride, and finally another 5k run, much of the route over hilly terrain. Another annual Gaylord event is the Alpine Cup Snowmobile Grass Drag Races. For this event, snowmobilers literally drive on the grass at speeds that may exceed 100 miles an hour.

Exit 282

The highway that crosses here, M-32, reaches far beyond Gaylord. It stretches nearly to the Lake Michigan shoreline to the west, and reaches eastward to the city of Alpena (al-PEE-nuh) that sits on the Lake Huron shoreline. At a population of more than 11,000, Alpena is the second-largest city in the northern half of the Lower Peninsula. Alpena has several notable features, one of which is its location on Lake Huron's Thunder Bay. Vacationers flock to the area for swimming and fishing, and also for diving in the Thunder Bay National Marine Sanctuary and Underwater Preserve. Covering 448 square miles, the preserve is the only national freshwater sanctuary in the nation. It protects at least 30 known shipwrecks and probably more than

into the Boogg, and then watch as the Boogg is set on fire. After that, they can forget their cares—they did after all just go up in smoke—and enjoy the activities. Area businesses join in the fun and have their employees suit up Swiss-style for the week. For the men, this means wearing knee-high socks; a pair of shorts, called lederhosen that are held up with suspenders; and often a jaunty hat sometimes decorated with a little feather. Other highlights of the festival include a variety of parades, a men's knee contest, concerts and a whole range of alpine food, some of it modeled after food served in Gaylord's sister city in Switzerland: Pontresina. The Michigan festival also holds Die Groeste Kaffe Pause, which is billed as the

187

100 others. The high number of shipwrecks is the result of a combination of dangerously shallow and rocky underwater shoals in the bay, sudden and fierce gales that occur in the Great Lakes, and all-too-frequent banks of rolling fog that can cut visibility to just a few dozen feet. The shipwrecks in the preserve mainly rest entirely underwater, but here and there a ship's hull breaks the surface to provide an eerie sight.

Divers from all over the country come to Alpena to explore the shipwrecks. The *Montana* is an example. This 236-foot, wooden, steam-powered freighter had its start in Port Huron where it was built in

Exit 282

THE ANSWERS

Concrete is a *combination of sand, gravel, and crushed stone that are held together with the cement*. Cement is a *mineral powder* that acts as a binder. As concrete dries, or cures, it undergoes a *chemical reaction that gives off heat*. The heat is especially evident when a short rain shower sprinkles the top of freshly poured concrete and quickly evaporates. The heat can be substantial, and for this reason, large concrete pours require elaborate cooling measures to release the heat without damaging the curing concrete. Alpena was a good location for a cement operation because of the large deposits of *limestone* in the area. Limestone is a sedimentary rock made out of the remains of sea animals that died many millions of years ago.

1872. On Sept. 6. 1914, a crew of 14 were aboard the *Montana* in Thunder Bay when a fire broke out just before dawn. It spread fast, and the men had no choice but to abandon ship. The crew leapt into the yawl, a small boat at the rear of the ship, and drifted away from the *Montana*. As they did, the *Montana* quickly burned all the way down to the waterline. Both another nearby ship, as well as a life-saving boat on Thunder Bay Island noticed the burning hulk and set off to help. The crew of the life-saving boat arrived, but found only empty water and assumed the worst. Luck was with the *Montana's* crew that day, however, because the nearby ship, which was named the *Alpena*, had already reached the *Montana*, picked up her men and steamed off before the life-saving boat reached the scene. The *Montana* herself was not so fortunate. The boat sank in 75 feet of water, and she has remained there ever since. Divers often swim down to look at her engine, propeller and other machinery, which are still intact, and to take a few underwater photos.

Shipwrecks aren't the only items of note at the bottom of Lake Huron. An Ojibwe legend tells of "image stones" that are now deep in the water. According to the story, a chief promised that after he died, he would return to his people at the site of the two large stones, which were located on land at a river mouth just a few miles south of the present-day city of Alpena. In an act of aggression, other Indians kidnapped a few members of the tribe, stole the stones and set off into Lake Huron. The crime brought the wrath of the spirits. Before the band of thieves got very far, the spirits made the water boil. The thieves drowned, but the captives survived, and when they swam to shore and scrambled back onto land, they found the stones once again standing at the river's mouth. The stones are no longer there because, the story continues, a fisherman used them as weights for his net, and lost them when he cast the net into the lake. The stones are still at the bottom of the lake today. The Ojibwe word for the image stones, *wawsineke*, is still remembered in the name of a small community at the approximate site of the stones. That community's name is Ossineke.

North of Mile Marker 284

Parmater Road recalls an early area settler named Dr. N.L. Parmater. In 1873, Parmater along with his brother and several others were among the first settlers to come to the Gaylord area on the new railroad through the area.

Before these settlers could arrive, however, another pioneer had to pave the way. This was Alfred Dwight, who first set foot in the county in the 1860s when it was still nearly impassable backwoods. His journey to this part of the state had its start three decades earlier when he came to Michigan from New England in the year 1833. He was 22 years old. The trip took him seven days by steamboat, and his first stop was Detroit. He provided a very revealing description of Michigan in an 1898 book called *Lumber and Forest History of the Northwest*. This is how Dwight described Detroit as he stepped off the steamboat:

"I found a quaint old French city of about 3,000 inhabitants, without sidewalks, paving, sewerage, or any of the like modern appliances of civiliza-

---

BRAINBUSTERS

While Gaylord has a whopping average of 12.5 feet snow every year, some areas get even more. One of them is the Keweenaw Peninsula, which juts out from the western Upper Peninsula into Lake Superior. The average snowfall there tops 200 inches, but the record is nearly twice that: 391 inches—more than 32 feet—in the 1978-79 season. It is not uncommon for the Keweenaw town of Houghton to get new snow every day for a month or more. In 1984-85, snow fell for 51 days straight, but even that wasn't a record. One year in the 1930s, the town got new snow every day for three months!

Basic: A university in the U.P. town of Houghton has an Institute of Snow Research that studies such projects as how to make anti-icing coatings for roads and bridges, and how to build a runway of packed, hard snow at the South Pole. What is the name of the university?

Intermediate: In the winter, drivers in Houghton attach tall-poled flags to their cars. Why?

Advanced: If water is clear, why is snow white?

See next page for answers.

tion. Its water system consisted of barrels drawn by French ponies, and the water delivered at dwellings at 10 cents per barrel."

He portrayed the community as a wilderness that had only a few roads. These were called "military roads" because their purpose was to transport soldiers to mainly Indian skirmishes outside of town. Before too many such roads were laid, however, the U.S. Supreme Court put a halt to government-funded, road-building projects in Michigan, citing that the Constitution did not authorize the construction of military roads in times of peace. According to Dwight: "Denied the aid of the government, these hardy settlers opened highways, constructed ditches, laid out villages and organized townships, built schoolhouses and churches, cleared farms and organized government, and out of these incipient stages of pioneer existence, have raised up a great state . . . ."

While in Detroit, Dwight became involved in the lumbering industry, and in 1860 set his sights on this region of the state, which he portrayed as "practically unexplored." In 1866, he and two other partners formed this county's first business, a lumbering company. The company quickly bought 32,000 acres (50 square miles) of prime forest near Otsego Lake, which is located a few miles to the south of this spot on I-75. Through his efforts, the nearby Au Sable River was widened,

THE ANSWERS

The home of the Institute of Snow Research is *Michigan Technological University.*

Like other towns near Lake Superior and in the path of its lake-effect snow, the amount of snow is staggering. Snow can sometimes completely encase the entire first floor of houses, but residents make due by digging out a narrow path to the front door. Walls of snow along the sides of roads can easily reach 6 feet tall, which presents a problem at many intersections because the drivers cannot see if any cross traffic is approaching. Residents here have learned to deal with this, too. *To help alert other drivers to their presence, they frequently attach a long pole to their cars with a brightly colored flag at the top, hopefully high enough to peek out over the towering piles of snow!* Depending on the severity of the winter, the flags may stay on the cars for several months out of the year.

Snow is white because sunlight is white, and the snowflakes, which are actually crystals, reflect almost all of that sunlight. Most other things absorb certain wavelengths of the sunlight and reflect back other wavelengths , which makes them look blue or red or some other color. Some things are clear, like liquid water, because the sunlight can pass right through.

cleared, and dammed when necessary to allow the floating of logs to mills farther downstream. He was also the driving force behind the construction of a state road that connected Otsego Lake with Torch Lake on the far western side of the state. The new road brought goods as well as people to this region. With Dwight's operation in full swing and the area showing promise, railroads made their way to the area, and the development of the county began in earnest.

North of Mile Marker 287

Winters is an appropriate name for the road that passes over I-75 here. This part of the state is known as the snow belt because of the annual, large dumping of the white stuff every year. The average snowfall here is 150 inches—that's 12.5 feet! That compares to less than half that amount in the Houghton Lake area, which is just 50 miles to the south. The amazing difference is due to what is called the "lake effect," a term that comes up in just about every northern Michigan weathercast.

What is the lake effect? It starts with the Great Lakes waters, which are so expansive that they cool down and warm up very slowly compared to the air above them. The next ingredient is the winter winds that usually blow from the north or northwest. This means that the winds have to cross Lake Michigan before they strike the west side of northern Lower Michigan. As the winds move over the warmer water, they pick up both speed from the heat of the lakes and moisture in the form of water vapor. The water vapor freezes and continues to travel with the wind. Once the wind reaches the land, the water-vapor-turned-snow drops to the ground in certain patterns, or bands, that can reach 30 or 40 miles inland. The exact position of the bands varies based on wind direction, but very often a band unloads snow in this area.

Weathercasts here also distinguish lake-effect from system snow. System snow comes from an actual weather system, the same kind that makes snow in states that are far away from the Great Lakes. Meteorologists can usually predict system snow much

BRAINBUSTERS

Drivers on this stretch of I-75 may see both white-tailed deer and the much-larger elk along the sides of the road . . . and sometimes standing almost defiantly right *in* the road.

Basic: A male elk is called a bull. What is a female elk called? What are the correct terms for a male and female deer?

Intermediate: If a driver sees a deer run across the freeway just ahead and head off into a field, why should the driver slow down?

Advanced: Deer and elk are ruminants (ROOM-ih-nents), so they chew their cud. What is cud and why do they chew it?

See page 193 for answers.

White-tailed deer. (USFWS/Ryan Hagerty)

for more on Mackinaw City and Mackinac Island.)

North of Mile Marker 293

Touted as Michigan's only 19-hole golf course, the Black Bear course on the southbound side of I-75 does indeed have an extra hole. The extra, par-three hole is at the beginning of the course, and gives golfers a chance to warm up and get rid of any jitters before step-

Exit 290
MM 293

more easily than lake-effect snow, because a lake-effect squall can leave behind a foot or more of snow in one place, but barely a dusting just a few miles away.

Exit 290

Just off this exit and through the town of Vanderbilt passes the newly surfaced 62-mile trail that starts to the south in Gaylord and runs all the way to the "tip of the mitt," or the northern edge of the Lower Peninsula. The trail is covered with compacted limestone to provide a good surface for bicyclists, hikers and horseback riders. In the winter, it is also used for snowmobiling. Along its route, the trail passes through marshes, next to the Sturgeon River (see mile marker 297), by the inland Mullett Lake (see exit 313) and by Lake Huron, and through a number of northern Michigan towns, including Mackinaw City. At Mackinaw City, bikers and hikers can continue their journey by boarding a ferry to Mackinac Island. (See miles 335–343)

THE ANSWERS

A female elk is known as a *cow*. A male deer is a *buck*, and a female is a *doe*.

Drivers should be especially careful if they see a deer racing across the freeway because *deer often travel in groups and will follow one another*, even across a road. This is especially true of mothers and their fawns, and of males that will group together during all but the mating season.

Deer and elk are ruminants, which means that they have extra stomach chambers to help them digest the vegetation that they eat. These stomach chambers mix the food they swallow with a digestive juice called bile. The deer regurgitates *the partially processed food*, called cud, into the mouth to chew it and *break it down even further*. This process allows the deer and elk to get nutrients out of foods that other animals could not digest.

192

A bull elk. (Hal Korber/PGC Photo)

Elk are native to Michigan, but they died out back in 1875. Residents didn't forget the elk, however, and in 1918, seven Rocky Mountain elk from Wyoming were reintroduced near Wolverine, which is a community a few miles north. The elk survived very well, and within just five decades, the original seven-member herd had increased to 1,500 animals. The future looked rosy, but the herd suffered setbacks from both poaching and poor habitat, and their numbers plummeted to 200 by 1975. Michigan's residents again stepped up to the plate and fought for the elk. As habitat improved and poaching declined, the herd rebounded to 850 by 1984. The Department of Natural Resources now manages the herd, and allows limited hunting to keep the herd to about 800–900 animals, as counted each winter. Any more than that causes too much damage to the habitat, because the elk eat not only plants in the summer, but twigs and bark from living trees in the winter. In addition, a herd that is too large will also spread out to find food wherever it can, and that includes nearby farm fields.

ping up to the "real" first tee. Golfers then proceed around the course, keeping score at holes 2 through 19.

***

Signs along this part of the freeway note that this is elk-crossing area. The impressive animals here in northern Michigan make up the only elk herd east of the Mississippi. While most of them seem content to stay in and around the Pigeon River Country State Forest, which is located to the east, some of them do try to cross I-75.

Even people who have never seen an elk can easily identify one. For one thing, it's huge. An adult elk can be anywhere from 6.5–9 feet long and weigh 500–1,000 pounds. On top of that, males (bulls) have enormous, reindeer-style antlers that they regrow every year. The only other animal in northern Michigan that looks anything like an elk is a white-tailed deer, but they are much smaller, reaching 5–7 feet long and weighing 100–300 pounds as adults, and the male's antlers look puny compared to an elk's.

The Pigeon River Country State Forest remains one of the best places to see an elk…or to hear one. The bulls blare out with loud whistling grunts, known as bugles. They do it for a few reasons, but primarily to keep females close and ward off other males. A male may have several mates, which stay together in a harem. The male has to stay on guard to keep other males from infringing upon his harem, and the bugle is one way to remind the others who's in charge. The male also uses the bugle to round up his harem, and keep them nearby as the herd moves from one place to the next.

Brown trout. (NOAA/Great Lakes Environmental Research Laboratory)

South of Mile Marker 295

This is the border between Otsego County to the south and Cheboygan County to the north. Otsego County is named for a county in New York that was the previous home of some Michigan settlers. Otsego is an Ojibwe (Chippewa) word that may mean either "place of the rock" or "clear water." (For more on Otsego County, see mile marker 269.) The word Cheboygan also has an Ojibwe base, and its origin is in question, too. According to the book *Michigan Place Names*, it may be a combination of Cehboys, which was another name for the Ojibwe Indians, and the word *gan*, which means water. In other words, Cheboygan may mean "Ojibwe water," probably in reference to the large river that runs through the county. The book *Indian Names of Michigan* favors a translation to big pipe. The "che" comes from the end of the word *kitchi*, which means big, and "boygan" comes from the word *o-paw-gan* that means pipe. Finally, the book *Michigan Gazetteer* adds another option, which is "place of entrance." A similarly named city in Wisconsin, Sheboygan, provides no help either, because historians there are also unsure of its origin.

Cheboygan County continues from here north to the Mackinac Bridge that separates the Lower and Upper Peninsulas. The county holds two of the state's biggest inland lakes: Burt and Mullett, which are described at exits 310 and 313. Its northern edge runs along the shoreline of Lake Huron and the Straits of Mackinac.

Mile Marker 297

Running beneath the freeway here is the Sturgeon River, a fast-flowing waterway that attracts canoe and kayak paddlers, who can find particular challenges where the river makes sharp turns or flows past various obstacles. It is also a well-known trout stream that is unusual for a population of particularly hardy brown trout. Fisheries biologists are now testing the fish in the hopes of using them to stock other Michigan waterways.

The interest in the Sturgeon River brown trout arose when fisheries biologists noticed that one of the three main strains that they normally used for stocking was winding down. This is common in fish that are raised in hatcheries over many years—eventually inbreeding makes the fish less fit and their survival rate starts to drop off. The biologists started searching for a new strain, and focused on the Sturgeon River because its fish are particularly adaptable. Some of them live year-round in the river, but others live most of their lives in the adjacent Burt Lake and only swim upstream into the river for spawning runs. This ability to live in both lakes and streams made them an especially good contender for the next new strain.

In 2006, an army of biologists, technicians and fisheries assistants from the Michigan Department of Natural Resources arrived at the river to collect 1,250 brown trout of varying sizes to transfer to the Oden State Fish Hatchery in nearby Alanson (uh-LAN-sun). Since then, the fish have undergone a series of health inspections, and in the fall of 2007 were expected to begin spawning. Once that happens, biologists will collect their eggs and rear the young at the hatchery. After a few more rounds of health checks and spawnings, biologists hope to start stocking the rivers, streams and lakes of Michigan with fish from their newest hatchery strain: Sturgeon River brown trout. If all goes well, they estimate that the first stockings of the strain will occur in either 2012 or 2013.

MM 297

Exit 301

The community of Wolverine, just west of the freeway here, has the same name as both the state animal and the mascot of the University of Michigan. Strangely, however, wolverines are not common Michigan mammals, and some say they have never lived in the wild here. So what exactly is the connection between the wolverine and Michigan?

Several stories exist about how the state got associated with the ornery and ferocious wolverine, which is a member of the weasel family. According to one tale, the name originated in a Michigan tavern. As told in the book *Michigan Gazetteer*, when customers would order steaks or any other kind of meat, the tavern owner would stop by the table and jokingly ask how they liked their "wolf steaks." One day, a little girl answered him, "Then I suppose I am a Wolverine?" From then on, according to the story, the tavern's customers started going by the nickname wolverines, and it soon spread beyond that restaurant and to all Michigan residents. Other stories give credit to the American Indians here, who may have used it as a derogatory term for the newly arrived and swiftly expanding white settlers in the early to mid-1800s. The wolverine had a reputation as a particularly nasty beast that would take far more than it could use, and the native people may have viewed the influx of the settlers as having similar qualities.

Somehow, Michigan residents have become associated with this animal, the wolverine. (US Dept. of Interior, National Park Service, 1968)

Still others believe that the nickname comes from an actual wolverine population that lived in the Upper Peninsula, where it was trapped for the fur trade up until the late 1700s and possibly early 1800s. Unfortunately, no incontrovertible evidence is available to confirm the animals' presence here, so the argument rages. At present, the wolverine's range is primarily in far northern Canada, in Alaska and in a few northwestern states.

That said, however, a lone wolverine did make a stir in the state a few years ago. In the winter of 2004, hunters near the town of Ubly in Michigan's Thumb reported that they had seen one of the animals, which looks a bit like a 25–35 pound bear that moves like a weasel. Their sighting was followed by another—and a clear shapshot—by a wildlife biologist, who was able to positively confirm it as a wolverine. Since then, additional photos as well as video footage of apparently the same wolverine have surfaced in 2005 and 2006. The sightings did nothing to quell the mystery, though: Was it part of a small but

Lake sturgeon. (NOAA/Great Lakes Environmental Research Laboratory)

clandestine wolverine population in Michigan? Was it a lone animal that had crossed the ice of the frozen Lake Huron from Ontario, Canada? Was it an escapee from an exotic animal farm? Wildlife experts seem to favor the latter two explanations, but the jury is still out on the animal's origin.

— — —

The community of Wolverine here in northern Michigan got its start in the 1880s as a sawmill and station on the Michigan Central Railroad. In this part of the state at the time, the railroad's primary purpose was to haul lumber and supplies for lumber camps and sawmills. In the southern part of the state, however, it also had a busy passenger component, delivering people to and from Chicago, Detroit and other hubs. Michigan Central Railroad continued to expand its tracks, reaching 9,100 miles in 1910. The expansion ended by the 1920s when the favored mode of transportation shifted to the automobile.

Currently this approximately 360-resident village is known mainly for its location on the Sturgeon River and its annual Lumberjack Festival. (For more on the festival, see exit 173.) Anglers will no doubt be familiar with lake sturgeon, even if they have never caught one. The prized lake sturgeon has a shark-like appearance, but with rows of bony

plates beneath the skin that give its back and sides a jagged look. It can grow to be very large. The Michigan record lake sturgeon, caught in 1974 in the nearby Mullett Lake, was 7 feet 3 inches long and 193 pounds! Nowadays, sturgeon fishing is highly regulated. It is no longer allowed on Mullett Lake or on most lakes in the state. In fact, one of the few places where an angler can catch and keep them in the state is about 20 miles to the northeast on Black Lake. There, and only there, anglers can harvest the fish by spearing them, but only if they have a special tag. To distribute the limited number of tags, the Michigan Department of Natural Resources holds a lottery and 25 winners a day have a chance to spear sturgeon on the lake during a nine-day season. Once the lucky anglers have together taken a total of five sturgeon, the season closes—even if that happens on the very first day of the season—and sturgeon spearing is off-limits once again.

Mile Marker 304

Rondo Road crosses the freeway south of this mile marker. It leads to a one-time community and station on the Michigan Central Railroad. The station's name was Rondo.

Look on the southbound side of I-75 for one of the many quarries that show up along I-75 at various points along its route. Some of them are operations for collecting sand, while others are extracting types of rock. Two common types of quarry rocks in Michigan are sandstone and

Remnants of Fiborn Quarry and its surrounding community still stand near the town of Trout Lake in the eastern Upper Peninsula. This quarry, active from 1905–1935, mined limestone, most of which was used in steel-making. (Leslie Mertz)

limestone. Sand and sandstone are both important resources for making concrete, cement, plaster, glass, paints, abrasives and many other construction materials. Limestone is used for building materials, and as a source of lime, which is used to make mortar and cement, and also as a soil additive to correct excessive acidity.

The origin of sandstone and limestone in Michigan lies in ancient history. As mentioned elsewhere in this book, a shallow sea covered Michigan hundreds of millions of years ago. The sand at the bottom of the sea packed together over time and minerals settling out of the water cemented together the sand grains to form sandstone. Usually this sandstone is buried underground, but in some places in Michigan, the sandstone is revealed. This is true in the Pictured Rocks National Lakeshore, which lies along Lake Superior in the central Upper Peninsula. Forces of erosion from the lake have shaped the exposed sandstone there into majestic and amazingly colorful sculptures, like the 200-foot-tall Miners Castle, that draw visitors from around the country and around the world.

Like sandstone, limestone also has its basis in the shallow sea. While sandstone is compressed sand, limestone is the compressed skeletons of various sea animals, like corals, clams and snails, mixed with the remnants of algae and other marine plants. By the time these animals became incorporated into the limestone, most of the animal skeletons had decomposed into tiny bits, but some remained either in large chunks or whole. As a result, limestone often has fossils in it. Some common fossils in Michigan limestone include crinoids, which have the shape of a flat round bowl with a hole in the middle. Most of the crinoids are an inch in diameter or less. In some cases the bowl is clearly made up of six, hexagonal pieces that look almost like the

MM 305

This natural formation, called Miners Castle, stands majestically over the waters of Lake Superior. (Stephen Zaglaniczny)

called stromatoporoids (pronounced stroh-muh-TOP-er-oidz).

Mile Marker 305

Most people think very little about power lines until they have a power outage. The power lines and poles visible on the southbound side of the freeway are typical throughout the state (and elsewhere). This is how it works: A power plant creates energy through any of a number of methods, including burning coal or splitting uranium atoms (see information on nuclear power in the Brainbuster on page 12). The plant sends out the energy over high-voltage transmission lines. These transmission lines are carried on enormous steel structures or towers.

petals of a geometric flower. When these creatures were alive—most are long extinct—they had a flower-like appearance with a stalk that held the bowl-shaped portion up above the substrate. In addition, the "bowl" had a number of long and feathery tentacles, or arms, that floated back and forth in the water current. Depending on the species, it could have five tentacles or several dozen. Other common fossils in Michigan are various types of coral, including petoskey stones (see the Brainbuster on page 7 for details), ridged tubes that are the remains of creatures called cephalopods (pronounced CEFF-uh-low-podz), and thick, striped sheets of material that are left from much bigger sponges

BRAINBUSTERS

Everything is made of atoms, and all atoms are made of even smaller particles, some of which are called electrons. The electrons carry a tiny negative charge, and when enough of them move together in a current, they produce electricity.

Basic: Electricity can be either DC or AC. What do DC and AC stand for?

Intermediate: What is it about the movement of electrons that makes DC and AC electricity different?

Advanced: Why do many power poles carry four lines?

See page 202 for answers.

The high-voltage lines continue on to a power substation that takes the power down a notch so it can be carried safely as it continues its journey. After the substation, the power fans out through a series of insulation-wrapped electrical lines to homes and businesses. Where the lines pass a power pole, additional care is taken and spiral- or cup-shaped devices are used to connect the line to the arms of the pole. These are called insulators. Without them, power from the line could possibly find a route down the pole and into the ground, causing a hazard for people passing by. Once the electricity reaches your home, the power goes through a box-shaped transformer drum that dampens down the power so it doesn't fry your appliances.

Mile Marker 306-308

If you are heading northbound, you will see signs warning that this is a strong wind area. No such signs are on the southbound side. Look at both sides of the freeway and see if you can figure out why.

Give up? The southbound side is at a lower elevation and is therefore more protected from the gusts of wind that can cause a problem on the northbound side.

Exit 310

Indian River and Burt Lake State Park are just to the west of I-75. Indian River is a 2,000-resident community that sits at about the midway point on the Inland Waterway, a 45-mile chain of rivers and lakes that can take boaters almost from one side of the state to the other. It runs from Pickerel and Crooked Lakes, which are just east of Lake Michigan, all the way to Lake Huron. The community is named for one part of the Inland Waterway, the Indian River, that connects Burt Lake and Mullett Lake. Burt Lake is Michigan's third-largest lake, and Mullett is the state's and fifth-largest. The community of Indian River sits on the south shore of Burt Lake, and Mullett Lake is about 4 miles to the northeast. (For more on the Inland Waterway and Mullett Lake, see mile marker 312 and exit 313.)

Besides its place on the Inland Waterway and Burt Lake, the community of Indian River is known for "The Cross in the Woods," which is said to be the world's largest crucifix. The cross has its origins in the story of an Indian girl who lived in New York. Kateri Tekakwitha (pronounced kah-tah-LEE tay-kah-WEE-tha) was the daughter of a Mohawk chief and an Algonquin Indian woman who was also a Catholic. In 1660 when Tekakwitha was 4 years old, a small pox epidemic swept her New York village, and she lost both parents and her only brother to the disease. She survived her own bout with small pox, but she had lingering effects from the illness, including weakness, scars and partial blindness. Her poor vision even resulted in her name, Tekakwitha, which means "walking while feeling the way." Now orphaned, the young girl went to live with two aunts and an uncle. Her life was similar to that of the other children until a Jesuit missionary set up a chapel nearby. Through the missionary's work, Tekakwitha recalled her own mother's religious teachings and decided to take up the Catholic faith. This did not sit well with her tribe, however, so she ran away. Despite her poor health and vision limitations, Tekakwitha traveled more than 200 miles to reach a Catholic mission in Montreal. She worked at the mission and, in her spare time, made small wooden crosses that she set up in the woods to remind her to take time for prayer. Her failing health caught up with her in 1680, and at just 24 years old, she died.

The Catholic Church didn't forget Tekakwitha, and in 1943, it took the first step toward making her a saint and declared her "venerable," which means that she is a role model of Catholic virtues. This served as the inspiration for Rev. Charles D. Brophy who wanted to remember her faith with another cross, and this idea led to the "Cross in the Woods"

THE ANSWERS

DC is short for *direct current*, and AC is short for *alternating current*.

In DC, the type of electricity in batteries, electrons all move in one direction in a nice, steady flow from the negative terminal on the battery to the positive, so direct current is an appropriate name. *In AC, electrons alternate: They bounce back and forth from negative to positive many times a second.* At the top and bottom of each bounce, they produce maximum power.

Many electrical power poles are strung with four lines, called distribution lines. *One of them is the neutral or ground line that completes the electrical circuit and shunts electrons into the ground, or earth. The other three lines carry slightly different "phases" of AC power.* This means that the bouncing electrons in one line are in sync—they all move together, so they produce maximum power at the same time. The timing of the bouncing electrons in the second line is slightly offset from the timing in the first line, and also offset from the timing in the third line. In other words, each of the three lines is achieving maximum power at ever-so-slightly different times. The average household appliance runs perfectly well on only one phase, but certain industrial motors and other types of power equipment need a consistent flow of maximum power. With three phases hitting their peaks at slightly offset times, this system can provide it. This is why power poles near factories often have four lines, while poles near houses often have only two (a ground and a line carrying one phase of AC power). In addition, towers leading from power generating plants typically have four lines, or two sets of four lines that eventually go to distribution points, called substations, where the power is divvied up and run to homes and businesses.

in an outdoor sanctuary near here in Indian River. A sculptor carved a seven-ton bronze sculpture of Christ, which hangs on a cross made from a redwood tree. The cross, which is 55 feet tall and 22 feet wide, has been standing here since 1954.

Since then, the Catholic Church has taken another step toward canonizing Tekakwitha as a saint. In 1980, Pope John Paul II beatified her. As a result, Tekakwitha is now known as a "blessed." The final step in the sainthood process is for the church to verify a posthumous miracle.

Thousands of people visit the "National Shrine of the Cross in the Woods" to see the crucifix, a separate statue of Tekakwitha and the grounds, and to participate in the year-round religious services.

The "National Shrine of the Cross in the Woods" in northern Michigan pays tribute to Kateri Tekakwitha, a Mohawk-Algonquin Indian girl who may one day become a saint. This statue of Tekakwitha stands in New Mexico. (Einar Einarsson Kvaran)

Another major attraction here is the Burt Lake State Park, a 400-acre, 306-campsite park on the shores of both Burt Lake and the Sturgeon River. Big draws are swimming and sunbathing along the 2,000-foot, sandy beach, and fishing in the lake. Other people select this as a good base camp from which they can visit towns on either Lake Michigan to the west or Lake Huron to the east, or head up to tourist destinations like Mackinac (pronounced MACK-ih-naw) Island and Fort Michilimackinac (pronounced mish-ill-ih-MACK-ih-naw) to the north.

Burt Lake's namesake is William Burt, an interesting man who lived the first half of his life in Massachusetts, and the second half in

Michigan. He came to the Michigan territory in 1824 when he was in his 30s. This was more than a decade before Michigan would become a state. Burt set about building his reputation as a solid citizen. He served a short stint on the Michigan territorial legislature, and became involved locally as postmaster and as a judge in and around his community of Mount Vernon, which is north of Detroit. He also spent time as an inventor, and in 1829 developed a machine called a typographer, which was a predecessor to the typewriter. In 1833, he had a chance to make a big contribution to his adoptive state by working here as a surveyor. The job involved traveling into the still-mysterious woodlands of the northern Lower Peninsula and Upper Peninsula, and dividing it into townships that could be further subdivided into identifiable parcels, which could then be bought and sold. Burt's first assignment was in Sanilac County in Michigan's Thumb, an area that at the time was covered with swamps that not only soaked Burt and his crew, but also bred an all-too-healthy population of mosquitoes.

Once he finished this first job, he got other assignments farther north, where he came across an odd problem. The compasses the surveyors used would give incorrect readings because they were keying in on the magnetic pull of the minerals in the area rather than the Earth's magnetic field. Burt found a novel way around the problem. He put his inventing skills to work and designed a solar compass that used the sun rather than the magnetic field to obtain accurate readings. The compass was so successful that other surveyors embraced it, and soon the federal government adopted it for its survey work, too.

One of Burt's most important tasks as a surveyor was to extend the principal meridian through the Upper Peninsula. The principal meridian is a north-south line that is used as a foundation for determining all other lines in a large region. The principal meridian had already been set in the Lower Peninsula, but Burt had to extend it across the Straits of Mackinac, through the difficult wilderness of the eastern Upper Peninsula and to Lake Superior. While

he was continuing survey work in the Upper Peninsula, Burt and his crew became the first to discover iron ore there. Soon, Michigan became the top iron-ore producer in the nation and remained so for about 60 years.

Burt stayed on as a surveyor for two decades, much of it spent trekking through land that was known only to a scattering of American Indians and perhaps a few French fur trappers.

Despite the challenges Burt faced—1) compasses the gave wild readings, 2) solar compasses that were less than satisfactory on cloudy days or in thick forests, 3) rugged terrain made more difficult by biting flies and mosquitoes, and 4) very long days in the field—his original surveys have stood the test of time. Even with the most modern and precise equipment available, surveyors today still find that Burt's lines are highly accurate. Such lines are used as the basis for identifying the boundaries for every parcel of property in Michigan (and elsewhere).

Mile Marker 311

On the northbound side of the freeway is the Calvin Campbell Municipal Airport, a small public facility. At the northern end of the airport is Onaway (pronounced ON-uh-way) Road. Onaway Road continues west and then south to meet up with another road that heads into the community of Onaway, a one-time sawmilling center. Some have said Onaway means awake, probably because of Longfellow's Hia-

The Cheboygan River, shown here passing through the city of Cheboygan, is part of the inland waterway (also known as the intercoastal waterway or inland water route). The waterway consists of a series of streams and lakes in northern Michigan that forms a navigable route for small craft connecting Lake Huron and Lake Michigan.

watha poem lines: "Onaway! Awake, beloved! Thou the wild-flower of the forest!" That doesn't seem to square with Ojibwe (Chippewa) Indian language, however. The poem may not have meant that the two successive words had the same meaning, as had been thought, but rather that Onaway was the name of an Ojibwe woman.

Mile Marker 312

The Indian River crosses I-75 a bit south of mile marker 312. Just beyond the freeway on both sides, the river widens out considerably making it an ideal water link for boaters moving between Burt Lake and Mullett Lake. The river connects to Burt Lake at its southeastern tip, and to Mullett Lake at its southwestern edge. The river here is part of the inland water-

way, sometimes called the intercoastal waterway, that starts in Pickerel Lake and Crooked Lake just to the east of Lake Michigan, then continues along the Crooked River until it meets Burt Lake on its western shore. Boaters can continue through Burt Lake to the Indian River and take it to Mullett Lake, exit at Mullett's northern shore into the Cheboygan (pronounced sheh-BOY-gen) River and take that river all the way up to the Straits of Mackinac.

The waterway can handle boats up to 60 feet long. To make the entire route, boats must clear two bridges—one at 20 feet in height and the other at 16.7 feet—and maneuver through two locks: one on the Crooked River and one on the Cheboygan River. The locks are necessary because the land is higher on one side of the river than

205

it is on the other. Without the locks, the water would tumble down the river resulting in dangerous rapids. The locks ease the transition by serving as a water "elevator": Boats enter a lock much as a person walks into an elevator, and reach the appropriate level as water inside the lock rises and lowers. The lock on the Cheboygan River dates back to 1869, when the Cheboygan Slack Water Navigation Co. ran a passenger and freight service on the water. As tourism blossomed in northern Michigan, visitors to the area would buy seats on the passenger boats for daylong trips on the waterway. Nowadays, the waterway is heavily used by recreational boaters.

BRAINBUSTERS

Exit 313

From 1944 to 2006, the U.S. Coast Guard cutter called the *Mackinaw* chugged through the waters of the Great Lakes, and had its home port in Cheboygan. Drivers and passengers crossing the Mackinac Bridge between the Upper and Lower Peninsulas often saw the large red-and-white ship passing under the bridge on its way from Lake Michigan to Lake Huron and back, and in the winter, would sometimes spot a freighter following right behind it.

Basic: What was the 290-foot-long *Mackinaw's* main job in the winter?

Intermediate: The *Mackinaw* had propeller at the bow of the boat. Twelve-feet-in-diameter, the propeller was helpful for the cutter's winter job. What was the propeller's main purpose?

Advanced: Among the specifications for the *Mackinaw* are a draft of 19 feet 2 inches and a standard displacement (or weight) of 5,252 pounds. What does "draft" mean, and how is a ship weighed?

See page 208 for answers.

Exit 313

The town of Topinabee (pronounced TOP-in-uh-bee) is about a mile to the southeast on the western shore of Mullett Lake. It is rather unusual because it didn't start out as a logging center, like so many other communities here did. Instead, it originated in 1881 as a tourist destination planned by officials at Michigan Central Railroad, who were well aware that the logging industry would be winding down over the next couple of decades as the forests fell to the lumberjacks' axes and saws. For the lumber companies, this simply meant pulling up stakes and moving to another state. The railroads, however, had a huge investment in their tracks and wanted to keep the trains running. Fortunately, another industry was blossoming, and this was tourism. People from southern Michigan and other nearby states had heard about the beauty of northern Michigan's multitude of inland lakes and started to consider vacations there. The railroad was a good way, and often the only way, to reach Michigan's interior. Michigan Central's railroad officials knew a good opportunity when they saw it, and planned Topinabee as a resort town.

Topinabee is named for a powerful Potawatomi (pronounced pot-uh-WOTT-oh-mee) chief who lived with his band in extreme southwestern Michigan (where some streets now carry his name). The chief's name is sometimes spelled Topenebee, Thupenebu or other variations, and likewise has alternative translations, including "Quiet Sitting Bear," "Great Bear Heart" and "Peacemaker." Topinabee was involved in treaty talks from the late 1700s to the 1830s. At first, he fought against the loss of Indian land, but later gave in to pressures from the American government and its military, and signed numerous treaties that relinquished land. One of those treaties ceded the land at the site of Fort Dearborn, which is present-day Chicago. As time passed, many American Indians abandoned Michigan for parts west, but Topinabee stayed on in southwestern Michigan, at one point living on a small reservation there on the St. Joseph River.

Topinabee is on the western shore of Mullett Lake, the fifth largest inland lake in Michigan. Like Burt Lake just to the west, it is named for a surveyor. In fact, John Mullett and William Burt together conducted the initial survey and set up the township lines in this area in 1840. Mullett and Burt didn't always work together. While Burt spent a great deal of his time in the Upper Peninsula, Mullett did a good portion of his surveying work in Wisconsin and in the Lower Peninsula.

Like Burt, he faced many obstacles, and on one occasion two of the men from Mullett's survey crew got in a horrible fight with two armed Indians (probably Potawatomi) in southern Michigan. The clash left both Indians dead and the two crewmen so distraught that they promptly resigned from their jobs. Since that time, the place of the fight has been known as Battle Creek.

Both Burt and Mullett lakes are about 10 miles long, but Burt Lake is wider, covering 17,300 acres to Mullett's 16,700 acres. By comparison, Burt Lake is about 15,700 football fields in size (not counting the end zones), and Mullett is about 500 football fields smaller. Mullett is considerably deeper than Burt, however, with a maximum depth of more than 140 feet. Burt reaches about half that.

Just as Burt Lake has a state park, Mullett has one, too. The name of Mullett's state park and a community there are Aloha, which seems a bit out of place here in northern Michigan. Once you know the story, however, it makes some sense. Like so many other towns in this part of the state, Aloha has a tie to the lumbering industry. According to the book *Michigan Place Names*, a local sawmill owner named James Patterson had made a trip to Hawaii back around the turn of the 20th century and recalled the trip by naming the town Aloha, which is a greeting in Hawaii. The state park is named after the town.

Mile Marker 317

The rest area here on the northbound side of I-75 has a scenic turnout that affords views of the countryside. The views are only available for part of the year however, because this is one of the rest areas in the state that the Michigan Department of Transportation closes in the winter months.

Rest areas like this one are common on highways throughout the state. Michigan was, in fact, the first state to develop a roadside park for travelers' use. That happened back in the early 1900s on U.S. 2 in Iron

THE ANSWERS

MM 317

The *Mackinaw* was an icebreaker. In the winter, it plied the Straits of Mackinac, a narrowing between Lakes Michigan and Huron, *to break up the ice so freighters following behind could make the passage.* During its six decades of service, it was the largest Coast Guard icebreaker stationed year-round on the Great Lakes. It is now moored in Mackinaw City, where it serves as a museum.

To accomplish its task, the *Mackinaw* used a 7.2-ton propeller on the bow *to pull water from underneath the ice up ahead and push the water back along the sides of the ship's hull.* Without the buoyancy of the water, the ice would sag and break up more easily as the ship's steel hull plowed into it. In addition, the water flow on sides of the ship served as a buffer of sorts to help to keep the ice away from the hull as the ship chugged through it. Besides this propeller, the *Mackinaw* also had a system in place that allowed it to slosh ballast water rapidly from one side of the ship to the other, and in so doing rock the ship. This maneuver was useful on those occasions when even the *Mackinaw* got stuck in thick ice. The rocking motion is called heeling, so the system is called a heeling system.

The standard displacement of a ship is its weight when fully manned, equipped and stocked, but not counting the fuel. To determine the standard displacement, the ship is not weighed on a scale. Rather, *its weight is determined by this formula:*

[the volume of the portion of the ship that is below the surface of the water] x [the density of the water, which in the case of freshwater is about 62.4 pounds per cubic foot]

In other words, a ship weighs as much as the water it displaces, so it is called the standard displacement. The draft is *the vertical distance from the waterline down to the bottom of the hull.* This is an important measurement when a boat is cruising through shallow waters or over underwater obstacles that jut high into the water column.

With the decommissioning of the original *Mackinaw*, the Coast Guard continued its icebreaking and other operations with a new 240-foot-long cutter, which has also been named the *Mackinaw*. The new *Mackinaw* is stationed at Cheboygan, and like its predecessor spends much of its winters crushing ice.

County, which is in the southwestern Upper Peninsula. There, the head of the local highway department had the idea for a park with tables and grills after he had trouble finding a spot to picnic one afternoon. He spearheaded a campaign, worked out the details, and watched as the park opened in 1918. Everyone loved it. Word about the park spread fast, and soon Michigan had many other roadside parks. Today, the Michigan Department of Transportation operates 81 rest areas throughout the state.

Mile Marker 318–319

Part of the Mackinaw State Forest lies to the east of the freeway here. It is a small part. In its entirety, the forest includes 660,000 acres—an area about two-thirds the size of Rhode Island—that cover considerable spans of land within the northern tip of Lower Peninsula. The section next to the freeway here is only a little bigger than a square mile in total size.

Mile Marker 319

For many years, a billboard stood on the side of the freeway about a half mile north of this mile marker, and the remnants of the billboard may still be visible on the northbound side. It advertised a Stuckey's store, one of a chain of roadside stores that were favorite stopping points a few decades ago for travelers looking for a pecan log roll or other treat. No Stuckey's stores are in Michigan anymore, but the chain still has shops in other states.

This stretch of the freeway is notorious in the winter for winds that sweep in from the north and west, and blow swaths of snow from adjacent land onto the road. As a result, drivers may encounter sudden, deep drifts in their paths. To compound the problem, this area is also prone to bands of lake-effect snow (see mile marker 287). These bands can be quite narrow, so drivers may find sunshine and clear roads alternating with dark gray skies and blizzard conditions. Winter drivers are wise to focus on the road and be prepared for swiftly changing conditions.

Mile Marker 321

Two miles to the west (southbound side of I-75) is the University of Michigan Biological Station, which is situated on the southern side of 4-mile-long-by-2-mile-wide Douglas Lake. The station opened in 1909. If that seems like an awfully long time ago, consider that the University of Michigan itself is the Michigan's oldest university and has been in existence since 1817, about two decades before Michigan had even become a state!

The biological station is set up like a small town with 70 one-room cabins, 30 larger cabins, a 14-room dormitory, a large dining hall capable of holding almost 300 people, a fully-stocked library, lecture hall, 100-foot and 150-foot towers to make meteorological and environmental measurements, a greenhouse, and an auditorium. A highlight is its 24,000-square-foot laboratory building complete with all manner of equipment and an attached boathouse that has direct access to the lake.

More than 100 college students arrive at the station each year for its four-week and eight-week spring and summer courses. The station faculty also offer weeklong mini-courses to the public. Mini-courses may include such topics as Michigan birds, plants,

nature photography or outdoor activities for kids.

Besides the classes, faculty and other scientists come to the station to conduct studies on everything from predator-prey relationships and preferred fish habitat to the effect introduced species have on native organisms, and the impact of elevated carbon dioxide levels (a greenhouse gas) on plants and on the animals that eat them. In all, researchers there publish two dozen or more scientific papers every year.

Exit 322

BRAINBUSTERS

At the University of Michigan Biological Station (UMBS) on Douglas Lake, more than 100 college students take a variety of nature-oriented courses every spring and summer.

Basic: One of the courses the UMBS frequently offers is mammalogy (pronounced mam-AHL-oh-gee), which is the study of mammals. Which of the following Michigan animals are mammals: bullfrogs, owls, mice, skunks, lizards and/or deer? What kind of an animal is a whale?

Intermediate: Other courses frequently offered at UMBS include botany, ornithology (pronounced or-nith-AHL-oh-gee) and entomology (pronounced en-toh-MAHL-oh-gee). What do these cover?

Advanced: What are these fields: malacology (pronounced mal-ah-CAHL-oh-gee), phycology (pronounced fie-CAHL-oh-gee) and herpetology (pronounced her-pet-AHL-oh-gee)?

See page 212 for answers.

Exit 322

On the northbound side of the freeway is a propane dealership. Here in northern Michigan, homeowners often do not have access to natural gas lines like people in urban areas do. As a result, they must find other ways to heat their homes and their water. Some use wood and electricity, but many rely on propane. This is the same propane that people may use in portable grills.

Propane is a colorless, odorless gas that occurs naturally on Earth by the same processes that make crude oil and gasoline. All of them result when organic matter, such as dead plants and animals, decomposes over vast periods of time. Propane gas is separated out from the gasoline, oil and other hydrocarbons, and refined to make it pure. It is then put under pressure to turn it into a liquid. This is an important step, because the liquid takes up far less room than the gas. A quantity of liquid propane takes up about 1/270th the space it would if it were a gas. This makes liquid propane easy to transport.

A homeowner typically has an above-ground, cylindrical storage tank near the house, and a propane truck arrives periodically to fill the tank, which is called a pig. A typical pig holds 500 gallons, and homeowners generally need refills several times a year.

— — —

This exit, Riggsville Road, leads to the tiny burg of Riggsville, which is about a half mile to the southeast, and to the much larger town of Pellston, which is about 8 miles to the west. Pellston is home to a regional airport that has a beautiful, new terminal centered with a massive, stone fireplace. Its commercial flights mainly run to and from Detroit Metropolitan Airport, where passengers can connect to other locations.

Mile Marker 325

A number of Christmas tree farms dot the sides of I-75 and other highways in Michigan. This state is one of the top producers of Christmas trees. According to the National Christmas Tree Association, Michigan placed second out of all states for the number of acres—60,520—planted with Christmas trees as of 2002. Only one state surpasses Michigan in acres planted, and that's Oregon at 67,800 acres. Michigan does top Oregon, and indeed all other states, in the number of varieties of Christmas trees grown commercially: 13! One of the most common Christmas trees planted in this state is the Scotch pine (some-

times called a Scot's pine). Introduced to the United States from Europe and Asia, the Scotch pine is very popular among consumers because of its full branches, the deep green color of its needles, its persistent piney scent and its ability to hold onto its needles for a long time after it's been cut down. Even when it's dry, the Scotch pine doesn't drop its needles as readily as other trees—a definite benefit when it comes to hauling the tree out of the house in January.

The Christmas tree industry is as trendy as any other, and one type of tree that is currently increasing in popularity for the holidays is the Fraser fir, a native of the eastern United States. It has stiff, neat branches decked out with sprays of short needles. Fortunately for Michigan tree farmers, its ability to grow well on sandy soils makes it a good choice for northern Michigan farms.

Exit 326

If you've been watching the sides of the freeway, you have probably seen at least one sign for Sea Shell City or its man-killing giant clam. Sea Shell City is just off this exit on the northbound side of the freeway. Exactly why ocean goods are attractive to tourists traveling through a freshwater state is anyone's guess, but this shop has survived in this spot since the 1950s and draws thousands of visitors, many of them second- and third-generation customers.

— — —

The road crossing the freeway here is County Road 66, also known as Levering Road to the west and Cheboygan (pronounced sheh-BOY-gen) Road to the east. Levering (pronounced LEV-er-ing) Road leads to the small community of Levering, a one-time railroad way station, about 7 miles to the west. (Way stations were stopping points between larger stations.) Continuing west another

---

THE ANSWERS

Exit 326

Mammals are animals that have the following characteristics: hair or fur on the body, milk glands (also known as mammary glands) and warm-bloodedness, which means that their body temperature remains fairly constant regardless of the temperature outside. Of the list, *mice, skunks and deer are all mammals*. In addition, *whales are mammals*, too, because they have a tiny bit of hair in the form of bristles, usually on the head; they are warm-blooded (and stay warm thanks in part to their thick layer of blubber); and the young suckle milk from their mothers' milk glands.

Botany, ornithology and entomology are the studies of plants, birds and insects, respectively.

Malacology delves into mollusks, such as clams. Phycology is the study of algae and blue-green algae (also known as cyanobacteria). Herpetology covers both amphibians (like frogs and salamanders) *and reptiles* (such as turtles, snakes and lizards).

13 miles from Levering is Cross Village, which is on the shore of Lake Michigan. Cross Village and the adjacent Bliss Township are interesting to birders because they are home to some of the few piping plovers (pronounced PLO-verz) in Michigan. In 2004, nine pairs of the small birds nested here. That may seem like a low number, but those nine pairs represented 16 percent of all known piping plover pairs in the entire state. A piping plover is a sandy-brown bird with a white underside and white ring at its neck. Adults also have a black blotch on the forehead and a black neck ring. Sometimes people mistake them for a similar-looking bird called a killdeer, but the plover's long legs give them away. Plover legs have a characteristically striking yellowish-orange color. Unlike killdeer, which may live quite far inland, piping plovers are mainly shore birds that run in fits and starts along beaches of the Great Lakes. They get their name from the high-pitched whistling, or piping, call they make.

Although this bird was once quite common on all of the Great Lakes beaches in Michigan, it is now an endangered species. The numbers underwent a particularly steep decline in the 1880s. The birds' small size apparently made them enticing targets for shooting practice. In addition, people hunted the birds for their feathers and for food, although plovers carry very little meat on their bones. Legislation put a stop to the hunting in the early 1900s, and the birds started to recover but never regained their previous abundance.

The killdeer (shown here) is sometimes confused for the much rarer piping plover. (Alan D. Wilson, 2007)

Exit 326

Efforts are under way to protect the piping plover, an endangered species. (USFWS/Gene Nieminen)

A big part of the reason is that more and more people started going to Great Lakes beaches for recreation. Human visitors to the beaches inadvertently disturbed the birds while they were breeding; built homes or cleared vegetation from the places where the birds bred; brought cats and dogs that chased the birds or ate their eggs; and accidentally stepped on the birds' nests and eggs. The latter was easy to do because the nests are little more than pebble-lined or driftwood-lined depressions in the sand, and their eggs have camouflage colors that make them all but invisible.

In 1986, the government listed the piping plover as an endangered species. Now, people who kill, harm or even harass the birds—intentionally or not—can face penalties of up to $100,000. If you are in or near piping plover habitat, the U.S. Fish and Wildlife Service offers this advice: 1) Keep your pets off of the beaches; 2) If you see plover, view them and their nests only from a distance; 3) Stay out of posted or fenced areas. These rules are especially important during

the bird's breeding season, which runs from late April to early May.

Cross Village isn't only interesting for its piping plovers. As far back as the 1700s, this region was known as L'Arbre Croche, which is French for "the crooked tree," apparently in reference to the shape of a certain pine tree. A band of Ottawa Indians lived there, mixing hunting and fishing with corn farming. Jesuit missionaries arrived in the 1800s and built a cross at the site. At that point, the Indians began calling the area Anamiewatigoing, which means "at the cross," and the French used La Croix, which also means "the cross." In 1875, the name was translated to English as Cross Village and has remained that way ever since.

Bois Blanc Island Lighthouse looks out over the Straits of Mackinac. (Carl Ter Haar)

Exit 326

Off to the east of the freeway, Cheboygan Road takes travelers the 7- to 8-mile distance to the city of Cheboygan, a 5,300-resident community on the Straits of Mackinac, the waterway that connects Lake Huron to the east with Lake Michigan to the west. A testament to the town's place in history is the presence of a restored opera house downtown. Originally built in 1877, the Cheboygan Opera House has remained part of the community despite two fires in 1888 and 1903 that burned it down, and a two-decade period in the 1960s and 1970s when it remained closed and in disrepair. It reopened in 1984, revitalized and renovated, and still operates today.

Another attraction for residents and visitors alike is the 40-minute ferryboat trip across the Straits of Mackinac to Bois Blanc (correctly pronounced BAH-blo, but sometimes locally pronounced as boyz blahnk) Island. This is not to be confused with the one-time amusement park of the same name (Bois Blanc or Boblo) located in Canadian waters of the Detroit River south of the city of Detroit. Bois Blanc Island here in northern Michigan is a large island about 11.5 miles long and 4.5 miles wide. Bois Blanc is French for white wood, probably named for the basswood on the island. Basswood is a tall tree with leaves shaped like lopsided hearts that have one lobe larger than the other. Basswood has light- or white-colored, soft and easy-to-carve wood. Some people know the tree as American linden. The name of the island likely came from the French voyageurs, a group of adventuresome men who plied Michigan waters in giant-sized canoes that were up to 36 feet long and 6 feet wide. The men would stop along shore, trading blankets, knives and other goods for furs provided by American Indians. The voyageurs, a word that means "travelers," would then heap a large payload of furs into the canoe, which was big enough to carry not only the cargo, but also eight or 10 men and all their provisions.

Today, Bois Blanc is an ideal place for people who want to get away from it all, since its 24,000 acres are mainly state land cut only occasionally by dirt roads and sprinkled infrequently with private summer cottages and year-round residences. Swimming, fishing, biking and hiking are popular activities. Camping is allowed on Bois Blanc, but it does not have campgrounds or any park facilities, so the camping is primitive. For those who do not like things quite so rustic, a limited number of rental cabins are available. The island also has a single

---

BRAINBUSTERS

River otters grow to about 3–4 feet long, while minks reach about 2 feet long. Minks live throughout the state, and river otters nearly do, except for the state's far southern reaches and the Thumb of the Lower Peninsula.

Basic: Both of these two animals are members of what family of mammals: the raccoon family, the weasel family, the rodent family or the dog family?

Intermediate: River otters are known as playful animals that people sometimes see repeatedly climbing up and sliding down slippery rocks or river banks to land with a splash in the water, or skidding along the snow- or ice-covered ground. They are also fast swimmers. Like other mammals, a river otter cannot breathe underwater, so it has to hold its breath. How long can a river otter stay underwater: 3 minutes, 8 minutes, 13 minutes or 18 minutes?

Advanced: During the summer, the mink is a predator that mainly hunts and eats crayfish. In the winter, its diet switches mainly to one type of mammal. What is it: mice, rats, shrews or muskrats?

See page 217 for answers.

general store, which has the island's only gas pump.

Mile Marker 327

Marshy and swampy areas are typical in much of northern Michigan. The wet area here along I-75 surrounds Mud Creek, a small waterway that eventually connects with Lake Paradise about 5 miles to the northwest. This habitat is specially conducive to such mammals as beavers, river otters and minks, and all were important to the vigorous fur-trapping and -trading industry in Michigan from the 1600s though the early 1800s. The demand for fur at that time came from Europeans, and they especially desired beaver pelts, which are extremely soft once the coarser outer hairs, or guard hairs, are removed. They used the pelts to make hats. These hats were so fashionable and so popular that trappers in western Europe and Russia had nearly gone through their combined beaver populations by the late 1500s. Beaver were in good supply in North America, however, so the rush was on.

The process of making a beaver pelt into a hat had several steps, one of them very dangerous. The first step was to remove the guard hairs. Hatters could buy the pelt and yank out the hairs from the pelt with a knife or a pair of tweezers; or buy the pelt with the guard hairs already removed. These pelts, called *castor gras* or coat pelts, came from American Indians, who had worn them as coats or other clothing and worn off the guard hairs. By wearing the pelts, their body oils

River otters are found in and near rivers, lakes and wetlands in Michigan. (USFWS/Dave Menke)

had also softened them. The next step was to brush on a solution to mat the remaining hairs, which are collectively called wool. This process, called carroting, turned the wool an orange-red color. The hatter then dried the pelt, shaved off the wool and used a complex procedure to press the shaved wool together to make the felt that would eventually become the hat. The solution in the carroting process was the dangerous part of the procedure, because it contained mercury, a poison that attacks the nervous system. As the pelt dried, the mercury in the solution would become airborne and the hatter would inhale it. Mercury accumulates in the body, and after a while, the hatter would start to have symptoms, like uncontrollable muscle twitches followed by problems walking, talking and finally thinking. Many of them died.

People began to notice a connection between the symptoms and individuals in the hat profession, and began to describe anyone who had a mental problem as being "mad as a hatter." It wasn't until well into the

20th century that hatters started to use new methods of making felt that didn't include mercury.

During the fur-trading heyday in Michigan, mink and river otter never had the stature that beaver did. Mink and otter fur would occasionally show up on a coat collar or cuff, but more as a fashion novelty than a fashion statement. That changed in the mid-1900s, and mink became one of the most highly sought-after furs. Mink and otter are still highly prized among some segments of the fashion industry.

Despite the past hunting and trapping pressure on beaver, river otter and mink, Michigan still has healthy populations of all three mammals. Part of the reason is that the Michigan Department of Natural Resources regulates the hunting and trapping of furbearing mammals, which helps to ensure that they aren't over-harvested.

Mile Marker 333

Periodically, signs along the sides of the freeway announce the Adopt-A-Highway program. Run by the Michigan Department of Transportation (MDOT), this program helps keep highway roadsides clear of litter by seeking volunteers to collect trash. Typically, an organization selects a stretch of road, usually at least 2 miles long, and picks up litter along that distance at least three times a year. Scout groups, community organizations, social clubs and other groups can adopt a piece of highway through this program. Every participating group gets safety vests and trash bags from MDOT, which arranges to pick up the filled bags after the clean-up. The volunteering group also gets a certificate for its hard work. About 3,000 groups participate, and beautify nearly 7,000 miles of highway within the state.

If you are heading north on a clear day, you can look ahead in the distance to see the Mackinac Bridge, which crosses the Straits of Mackinac and connects Lower and Upper Peninsulas. The bridge opened to traffic on Nov. 1, 1957, but its construction started three years earlier, and its planning long before that. Organized transit across the bridge started with a ferry operation in 1881. Run by the railroads, it transported passengers and railroad cargo back and forth. Once automobiles started to become more popular, the ferries would also transport them, too, but only at a stiff price. After hearing from disgruntled car owners/tourists, the state government started up its own cheaper version of the car-ferry service in 1923.

THE ANSWERS

Minks and river otters are both members of *the weasel family*, which is also known as the Mustelidae (pronounced moo-STELL-ih-dee) family. Michigan has nine species of weasels. The river otter and the mink both have the characteristic long and thin body of a typical weasel. Other long and thin members of this family are the American marten, fisher, ermine, long-tailed weasel and least weasel. Two rather un-weasel-like members of this family are the American badger, which has a squat and stocky body; and the striped skunk that has more of a pear-shaped body.

The river otter splits its time between the water and land, but its speed is in the water. There, it can swim at speeds of 6–7 miles per hour and dive to depths of as much as 50–60 feet, where they may capture fish for dinner. River otters can stay underwater for *8 minutes*. In the winter when ice covers the water, the river otter can appear to stay underwater longer. Actually, however, it breathes periodically from small pockets of air that are trapped beneath the ice, and moves from one pocket to the next.

In the summer, the mink diet is mainly crayfish with a fish, frog, and small duck or mammal occasionally added to the mix. In the winter, the main part of a mink's diet is *the muskrat*, even though the muskrat and the mink can grow to similar size, about 2 feet long. Mink are faster swimmers than the average muskrat, and have four prominent canine teeth to help them attack their prey. As is the case in many predator-prey relationships, minks often target slower and/or weaker members of the prey population, and in so doing remove many diseased muskrats from the wild.

The Mackinac Bridge is a suspension bridge: The bridge deck is literally suspended by cables. (Travel Michigan)

The 4-mile and 45-minute ferry ride wasn't bad, but the wait could be. At certain times of the year, such as hunting season, traffic could back up for 10–15 miles, resulting in up to 19-hour waits for the ferry. To imagine the extent of the traffic jam, consider that you are now about 4.5 miles south of the straits.

Soon, people were calling for a bridge to link the two peninsulas. One of the earliest bridge proponents was U.S. Senator Prentiss Brown of St. Ignace on the U.P. side of the straits. In 1934, just 11 years after the state initiated its car-ferry service, he helped nudge the state legislature to establish a Mackinac Bridge Authority that would conduct initial engineering studies. The construction of a causeway, or an elevated bank, on the St. Ignace side of the straits started. This cause-way would eventually connect with the bridge. World War II put a stop to the bridge plans, but by 1950, then-Gov. Mennen Williams got on the bandwagon and with Brown and others, put the bridge project back on track. The legislature wasn't as thrilled with the prospect and the cost, but went along and authorized the bridge authority to issue bonds that would eventually be paid back through bridge tolls.

Construction on the bridge started in 1954, and with the help of 11,000 workers, (including 350 engineers and 3,500 men at the bridge site), it opened just 42 months later. The year 2007 marked the bridge's 50th year of operation. Currently, about 3.5–3.7 million vehicles cross the bridge every year. That amounts to an average of about 10,000 vehicles a day.

Nicolet Street runs north into Mackinaw City. Its name calls to mind Jean Nicolet, who was the first white man to explore what is now Michigan. A French explorer and fur trader, he came down from Canada past what is now Sault Sainte Marie, Mich., and then along the St. Marys River at the eastern edge of the Upper Peninsula to reach this part of the state in 1634. Nicolet came to this region under orders from the noted navigator and map-maker Samuel de Champlain to find a passage to . . . China. At that time in history, the French believed the New World was a much narrower land mass than it actually is, and shortly beyond its western boundary, they hoped to find the Asian coast, where China and the Indies were located. If it could find a short passage to the Orient through the New World, France would have at its disposal an extremely lucrative trade route.

Champlain selected Nicolet for the job because he could speak two Indian languages: Algonquin and Huron. Nicolet learned both languages over the several years he spent living first with an Algonquin tribe and then with a Huron tribe as part of his assigned job of interpreter. While living among these people, they told him about another tribe that he interpreted to mean "people of the salt water" or "people of the bad-smelling water." He assumed this referred to the residents of China or the Indies, who lived on the ocean. After all, ocean water was salty and it did have a definite aroma compared to fresh water.

He reported his discovery, and Champlain sent Nicolet off to find his way to Asia. This led Nicolet to this region, and then across a wide expanse of water to what he was sure would be Asia. He even donned a traditional, ornate damask robe so he would be suitably dressed when he came ashore. Instead of finding the Orient, he encountered a tribe of American Indians known as Ho-

BRAINBUSTERS

In the days before the Mackinac Bridge, drivers had to wait for a car ferry to cross the Straits of Mackinac. During the summer and the hunting season, lines for the ferry could back up for miles.

Basic: The wait was made at least semi-tolerable by vendors who would walk among the cars selling pasties (pronounced PASS-teez). What is a pasty?

Intermediate: Pasties are frequently associated with the Upper Peninsula, but they did not originate there. Where did they come from, and what made them so popular in the U.P.?

Advanced: People from the western Upper Peninsula can often identify which customers are non-native by what they put on their pasties. What is the give-away? Also, what do Yoopers (the nickname for Upper Peninsula residents) put on their pasties, if anything?

See next page for answers.

Emmett County is named for Irish patriot and orator Robert Emmett. (Library of Congress, N.Y.: Publ. & Print. by Th. Kelly, circa 1874.)

1634, four decades passed before a fur-trading post finally opened here in 1673.

— — —

The border between Cheboygan (pronounced sheh-BOY-gen) and Emmet County passes just north of this exit. The two counties sit side by side with Cheboygan County to the east and Emmet County to the west. I-75 runs along the border between the two counties from here to the Mackinac Bridge. The name Cheboygan has an Ojibwe (Chippewa Indian) base, but

Chunks, sometimes called Winnebagos, who were quite astonished by the sight of the traveler in the silken robe. He had landed not in China, but near what we now know as Green Bay, Wisconsin. Apparently the translation on which Nicolet had based his journey did not refer to ocean salt water, but to some other characteristic of the area where the tribe lived, perhaps some malodorous, stagnant or algae-filled waters of a local lake or river.

Although Nicolet hadn't found a route to China on this expedition, he had become the first European to traverse Lake Michigan and set foot in Wisconsin. In addition, his regal arrival in the flowing robe had so impressed the Ho-Chunks that they were open to fur-trade negotiations, which was a definite plus for the French.

After Nicolet's historic journey through northern Michigan and past this tip of the Lower Peninsula in

THE ANSWERS

A pasty is rather like a calzone or hand-held pot pie. It is *a folded pastry filled with beef, rutabagas and other vegetables.*

Pasties originated in Cornwall, which is in southwestern England. Cornish immigrants brought the food with them when they came to the western Upper Peninsula looking for work in the copper and iron mines. *The food's portability made it popular* with other miners—it could easily be carried to work in a pocket—and pasties soon became commonplace.

Now, many sit-down restaurants and roadside diners in the Upper Peninsula and in the northern Lower Peninsula include pasties on their menus. *Yoopers typically put ketchup on their pasties, but visitors to the area often ask for gravy.*

its exact meaning is unknown. Some con-tend that it means "Ojibwe water" in reference to the large river that runs through the county, while others say it means "big pipe" or "place of entrance."

Emmet County is easier to explain. It is named for Irish patriot and orator Robert Emmet. In the late 1700s, when Emmet when was in college, he joined with many other young people who were calling for an end to British rule and religious oppression. He spent some time in exile in France, but returned to his homeland to lead a rebellion in the spring of 1803. He was 26 years old. Although he was involved in making explosives and other weapons, he cringed when the fighting turned too violent, and called off the uprising. He then went

into hiding, but British authorities were able to capture him in August when Emmet left his hideaway to try to reach his fiancée. Found guilty of treason, Emmet died by execution on Sept. 20, 1803.

Mile Markers 337–338

A windmill rises above the trees about halfway between mile markers 337 and 338. This is one of Mackinaw City's two energy-producing windmills. The three 85-foot-long blades are set on a 230-foot-tall tower. The blades can spin at up to 22 revolutions per minute, which means that the blade tip can be revolving at speeds of more than 100 miles per hour. The two 900-kilowatt windmills went online in 2001,

BRAINBUSTERS

Standing sentinel along the shores of the Great Lakes in Michigan are 124 lighthouses, a greater number than in any other state in the union.

Basic: Some Michigan drivers have license plates sporting a boldly colored red-and-white lighthouse. What does this signify?

Intermediate: The state's first lighthouse was the Fort Gratiot Light, built in 1825 at the southern entrance into Lake Huron from the St. Clair River. The lighthouse burned down four years later, perhaps because its illumination came from flames generated by burning wood, kerosene, whale oil and other fuels. After the fire, a new lighthouse made

of bricks replaced it, and it still stands as the oldest lighthouse in Michigan. What is the name of the Michigan-to-Ontario bridge near the current Fort Gratiot Lighthouse?

Advanced: Both before and after lighthouses switched from flames to electricity to provide their illumination, many of them used so-called Fresnel lenses. These lenses were made up of a collection of concentric prisms that could gather light and project it in a narrow beam over distances exceeding 20 miles. With all of the competing lights, how did captains tell one lighthouse's beacon from another on dark nights?

See next page for answers.

221

and can produce enough renewable energy in a year to power 600 homes.

Energy from these windmills and other power plants all flows into a general electrical grid. This energy is then distributed to homes and businesses. Homeowners can support these wind turbines as well as other present and future alternative-energy sources by purchasing their power for a slightly higher cost through the Green Generation program of Consumers Power.

Other windmills are now popping up in Michigan, particularly in the Thumb region. Advocates point out that these alternative-energy sources reduce our dependence on foreign oil; create local jobs in construction, and in facility operation and maintenance; and add to the tax base of local communities where the facilities are located. In addition, farmers who have windmills placed on their farm fields and among their crops also receive added income. Preliminary plans are now under way to construct wind-turbine fields in the state to take advantage of the quite steady and often strong breezes that blow off of the Great Lakes.

THE ANSWERS

Exit 338

Michigan has a number of specialty license plates that drivers can purchase in lieu of the standard blue print on a white background. One of these is the *lighthouse-preservation plate*. The specialty plate costs an extra $35, $25 of which goes toward efforts to preserve Michigan's 124 lighthouses, many of which have fallen into disrepair since their heyday decades ago when they were manned by lighthouse keepers. The slogan at the bottom of the lighthouse-preservation plate reads, "Save Our Lights."

The Fort Gratiot Lighthouse stands near the *Blue Water Bridge*, which connects the city of Port Huron, Mich., with the community of Sarnia, Ontario, Canada.

In the days when ship captains relied on lighthouse beacons as key navigational points, lighthouses had *unique blink patterns that distinguished them from one another*. A captain had only to watch the pattern to know the identity of the lighthouse.

Exit 338

About 3.5 miles east of this exit down US-23 is Mill Creek State Park. It is set on the site of a lumber mill, which was built in 1790 to saw logs into lumber for use on Mackinac Island about 8 miles north across the Straits of Mackinac. The mill remained in operation until about 1839, but was then abandoned. It deteriorated over the next century and fell from memory, but its rediscovery in 1972 led to extensive archaeological work and renovation of the mill, the dam, a workshop and a millwright's house. Today, visitors to the park can witness the working sawmill and learn about life at the turn of the 18th century.

This exit in Mackinaw City leads to the state historic park called Colonial Michilimackinac (pronounced mish-ill-ih-MACK-ih-naw) and to the boat docks for passenger ferries to Mackinac Island. In that sentence, Mackinac and Mackinaw are pronounced the same (Mack-ih-naw), but spelled differently. This is no surprise because often, the spelling is the English interpretation of the French version of the original Indian word. In this case, one place got a "c" at the end (Mackinac), and the other got a "w" (Mackinaw). Both words probably go back to the original Ojibwe (Chippewa) word for turtle, and Michilimackinac likely means big turtle.

A state historic park, Colonial Michilimackinac is a reconstruction of a 1700s fort. (Travel Michigan)

Exit 339

Colonial Michilimackinac is a detailed reconstruction of the fortified village that once occupied this site in the 1700s. It contains 13 buildings, all staffed by employees who dress in the clothing of the time and take on the roles of the British redcoats or villagers who would have lived here at the time. The re-creation is built on evidence that has been collected during what is the longest archaeological excavation in the United States.

The French built the fort in 1715 as a way to both foster better relationships with local American Indians and ensure that the English could not expand into this region. The French continued to occupy Fort Michilimackinac for more than four decades, but pressure from the

British eventually forced them to surrender it in 1760. Unlike the French, who had managed to develop a fairly good if tenuous relationship with the local Indians, the British fared less well and tensions quickly escalated. In 1763, several Indian tribes in Michigan formed an alliance and planned simultaneous attacks on Fort Michilimackinac and another important fort in Detroit. The uprising in Detroit did not succeed (see mile marker 42), but the revolt at Michilimackinac did. The local Ojibwe who lived near the fort devised a plan, and on June 2, 1763, the men started to play a game of ball, called baggatiway, outside the fort as the women moved inside and took up positions there. The fort commandant was

The magnificent Grand Hotel on Mackinac Island is a stunning sight. Information about the hotel is on page 230. (Stephen Zaglaniczny)

not alarmed, and he and many of his men even went outside the fort to watch the game, which went on all morning. At about noon, one of the players threw the ball over the wall, and the other players rushed past the commandant and the soldiers to the women, who gave them hatchets they had concealed in their blankets. The assault began. The surprised soldiers had little chance, and the Ojibwe took over the fort. Their success didn't last, however, and British forces were able to retake the fort a little more than a year later.

Fort Michilimackinac remained in operation and under British control until 1779, when fears of an attack by a new enemy, the Americans, prompted the British to begin the arduous job of moving the fort to Mackinac Island. The reasoning was that Mackinac Island would be much easier to defend. As the soldiers dismantled Michilimackinac over the next few years, they took most of the buildings and their contents with them. Slowly, sands blown in from Lake Michigan began to bury any remaining structures and equipment, and the last of the fort disappeared from view if not from memory. It remained mainly untouched for more than a century, but in 1909, it became a state park. Not long afterward, workers began uncovering bits and pieces of the old fort. By the 1930s, reconstruction was underway. With the addition of a professional archaeological dig that started in 1959 and has continued during every summer since, the park is now the site of the longest ongoing, historical archaeological excavation in the nation.

Visitors to Mackinac Island watch a re-enactment at Fort Mackinac, which was constructed by the British in the late 1700s. (Travel Michigan)

Ferries to Mackinac Island, which is about 7 miles to the northeast, leave from boat docks both here in Mackinaw City and from St. Ignace on the other side of the Mackinac Bridge. The boats make the passage from Mackinaw City to the island in anywhere from 15 minutes to 35 minutes, depending on the style of boat. The three big ferry companies are Shepler's, Arnold Transit and Star Line.

Shepler's started in 1945 with a charter service to the island, and later added more boats, including a vessel in the 1950s that brought the curious to the middle of the straits so they could watch as the new Mackinac Bridge was being built. Shepler's now has five passenger ferries in its fleet, four of which are named after historical vessels that plied the Great lakes in the 17th century. They include *The Welcome*, *Felicity*, *The Hope* and *Wyandot*. The fifth vessel is the Capt. Shepler.

Arnold Transit's history goes back even farther. Three partners who founded a lumber company on Mackinac Island in 1878 also started the Arnold and Coats Ferry Line, which eventually became Arnold Transit. The early boats were steamers that made the trip to the island in about an hour. The company has changed hands over the years, but has never stopped its operation. Arnold Transit now has a fleet of five classic ferries (*Algomah II*, *Chippewa*, *Huron*, *Ottawa* and *Straits of Mackinac II*) and three catamarans (*Straits Express*, *Mackinac Express* and *Island Express*) to carry people to and from Mackinac Island.

Star Line's boats, which the company calls hydro-jets, are recognizable for the large roostertails they produce. According to the company, the waterjets add about 3 mph to the vessels' speed, and the plume of water reaches about 35 feet.

Besides the island runs, the ferry companies offer a variety of cruises. Shepler's, for instance, has a lighthouse cruise, and Arnold Transit offers a tour of area island channels.

The North Country National Scenic Trail extends through much of the Lower Peninsula to about here. From

BRAINBUSTERS

A few areas of Mackinac Island are privately owned. The remainder is a state park.

Basic: Before it was a state park, however, Mackinac Island was a national park. In fact, it became the second national park in the United States in 1875. What was the first?

Intermediate: One of the more bizarre stories from Mackinac Island's past is that of Dr. William Beaumont (pronounced BO-mont), who conducted experiments in the 1820s to learn how the human digestive system worked. He did much of this work on a patient named Alexis St. Martin. What was so unusual about St. Martin that allowed Beaumont to do his experiments?

Advanced: Mackinac Island has a number of interesting limestone formations with colorful names. Arch Rock, for instance, is a 149-foot-tall, 50-foot-long rock bridge. Another formation is known as Skull Cave, also sometimes called Henry's Hiding Place, which was used by fur trader Alexander Henry in 1763. Why is it called Skull Cave, and what was Henry hiding from?

See page 228 for answers.

this point, hikers can make their way to the Upper Peninsula segment of the trail, but only after they have crossed the Straits of Mackinac. One way they can traverse the straits is by taking a ride over the Mackinac Bridge on a shuttle bus operated by the Mackinac Bridge Authority. Another option is to hop on a ferry to Mackinac Island, and then take another ferry to St. Ignace on the U.P. shore. The only day they cross the bridge on foot is on the morning of Labor Day during the state's annual bridge walk. At that time, tens of thousands of people take the 5-mile trek from one side of the bridge to the other. Once hikers enter the U.P., the North Country Trail continues north and then west across the Upper Peninsula and into northern Wisconsin.

Not all of the North Country Trail is complete, but most of it is, and the remainder is under development. In some places, the path meanders through wilderness areas, but in others it tracks through cities or farmland. Eventually, the non-profit North Country Trail Association and its hundreds of volunteers hope to continue to work with the National Park Service to develop a continuous, 4,600-mile, off-road trail from central North Dakota through Minnesota, the tip of Wisconsin, the Upper and Lower Peninsulas of Michigan, Ohio, and western Pennsylvania, finally ending in eastern New York state. When it is completed, the multi-state trail will be the longest off-road hiking trail in the nation—longer than both the Appalachian National Scenic Trail in the eastern United States, and the Pacific Crest Trail that runs from Mexico to Canada through the western United States.

Southern End of the Mackinac Bridge

A lighthouse stands on the shoreline just to the east of the southern ramp onto the Mackinac Bridge. Built in 1892, the lighthouse's function was to assist passing ships at night, in the fog and during storms. To do this, it had a lens that projected light up to 16 miles away. Besides the 50-foot-tall lighthouse tower, the building included a two-story, red-roofed, double residence that had separate accommodations built for the lighthouse keeper and the assistant keeper. This location of this lighthouse right in Mackinaw City was a definite plus for the keeper, assistant keeper and their families. Often, lighthouses were on islands or in remote wilderness areas with little connection to civilization or even other people, but here in Mackinaw City, the children could attend school and make friends, and the adults could take advantage of the benefits of living in a community. At the same time, however, this lighthouse had almost too much exposure to people. This is because the surrounding land had been declared part of the Michilimackinac park (see exit 339), and the keepers had expressed instructions to provide a courteous welcome to visitors whenever possible. The park could become quite busy in the summer, particularly as automobile traffic increased, so the keepers spent many an hour explaining lighthouse operation to visitors. Although they never let lapse their attention to the light itself, they had to scramble at times to both cater to tourists and attend to their other duties, which included keeping the lighthouse building and grounds meticulously well-kept.

Next to the lighthouse is a building with the tall chimney and copper roof. This housed a large, steam-powered fog signal to help passing boats navigate in bad weather. Both the lighthouse and the fog-signal building operated until 1957. In that year, the Mackinac Bridge opened for business, and it had its own lights and fog signal.

Today, visitors to the park can again tour the lighthouse building and learn about life a century ago.

— — —

A definite highlight of this part of Michigan is, of course, the Mackinac Bridge (see photo on page 218). Its design was the brainchild of engineer David Steinman, who was a superstar of bridge building and had already designed or helped to design bridges in Brazil, California, Rhode Island, Oregon, Maine and New York, among other places. A native New Yorker, he took on the job of design engineer for the Mackinac Bridge in 1954. His plans called for a bridge deck (the roadway) that would be suspended from cables, which would themselves be hung from two main towers. Photographs from the construction project are jaw-dropping, with workers standing on cable strung hundreds of feet in the air ... and without any safety

Exit 339

227

harnesses in sight. During the 42 months of construction that continued through good weather and bad, five workers died. One was a diver who was working 140 feet underwater, surfaced too quickly, and got a fatal case of the bends. A second lost his balance and fell to his death from a height of 40 feet, and a third fell from only 4 feet and may have suffered a heart attack.

The final two men died when a catwalk collapsed near the north tower.

Despite the deaths, the bridge work went on and the structure opened to traffic in 1957. In its completed form, the two main towers rise 552 feet—about the height of a 55-story building—above the water surface. The bridge itself is almost 5 miles long, making it one of the longest suspension bridges in the world.

THE ANSWERS

Exit 339

The first national park in the United States was *Yellowstone*, which was established in 1872. Yellowstone is a huge park in the western United States. The much-smaller national park at Mackinac Island was established three years later. In 1895, two decades after Mackinac was designated a national park, Michigan took control and has since operated it as a state park.

Dr. Beaumont learned about the digestive system through Alexis St. Martin, a young fur trader known as a voyageur, who came to see the doctor on Mackinac Island because of a point-blank bullet wound to his upper abdomen. The wound healed, but despite Dr. Beaumont's attempts to close it, *the nearly inch-wide hole in St. Martin's side remained open.* This gave Dr. Beaumont an idea. If he inserted pieces of meat or other foods through the hole and into St. Martin's stomach, and then extracted them after a period of time, he would be able to document how diges-

tion proceeded and how quickly it worked. He did just that, tying strings around chunks of beef, chicken or other foods, and then dangling them through the hole and into the stomach before taking them out to check on the progress. Beaumont experimented on St. Martin for several years, and eventually chronicled his work in 1833 in what has become a classic book on the subject.

In 1763, Alexander Henry fled to Mackinac Island *to escape a famous Indian attack on British-held Fort Michilimackinac* on the other side of the Straits (see pages 223–224). There, he found Skull Cave with the help of an Indian friend. Henry spent the night there. As day broke, he found that *he was surrounded by piles of human bones, including skulls.* Henry assumed they were the remnants of Indian-held prisoners who had been killed and possibly cannibalized, but current hypotheses suggest that the site was simply a burial grounds used by an early tribe.

Middle of the Mackinac Bridge

One of the things that people often mention on crossing the bridge is the open steel grate that makes up much of the roadway and provides a rather-shocking view of the water some 200 feet below. This was done for a specific purpose. Because of the open-grate design, wind blows through the grate rather than rocking the bridge decking. With this feature and others, engineers designed the bridge to withstand winds of more than 600 mph. Wind speed has never reached 600 mph at the bridge, but it does blow mighty hard. Wind at the bridge has been clocked with sustained blows nearing 80 mph and gusts topping 100 mph. During these severe blows, the bridge can actually ever-so-slowly shift as much as 35 feet to one side or the other. When the gale finally lets up, it then slowly returns to its original position.

To help ensure the safety of the traveling public, the Mackinac Bridge Authority provides escorts for tall, or "high-profile," vehicles on particularly windy days, and will even close the bridge to traffic if sustained winds top 65 mph for a set length of time. Even these safety measures and the solid construction of the bridge are not enough for some people. Passengers with various water, height or other phobias sometimes make the crossing with their eyes closed or by crouching down on the floor of the car. Employees of the Mackinac Bridge Authority will also take the wheel for car owners who don't feel comfortable driving the span themselves.

From this vantage point at the center of the bridge, travelers can see two islands toward the west. The closest, at about a mile away, is the tiny Green Island. It pokes above the surface just off the shore of Pointe La Barbe, a small jut of land that extends from the U.P. mainland.

Green Island is actually the exposed part of an underwater shoal, so as the water levels rise and fall in the Great Lakes, the island becomes smaller or larger, respectively. It is close enough to Pointe La Barbe that deer can swim there from the mainland. The most noticeable animals on the island, however, are the herring gulls, or what people generally call "seagulls." Herring gulls, some of which you can probably see soaring in the sky near the bridge now, have a gray back and black-tipped gray wings on a mainly white body. They also have a yellow beak that, although not especially obvious, has an orange spot on the lower bill. The spot has an unusual purpose that has to do with feeding. Many birds feed their young by going on foraging missions, swallowing up acceptable food items, and then regurgitating them into the mouths of their waiting chicks. Gulls do the same thing. Adults search for small fish and whatever else they can find, and return to the nest. The young chicks peck at the orange spot, and this triggers the adult to regurgitate. For gull chicks, nothing says "parental care" quite like a partially digested fish from mom or dad.

Another 6 miles west-northwest of Green Island is St. Helena Island, which has a lighthouse on its eastern shore. St. Helena Island is about a mile long and a half mile wide, large enough in the 1800s to call itself home to a number of families that made a living through fishing. In 1873, the island also got a lighthouse with a 78-foot-tall, white-painted tower for the beacon. A string of lighthouse keepers lived there until 1923 when the lighthouse was automated. Without a keeper's constant attention, the building suffered, but in 1989, Boy Scouts and volunteers from an organization called the Great Lakes Lighthouse Keepers Association got to work. Thanks to their work, the light still shines at the now-restored lighthouse, and it is open to the public by appointment.

Exit 339

On the east side of the bridge, although underwater, is the 148-square-mile Straits of Mackinaw Bottomland Preserve where nine major shipwrecks rest. Although the water is 300 feet deep in much of the straits, including the part under the middle of the Mackinac Bridge, much of the preserve is only 80–100 feet deep. These shallower depths are ideal for divers who want up-close views of the shipwrecks, which have been well-preserved in the cold, clear freshwater of the straits.

Northern End of the Mackinac Bridge

Unless it's extremely foggy or nighttime, a row of three fairly close islands are visible in the water to the east (the northbound side of I-75). The northernmost of the three is Macki-nac Island; the small, middle island is Round Island; and the largest one that is farthest is Bois Blanc Island (pronounced BAH-blo, but sometimes boyz blahnk).

The prominent landmark on Mackinac Island is the Grand Hotel, the large white building that is apparent even from this distance on the bridge. The huge structure (see photo on page 324) has 385 rooms—no two decorated exactly alike. It also has a sweeping porch with panoramic views of the straits and shores beyond, and lovely gardens that in season provide a sweet-scented vista in every direction. The hotel is particularly enchanting set as it is on an island where automobiles are banned, and transportation is mainly by horse or bicycle, or on foot.

Today, the island is a major tourist destination, but it hasn't always been that way. The first inhabitants were aboriginal people who were the ancestors of the Ojibwe Indians. According to Ojibwe lore, they arrived from the East Coast of North America thousands of years ago. As the years passed, the island became a meeting and trading place for various Indian tribes, some of which buried high-ranking individuals there. The first white men to see the island were part of Jean Nicolet's famed journey that traveled from Canada through the Straits of Mackinac here in 1634 on his way to what he thought would be the Orient. (For more on Nicolet's expedition, see exit 337.) The next milestone in the island's history came a few decades later when a Catholic priest named Father Jacques

Marquette (pronounced mar-KET) established a mission on the island. With him came a group of displaced Huron Indians, who hoped to farm on the land there. The soil on Mackinac Island, however, wasn't suitable for crops, so the mission pulled up stakes and moved onto the mainland of the Upper Peninsula in St. Ignace. (See exit 344.)

Back on Mackinac Island, things started to pick up when fur traders began flooding into the area. The island became a popular location for Europeans to trade knives, cloth, kettles, axe handles and other goods to the Indians for their fur pelts. The Europeans did very well on the exchange. A pelt that cost them a knife or a few woolen blankets, brought enough income back in Europe to buy several knives or a whole pile of blankets. The profitability of the fur trade brought many traders, some fair and some not, to the region. It also caught the attention of the French and English governments, who both sought to gain the lion's share of the market. At first, the French had the upper hand. They constructed Fort Michilimackinac in 1715 on the Lower Peninsula side of the straits (see exit 339) and also developed a settlement on Mackinac Island. By 1760–61, the tide had turned, and the British took control of the fort.

Except for a yearlong occupation by local Indians and the French in 1763–64, the British continued to hold Fort Michilimackinac for almost two decades. Times, however, were changing once again. By now, the threat was coming not from the French but from the upstart Americans. As the Revolutionary War waged on, the British decided that they needed a more defendable location than was provided at Fort Michilimackinac, so they moved to Mackinac Island. From the island, they reasoned, they could control boat traffic on the straits and more easily guard against an attack from the Americans. All their work was for naught. In 1783, a peace treaty essentially ended the war and gave the fort to the Americans. The British troops refused to leave, however, and remained at the fort until U.S. soldiers arrived in 1796. That was still not the end. At the beginning of the War of 1812, a 1,000-strong army of British soldiers, trappers and Indians secretly crossed the straits at night, landed on the island, and pointed two cannons at the fort. The Americans had not yet heard that a war had been declared, so they did not have the proper precautions in place. The British attack was swift and the Americans had little choice but to surrender. They didn't give up. The Americans launched their own offense by using two ships to prevent supply boats from bringing food to the English troops. They might have been successful in starving out the troops, but the English had a plan of their own. Again at night, about six dozen British soldiers quietly rowed out to one of the American ships and took the crew by surprise. They manned the boat, and with the American flag still run up the pole, they sailed into range of the unsuspecting second American boat, opened fire and quickly sank her. With control of one American ship, and the other now at the bottom of the water, the supply line opened again. More wary, the British were able to hold onto Mackinac Island until the war ended in 1815, and the Americans regained control permanently.

Visitors to Mackinac Island today can recall the tumultuous past of the fort and the straits area through a tour of the 14 restored buildings of Fort Mackinac on the island, and by watching performances by park interpreters who dress in 1880s soldier uniforms, play military music, and fire both rifles and cannons.

Exit 339

Once the War of 1812 was over and the Americans had permanent control of Mackinac Island, its busy fur trade could carry on uninterrupted. One of the most prominent fur traders on the island, and indeed in the entire country, was John Jacob Astor (see photo on next page). Astor came to the United States from London in 1784 when he was 20 years old and quickly built a tidy fortune by running a fur operation in New York City. In 1808, he started the American Fur Co. and in 1817, made Mackinac Island the hub of the company activities. Island visitors today can learn more about Astor's story and that of fur trading at the Stuart House Museum.

The fur-trading industry continued until the 1830s, but then faded off as fur-bearing animals became more scarce. At the same time, however, tourism was on the upswing. By the 1860s and 1870s, Mackinac Island was becoming a popular vacation spot and people arrived by boat and by rail from Detroit, Chicago, and as far away as Buffalo. Lodging for the growing number of mainly summertime visitors was in short supply, and getting shorter every season. In 1886, two railroad outfits and a steamship business joined forces to create the Mackinac Island Hotel Co., and started to build the massive Grand Hotel that you can see from the Mackinac Bridge today. It opened the following year, adding its expansive porch and another wing in the 1890s. Over the years, many famous people have come to the hotel, including five U.S. Presidents: Harry Truman, John Kennedy, Gerald Ford, George H.W. Bush and Bill Clinton. Several films have been set at the hotel, too. These include: *This Time For Keeps*, which starred Jimmy Durante and Esther Williams in 1946; *Somewhere In Time*, which starred Christopher Reeve, Jane Seymour and Christopher Plummer in 1980; and *Mr. Art Critic*, which starred Bronson Pinchot, John Lepard and Michigan-born actress Toni Trucks in 2008.

Today, Mackinac Island may have as many as 15,000 visitors a day during the busy summer tourist season. Some come to bike or hike the trails through forests or to take a horse-drawn carriage ride. Some come to snack on the island's famous fudge, to relive Michigan's history, or to marvel at the cascading blooms during the annual Lilac Festival. Whatever the reason, Mackinac Island is one of the premier vacation destinations in the state.

The small island just to the south of Mackinac Island is Round Island. On its northern end, a thin spit of land reaches out into the straits, and at its tip is a red-and-white lighthouse. Built in the 1890s, the lighthouse helped boat crews navigate until 1947 when another nearby light at Mackinac Island became operational. Once the usefulness of the Round Island lighthouse ended, the building fell into disrepair and was nearly lost when water erosion from a ferocious storm in 1972 clawed a hole into the foundation. Following a groundswell of public support, the lighthouse was placed on the National Register of Historic Places. Preservationists have since worked with federal and state agencies to restore the lighthouse to its former glory.

Today, visitors can get a close-up view of the lighthouse from the Mackinac Island ferries or from the Round Island grounds. The lighthouse itself, however, is closed to the public.

For information on Bois Blanc, the large island south of Round Island, see exit 326.

– – –

The tollbooths for the Mackinac Bridge are located here at the northern end of the bridge. These tolls are critical to the bridge because they pay for its day-to-day maintenance. Some of the typical maintenance projects include inspecting the huge cables that hang from the two main towers, replacing the open grating on the deck of the bridge, resurfacing the

John Jacob Astor, shown here in a detail from a 1794 painting by Gilbert Stuart, once ran his fur company from Mackinac Island.

Exit 343

right-hand lanes of the road, and lots and lots of painting.

Exit 343

Depending on your direction, you are now either entering or leaving the Upper Peninsula, which at more than 16,400 square miles is larger than Massachusetts, Connecticut and Delaware combined. It is still a wild land. More than 90 percent of the U.P. is forested, and it has more than 1,700 miles of shoreline on the Great Lakes. It also contains more than 4,000 inland lakes and some 12,000 miles of trout streams. Despite the land size, it doesn't have many residents. According the U.S. Census Bureau, the population in the Upper Peninsula as of 2006 was about 312,000, approximately 3 percent of the Michigan's entire population of 10.1 million. By comparison, the smallest state in the union, Rhode Island, has more than three times the population of the Upper Peninsula even though it is just 1/15th the size of the U.P. That means that Rhode Island has about 1,000 people per square mile, whereas the Upper Peninsula has about 19.

BRAINBUSTERS

Father Jacques Marquette (pronounced mar-KET), was born in France in 1637. He became a Jesuit priest. Jesuits are members of the Society of Jesus, an order of the Roman Catholic Church.

Exit 344

Basic: In 1666, at the request of the church, he set out for Québec (pronounced kweh-BEK or keh-BEK), now in Canada. What was his job there?

Intermediate: In a couple of years, Marquette accepted instructions to head westward to the Great Lakes region. During his travels and discussions with members of various American Indian tribes, he learned of a large river that flowed beyond the Great Lakes. After establishing himself in St. Ignace, which is on the north side of the Mackinac Bridge, he set off again with a French-Canadian explorer named Louis Joliet, to locate that waterway. What river did they find?

Advanced: Marquette was on his way back to St. Ignace in 1675 when he died, probably from complications due to a case of dysentery he had picked up on his journey. He is remembered in the names of many Michigan places, including a city and a county in the Upper Peninsula. Dysentery was not uncommon among early explorers, and many of them got the illness from doing what?

See page 236 for answers.

Travelers often take this exit to the west to spend a few moments enjoying the full expanse of the Mackinac Bridge from the vantage point at Bridge View Park. The park is almost immediately off the exit and is set right on the shore of the straits. To the right of this exit is one of the Welcome Centers/rest areas that are operated by the Michigan Department of Transportation. In addition to banks of tourist information, the center also holds a scale model of the bridge and details about its construction.

Exit 344

To the west, this exit leads onto US-2, a highway that continues to the other side of the Upper Peninsula and then runs clear to the state of Washington. Although it appears that its intersection here with I-75 is the easternmost point of US-2, the highway has a separate expanse in the eastern United States, where it stretches from the northeastern tip of New York eastward to Maine. This is quite unusual. Most major highways in the country are continuous.

To the east, this exit leads to the city of St. Ignace. With 2,700-residents, St. Ignace overlooks the Straits of

Mackinac and Mackinac Island, which is only about 3 miles distant. A missionary named Father Jacques Marquette (mar-KET) established the settlement in 1671. This makes it the second-oldest settlement in the state. The oldest is in Sault (pronounced SOO) Sainte Marie, which is another 50 miles north. Marquette decided to name the settlement St. Ignace after St. Ignatius Loyola, a 16th century Spanish soldier-turned-religious man who founded the Catholic order known as the Jesuits. Marquette was a Jesuit. Marquette's arrival in the Upper Peninsula was noteworthy because he was one of the first Europeans to come to Michigan and therefore made some of the initial contacts with the local Ojibwe Indians.

After Marquette had begun establishing the mission at St. Ignace, French fur trappers started trickling into the area. With great wealth beckoning from the fur industry, St. Ignace soon became a fur-trading center. Within two decades of Marquette's arrival, the fur trade was so busy that the French decided a fort was necessary to protect the fur trade, and soldiers constructed Fort de Buade next to the mission in about 1690. At that time, this region was part of New France, which was the name of the area encompassing present-day Canada and some of the northern United States.

As more and more English traders moved into the area, the governor general of New France became increasingly concerned about control of the fur trade. In response, he named Antoine de la Mothe Cadillac, an up-and-coming soldier/explorer, as commandant of the fort. While he was there, Cadillac came to believe that the best way to prevent the British from encroaching on the fur trade was to cut off their entry into Michigan from the south. He went overseas to France and urged government officials there to fund a massive fort and settlement at the southern end of the Lower Peninsula where soldiers could block the travel route that passed from Lake Erie to Lake Huron. The government agreed to a fur-trading post, but not a settlement on the scale that Cadillac wanted. Nonetheless, Cadillac returned to the New World, gathered his soldiers from the northern Michigan fort and made the move south to establish what is now Detroit. (See exit 46 for details.)

Historians sometimes ponder what would have happened had the French government granted Cadillac's wish: If Detroit had become a fully fortified and large settlement in the early 1700s, would it have been able to resist the English invasion that would ultimately occur? Furthermore, would Michigan today have been a part of Canada rather than the United States?

Although the fort in St. Ignace closed as of 1697, the community remained busy with a healthy fur-trapping business. Visitors today can learn about the region and its history from a number of museums in town. They include the Museum of Ojibwa Culture and the Fort de Buade Museum.

Visitors can also tour the Father Marquette Memorial, which is within the Straits State Park. The park extends to both sides of I-75. The memorial is on the west side of I-75, and the camping and main picnic areas are on the east side. The park is ideally situated for viewing the Mackinac Bridge, freighter traffic, and the ferries traveling between St. Ignace and Mackinac Island.

— — — —

Like many other places in Michigan, St. Ignace is also home to a casino owned by a local American Indian tribe. The Sault band of Ojibwe Indians owns this casino, which is called Kewadin (pronounced kee-WAY-din) Shores. This band also has four other casinos in the Upper Peninsula. Because American Indian tribes are

sovereign nations and therefore independently governed, their casinos do not fall under state regulations. Instead, the National Indian Gaming Commission and/or the government of the associated tribal community regulates them.

Michigan's Indian-run casinos all opened after the 1988 passage of the Indian Gaming Regulatory Act by the U.S. Congress. Michigan currently has 12 federally recognized tribes, and as of January 2008, a total of 19 Indian-operated casinos.

Mile Marker 346

Just south of mile marker 346 is Cheeseman Road. Cheeseman has long been a common name in St.

THE ANSWERS

In 1666, Father Marquette arrived in Québec with the job of *converting American Indians to the Catholic faith*.

Marquette left Québec and moved west in 1671. He established a short-lived mission on Mackinac Island and then a more-permanent one in St Ignace. During the travels that ultimately brought him to St. Ignace, Marquette had heard from various Indians about a great river that cut through the land beyond the Great Lakes. In 1673, Marquette set off with a Louis Joliet (sometimes spelled Jolliet) on an expedition to find that river. They did. In June of 1673, they became the first Europeans to enter, explore and map the mighty *Mississippi River*. The Joliet-Marquette

expedition traveled down the river nearly to the Gulf of Mexico before heading north again.

Dysentery struck Marquette during his and Joliet's exploration of the Mississippi River. *Dysentery at the time was typically caused by eating food and drinking water that was contaminated with microorganisms, either parasites or one of several types of bacteria.* Dysentery can also spread through contact with a person who already is infected. The primary symptoms are stomach pains and severe, often bloody diarrhea, sometimes accompanied by fever and vomiting. Left untreated, it can cause extreme weakness, dehydration and death.

Ignace and the area surrounding this community. Ancestors of the Cheeseman family migrated here from New York in the mid-1800s, and many of their descendants have remained. Just south of Cheeseman Road is Chain Lake, which is visible on the southbound side of I-75. Although it doesn't look very big from the freeway, it is about a mile long, and widens to approximately a half mile at its broadest spot. Anglers come to the lake for panfish and bass.

Mile Marker 347

Watch for Mackinac County Airport, which is on the northbound side of I-75. This airport is an important one for the residents of Mackinac Island. In the spring, summer and fall, island residents can ride across the straits to the mainland on a ferry or in a personal boat. Once the water freezes over, however, their choices are limited. If the ice is thick enough, snowmobiles can make the crossing. If not, or if a resident prefers to avoid the inherent dangers of riding a machine on surface ice over deep water, the other option is flying. Flights between the island and this airport are available year-round. Since Mackinac Island has no motorized transportation, visitors arriving at the airport there have to arrange other transportation to their final destination on the island. Skiing is always an option, but many people who arrive on the island call ahead to schedule a "winter taxi," a carriage drawn by two horses. Besides transporting people, the carriages also pick up and deliver mail and freight.

Mackinac Island Carriage Tours, which operates the carriages all year long, has about 400 horses on the island in the summer. When winter approaches, the company ships most of them to farms on the mainland where they spend the coldest months, and keeps only about a dozen on the island to serve the approximately 500 residents who live there all year long.

Exit 348

Hikers can pick up the U.P portion of the North Country Trail National Scenic Trail here off Castle Rock Road. It is part of what will be a 4,600-mile, off-road trail reaching from North Dakota to New York. The trail from St. Ignace heads northwest to the mouth of the Two Hearted River, which is on Lake Superior, and then continues west. Most of the stretch in the eastern Upper Peninsula is through uninhabited wilderness, and some of it cuts through marshy areas. Before heading out, hikers should have a good map since parts of the trail may not be well-marked or easily visible, and they should have sufficient supplies. The latter is important, because hikers will find few stores over the next 200-plus miles. For those who are properly prepared, however, the trail offers one of the increasingly rare chances to truly get back to nature. (For more on the North Country trail, see exit 339.)

Mile Marker 348

Castle Rock on the southbound side of I-75 is hard to miss. This approximately 200-foot-tall outcropping is made of natural limestone carved over the millennia into a tower-like shape by the action of wind and, in years past, the forces of water erosion. Much of the rock in the eastern Lower Peninsula is limestone like this that formed some 360–540 million years ago. Compared to the western Upper Peninsula, however, this rock is very young. Some of the oldest rocks on the planet are right at the surface in the western U.P. These rocks resulted from volcanic eruptions as much as 3.5 billion years ago, long before plants and animals evolved.

MM 349

According to one long-ago legend reported in *Michigan: A Guide to the Wolverine State*, the rock has significance as the clandestine rendezvous point for an Indian woman and a white man who were sweet on each other. Their meetings didn't remain a secret. Other men who had hoped to gain the woman's attentions learned of her relationship and hurled her lover from the top of the rock and to his death. Their action had unintended results. The woman was so distraught at losing her sweetheart that she climbed the rock and likewise flung herself into the void. Beyond the legend, local Ojibwe (Chippewa) Indians did come to the rock, but not to toss anyone from the side. Rather, they used it as a lookout. Today, Castle Rock is a tourist attraction that has been in the family of current owner Mark Eby since the 1920s. Visitors can pay a nominal fee to climb to the top, and appreciate the view of the straits and nearby

This sundew plant is one of Michigan's carnivorous plants. (Jan Wieneke)

islands much as the Ojibwe did in centuries past.

Mile Marker 349

If you are driving through this area in the fall, you may be surprised to see that the needles on some of the pine trees—like those on the side of I-75 north of mile marker 349—are all brown. No, they are not dying. These trees are tamaracks (pronounced TAM-ar-ax) that are one of the few conifers (cone-bearing trees, like pines) that lose their needles every year and regrow them in the spring. Another name for the tamarack is the eastern larch. Tamaracks grow to about 50–60 feet tall and have branches filled with bunched sprays of short needles, and small cones that have a rose-like appearance. They grow throughout the northern United States and Canada in very wet, often poor soils that aren't suitable for other types of pines.

Often, tamaracks are accompanied by other plants that people rarely see. Two of the most unusual are the northern pitcher plant and the round-leaved sundew, which are both carnivorous—they eat meat!

The pitcher plant has 4- to 12-inch-tall leaves that curl around to form a vase-like structure. The structure, the "pitcher," collects water. The inside walls of the pitcher also have downward-facing hairs, so an insect can crawl down into the pitcher, but it can't crawl back out. Eventually the insect falls into the water and drowns. There, bacteria go to work breaking down the insect, and plant enzymes in the water also do their part to digest it. As the insect decomposes into basic nutrients, the plant takes them up.

The sundew works differently. It is a tiny plant that may only be an inch tall. Its stems fan out to the sides and each is tipped with a round leaf that is covered with red hairs. Each hair seeps a sticky substance from its end. Insects land on and stick to the hairs, the plant oozes enzymes that digest the insect, and the proteins from the digested insects feed the plant.

MM 349

The cup-like leaves of the pitcher plant trap insects inside, and the plant digests them. (USFWS/Dr. Thomas G. Barnes)

Often, the best way to spot a pitcher plant is to look for its flower (shown here), which rises tall above its leaves. (USFWS/Dr. Thomas G. Barnes)

Mile Marker 350

The freeway crosses a small stream called Rabbit Back Creek here. The creek flows to the east about a mile or so where it empties into Lake Huron's Horseshoe Bay. To the west, Rabbit Back Creek continues on a serpentine path to Hay Lake, which as the crow flies is only about 1.5 miles away. Hay Lake curls around to form a 1.5-mile-long and half-mile-wide, comma-shaped basin of water. The lake's small size and its surrounding swampy land do not make it a favorite inland fishing spot. Instead, most anglers head a few miles farther west to the larger and much more accessible Brevoort (pronounced BREE-vort) Lake, which was named for 19th century surveyor Henry Brevoort. At about 5 miles long and up to 2.5 miles wide, Brevoort Lake is big enough to support many game species including walleye, northern pike, muskellunge (also known as muskies) and smallmouth bass. It attracts considerable numbers of visitors who

MM 350

BRAINBUSTERS

Some people who live in the Upper Peninsula, particularly in the central and western regions, equate themselves more with Wisconsin than with the Lower Peninsula. One indicator of this is the newsstands: The farther west the newsstand, the more likely that it carries a daily newspaper from Wisconsin instead of a *Detroit News* or *Detroit Free Press*.

Basic: Over the years, some people in the Upper Peninsula have complained that the U.P. doesn't get the attention it deserves from the Michigan political structure and have called for the U.P. to secede from Michigan and become the 51st state. They have even come up with a name for the new state that takes after one of its largest features. What is the name?

Intermediate: Travelers to the central and western U.P. often note a different, rather Canadian accent among some local residents, particularly those with a Finnish ancestry. This accent has a sing-song quality, and is reflected in a popular bumper sticker that reads: Say yah to da U.P., eh." Not all Yoopers have the accent, but many do pronounce certain words differently than most other Americans. One of the words is sauna. How is this word pronounced in the "Yooper accent?"

Advanced: Besides pasties (see the Brainbuster near mile marker 335), the Upper Peninsula has a good variety of other unusual foods. For instance, several restaurants are known for their enormous cinnamon rolls (the size of a child's head!), thimbleberry jam made from especially sweet strawberries, Trenary toast, and cudighi. What are Trenary toast and cudighi?

See next page for answers.

241

stay in a large campground that has two sections, one with campsites on Brevoort Lake and one with sites on Lake Michigan.

Mile Marker 351

Numerous roadside signs announce the Lake Huron Circle Tour. This is literally a tour that circles Lake Huron. From here, the tour proceeds north to Canada, sweeps east around the North Channel and the huge Georgian Bay of Lake Huron, continues down the eastern shore of Lake Huron to re-enter Michigan south of the Thumb in the Lower Peninsula, and then returns north along the western shore of the lake, across the Mackinac Bridge and back into the Upper Peninsula. Other Great Lakes circle tours circumnavigate the other four Great Lakes. In all, the circle tours cover 6,500 miles. That's about the distance from Seattle to New York and back, plus another trip

THE ANSWERS

Proponents of turning the U.P. into its own state generally call the proposed state *Superior*, sometimes Superiorland, after Lake Superior. Occasionally, advocates have even included parts of the northern Lower Peninsula and a slice of northern Wisconsin in the wished-for 51st state. The call for statehood has ebbed and flowed since the 1850s, with one of its most recent pushes coming in 1978 when Dominic Jacobetti, a state representative from the U.P., introduced a bill to put the question on the ballot. Too few other legislators supported his idea, however, and it never proceeded.

People from the central and western U.P. often pronounce sauna as *SOW-nuh*. A traditional sauna, or steam room, in this region is a small shack with a wood stove in the center. A fire in the stove heats a pile of rocks, and water sprinkled on the rocks provides the steam. Locals often spend time in the sauna during the winter, and once they are good and hot, rush outside to cool off in the snow.

Trenary toast is *cinnamon toast* made in the Trenary Home Bakery, which is located in the central Upper Peninsula. The bakery delivers the toast, a Finnish favorite, in brown paper bags. Most people buy it to dunk in coffee. Cudighi (pronounced coo-DEE-gee, not coo-DEE-jee) is a *spicy, Italian-style sausage patty* sold mainly in delis and grocery stores. It is especially common in the north-central cities of Negaunee (pronounced neh-GAW-nee), Ishpeming (ISH-peh-ming) and Marquette (mar-KET). Besides pork, the sausage contains spices including garlic salt, pepper, cinnamon and cloves. The cooked sausage is typically served on an Italian roll, usually with mustard, onions and melted cheese, but sometimes also with pizza sauce or other toppings.

242

from Seattle to Chicago. Eight states and two Canadian Provinces worked together with the Great Lakes Commission in the late 1980s to develop the circle tours and to install the signs as a way of encouraging tourism.

This exit leads to Michigan highway M-123, which swings in a large arc first northwest, then north, and finally southwest. Along the way, it passes through the towns of Moran and Trout Lake, then veers north all the way to the community of Paradise on the shore of Lake Superior's Whitefish Bay before heading southwest past Tahquamenon (pronounced tuh-QUAH-meh-non) Falls and into the relatively large city of Newberry. Each of these places has its own story to tell.

Co. was a group of 27 men from Detroit who in the late 1800s bought land here, divided it into lots, and then advertised the individual lots for sale at a profit.

The men abandoned the name of Jacob City when the group's president was caught in some fraudulent activity, and instead selected the town name of Moran after one of its members, William Moran, who was the primary investor. In the late 1800s, a train brought people and supplies to Jacob City/Moran, which was surrounded by a busy lumbering industry. The lumber boom ended about a century ago, and the train tracks are gone, but Moran still exists. Today, the entire, nearly 100-square-mile Brevort Township, including the village of Moran, has approximately 650 residents.

Moran is a small community that is confusingly located in Brevort Township rather than Moran Township, which is right next door. To make matters worse, the nearby village of Brevort is actually located in Moran Township. The mismatched placement of the two villages happened when the state government in 1881 removed a piece of Moran Township and made it into Brevort Township. Unfortunately, the move took the village of Moran with it and left the village of Brevort behind.

   Actually the village of Moran didn't start out with that name. It began as Jacob City, which reflected the last name of the president of the German Land Co. The German Land

Trout Lake is another small U.P. community with an odd story. In the late 1800s, two sets of railroad tracks—one from the west and one from the northwest—crossed. In 1881, that junction became the settlement now known as Trout Lake. Strangely, however, the town of Trout Lake was located not on a similarly named lake, but on the shore of Carp Lake. Even though Carp Lake had no trout, people started calling it and the town Trout Lake. The latter became the official town name, but many maps today still show the lake's name as Carp Lake.

   People often drive through Trout Lake and head north on M-123 in the fall just to take in the strikingly

The copper-colored water of the Upper Falls at Tahquamenon Falls cascades 50 feet to churn up billows of foam. (Stephen Zaglaniczny)

colorful trees on either side of the road. The trip is made even more pleasant by a sign posted for drivers heading out of Trout Lake. It reads "Good luck from us."

From Trout Lake, M-123 continues north through mainly forested land for about 28 miles to Whitefish Bay. Whitefish Bay is a large bay at the far eastern end of Lake Superior. About 5 miles farther up the shore is the town of Paradise (pronounced PAIR-uh-dice), which started out in 1925 as a tourist destination. Ever since, it has drawn summer vacationers to its sandy beaches for swimming, fishing and rockhounding. Today, it also draws thousands of snowmobilers who take to the trails that intersect in town and fan out over the eastern

Upper Peninsula. People who read detective novels may also recognize Paradise as the setting for a series of books written by award-winning author Steve Hamilton, who is a native Detroiter.

— — —

About 10 miles west of Paradise is Tahquamenon Falls State Park which holds one of the largest waterfalls east of the Mississippi River. It is also the state's second-largest state park.

At the so-called Upper Falls, which are just a short walk from a parking area, the water from the Tahquamenon River crashes nearly 50 feet over a sandstone cliff. The Upper Falls are 200 feet wide and set in a rich northern forest. The 100-mile-long river is the color of tea, which results from the natural chemicals, called tannins, that seep from the cedar, spruce and hemlock trees lining the shoreline. The chemicals have another effect. As the water crashes over the falls, the force combines with the tannins to generate mounds of foam that settle in big white and tan billows along the edge of the river. Visitors often assume the foam is the result of pollution, but it is a perfectly natural phenomenon.

Although the Upper Falls attract most of the attention, the park also has a smaller but also quite beautiful set of falls a few miles away. These are the Lower Falls, a series of cascades and rapids that visitors can approach by rowboats that are rented onsite. In addition, the park has numerous hiking trails and large camping areas.

Although not as tall as the Upper Falls, the Lower Falls at Tahquamenon Falls State Park are nonetheless quite spectacular. (Stephen Zaglaniczny)

Exit 352

The name of the river and the falls is no doubt derived from an Ojibwe word, but its meaning is unclear. This is because the earliest written records were attempts by explorers and voyageurs (fur traders) to sound out the long word. Spellings over the years have ranged from Outakouaminan to Tequoimenon, and Jackwaminan to Otikwaminag. Even Henry Wadsworth Longfellow took a stab at it and spelled out Tahquamenaw in his poem "Hiawatha." Several hypotheses exist about the word's meaning. One suggests that the word means "dark water," which makes sense given the amber hue of the river. Another asserts that the word actually has no direct connection to the river or the falls at all, but instead refers to a shortcut near what is now Sault Ste. Marie many miles to the east. The original meaning of the word, and its exact pronunciation, may be lost to the ages.

— — —

From the Upper Falls at Tahquamenon Falls State Park, M-123 continues about 30 miles through mainly uninhabited forest land to reach the city of Newberry, which at about 2,700 residents, is quite large by Upper Peninsula standards. The city proudly calls itself the "official moose capital of Michigan" and claims that the surrounding county has more moose sightings than any other county in the state.

Newberry started out in 1882 with the name Grant's Corner. It was a logging center located between the two major settlements of Marquette about 90 miles to the west and Sault Ste.

245

Campers enjoy the fall at Muskellonge Lake State Park north of Newberry. They occasionally see a moose wandering through the park and into the lake. (Leslie Mertz)

Marie about 60 miles to the east, and became the headquarters for the Vulcan Furnace Co. The company didn't make furnaces. Rather, its employees used charcoal furnaces for iron smelting, which is the process that extracts iron from mined iron ore.

The town's name soon switched to Newberry in tribute to rising Republican politician Truman Newberry, a Detroit businessman who was a founder of the Packard Motor Car Co. Newberry also served in the U.S. Navy, and spent a few months as the secretary of the navy during part of Theodore Roosevelt's term as U.S. president. In 1919, Newberry won a seat as U.S. senator from Michigan. Soon after, allegations arose about financial and other improprieties stemming from his successful Senate bid against automobile mogul Henry Ford. He was cleared once,

but when additional inquiries surfaced, he resigned his Senate seat in 1922—three-and-a-half years after taking office—and went back to a career as a manufacturing businessman. Despite the shadow cast over his career, the town of Newberry retained his name and still holds it today.

Mile Marker 356

The road called Mackinac Trail crosses I-75 near here, and a bit farther north, the Carp River passes under the freeway. Before the days of I-75, Mackinac Trail was the main north-south driving route through the eastern Upper Peninsula. Construction on the Mackinac Trail began around 1913 and full route finally opened in 1920 when a bridge was built over the Carp River. The bridge, which still stands immediately west of I-75, is a 60-foot concrete-arched structure. The bridge and the road were later widened to accommodate increased traffic, but when I-75 opened, the number of cars on the Mackinac Trail dropped off.

The Mackinac Trail is not only known by that name. It also goes by the name of county highway H-63, and is so marked over much of its length. The Mackinac Trail approximately parallels I-75, sometimes passing along just to the side of the freeway and sometimes crossing it, as it does here.

The Carp River snakes its way east from I-75 to the St. Martin Bay of Lake Huron, which is about a mile to the east. To the west, the river first drops about a mile south before swinging back north through the Carp River Campground. The campground has 44 campsites that are designated as rustic, which means no electrical hookups are available and water is by hand-pump. The Carp River is unusual because a long stretch of it is federally designated as "wild and scenic." The federal government has conferred the designation on 165 rivers in the nation because they "possess outstandingly remarkable scenic, recreational, geologic, fish and wildlife, historic, cultural or other similar values." Besides the Carp River, Michigan has more than a dozen other wild-and-scenic rivers, including the Au Sable and Sturgeon rivers in the Lower Peninsula, and the Tahquamenon River in the U.P.

Carp River is popular with paddlers in canoes and kayaks, and draws anglers who fish for brook, rainbow and brown trout. Seasonal fishing for salmon and steelhead occurs at the mouth of the river at St. Martin Bay. (Steelhead is the

BRAINBUSTERS

The Upper Peninsula hosts a number of sled dog races every year, including the U.P. 200 that covers a 240-mile route from Marquette in the north-central Upper Peninsula to the small town of Grand Marais (pronounced mah-RAY) and back to Marquette. Much of it goes through the Hiawatha National Forest. Up to 40 mushers, each leading a 12-dog team, enter the race every year. The U.P. 200 is a qualifying race for the Iditarod Trail Sled Dog Race, which is held in Alaska.

Basic: At 240 miles, the U.P. 200 is considered a mid-distance race. The Iditarod, on the other hand, is a distance race. How many miles long is the Iditarod: 450 miles, 750 miles, or 1,150 miles?

Intermediate: Mushers are often heard yelling commands to their dogs during a race. The following are common commands, but what does each mean? Hike up! Gee! Haw!

Advanced: Two other common terms are On by! and Trail! The musher calls out one of these to his or her dog team, and the other to a nearby musher. What do they mean? Also, what is pedaling?

See next page for answers.

MM 356

Sled dog races are held in several parts of Michigan each winter. (Kalamazoo Nature Center)

tive for sailing, boating and fishing. The islands, each of which has its own individual name, are collectively called Les Cheneaux, which means "the channels" in French. Before the French named them, the local Ojibwe Indians also referred to them as "the channels," but in their own language. Today, visitors may hear Les Cheneaux

THE ANSWERS

The Iditarod is *1,150 miles long*. Its route passes through mountains, forests and open tundra on its way from Willow, which is north of Anchorage in south-central Alaska to Nome, which is on the west coast of Alaska.

name for rainbow trout when they migrate upstream to spawn.)

Exit 359

This exit is the gateway and M-134 is the route to the far eastern Upper Peninsula, and such places as De Tour Village, Drummond Island and the Les Cheneaux (pronounced lay shen-O) Islands.

From I-75, M-134 runs east, mainly following the shoreline of a series of Lake Huron bays before reaching the region of the Les Cheneaux Islands. These are a series of three dozen, mainly thin islands that stretch out finger-like into Lake Huron. Among the islands, which are often just a quarter to a half mile apart, are a collection of small bays and channels that are especially attrac-

Besides the soft padding of paws and the swoosh of the sled's runners on the snow, often the only noise made by a passing sled is the musher's occasional commands to the dog team. "Hike up" can tell the team to either *start running or run faster*. "Gee" means to *turn or veer right*, and "haw" means to *turn or veer to the left*.

When one sled wishes to pass another, the passing musher yells out "Trail!" This tells the other musher to *yield the trail so the approaching team can pass*. The passing musher tells his or her team "On by" to instruct the dogs to *pass the other sled and team*. Pedaling is *a maneuver by the musher in which he or she keeps one foot on the sled's runner, while pushing along the ground with the other* as a child would on a scooter. This helps speed along the team.

248

The Les Cheneaux Islands are popular for sailing, boating and fishing. (Raymond J. Malace)

pronounced "The Snows," which is not necessarily precise, but certainly descriptive in the cold winters.

From the Les Cheneaux Islands, M-134 continues east to De Tour (DEE-toor) Village, which is at the easternmost tip of the U.P. mainland. Early European explorers and fur traders all came into Michigan—or rather, what would eventually become Michigan—by boat and from the north, navigating down the St. Marys River, and around the projection of land where De Tour is located, and toward the straits, Mackinac Island and the Lower Peninsula. The Ojibwe Indians, who were already well-acquainted with the geography here, named it Giwideonaning, which translates roughly to "the place we go around." In 1856, the community got the name of Detour (then written as one word), which also means "to go around," but in French rather than Ojibwa. Situated as it was at the

turn in a primary navigational route, Detour became a busy trading center for north- and southbound lake and river traffic.

The name of Detour held until 1953, when the spelling changed to De Tour. In 1961, it underwent its last name change, adding the word "village" to the name. This was no doubt helpful for travelers who may have seen a sign for De Tour and assumed it meant they were being rerouted!

One of the biggest town boosters in De Tour's long history was Theodore Bateski, a Catholic priest who arrived in the community in 1904 to run what was his very first parish. He found the church and church house to be in such bad shape that he spent his initial two weeks at the local hotel while getting the buildings in order. His job also included responsibility

249

In many areas, Lake Superior's rocky shoreline rises steeply from the water. (Leslie Mertz)

time—in less than a year. That church still stands and remains an active parish today.

Although Bateski had plenty to keep him busy, his life wasn't all work. He bought and had shipped in what was the first automobile to grace the De Tour area. It was a 1908 Reo runabout. Shortly thereafter, the priest decided he preferred a Ford instead. To keep his costs down, he took the necessary steps to obtain a Ford dealership ... and kept it just long enough to get the dealer's discount on the car he wanted.

By 1922, the population of the area had grown enough to warrant separate pastors for the two churches, so Bateski was able to concentrate his efforts in De Tour. He went to work on a replacement church, which became the large Sacred Heart church that remains to this day. He also toiled tirelessly to build up the community and became involved in local politics, even serving as president of the village council for six years in the 1930s and starting up the local chamber of commerce. These contributions earned him the nickname of "the fighting priest of De Tour." The Catholic Church recognized his good work in 1954 by promoting him to monsignor. Bateski remained at Sacred Heart until he finally retired in 1960, 56 years after he had arrived. He passed away five years later, but his legacy lives on in this corner of the Upper Peninsula.

Not far off the shore of De Tour Village is Drummond (DRUMmund) Island, the largest U.S. island

for a nearby mission, which was about 12 miles to the northwest in Goetzville. When he made the trek there, he found a tiny log church in even worse condition than the church in De Tour. The mission had been abandoned and neglected for years. It was a daunting first assignment for a new priest, but Bateski jumped right in. In between his other priestly duties, he traveled to and from Goetzville in a horse-drawn buggy to lead the construction of a new mission church. In just one year, the church was completed and named St. Stanislaus. A suspicious fire burned down the church just 17 months later, but even that wasn't enough to dampen the priest's spirit and he again spearheaded a construction effort that rebuilt the church—even bigger this in the Great Lakes. It measures about 20 miles from east to west and about 12 miles from north to south at its broadest reaches. Various points, coves and bays give the island a shoreline that runs 150 miles. The interior of the 87,000-acre island holds 40 lakes. The majority of the island is state land, so visitors have an opportunity to explore its lakes, forests and interesting geology. A type of rock called dolomite is visible at the surface at various locations around the island. This typically white rock is used in iron smelting, which is the process that extracts usable iron from mined iron ore.

The name of Drummond Island comes from a British commander named Sir Gordon Drummond who ordered his men to construct a fort on the island during the time of the War of 1812 when forces from the United Kingdom and its colonies, including Canada, clashed with those from the United States. At one point in the three-year war, the British/Canadian army was even able to capture Detroit temporarily (see exit 46). During the skirmishes, Gordon Drummond was working feverishly on the U.K. side to shore up key locations along the U.S.-Canada border, and he saw Drummond Island

BRAINBUSTERS

The large number of shipwrecks on the Great Lakes have spawned many stories, some true and some perhaps not. One of the most haunting tales centers on the *Myron*, an approximately 50-foot-long, wooden steamer known as a "lumber hooker" because it was able to connect to a lumber-carrying barge. The *Myron* was in this configuration when she set sail on Lake Superior in November 1919 on what was to be her last run of the season. A winter storm set in, and between the lake water freezing on deck and the wind-whipped snow, the passage was a nasty one. When the ship started to break apart, its captain, Walter Neal, gave the order to release the barge. It wasn't enough. He called for his crew to abandon ship, but he stayed with the *Myron*, clinging to a large piece of the ship as he watched his crew row away in the lifeboats.

Basic: The lifeboats apparently reached the rocky cliffs along the shore, but the men never made it onto the safety of land. Why not?

Intermediate: During the two-decade period of 1878–1898, the number of ships seriously damaged on the Great Lakes most closely averaged: one per month, one per week or one per day?

Advanced: The Great Lakes are large, but not as immense as the oceans. Nonetheless, hundreds of shipwrecks have occurred on the Great Lakes over the years. Why does their smaller size make them especially hazardous in comparison to the oceans?

See next page for answers.

and its position near the entrance to the St. Marys River as particularly critical. Once the fort was built, the British held the fort, even retaining it after the War of 1812 was over. Part of the reason was the uncertainty of the U.S.-Canada border: Was Drummond Island part of Canada or part of the United States? Until they knew for sure, the Brits stayed put. Even when word came in 1822 that the island was indeed part of the United States, the exodus was a slow one. The British/Canadian forces didn't completely abandon the fort for another six years, which makes Drummond Island one of the last—

Exit 359

if not *the* last—British-occupied locations in the United States.

Between De Tour Village on the mainland and Drummond Island lies the mile-wide De Tour Passage that boaters now and in the past have used to travel between the St. Marys River and Lake Huron. The narrowness of the passage and the storms that can brew on the Great Lakes, however, have combined to spell disaster for a number of ships. A De Tour Passage Underwater Preserve protects the shipwrecks in the area, and many divers visit each year to see them. One of the particularly popular shipwrecks is that of the *John B. Merrill*. Built in

THE ANSWERS

The men in the lifeboats presumably were unable to reach safety because, like the ship, *the steep and rocky shoreline was covered with ice.* Even in the summer, the shoreline is difficult to climb, but with a slick coating, it was no doubt impassable. A mail carrier who was making his deliveries by dog sled to nearby lumbering camps is said to have found eight of the *Myron's* 16 crewmen completely encased in ice, some of them appearing as if they were standing upright. The only survivor of the shipwreck was Capt. Neal, who was able to stay afloat for 20 hours until he made it to safety.

From 1878–1898, 6,000 vessels were reported wrecked on the Great Lakes. That averages 300 per year, or nearly one a day. Of those 6,000, about 1,100 were total losses.

The smaller size of the Great Lakes compared to the oceans make them especially prone to shipwrecks for several reasons. One is that the lakes are shallower. The captain of a vessel on the ocean can often ride out a storm without worrying about being blown too close to shallow waters near shore or over a shoal. *Lake-going vessels, however, have less room to navigate and often run aground, where they can sustain serious damage. In addition, wind over the comparatively shallow water of the Great Lakes can cause waves to rise quickly and more sharply, often with little warning.* On the oceans, waves may become taller, but they are usually slow-rolling and more predictable, giving a crew time to maneuver the ship into the most advantageous position.

Milwaukee in 1873, the *Merrill* was a wooden, three-masted schooner that sailed the Great Lakes for more than two decades before meeting her fate on Oct. 14, 1893. On that date, the 189-foot-long *Merrill* sank when it struck a shoal south of Drummond Island during a fierce gale. The crewmen were able to abandon ship, but the *Merrill* went down. The schooner remained under the waves, its exact location unknown to boats passing overhead until she was rediscovered in 1992—99 years after she sank—in about 65 feet of water. The *Merrill* still has onboard or in the surrounding debris field some of the crew's personal effects, ship tools, the anchor and other pieces of ship hardware.

Mile Marker 365

Michigan has several Pine rivers within its boundaries. The Pine River that crosses here starts to the northwest, flows generally eastward until it reaches about 10 miles to the north of this point on I-75, and then turns southward. Once it crosses I-75 here, it continues down into Lake Huron's St. Martin Bay. For much of its distance, the Pine River travels through land within the Hiawatha National Forest, which covers two large slices of the Upper Peninsula, one here in the eastern U.P. and another in the central U.P. A century ago, the 880,000 acres now in the forest were mainly barren. The trees had been cut during the logging era and subsequent fires had cleared even the leftover branches from the ground. Regrowth was very limited, but the forests were able to mount a substantial recovery in the 1930s when the Civilian Conservation Corps began a massive tree-planting initiative here and throughout the state. (See exit 244 for details.)

BRAINBUSTERS

The Upper Peninsula is home to many legends, some surrounding the local Ojibwe Indians, and others about French trappers and fur traders.

Basic: One of the most well-known legends of northern Michigan is that of the loup garou (pronounced loop ga-ROO) or roup garou, as they are known in the St. Ignace area. A number of horror movies have featured these creatures, although they are called something else. What is it?

Intermediate: A common legend is that some U.P. Indians and/or fur trappers were bloodstoppers. What unusual skill did a bloodstopper have?

Advanced: An Ojibwe legend tells of a bearwalker, an individual who at night has the ability to turn into an animal. The animal is often a bear, but sometimes an owl, insect or other creature. The bearwalker could approach a person, cause him or her to become drowsy, then fall ill and finally die. According to the legend, how could a person tell the difference between a bearwalker and a real animal?

See next page for answers.

MM 365

Mile Marker 369

Near here, I-75 crosses the border between Chippewa County to the north and Mackinac County to the south. Mackinac County continues south to about halfway across the Mackinac Bridge that separates the Upper and Lower Peninsulas. Its name goes back to an Ojibwe (Chippewa) Indian word, which means "turtle." Originally, the county was called Michilimackinac, which means "big turtle." Chippewa County gets its name from the local Indians, who lived here long before the Europeans arrived in the 1600s. Chippewa is a pronunciation of Ojibwe with the initial "o" silent. Sometimes, Ojibwe individuals will refer to themselves not as Ojibwe, but as Anishinaabeg, which means "original people" or "good people on the proper path." The word *ojibwe* is often translated as "puckered" in reference to the puckered look of their traditional moccasins.

The Ojibwe are one of the largest Indian groups in North America, and today have 150 bands, mainly residing in the Great Lakes region and westward to south-central Canada.

THE ANSWERS

Loup garou is the French version of werewolf. The U.P. legend of these beasts can be traced to the French fur trappers and traders who once frequented this region. According to the story, people who had fallen on hard times would become engaged to the devil for a certain number of months in exchange for money. As a result, the person would become a wolf, or perhaps another type of animal, such as a bear or an owl, and would then attack other people. Once the months of service were up, the loup garou would not simply revert into a human. Instead, it had to incur a bloody wound at the hand of another person. The blood caused the release of the animal skin, which would fall from the body and reveal the naked person underneath.

A bloodstopper was a person who was able to end the bleeding from a wound simply by whispering a few words. The bloodstopper could accomplish the task even from a great distance. According to the legend, the bloodstopping abilities often fell on men who were the seventh sons of seventh sons. In addition, a bloodstopper could confer the ability to another member of his or her family by reading certain passages from the Bible.

The telltale clue that an animal was actually a bearwalker in disguise was a glow that emanated from the animal. A bearwalker maintained its power by going to its victim's final resting place, and taking a small piece of flesh from the person, usually the tip of a toe, finger or tongue, and keeping it in a medicine sac. The only way to stop a bearwalker was to shoot it with a gun during the night when it was in the form of an animal.

Mile Marker 371

People are often shocked to see farms in the Upper Peninsula, but farmers are able to plant and harvest select crops, like hay or corn, even this far north. Besides the more-typical farms like those along I-75 here, the Upper Peninsula is also home to the historic Centennial Cranberry Farm. This farm, located another 40 miles north and just off the shore of Lake Superior, has been producing cranberries since 1876—and has remained in the same family all that time. Cranberries grow in moist, acidic soil. Harvesters gather juice berries by flooding the field when the berries are ripe. The plump, red berries float to the surface, and workers gather up the harvest with specialized equipment. To harvest berries to sell fresh, harvesters dry-pick them off the vine to make sure the fruits aren't damaged.

Exit 373

This exit leads to the communities of Rudyard and Pickford.

Rudyard is located about a mile and a half to the west. Rudyard's original name was Pine River, after a waterway that flows just to the west of town. (See mile marker 365 for more information on the Pine River.) This caused a bit of confusion, however, because the state had a number of other rivers with that name. Fred Underwood, who was the general manager of the Soo line of the Baltimore and Ohio Railroad, had a solution. He suggested the replacement name of Rudyard to honor English author Rudyard Kipling. Kipling had written a number of highly respected novels, including *Jungle Book* in 1894 and *Gunga Din* in 1890. The town's name became Rudyard in 1891, 16 years before Kipling would win the Nobel Prize for Literature.

The naming of the town did not go unnoticed by Kipling. According to *Michigan: A Guide to the Wolverine State*, the author acknowledged the naming of the Upper Peninsula community by sending a photograph to Underwood with a poem written on the back. Part of it read:

> "'Wise is the child who knows
>   his sire,'
> The ancient proverb ran,
> But wiser far the man who knows
> How, where and when his offspring
>   grows,
> For who the mischief would suppose
> I've sons in Michigan?"

The community of Pickford is about 10.5 miles to the southeast of I-75 as the crow flies. By road, it's about 5 miles farther. Named for its first settler, this small berg is located on the Munuscong (pronounced muh-NUSS-kahng) River. The river gets its name from the bay into which the river eventually flows. This bay is known as Munuscong Bay or Munuscong Lake, and it sits off to the side of the Saint Marys River that runs along the eastern edge of the Upper Peninsula and connects Lake Superior to Lake Huron. Munuscong is an Ojibwe word for "bay of the rushes." At one time, the Ojibwe collected the long, slender leaves of the rushes and

With all the water around and in the state of Michigan, fishing is a big recreational sport. (Leslie Mertz)

weaved them together to make floor rugs or seating mats.

Today, the shallow waters of Munuscong Bay are known primarily for their fishing opportunities. Anglers regularly take nice catches of northern pike, walleye, muskellunge and perch. The one state-record fish caught on Munuscong Bay, however, was none of those species. It was a 40-inch-long, 18.25 pound burbot (pronounced BUR-but) captured in 1980. A burbot, sometimes called an eelpout, is a freshwater cod. Although most anglers in Michigan throw them back, the meat is nutritious and can be quite tasty. In fact, some describe boiled and buttered burbot as tasting similar to lobster. In addition, burbot is an excellent source of cod liver oil, a supplement some people use to bolster their vitamin D intake or to treat various health conditions, such as arthritis.

Exit 378

The very small community of Kinross is to the west, and the town of Kincheloe (pronounced KINCH-lo) is to the east. Kinross is the older of the two, and was settled by Scottish-Irish families who traveled south to this location from Canada. They named it Kinross after the county of the same name in Scotland.

Kincheloe arose in 1941 as an air field for the U.S. Air Force, which was then known as the U.S. Army Air Force. Originally named the Kinross Auxiliary Field, its name changed in 1947 to Kinross Air Force Base and then to Kincheloe Air Force Base in 1959. The name Kincheloe paid tribute to Captain Iven Kincheloe, a Michigan native who was a jet ace in the Korean conflict of the early 1950s, and then a test pilot for the F-100 Super Sabre and the F-104 Starfighter. Developed in 1954, the Super Sabre was the first U.S. jet fighter that could reach supersonic speeds in a level flight, which means that it could break the sound barrier even when it wasn't in a dive. The Starfighter came four years later in 1958, and was also capable of supersonic flight. Some safety issues arose with the Starfighter, and it was while flying one of the first of these aircraft that Capt. Kincheloe crashed and died. Before that fateful flight, however, Kincheloe was able to make another mark in aviation history. In 1956, he flew a rocket-powered research craft known as a Bell X-2 Starbuster, to a new world record for altitude: 126,200 feet. That's a height of almost 24 miles. Had he not died when he did, Kincheloe would likely have become America's first spaceman because he had been selected to fly the X-15, an aircraft that was in the works to fly more than twice as high as the X-2 and therefore reach space. Due to his death, Kincheloe's alternate instead got the X-15 assignment and in 1962 flew at 4,105 miles per hour to an altitude of 314,750 feet—about 60 miles—on July 17, 1962.

Exit 378

BRAINBUSTERS

Occasionally, drivers see wolves crossing I-75 here, and on at least one occasion, a driver has hit one.

Basic: Both gray wolves and coyotes live in the Upper Peninsula. They look somewhat similar, but wolves are larger. A typical adult coyote will weigh between 25 and 45 pounds. What is the weight range for a typical adult gray wolf: 30-90 pounds, 55–115 pounds, or 80–140 pounds?

Intermediate: For many years, researchers have been studying gray wolves on Isle Royale (pronounced ROY-ul), an island national park located in western Lake Superior. Scientists are interested in the relationship between the size of the wolf's population and that of its primary prey. What is the wolf's primary prey species on Isle Royale?

Advanced: Gray wolves were once common throughout Michigan, but overhunting—often spurred by a bounty on the animals—exterminated them completely from the Lower Peninsula by 1910, and nearly eliminated them from the Upper Peninsula by the time state lawmakers finally took action to protect them in the 1960s. In fact, biologists in 1973 estimated that outside of Isle Royale, only six wolves lived in the entire state, all of them in the Upper Peninsula. In 1989, however, biologists were heartened when they found some evidence that suggested the wolves might start breeding again in Michigan, and therefore could possibly make a recovery after all. What evidence did they find?

See next page for answers.

Kincheloe Air Force Base is no longer open. It closed in 1977, and the airfield was converted into the Chippewa County International Airport, which added a passenger terminal in 2002. The airport has four regularly scheduled commercial flights a day: two outbound and two inbound.

Exit 379

The community of Barbeau (pronounced bar-BO) is several miles to the east of I-75. If you ventured another 3 miles beyond the town, you would see the large Neebish Island just offshore and nearly filling the St. Marys River. On the island's opposite side, it almost touches Ontario, Canada. "Neebish" comes from an Ojibwe word meaning "where the water boils," which is a reference to the tumultuous rapids that once ran along the island's west side. The days of the rapids disappeared when locks were installed on either side of the island: one for southbound freighters and one for northbound water traffic. First-time boaters and other visitors to the island are often flabbergasted at the sight of an enormous freighter slowly (and barely!) skirting the shores of the island—and often rising taller than the surrounding trees.

Mile Marker 382

The wetlands on the southbound side of I-75 look much like those found in the Lower Peninsula, but they may hold a few different species, particularly when it comes to amphibians and reptiles.

One reason is the glacier that once covered the state and eliminated any

THE ANSWERS

Adult gray wolves weigh between 80 and 140 pounds. They are the largest wild members of the dog family.

The researchers on Isle Royale are studying the relationship between gray wolves and the main component of their diet: *the moose*. Scientists are also interested in how the size of the moose population's affects the number of fir tree samplings, which is the food the moose eat. The study is one of the longest ongoing studies ever conducted: It has been running continuously for approximately 50 years.

In 1989, scientists found *two adjacent sets of wolf tracks*. This suggested that a male and female had paired off and might start breeding. Their suspicions were correct. In 1991, this pair produced pups. It marked the first time in 35 years that wild gray wolves had bred in Michigan outside of Isle Royale. Since then, the wolf population in the Upper Peninsula has climbed considerably. Estimated at just 20 wolves in 1992, it jumped to 216 in 2000, and 434 in 2005. In addition, state wildlife officials in 2004 confirmed the presence of three gray wolves in the Lower Peninsula—the first since 1910.

already-existing amphibians and reptiles from Michigan. When the glacier receded back north, about 11,000–13,000 years ago, amphibians and reptiles slowly began returning to the Lower Peninsula from Ohio, Indiana and Illinois. Over the centuries that followed, those that could survive in the Michigan climate crept father and farther north, but some found the Straits of Mackinac to be a barrier they just couldn't cross. For this reason, the Lower Peninsula is home to certain species, like the eastern Massasauga (pronounced mas-suh-SAW-guh) rattlesnake and the northern ribbon snake, but the Upper Peninsula is not. Although it may be startling to think that the Lower Peninsula had rattlers, Massasaugas (scientific name: *Sistrurus catenatus catenatus*) are shy creatures that would much rather run from or hide from a human than encounter one. These chunky but small snakes (reaching just 2–3 feet long) have short fangs that are hard-pressed to penetrate a boot or even a pair of sturdy blue jeans, so they seldom inject their venom into a person even on the rare occasions when they strike. In fact, experts say most people who are bitten by this little rattler are teenage boys and young men who harass a Massasauga … frequently at the urging of their peers and often with their judgment clouded by alcohol. If a person does get a penetrating bite, it is rarely fatal but still requires immediate medical attention. Ribbon snakes (*Thamnophis sauritus septentrionalis*), on the other hand, are non-venomous, as

Exit 379
MM 382

The numbers of moose (top) and gray wolves on Isle Royale in Lake Superior are interconnected because moose are the primary prey of the wolves, and wolves are the sole predators of moose. (Moose: USDA Forest Service, Superior National Forest; Wolf: USFWS/John and Karen Hollingsworth)

are all other wild snakes in Michigan. They are thin, brown-and-black snakes with three cream-colored stripes running the length of the body. To an untrained eye, they look like garter snakes.

Besides the Massasauga rattler and the ribbon snake, several other snakes are found in the Lower Peninsula, but only in small areas of the Upper Peninsula. For instance, both the brown snake (*Storeria dekayi*) and the eastern hognose snake (*Heterodon platyrhinos*) live throughout the Lower Peninsula, but only exist in the far southern Upper Peninsula at the border with Wisconsin. The population in the U.P. did not cross the straits, but instead came up through Wisconsin.

One species of amphibian—the mink frog—made its way into the Upper Peninsula, but has as yet never crossed the straits or otherwise entered the Lower Peninsula. This mottled brown-and-green frog lives in ponds, lakes, slow streams and other wetlands that are heavy with vegetation, like cattails and/or lily pads. A lucky driver past this wetland on I-75 might be able to hear the male mink frogs' deep, knocking call during their breeding season in June and July.

Exit 386

M-28 proceeds west from I-75 across the Upper Peninsula. For the most part, it runs more or less through the center of the U.P., but the 43-mile stretch between the cities of Marquette (pronounced mar-KET) and Munising (MYOO-nih-sing) in the central U.P. closely follows the shore of Lake Superior. In the winter, lake-effect snows and winds from the north can produce extremely low visibility, sometimes barely beyond the hood of the car. These conditions, called a whiteout, sometimes force officials to close this stretch of highway until the weather clears up.

Heading to the west from I-75, M-28 takes travelers through mainly forest and swamp, but it does pass by a few small communities. Two of them stand out: Seney (75 miles from

I-75) and Shingleton (about 101 miles west of I-75).

Today, Seney (pronounced SEE-nee) is a small and quiet community, but in the lumbering era, it had a reputation as the roughest logging town in the Upper Peninsula … and the U.P. had a good share of wild logging towns. Considering the many stories about Seney and the men who frequented it, the reputation was well-deserved. One book, called *Michigan: A Guide to the Wolverine State*, includes a section on some of the legendary men who lived in or passed through Seney:

- P.J. "Snap Jaw" Small, who bet and won drinks by biting off the heads of live snakes and frogs, and once nipped the head off of an owl
- "Protestant Bob" McGuire, who seldom fought but when he did, clawed at his opponent with his thumbnails, which he had shaped into knife-like points
- "Stub Foot" O'Donnell and "Pump Handle Joe" who would literally shake down new arrivals to town by flipping them upside down and shaking the money out of their pockets
- native Michigander Leon Czolgosz (pronounced CHAWL-gosh), who spent some time as a railroad section hand in the Upper Peninsula before moving to New York, where in 1901, he assassinated U.S. President William McKinley. Czolgosz walked up to the president and in front of a crowd of witnesses, drew a .32 caliber gun and fired two rounds at point-blank range, kill-

LESLIE'S WEEKLY
McKINLEY EXTRA

Vol. XCIII—EXTRA NUMBER   New York, September 9, 1901   PRICE 10 CENTS

LEON F. CZOLGOSZ, THE ASSASSIN.

Leon Czolgosz, who spent time working on the railroad in the Upper Peninsula, is shown in jail after he moved to New York and assassinated President McKinley in 1901. (Library of Congress. Leslie's weekly, McKinley extra, Sept. 9, 1901)

ing McKinley. Within a matter of weeks, Czolgosz was tried, convicted and executed by electrocution.

With its wild logging days behind it, Seney is now a small community best known for the Seney National Wildlife Refuge, which is a few miles south of town. Established in 1935, the refuge covers more than 95,000 acres in the Great Manistique (mann-ih-STEEK) Swamp and provides a stopover point for thousands of migratory birds in the spring and fall. One of the birds that always draws attention is the trumpeter swan. Large

white birds with black bills, the swans had disappeared from the Upper Peninsula and most of North America by the late 1800s. In 1991, however,

BRAINBUSTERS

Michigan has had a long line of interesting governors.

Basic: G. Mennen Williams, who won six terms as governor from 1949–1961, had an unusual nickname. What was it, and what did it signify?

Intermediate: George Romney was the governor in Michigan from 1963–1969. He was born in Mexico because his family had moved there to avoid a certain law in the United States. What did that law prohibit?

Advanced: One of the most colorful of Michigan's governors was Chase Salmon Osborn, who served from 1911–1912. He had already had a rather-too-thrilling career as a newspaperman in northern Wisconsin where he survived assassination attempts from a murderous gang that was running a white-slavery ring there. After shutting down the ring, he moved to the U.P.'s Sault Sainte Marie, where he developed a skill for predicting the location of iron ore deposits, and amassed a considerable fortune. He also started to take an interest in politics, and eventually became governor. He is perhaps best known, however, for adopting an orphan named Stella Lee Brunt. What was unusual about the adoption?

See page 263 for answers.

Exit 386

After disappearing from the Upper Peninsula and indeed most of North America by the late 1800s, trumpeter swans are now making a comeback.

MM 387

wildlife biologists embarked on an effort to reintroduce the birds to Seney. Over a three-year period, they released 44 two-year-old trumpeter swans at the refuge with the hope that the birds would mate and start a new population. The plan worked. By 2005, the refuge had a healthy population of more than 200 swans, and at least 30 nests.

In addition to bird-watching opportunities, the refuge has miles of hiking, cross-country skiing and biking trails, two rivers for paddling, and a 7-mile-long wildlife drive with observation decks along the way for drivers and passengers to get out of the car and soak up the sights and sounds of nature in the Upper Peninsula.

The community of Shingleton, about 26 miles to the west of Seney, got its name from a shingle-making operation dating to the late 1800s. Today, it is perhaps best known for Iverson's snowshoes. This company makes traditional snowshoes from the wood of the white ash tree. At the company's shop, workers steam and bend the wood to the proper shape,

dry it in a kiln, and then lace the snowshoe either with the traditional rawhide or with neoprene. As a final step, they dip the snowshoe in lacquer to help keep snow from sticking to the shoe as the wearer is hiking along. Besides the snowshoes, the company also makes furniture and decorating items with a snowshoe flair, and is starting to make trout-fishing nets.

— — —

Brimley State Park is about 7.5 miles northwest of this point on I-75. Brimley is a 237-campsite park in on the water's edge in the area where the St. Marys River opens into Lake Superior's Whitefish Bay. Many people come to the park to take advantage of its swimming beaches, fishing opportunities, boat launch and hiking trails. Others come to Brimley because it's centrally located to numerous U.P. attractions, including Tahquamenon Falls (see exit 352), the Hiawatha National Forest (see exits 198 and 365) and the Soo Locks in Sault Ste. Marie (see exit 394).

Mile Marker 387

Signs along the freeway announce that this northernmost stretch of I-75 is part of the Lake Superior Circle Tour. The tour takes travelers through the Upper Peninsula, and parts of Wisconsin, Minnesota and Ontario as it winds its way approximately 1,300 miles around Lake Superior, the largest of the Great Lakes.

In all, the surface area of Lake Superior approaches 32,000 square miles, which is about the size of South Carolina. Lake Superior is also the deepest of the Great Lakes, averaging 500 feet deep and in some spots dropping to 1,332 feet deep. The considerable depth makes for some cold water, and even on the hottest summer days, few people will take even a short dip in Lake Superior. After all, the average water temperature is a bone-chilling 39–40 degrees Fahrenheit. That extreme cold is the reason that Lake Superior is known to never give up its dead, meaning that the body of a person who drowns in the lake's deep water will never float to the surface. Why does this happen? Bacteria feed off decaying organisms, even under water. As they do, they release gases that accumulate in the body and eventually buoy it up to the surface. The water in Lake Superior is so cold that bacteria don't grow well, so a sunken body remains sunken. The bays of Lake Superior are generally shallower and a bit warmer in the summertime, and there, the lake does yield drowning victims.

THE ANSWERS

Gerhard Mennen Williams was nicknamed *"Soapy,"* because *he had inherited the family fortune, which was made in the soap business.*

George Romney's family was Mormon, and his father and grandfather could not abide *the U.S. law that prohibited polygamy.* Like many other Mormons at the time, his family moved to Mexico, where the future Michigan governor was born. His family later moved back to the United States, where Romney held jobs as a political speechwriter and lobbyist before becoming involved in the automobile industry and eventually moving into the job of president of American Motors Corp. He remained interested in politics, and made a successful run for governor of the state of Michigan, taking office in 1963. In 1967, he made a bid for U.S. president, but pulled out of the race early the following year. He resigned his post as Michigan governor in 1969 to become U.S. Secretary of Housing and Urban Development under U.S. President Richard Nixon.

When Chase Osborn adopted Stella Brunt in 1931, he was 71 and *she was 37.* The two had become acquainted through correspondence 10 years earlier, at which time Osborn was married. Osborn and Brunt finally met in person in 1924, and soon afterward she became his secretary. By 1931, with Osborn then separated from his wife, he adopted Brunt who promptly moved in with him. The arrangement continued until April 9, 1949, when on his death bed, Osborn annulled the adoption and married her. He died two days later of complications from pneumonia.

Six Mile Road crosses in this area. It is six miles south of Sault Ste. Marie.

At this point, travelers are less than 7 miles to the west of the St. Marys River. Although "Marys" should have an apostrophe to be grammatically correct, its official name is indeed St. Marys without the apostrophe. The river, which was named by early French explorers, wraps around the eastern side of the Upper Peninsula, starting at the bottom of Lake Superior's Whitefish Bay, which is about 12 miles to the northwest and then passing between two cities with the same name: Sault Sainte Marie in Michigan and Sault Sainte Marie in Ontario, Canada. From there, the river curves south between the U.P. and a large island, called Sugar Island, and then squeezes past Neebish Island before continuing south past Drummond Island and into Lake Huron.

For many years, the river was a navigational nightmare, because the water drops a full 22 feet in elevation and has a series of difficult rapids. The first travelers on the river were American Indians. When the white men arrived in the 1600s, they found that the local Ojibwe Indians had already developed a well-worn land path so they could haul their canoes out of the river and portage around the worst of the rapids.

The first of the white men to reach the St. Marys River was Étienne Brûlé (pronounced AY-tee-ane broo-LAY) in 1618. Étienne is the French version of Stephen. Brûlé came up from the south, and made his way upstream through the treacherous St. Marys rapids to become the first non-Indian to step onto Michigan soil in what is now known as Sault Sainte Marie (see exit 394). Unfortunately, Brûlé was illiterate, so the details of this voyage were never recorded.

By the time he had reached Michigan, Brûlé was already a seasoned adventurer. He had been born in France, but when he was only 16 years old, he set sail for the New World and landed in Québec, a settlement only recently founded by the highly respected French explorer Samuel de Champlain. Champlain took notice of the young man, and as he would do with another eventual Michigan adventurer named Jean Nicolet (see exit 337), he instructed Brûlé to live among the Huron Indian people, and learn their language and customs so he could become an interpreter and scout for Champlain's expeditions into unknown lands. One of Brûlé's trips with Champlain was into the Great Lakes of Huron and Ontario in 1615. That voyage was successful, but the following year would be difficult for Brûlé. In 1616, a group of Iroquois Indians captured and tortured him, but he survived the encounter. Two years later, Champlain sent Brûlé out to explore farther north into Lake Huron, and it was this trip that brought him through the St. Marys River and to Sault Ste. Marie.

After this journey, Brûlé grew weary of colonial life and its social and religious restrictions, and he spent most of the rest of his life living among the Huron Indians and conducting fur-trading transactions. Champlain was disappointed with Brûlé's preference for life in the wilds. That displeasure came to a head in 1629 when Québec fell to a British attack, and Champlain accused Brûlé of acting as a scout for the enemy. Fortunately for Brûlé, little came of the accusation and he was able to continue his life among the Indians. Three years later, however, his relationship with the Huron Indians took a severe turn, and Brûlé died at their hands. The details of Brûlé's final days and his death remain a mystery, but one hypothesis suggests that the Hurons believed he had begun trading with an enemy tribe, and viewed him as a traitor.

BRAINBUSTERS

People who are born and raised in the Upper Peninsula are called Yoopers. Some of them, particularly those from the central and western U.P., may use terminology that is unfamiliar to visitors.

Basic: Yoopers sometimes say "Holy wah!" Others may say they are "going to the IGA" or "going Shopko." What do each of these mean?

Intermediate: Explain "swampers," "choppers" and a "touke" (pronounced chook).

Advanced: Explain "Toivo and Eino," "sparklers" and the phrase "start with me last."

See page 267 for answers.

Exit 392

Large flocks of small black birds called starlings are common here. Although they are so plentiful throughout Michigan to frequently become a nuisance, they are not native to Michigan nor to North America. They are one of several European species that were released in New York City's Central Park in the early 1890s by a group called the American Acclimatization Society that wanted to introduce to the United States all of the birds that appeared in the works of Shakespeare. The group shipped over and set free 60–100 starlings, and from that stock arose the more than *200 million* starlings that now live in North America.

A large population of Ojibwe (Chippewa) Indians lives in this region. They are part of the Sault Tribe whose ancestors in the region date back hundreds of years. Despite this long history, the tribe's current governmental structure is fairly recent. In the 1940s, a few individuals set in motion a plan that would eventually gain them federally recognized status as the "Sault Ste. Marie Tribe of Chippewa Indians" in 1972. Today, this tribe has 29,000 members, although not all of them live in the Upper Peninsula. It is associated with five very successful U.P. casinos, the first of which opened in 1984. Together, these five casinos are one of the largest employers in the Upper Peninsula.

This exit leads into the city of Sault (pronounced soo) Sainte Marie, which is often shortened to "the Soo." A city of more than 14,000, it is one of the largest municipalities in the Upper Peninsula. It is small, however, in comparison to the much larger city just across the St. Marys River in Ontario, Canada. This city, also called Sault Ste. Marie, has a population of nearly 75,000. The two share a common name because they were considered to be one community for many years.

Originally, Ojibwe Indians gathered here to catch whitefish, numerous schools of which would pass through the river at certain times of year. The Ojibwe named this spot Baawitigong (sometimes spelled Bawating), which translates to "place of the rapids." The rapids here were quite strong, because the river narrows through this region on its way from Lake Superior to Lake Huron. They are also strong here because the water is actually falling 20–22 feet in elevation from the higher Lake Superior to the lower Lake Huron. The rapids were fierce enough along this stretch that the Ojibwe Indians had a set, overland route so they could portage their canoes around the rapids. That route is remembered today in the name of a Sault Sainte Marie street: Portage Avenue.

The first European, Étienne Brûlé (pronounced AY-tee-ane broo-LAY), made his way here by canoe from Québec as early as 1618, although some historians say it may have been a couple of years later. Regardless, it was definitely early in America's history. After all, the Mayflower was only just making its landing at Plymouth Rock in 1620! Brûlé named the place Sault de Gaston (pronounced goss-TONE). Sault is an archaic French word for rapids, and Gaston was the Duke of Orléans and the brother of Louis XIII, the king of France. Brûlé didn't stay in the Upper Peninsula, but his explorations here and throughout four of the five Great Lakes opened up the region to French fur traders and trappers. (For more on Brûlé, see mile marker 389.)

The name of Sault de Gaston changed in 1668—about 50 years after Brûlé set foot here. A catholic priest, Father Jacques Marquette (pronounced mar-KET), arrived to establish a settlement, and he christened it Sault Sainte Marie, or the "rapids of St. Mary," in honor of the Virgin Mary. Sault Sainte Marie became the first permanent settlement in Michigan, and also one of the first cities in the United States. After establishing the mission here, Marquette traveled to other areas, including St. Ignace (see exit 344), and was one of the explorers to discover the upper reaches of the Mississippi River.

The settlement in Sault Sainte Marie continued to thrive and grow, and became a major fur-trading hub. To protect its interests in the very profitable fur trade at a time when the British were expanding into the region, the French constructed a small fort, called Fort Repentigny, in Sault Sainte Marie in 1751. The British were able to gain control of the fort in 1762, but it burned down shortly thereafter. At that point, Sault Sainte Marie was part of a British province called Upper Canada that curved along the northern and eastern shores of the Great Lakes Superior, Huron, Erie and Ontario. The Upper Peninsula became the property of the United States following the Revolutionary War and the Treaty of Paris in 1783, but British soldiers didn't pull out of Sault Sainte Marie—or much of the U.P. for that matter—until 1797 following a second treaty, called the Jay Treaty, that tied up some loose ends.

The disputes over boundaries weren't over. When the War of 1812 started, old tensions between the U.S. and Great Britain generated skirmishes between soldiers and ships stationed on either side of the St. Marys River. Although the war ended three years later, the British still desired control over the Upper Peninsula, where they had been able to form lucrative fur-trading relationships with the local Ojibwe Indians. With hostility mounting once again, American soldiers arrived in 1822 and began to build a fort, called Fort Brady after its commander Col. Hugh Brady. Once the fort became operational, the

THE ANSWERS

"Holy Wah!" is the Yooper equivalent of "Holy cow!" "Going to the IGA" or "going Shopko" means that the person is *going shopping*. Yoopers often call any grocery store an IGA, even though IGA (the Independent Grocery Alliance) is only affiliated with some of them. Shopko is a chain of department stores with locations in the U.P.

Swampers are *tall rubber boots* used to walk through a swamp or other muddy terrain. Choppers are *leather or deer-hide mittens* that are worn over a second pair of cotton or wool mittens. Sometimes choppers instead have a cotton or wool lining. A touke is a *winter hat with a long tassel*, often called a stocking hat outside of the U.P.

Toivo and Eino are *Finnish characters that are the butt of many a Yooper*

joke, as in "So Toivo and Eino go to deer camp . . . ," Sparklers are a pair of *brand-new white socks*. "Start with me last" is sometimes heard during a card game and is a *request that others take their turns first*.

Here are a few other words you might hear while driving through the Upper Peninsula:

- "Give 'er tarpaper," which means to "give it your all" or "put in a big effort."
- "Side by each," which means "side by side."
- Heikki Lunta, who is a fictional backwoods character said to be able to do a magical dance and cause the snow to fall. Yoopers sometimes "pray to Heikki Lunta" to make it snow.

conflict between the British Canadians and the Americans ended, and life in Sault Sainte Marie settled back down. Over the following decades, Canada would become its own country, and the United States and Canadian governments would engage in a much more fruitful relationship, eventually working together to construct a bridge across the St. Marys River at Sault Sainte Marie to connect the two nations (see the following exit).

Int'l. Bridge

By the mid-1800s, shipping had become an important part of life in Sault Sainte Marie. The discovery of iron ore in the Upper Peninsula in the 1840s (see exit 310) led to an ore-mining boom, and much of that material made its way on ships to Sault Sainte Marie. Ships carrying lumber harvested from the Upper Peninsula also headed to the Soo. As they had in the past, however, the rapids in the river proved an insurmountable barrier to river transit, so workers had to offload the ships on one side of the rapids, transport the cargo over land to the other side of the rapids, and then reload the cargo onto ships waiting there. That all changed in 1855, when the state of Michigan got funding to construct and open to traffic a set of two locks on the river. The locks were immediately busy. Plans started soon afterward for another lock, which opened in 1881. Those locks have since been replaced, and four locks are currently located at Sault Sainte Marie, essentially serving as water elevators to raise and lower about 10,000 vessels

every year so they can safety navigate the river. (See the following exit.)

Throughout the lock-building era, Fort Brady remained in the Soo, although its location changed. In 1893, the U.S. Army ordered it dismantled and rebuilt on top of a hill overlooking the locks. Dubbed the "New Fort Brady," it remained a fairly quiet place until World War I and World War II, when military strategists feared that enemies could strike a serious blow against American steel production by targeting the locks, through which much of the iron ore passed. To counter the threat, the U.S. Army assigned thousands of soldiers to the fort and installed antiaircraft weapons to protect the locks. Once the wars were over, the fort closed for good. Many of its buildings still stand, however, and are part of Lake Superior State University, a 115-acre, nearly 3,000 student public university that sits on the former site of the fort.

At the International Bridge

The Sault Sainte Marie International Bridge here at the northernmost point on I-75 spans the St. Marys River that flows between the two cities of Sault Sainte Marie in Michigan and Sault Sainte Marie in Ontario, Canada. The bridge has three arched trusses, two on the American side and one on the Canadian side. The two on the American side extend over a canal through which freighters pass.

Construction on the International Bridge started in 1960 when Michigan and Ontario officials were able to agree on a plan as well as funding for

The Soo Locks make navigation possible through the rapids on the St. Marys River. (Travel Michigan)

the river crossing. The bridge cost $16 million and opened to traffic in 1962. Before the bridge was in place, most travelers between the twin Sault Sainte Maries took a car ferry across the river. Today, drivers need only pay a small toll and drive the span themselves. By the year 2000, the tolls collected at the bridge finally paid off the last of the bonds used to fund its construction, and the state of Michigan and Canada created a Joint International Bridge Authority to manage and operate the bridge. The arrangement has worked out very well, and many people point to the Sault Sainte Marie International Bridge as a shining example of how cooperation between two countries can benefit the common good.

To the east of the bridge's double arches are four locks that look like very narrow channels alongside long and thin islands. The locks eliminate the need for boats to go through the rapids that are visible just north of the locks (see exit 40 for information on lock operation). The rapids are considered a waterfall, and are one of the more than 150 waterfalls in the Upper Peninsula. These falls, called the Soo Rapids Falls, do not look particularly dramatic from the bridge, but from up close, they are a pleasure to watch as the water tumbles down. The bulk of the U.P.'s waterfalls are farther to the west, where they are quite numerous. The Tahquamenon Falls are the largest, but the smaller falls are no less spectacular. Some of them are well-marked, but not all. First-time drivers to the Upper Peninsula are often shocked to see small waterfalls along the side of the road, or surprised to find only a

Laughing Whitefish Falls (Leslie Mertz)

tiny wooden sign at a rest stop that simply reads "Falls" and points to a path. The trip down such a path can be very rewarding: a soft sound that gets louder with every step until the hiker realizes it is the rush of the waterfall; then views of the fast-flowing river; and finally an opening in the forest that reveals a wide wall of white pouring over rocks or a veil-like stream plummeting off of a cliff. Each waterfall is unique and each is mesmerizing.

Another point of interest visible from the bridge is a quarter-mile-long building that straddles a canal just beyond the locks. This is a hydro-electric plant now owned and operated by the Edison Sault Electric Co. More than a century old, it is the longest hydroelectric plant in the world. Construction of the plant began with the excavation of a 24-foot-deep and 200- to 220-foot-wide canal during the years 1898–1900. From 1900–1902, workers used steel as well as stone from the canal excavation to build the plant. They installed 41 turbines, the blades of which turn as the water rushes past. The energy from that action drives generators that produce electricity. Workers added another 33 turbines in 1915-16, giving the plant a total of 74 turbines, which still operate today. Through these turbines, up to 13.5 million gallons (30,000 cubic feet) of water pass every minute. According to the Edison Sault Electric Co., the plant produces 225 million kilowatt-hours annually, which is about 20 percent of the power needs of the entire eastern Upper Peninsula.

At the Ontario-Michigan Border

Depending on whether you're heading north or south, you are either entering or leaving a unique state. Geographically, Michigan is distinctive for many reasons, but most notably for its two peninsulas which together touch four of the five Great Lakes. This arrangement affects the state's weather, its crops, the distribution of its animals, and its rich cultural, political and industrial history.

BIBLIOGRAPHY

Numerous books detail the history of Michigan, including the naming of its counties and communities. Important resources for *Driving Michigan: Mile by Mile on I-75* included:

Baller, Clinton, and Joe Grimm (eds.). *Great Pages of Michigan History From The Detroit Free Press*. Detroit: Wayne State, 1987.

Callahan, Leo F. *My Story of Michigan Geography*. Hillsdale, Mich.: School Supply Co., 1948.

Cook, Webster. *Michigan: Its History and Government*. New York: The McMillan Co., 1905.

Dodge, R. L.. *Michigan Ghost Towns of the Lower Peninsula*, Las Vegas, Nev.: Glendon Publishing. 1970 and 1971

Dorson, Richard M. *Bloodstoppers and Bearwalkers: Folk Traditions of the Upper Peninsula*, Cambridge: Harvard University Press copyright 1952, second printing 1972.

Dunbar, William F. *Michigan*. Grand Rapids, Mich.: William B. Eerdmans Publishing Co., 1980.

Freedman, Eric. *Pioneering Michigan*. Franklin, Mich.: Altwerger and Mandel Publishing Co., 1992.

Grimm, Joe (ed.). *Michigan Voice*. Detroit: *Detroit Free Press* and Wayne State University Press, 1987.

Hemans, Lawton T. *History of Michigan*. Lansing, Mich.: The Hammond Publishing Co. Ltd., 1906.

Kelly, R.W., and W.R. Farrand. *The Glacial Lakes Around Michigan*. Michigan Geological Survey Bulletin. Lansing, Mich.: Speaker-Hines and Thomas Inc., 1967.

Michigan Gazetteer. Wilmington, Del.: American Historical Publications, 1991.

Romig, Walter. *Michigan Place Names*. Detroit: Wayne State University Press, 1986.

Savela, Judith A. *Michigan Municipalities*. Sterling Heights, Mich.: Sterling Heights Public Library: 1989.

Sommers, Lawrence M. *Michigan: The Geography*. Boulder and London: Westview Press, 1984.

Vogel, Virgil J. *Indian Names in Michigan*. Ann Arbor: University of Michigan Press, 1986.

Workers of the Writers' Program of the Work Projects Administration in the State of Michigan. *Michigan: A Guide to the Wolverine State*. Oxford University Press, 1941.

Some of the information on Michigan plants, trees and wildlife was drawn from the author's own experience as a field-biology instructor for programs offered through Wayne State and Eastern Michigan universities. Additional resources on these topics included:

James Harding and J. Alan Holman. *Michigan Turtles and Lizards.*
J. Alan Holman, et al. *Michigan Snakes*
James Harding and J. Alan Holman. *Michigan Frogs, Toads and Salamanders.*
Dunn, Gary. *Insects of the Great Lakes Region.* Ann Arbor: University of Michigan Press.
Barnes, Burton V. and Warren H. Wagner Jr. *Michigan Trees.* Ann Arbor: University of Michigan Press.
Kurta, Allen. *Mammals of the Great Lakes Region.* (Revised Edition.) Ann Arbor: University of Michigan Press.
Peterson, Roger Tory. *Eastern Birds* (Peterson Field Guides). Boston: Houghton Mifflin Co., 1980.
Ehrlich, Paul R., David S. Dobkin and Darryl Wheye. *The Birder's Handbook: A Field Guide to the Natural History of North American Birds.* New York: Simon and Schuster, 1988.
"Master Angler State Records," Michigan Department of Natural Resources, http://www.michigandnr.com/MasterAngler/MasterAngler.asp.

Demographic information about Michigan and other states is available through the U.S. Census Bureau at http://quickfacts.census.gov/qfd/states/.

Specific helpful resources for other exits mile markers and Brain Busters are listed below. The Brainbuster resources are listed with a nearby mile marker or exit. (All websites were current as of February/March, 2008.)

At the Ohio-Michigan border

"The Toledo War Song - Background Reading," State of Michigan History, Arts and Libraries, http://www.michigan.gov/hal/0,1607,7-160-17451_18670_18793-80167--,00.html.

Exit 15

"Monroe County Since 1817," Monroe County Convention and Tourism Bureau, http://www.monroeinfo.com/historicsites.html.
Rosentreter, R., "Remember the River Raisin," *Michigan History*, Nov./Dec. 1998, pp 40-48.
Additional newspapers excerpts about Gen. Custer's "Last Stand" area available online at http://www.custerslaststand.org/source/extra.html.

Exit 18

"Detroit River-Western Lake Erie Basin Indicator Project," U.S. Environmental Protection Agency, http://www.epa.gov/med/grosseile_site/indicators/whitefish.html.

Exit 29

"Enrico Fermi Biography," Fermi National Accelerator Laboratory, http://www.fnal.gov/pub/about/whatis/enricofermi.html.

"Fermi 2 Facts," Detroit Edison/DTE Energy, http://web.archive.org/web/20010215211229/www.detroitedison.com/aboutus/whoweare/fermi_facts.html.

Information about Lake Erie Metropark is available through the park's website at http://www.metroparks.com/parks/pk_lake_erie.php.

Mile Marker 37

"President Zachary Taylor and the Laboratory: Presidential Visit from the Grave," Oak Ridge National Laboratory, http://www.ornl.gov/info/ornlreview/rev27-12/text/ansside6.html.

"Zachary Taylor," American Presidents: Life Portraits, http://www.americanpresidents.org/presidents/president.asp?PresidentNumber=12.

"Zachary Taylor," The Internet Public Library, http://www.ipl.org/div/potus/ztaylor.html.

Exit 37

"Airport Information: Airport History," Willow Run Airport, http://www.willowrunairport.com/information/history.asp.

"Consolidated B-24 Liberator," http://www.daveswarbirds.com/usplanes/aircraft/liberatr.htm.

"Detroit Metro Airport Sets All-Time Record: Handles more than 36 million passengers in 2005," press release, Wayne County Airport Authority, http://www.metroairport.com/uploads/docs/NR_2005_Stats.pdf.

"What is the history of Detroit Metropolitan Airport?" Plymouth District Library, http://plymouthlibrary.org/faqmetro.htm.

"Welcome to Detroit Metro Airport," Detroit Metropolitan Wayne County Airport, http://www.metroairport.com/.

Exit 40

Rosenberg, Matt. "Erie Canal," About.com: Geography, http://geography.about.com/od/urbaneconomicgeography/a/eriecanal.htm.

Mile Marker 42

"Amherst, Jeffrey," William L. Clements Library, The University of Michigan, http://www.clements.umich.edu/Webguides/Arlenes/A/Amherst.html.

Hochman, Louis C. "Right time for the Tucker: Marlboro's Robert Ida has plans to produce vintage 1940s auto," News Transcript, http://newstranscript.gmnews.com/News/2000/1004/Front_Page/02.html.

"The 1948 Tucker," The Henry Ford, http://www.hfmgv.org/exhibits/showroom/1948/tucker.html.

Exit 43

"Rouge River Watershed Initiative," Michigan Department of Environmental Quality, http://www.michigan.gov/deq/0,1607,7-135-3313_3682_3718-14569--,00.html.

Wesley, Tony. "Significant Events in the History of the Edmund Fitzgerald," http://www.wideopenwest.com/~awesley5155/edm-fitz.html.

Exit 46

"Battle of Fallen Timbers," Ohio History Central, http://www.ohiohistorycentral.org/entry.php?rec=473.

"Nautical Terms and Phrases... Their Meaning and Origin," Naval Historical Center, http://www.history.navy.mil/trivia/trivia03.htm.

Exit 48

"Ste. Anne de Detroit," http://www.ste-anne.org/.

"St. Anne Roman Catholic Church Complex," National Park Service, http://www.nps.gov/history/nr/travel/detroit/d39.htm.

Exit 49

"Comerica Park," Ballparks, http://www.ballparks.com/baseball/american/detbpk.htm.

Draeger, C. "Girls of Summer," *Michigan History*, Sept./Oct. 1997, pp. 16-20.

"Glorious Detroit: Word on the Street," http://www.motorcityrocks.com/stree.htm.

Hamilton, Jim. "For More Than A Century, Tigers Have Never Been a 'Blah' Team," *The Daily Star*, April 24, 1999.

"Tiger Stadium, a.k.a. Briggs Stadium (1938-1960)," ESPN, The Magazine, http://www.baseball-statistics.com/Ballparks/Det/Tiger.htm.

Exit 50

"Comerica Park: Home of the Tigers," Official Site of Major League Baseball, http://detroit.tigers.mlb.com/det/ballpark/index.jsp.

"Fox Theatre," Olympia Entertainment, http://www.olympiaentertainment.com/venues/foxtheatre.jsp?dispPos=1.

"Fox Theatre Building," State of Michigan History, Arts and Libraries, http://www.michigan.gov/hal/0,1607,7-160-17449_18638_20846-54585--,00.html.

Winchell, R. "Houdini's Final Act," *Michigan History Magazine*, September/October 2000, pp. 46-47.

Exit 54

"Fisher and New Center Buildings," State of Michigan History, Arts and Libraries, http://www.michigan.gov/hal/0,1607,7-160-17449_18638_208 46-54575--,00.html.

"Fisher History," Nederlander Detroit, http://www.nederlanderdetroit.com/fisher/history.htm.

"The Fisher Brothers — Their Life and Times," Fisher Body Online, http://www.geocities.com/sponcom26/Life-TimesChapt8.html.

Exit 57

"Detroit Golf Club," Detroit Golf Club, http://www.detroitgolfclub.org/.

"History of Marygrove," Marygrove College, http://www.marygrove.edu/about/history.asp.

"The History of UDM," University of Detroit Mercy, http://www.udmercy.edu/mission/university/history/index.htm.

Exit 59

"History of the Michigan State Fair," State of Michigan History, Arts and Libraries, http://www.michigan.gov/mistatefair/0,1607,7-109--12804--,00.html.

Mile Marker 63

"Detroit Zoo," Detroit Zoo, http://www.detroitzoo.org/.

Marsden, Graeme, "The Royal Oak," The First Foot Guards, http://footguards.tripod.com/06ARTICLES/ART26_royal_oak.htm#king.

"Take A Tour," Elmwood Historic Cemetery, http://elmwoodhistoriccemetery.org/pages/takeatour.html.

Mile Marker 68

"'Detroit's Own' Polar Bear Memorial Association," http://pbma.grobbel.org/.

Mile Marker 69

"Cranbrook House and Gardens," Cranbrook, http://www.cranbrook.edu/housegardens/Default.asp?bhcp=1.

Mile Marker 77

"Foamade Industries: The History," Foamade Industries, http://www.foamade
.com/about/about.htm.

Exit 78

"Biography: Walter P. Chrysler," Answers.com, http://www.answers.com/
topic/walter-chrysler?cat=biz-fin.

"History," Walter P. Chrysler Museum, http://www.chryslerheritage.com/
pg500.htm.

Exit 79

"Biography: Dodge Brothers," Answers.com, http://www.answers.com/topic/
dodge-brothers.

"Meadow Brook Hall and Gardens," Oakland University, http://www2
.oakland.edu/oakland/OUportal/index.asp?site=87#.

"Oakland University Timeline," Oakland University, http://www3.oakland
.edu/oakland/aboutou/popups/history_timeline.htm.

"The Life of Matilda Dodge Wilson," Oakland University, http://www3
.oakland.edu/oakland/aboutou/popups/history_matilda.htm.

"This Date in Michigan History: April 15, 1859," Michigan History Online,
http://www.michiganhistorymagazine.com/date/april03/04_15_1924
.html.

Exit 81

"Detroit Pistons: 2000–Present," National Basketball Association, http://
www.nba.com/pistons/history/.

"Fred Zollner," Hoopedia, National Basketball Association, http://hoopedia
.nba.com/index.php/Fred_Zollner.

Herron, Jerry. "Downtown Time Capsule: Fading echoes fill Detroit's Capitol
Park," Metro Times, July 28, 1999, http://www.metrotimes.com/editorial/
story.asp?id=2326.

"History of Lapeer, Michigan," City of Lapeer, Michigan, http://www.ci.lapeer
.mi.us/web/res-history.htm.

"The Life of Matilda Dodge Wilson," Oakland University, http://www3
.oakland.edu/oakland/aboutou/popups/history_matilda.htm.

Exit 83

"Bald Mountain Recreation Area," Michigan Department of Natural
Resources, http://www.michigandnr.com/parksandtrails/details.
aspx?id=435&type=SPRK.

"Olde World Canterbury Village," http://www.canterburyvillage.com/.

"Scripps Estate: A Brief History," Orion Historical Society, http://www
.orionhistoricalsociety.org/Scripps%20Brief%20History.htm.

Exit 89

Basinger, Susan. "Clarkston's History: A Synopsis," Independence Township Library, http://www.www58195.w1.com/cin/history/chd/misc/clarkston_history.shtml.

"Chief Sashabaw," Clarkston Community Historical Society, http://www.clarkstonhistorical.org/chief_sashabaw1.htm.

Pokagon, Chief, "The Red Man's Rebuke," Hartford, MI: C.H. Engle, Publisher, 1893.

Exit 91

Basinger, Susan. "Clarkston's History: A Synopsis," Independence Township Library, http://www.www58195.w1.com/cin/history/chd/misc/clarkston_history.shtml.

"Kid Rock: Biography," Kid Rock, http://www.kidrock.com/.

Mile Marker 92

Gross, Bob. "Controlled burn planned at fen: Action necessary to help kill off invasive species in rare wetlands area," Oakland Press, April 1, 2005, http://www.theoaklandpress.com/stories/040105/loc_20050401014.shtml.

Exit 93

Henze, Doug. "Market Plan Angers Neighbors: Developers plan to build shopping center on site of church," Oakland Press, August 19, 2006, http://www.theoaklandpress.com/stories/081906/bus_2006081944.shtml.

Lombardo, Natalie. "Church could give way to shopping: Residents vehemently argue against development," Oakland Press, August 23, 2006, http://www.theoaklandpress.com/stories/082306/bus_2006082343.shtml.

"The Underground Railroad," State of Michigan History, Arts and Libraries, http://www.sos.state.mi.us/history/museum/explore/museums/hismus/prehist/civilwar/undergro.html.

"Underground Railroad," National Geographic Society, http://www.nationalgeographic.com/railroad/j3.html.

Exit 98

Angelo, Linda. "Holly Gets Ready for Carry Nation Festival," The Flint Journal, September 5, 2007, http://blog.mlive.com/flintjournal/newsnow/2007/09/holly_gets_ready_for_carry_nat.html.

"Carry Nation Festival," carrynation.org, http://www.carrynation.org/index.htm.

"Dickens Olde Fashioned Christmas Festival, Holly Area Chamber of Commerce, Michigan, http://www.hollymi.com/HACCdickens.htm.

"Our History," Village of Holly, http://www.vi.holly.mi.us/history.asp.

Exit 101

"Gage Cemetery, Fenton Township, Genesee County," Michigan Tombstone Photo Project, http://www.rootsweb.com/~usgenweb/mi/tsphoto/genesee/gage.htm.

"William and Sarah Gage, Township's First White Settlers," Centennial Anniversary Edition, *Holly Herald*, June 30, 1938.

Mile Markers 101–102

"Michigan Renaissance Festival," Michigan Renaissance Festival, http://www.michrenfest.com/.

"Mount Holly," http://www.skimtholly.com/about.aspx.

Mile Marker 116

"Flint Metal Center," GM Global Operations, http://www.gmdynamic.com/company/gmability/environment/plants/facility_db/facility_summary.php?fID=146.

"Flint's Bishop International Airport Dedicates the "Mayor James A. Sharp, Jr. Conference Room" Today at 11:30am," press release, Flint Bishop Airport, February 23, 2007, http://www.bishopairport.org/press-releases/new-conference-room.htm.

"Gerald R. Ford," The White House, http://www.whitehouse.gov/history/presidents/gf38.html.

Exit 118

"General Cougar Questions," Michigan Department of Natural Resources, http://www.michigan.gov/dnr/0,1607,7-153-10370_12145_43573-153232--,00.html.

"Hiding the Cougar: Denying the East its apex predator," Michigan Wildlife Conservancy, October 25, 2006, http://www.miwildlife.org/news-detail.asp?id=20.

"No Evidence of Cougars in 2006," National Park Service, U.S. Department of the Interior, http://www.nps.gov/slbe/parknews/cougarsnotfound.htm.

"Owosso Michigan History Index," Shiawassee County, Michigan, History, http://www.shiawasseehistory.com/owossohistoryindex.html.

Mile Marker 119

"Billy Durant and the Founding of General Motors," Mackinac Center, http://www.mackinac.org/article.aspx?ID=651.

"HUMMER History," Edmunds.com, http://www.edmunds.com/hummer/history.html.

Wright, Richard. "The Free-Wheeling Gambler Who Created Conservative General Motors," Detroit News, July 30, 1996, http://info.detnews.com/history/story/index.cfm?id=100&category=business.

Mile Marker 122

"Michigan History Series: Fires ravaged Michigan's thumb in 1871, 1881," University of Michigan News Service, Aug. 26, 1996, http://www. ns.umich.edu/htdocs/releases/story.php?id=1245.

Exit 126

"The Birth of Better Made® Potato Chips," Better Made Snack Foods, http:// bettermadenorth.com/history.htm.

Kelly, Carolyn. "Michigan Cherries," Absolute Michigan, http://www.absolute michigan.com/search/?articleid=2855.

"The Huckleberry Railroad," Crossroads Village and Huckleberry Railroad, Genesee County Parks and Recreation, http://www.geneseecountyparks. org/huckleberry_railroad.htm.

Mile Marker 129

"Architect of Innovative Construction Contract, MDOT District Engineer John J. Kelsch Retires," press release, Michigan Department of Transportation, June 3, 1997, http://www.michigan.gov/mdot/0,1607,7-1 51-9620_11057-94518--,00.html.

"Clio Rest Area 612," Michigan Department of Natural Resources, http:// www.michigan.gov/mdot/0,1607,7-151-9621_11041_21800_21802_227 29-63912--,00.html.

Mile Marker 130

"Elf Khurafeh Shrine Center," Elf Khurafeh Shrine Center, http://www .ekshrine.com/history.htm.

Exit 131

"History of the City of Clio," Clio, Michigan, http://www.clio.govoffice.com/ index.asp?Type=B_BASIC&SEC={6906C14D-1978-4BE9-B79F-01657FAD2A54}.

Exit 136

"Prime Outlets at Birch Run," Michigan Economic Development Corp., http://michigan.org/travel/detail.asp?m=&p=G7908.

"Prime Outlets: Birch Run," Prime Outlets, http://www.primeoutlets.com/ cntrdefault.asp?cntrid=1015.

Exit 144

"Bavarian Inn of Frankenmuth," Bavarian Inn of Frankenmuth, http://www .bavarianinn.com/.

"Frankenmuth: Say hello to fun!" informational brochure published by the Frankenmuth Convention and Visitors Bureau.

"Frankenmuth's Wooden Covered Bridge," Michigan Economic Development Corp., http://www.michigan.org/travel/detail.asp?p=G15956.

"Welcome to the Historic Frankenmuth Brewery," Frankenmuth Brewery, http://www.frankenmuthbrewery.com/.

"Zehnder's of Frankenmuth," Zehnder's of Frankenmuth, http://www.zehnders.com/.

Exit 149

"City of Holland, Michigan," Holland Area Chamber of Commerce, http://www.cityofholland.com/Brix?pageID=5.

"Native Languages of the Americas: Ottawa (Odawa, Odaawa), Native Languages of the Americas, http://www.native-languages.org/ottawa.htm.

Mile Marker 154

"Hartwick Pines State Park Old Growth Forest 'Virgin Pines' Foot Trail," brochure, published by the Michigan DNR Parks and Recreation Division, April 1997.

Moore, Sam. "Let's Talk Rusty Iron: Cant Hook or Peavey?" Rural Heritage Logging Camp, http://www.ruralheritage.com/logging_camp/peavey.htm.

"The Zilwaukee Bridge," Michigan Highways, http://www.michiganhighways.org/indepth/zilwaukee.html

Exit 155

"Inga Arvad," Wikipedia, http://en.wikipedia.org/wiki/Inga_Arvad.

Mroczek, John. "Inga Marie Arvad," Find A Grave, http://www.findagrave.com/cgi-bin/fg.cgi?page=gr&GSlh=1&GRid=22456735&.

Newton, Mike. "Col. Tim McCoy: Man of Destiny," http://www.classicimages.com/1998/september98/mccoytim.html.

"Shiawassee National Wildlife Refuge," U.S. Fish & Wildlife Service, http://www.fws.gov/Midwest/shiawassee/.

"Tim McCoy," Wikipedia, http://en.wikipedia.org/wiki/Tim_McCoy.

"Women's Bios: Serena Williams," U.S. Open, http://2007.usopen.org/en_US/bios/profile/ws/wtaw234.html.

"Women's Singles Championships," U.S. Open, http://2007.usopen.org/en_US/about/history/wschamps.html.

Exit 160

"Delta College Planetarium and Learning Center," Delta College, http://www.delta.edu/planet/.

"The History of SVSU," Saginaw Valley State University, http://www.svsu.edu/svsuhistory/.

Exit 162

"Herbert H. Dow," Harvard Business School, http://www.hbs.edu/
leadership/database/leaders/230/.

"Herbert Henry Dow," Clarkson University, http://people.clarkson.
edu/~ekatz/scientists/dow.html.

"Pipes - Wood," Sewerhistory.org, http://www.sewerhistory.org/grfx/
components/pipe-wood1.htm.

Exit 164

"Corn (Maize)," Kansas State University, http://www.oznet.ksu.edu/
kansascrops/corn_origin.htm.

Sugarbeet," University of California, Davis, http://sugarbeet.ucdavis.edu/
sbchap.html.

Mile Marker 167

"Facts about Oil and Gas in Michigan," Western Michigan University, http://
www.wmich.edu/geology/corelab/Michigan_oil_gas_facts.htm.

Freudenrich, Craig C., ìHow Oil Drilling Works,î How Stuff Works, http://
science.howstuffworks.com/oil-drilling.htm.

Exit 168

"Ruddy Duck," Cornell Lab of Ornithology, http://www.birds.cornell.edu/
AllAboutBirds/BirdGuide/Ruddy_Duck.html.

"Ruddy Duck," Stanford University, http://www.stanford.edu/group/
stanfordbirds/text/species/Ruddy_Duck.html.

"Saginaw Bay Visitor Center," Michigan Department of Natural Resources,
http://www.michigan.gov/dnr/0,1607,7-153-10365_10887-31276--,
00.html.

"Tobico Marsh," Michigan Department of Natural Resources, http://www
.michigan.gov/dnr/0,1607,7-153-30301_31154_31260-54037--,00.html.

Exit 173

"Festival History," Woodtick Music Festival, http://www.woodtickfestival.
com/Pages/History.htm.

"Gizzard Fest Activities – Potterville – June 13-15," City Pulse, June 11, 2003,
http://www.lansingcitypulse.com/030611/events/index2.html.

"Munger Potato Festival," Munger Potato Festival, http://www.
mungerpotatofest.com/index.php.

"National Asparagus Festival, Hart, Michigan," Silver Lake
Convention and Visitors Bureau, http://www.silverlakecvb.org/
nationalasparagusfestivalhartmichigan.html.

"National Baby Food Festival," National Baby Food Festival, http://www
.babyfoodfest.com/.

"The Great Morel: A Tribute to Shroomers," The Great Morel. http://
thegreatmorel.com/falsemorel.html.

"Welcome to Yale," Yale Area Chamber of Commerce, http://www.yale
chamber.com/new.php?id=49.

"Wolverine Lumberjack Festival," Wolverine Lumberjack Festival http://www
.wolverinelumberjackfest.com/.

Exit 181

"Jerusalem Artichoke," Alternative Field Crops Manual, University of
Wisconsin/University of Minnesota, Purdue University, http://www.hort
.purdue.edu/newcrop/afcm/jerusart.html.

"The Pinconning Cheese Co. and Fudge Shop," The Pinconning Cheese Co.
and Fudge Shop, http://pinconningcheese.com/.

Exit 188

"Rainbow Smelt," University of Wisconsin Sea Grant, http://www.seagrant.
wisc.edu/greatlakesfish/rainbowsmelt.html.

"Smelt Dipping," Michigan Department of Natural Resources, http://www
.michigan.gov/dnr/0,1607,7-153-10364-21769--,00.html.

Exit 190

Nolan, Jenny. "Chief Pontiac's Siege at Detroit," Detroit News, June 14, 2000,
http://info.detnews.com/redesign/history/story/historytemplate.cfm?id=1
80&CFID-8083290&CFTOKEN=98394864.

"Standish Maximum Correctional Facility (SMF)," Michigan Department of
Corrections, http://www.michigan.gov/corrections/0,1607,7-119-1381_
1388-5268--,00.html.

Mile Marker 198

"Hartwick Pines State Park," Michigan Department of Natural Resources,
http://www.dnr.state.mi.us/publications/pdfs/wildlife/viewingguide/
nlp/59Hartwick/index.htm.

"Forest History," State of Michigan, http://www.michigan.gov/documents/
2-ForestHistory_165779_7.pdf.

"Forest Facts," Michigan Society of American Foresters, http://michigan
saf.org/ForestInfo/Newspaper/057-0203.htm.

Exit 202

"Alger, Russell Alexander," Biographical Directory of the U.S. Congress,
http://bioguide.congress.gov/scripts/biodisplay.pl?index=A000107.

Bourasaw, Noel. "Russell A. Alger, logging capitalist, Michigan governor,
Secretary of War," Skagit River Journal, http://www.stumpranchonline
.com/skagitjournal/WestCounty/Burl-NW/Pioneer/Alger2-Russell.html.

Donnelly, Francis. "Believers Hear Bigfoot's Howl," Detroit News, http://www.detnews.com/apps/pbcs.dll/article?AID=/20070714/ METRO/707140364/1003 and other sources.

"Michigan MUFON Meeting Schedules," Michigan MUFON Inc., http:// mimufon.org/MiMufonSpecific/Meetings.html.

Mile Marker 205

Barnett, LeRoy. "Land for family and friends: the Saginaw Treaty of 1819," *Michigan History Magazine*, September-October 2003, page 28.

Bradsher, Keith. "Michigan Pact Resolves Battle Over Limits on Indian Fishing," The New York Times, August 8, 2000, http://query.nytimes.com/ gst/fullpage.html?res=9F07E2DC113CF93BA3575BC0A9669C8B63&n =Top/Reference/Times%20Topics/Subjects/F/Fishing,%20Commercial.

"United States of America et al., Plaintiffs, v. State of Michigan et al., Defendants. No. M26-73 C.A. United States District Court, W.D. Michigan, N.D. May 7, 1979,î http://www.1836cora.org/pdf/usvmichigan fox1979.pdf.

Mile Marker 210

"Bald Eagle (Haliaeetus leucocephalus)," Michigan Department of Natural Resources," http://www.michigan.gov/dnr/0,1607,7-153-10370_12145_1 2202-32581--,00.html.

Dewey, Tanya. "Buteo jamaicensis—Red-Tailed Hawk," Animal Diversity Web, University of Michigan Museum of Zoology, http://animaldiversity.ummz .umich.edu/site/accounts/information/Buteo_jamaicensis.html.

"Eagle Biology: Reproduction," American Eagle Foundation, http://www .eagles.org/vueaglewebcs/bio_repro.htm.

Exit 212

Tanger Outlet Centers, West Branch, Michigan, http://www.tangeroutlet .com/westbranch.

Mile Marker 213

Conrad, Jon. ìOpen Access and Extinction of the Passenger Pigeon in North America,î Applied Economics and Management Cornell University, http:// aem.cornell.edu/faculty_content/Conrad_PassengerPigeons.pdf.

Sheltrown, Jennifer. "Smiley Days," MSNBC TV/Citizen Journalist, http:// www.msnbc.msn.com/id/8006389/.

"Smiley Photos From Around the World," www.smileycollector.com, http:// www.smileycollector.com/smileyphotos3.htm.

"The Passenger Pigeon," Encyclopedia Smithsonian, Smithsonian, http:// www.si.edu/Encyclopedia_SI/nmnh/passpig.htm.

"West Branch City Police Department," Town Safety, http://www.townsafety.com/news/West%20Branch%20Safe%20Community%20Coalition.html.

"West Branch: Smiley Connection," City of West Branch, http://www.westbranch.com/.

Mile Marker 216

"Ogemaw Hills," Michigan Department of Natural Resources, http://www.michigandnr.com/parksandtrails/details.aspx?id=76&type=SFPW.

Mile Marker 218

Frawley, Brian J. "Michigan Deer Harvest Survey Report: 2006 Seasons," Michigan Department of Natural Resources, http://www.mich.gov/documents/dnr/deer_06harvest_198710_7.pdf.

Humphries, Rebecca. Radio address, Michigan Department of Natural Resources, http://www.michigan.gov/documents/gov/Gov67_Full_178396_7.mp3.

Moldenhauer, Phil. "A dream of a course comes to life in the wilds near West Branch," Booth Newspapers, April 17, 1997, http://www.teedream.com/mlivedream.html.

"The Dream Golf Course," The Dream, http://www.teedream.com/.

Mile Marker 220

"Dead Stream Swamp," Michigan Department of Natural Resources, http://www.michigan.gov/dnr/0,1607,7-153-30301_31154_31260-54005--,00.html.

"Osprey," Cornell Lab of Ornithology, http://www.birds.cornell.edu/AllAboutBirds/BirdGuide/Osprey.html.

"State, Local Conservation and Property Groups Call for Continued Cooperation Over proposed U.S. – Michigan – Tribal Treaty Agreement," Michigan United Conservation Clubs, http://www.mucc.org/policy/tribal/release.php.

"Wood Duck," Cornell Lab of Ornithology, http://www.birds.cornell.edu/AllAboutBirds/BirdGuide/Wood_Duck_dtl.html.

Exit 222

Milius, S. "Bluegill Dads: Not Mine? Why Bother?" Science News, April 19, 2003.

"St. Helen Bluegill Festival," St. Helen Bluegill Festival Committee, http://www.bluegillfestival.org/.

Mile Marker 225

"Hartwick Pines State Park Old Growth Forest 'Virgin Pines' Foot Trail,"
informational brochure, Michigan DNR Parks and Recreation Division,
April 1997.

Laidly, Paul R. and Robert G. Barse, "Spacing Affects Knot Surface in Red
Pine Plantations," Research Note, North Central Forest Experiment
Station, http://ncrs.fs.fed.us/pubs/rn/rn_nc246.pdf.

Mile Marker 235

"American Crow," Cornell Lab of Ornithology, http://www.birds.cornell.edu/
AllAboutBirds/BirdGuide/American_Crow_dtl.html.

"Common Raven," Cornell Lab of Ornithology, http://www.birds.cornell.edu/
AllAboutBirds/BirdGuide/Common_Raven_dtl.html.

Exit 239

Benedict, Brandy, "Super-rare warbler is nesting in Wisconsin: Birds found
only in jack pine forests," JS Online, Milwaukee Journal Sentinel, June 23,
2007, http://www.jsonline.com/story/index.aspx?id=623852.

"Michigan Firemen's Memorial Festival," Michigan Firemen's Memorial Festival
Committee, http://www.firemensmemorial.org/index.htm.

Exit 244

Barnett, LeRoy. "U.S. Surveyors," Michigan History, September/October 1982,
http://www.michiganhistorymagazine.com/extra/surveying/upsurveying.
html.

"Civilian Conservation Corps Museum," informational brochure published by
the Michigan Historical Center, April 1996

Rosentreter, Roger L., "Roosevelt's Tree Army: Michigan's Civilian
Conservation Corps," State of Michigan History, Arts and Libraries, http://
www.michigan.gov/hal/0,1607,7-160-17451_18670_18793-53515--,00
.html.

Mile Marker 244

Berkebile, Tanya, "Mystery of the Canal Freeze, Thaw Revealed," Cadillac
News, Dec. 8, 2006, http://www.cadillacnews.com/articles/2006/12/08/
news/news03.txt.

"Volume 6," Ohio History, Ohio Historical Society, http://publications.
ohiohistory.org/ohstemplate.cfm?action=detail&Page=00062.html&StartP
age=1&EndPage=34&volume=6&newtitle=Volume%206%20Page%201.

Exit 251

"Grayling Generating Station," Decker Energy International Inc., http://www
.deckerenergy.com/52863/53001.html.

"Weyerhaeuser Facility in Grayling Designated 103rd Clean Corporate Citizen," press release, Michigan Department of Environmental Quality, July 1, 2004, http://www.michigan.gov/deq/0,1607,7-135-3585_4129_4190-96783--,00.html.

Mile Marker 251

"District Engineer, Bridge Executive Monte Endres Retires," Michigan Department of Transportation, April 7, 1997, http://www.michigan.gov/mdot/0,1607,7-151-9620_11057-94597--,00.html.

Exit 254

"Crawford County Historical Museum," Crawford County Historical Society, Inc., http://www.grayling-area.com/museum/.
"Fred Bear," Bowhunters Hall of Fame, http://www.bowhuntershalloffame.com/members/bearfred/index.html.
"History," Grayling Visitors Bureau, http://www.grayling-mi.com/history.html.
"Range 40 Complex," Michigan Army National Guard, https://www.mi.ngb.army.mil/grayling/range40.asp.

Mile Marker 255

"Crawford County Historical Museum," Crawford County Historical Society, Inc., http://www.grayling-area.com/museum/.
"Michigan Grayling Only A Memory," Michigan Department of Natural Resources, http://www.michigan.gov/dnr/0,1607,7-153-10364_18958-53612--,00.html.

Exit 259

"Food in the Logging Camps," East Tennessee State University, http://www.etsu.edu/cass/Archives/Subjects/Hardwoods/Page6.htm.
"Hartwick Pines," brochure, Hartwick Pines State Park, undated.
"Hartwick Pines State Park," Michigan Department of Natural Resources, http://www.michigandnr.com/parksandtrails/Details. aspx?id=453&type=SFCG.
"Hartwick Pines State Park Old Growth Forest 'Virgin Pines' Foot Trail," informational brochure, Michigan DNR Parks and Recreation Division, April 1997.
"Hartwick Pines State Park Visitor Center and Logging Museum," brochure, Michigan DNR Parks and Recreation Division, March 1997.

Mile Markers 262-63

"Facts and Figures," Michigan Maple Syrup Association, http://www.mi-maplesyrup.com/Information/info_ref.htm.
Great Lakes Pilot, Vol. 6, No. 2, 2000.

"History" Michigan Maple Syrup Association, http://www.mi-maplesyrup
.com/Information/info_hist.htm.

"How to Tap Maple Trees and Make Maple Syrup," The University of Maine
Cooperative Extension, http://www.umext.maine.edu/onlinepubs/
PDFpubs/7036.pdf.

Exit 264

"Snowmobiling in Michigan," Michigan Department of Natural Resources,
http://www.michigan.gov/dnr/0,1607,7-153-10365_14824-32291--,
00.html.

"Snowmobiling Major Revenue Generator For Local Economies," International
Snowmobile Manufacturers Association, http://www.snowmobile.org/
features_revenue.asp.

"Welcome to Frederic, Michigan," http://www.frederic-mi.com/.

Mile Marker 267

"Why Leaves Change Color, U.S. Forest Service, http://www.na.fs.fed.us/
spfo/pubs/misc/leaves/leaves.htm.

South of Mile Marker 269

"Brief History of Otsego County," Otsego County Historical Society, http://
www.otsego.org/ochs/d-tour/otsegowalkdrive.htm.

"Historical Context," Otsego Lake Township, http://www.otsegolaketownship
.org/townshiphistory.cfm

"Otsego Lake," Michigan Interactive, http://www.fishweb.com/maps/otsego/
otsegolake/index.html.

"Otsego Lake State Park," Michigan Department of Natural Resources, http://
www.michigandnr.com/parksandtrails/Details.aspx?id=482&type=SPRK.

South of Mile Marker 270

"Lake Marjory State Forest Campground, Michigan Department of Natural
Resources, http://www.michigandnr.com/parksandtrails/Details.
aspx?id=615&type=SFCG.

"State Forest Campgrounds," Michigan Department of Natural Resources,
http://www.michigan.gov/dnr/0,1607,7-153-10365_10883-21791--,
00.html.

Exit 270

"Historical Context," Otsego Lake Township, http://www.otsegolaketownship
.org/townshiphistory.cfm

North of Mile Marker 271

Obrey, Tim, "Why Splake?" Maine Department of Inland Fisheries and Wildlife, http://www.maine.gov/ifw/fishing/species/splake.htm.

Mile Marker 273

"Otsego Lake State Park," Michigan Department of Natural Resources, http://www.michigandnr.com/parksandtrails/Details.aspx?id=482&type=SPRK.

North of Mile Marker 277

"Marsh Ridge Golf Course and Resort," Marsh Ridge Golf Course and Resort, http://www.marshridge.com/.

"The Loon Golf Club," Travel Michigan, http://www.michigan.org/Property/Detail.aspx?p=B5409.

Exit 279

"1994-95 Edition of the Gaylord Area Travel Planner," publication, *Gaylord Herald Times*, 1994.

"Gaylord, Michigan: Festivities Abound Year Round: A Guide to special events in the Gaylord area," publication, Gaylord Information Center, undated.

"Starker-Mann Duathlon," 3 Disciplines Racing, http://www.3disciplines.com/index.php?option=com_events&task=view_detail&agid=32&year=2008&month=05&day=18&Itemid=0.

Mile Marker 281

"Call of the Wild," Call of the Wild and Bavarian Falls Park, http://www.gocallofthewild.com/.

Exit 282

"Events," Gaylord Area Convention and Tourism Bureau, http://www.gaylordmichigan.net/.

"City of Alpena," City of Alpena, Mich., http://www.alpena.mi.us/.

"County Centennial Newspaper 1975," Otsego County Historical Society/Otsego County Herald Times, Aug. 21, 1975, http://www.otsego.org/ochs/county_centennial_paper/cent_paper_1975.htm.

"The Old Montana Burns to the Water's Edge," Michigan State University Extension, http://web1.msue.msu.edu/iosco/montana.htm.

"Thunder Bay National Marine Sanctuary," Thunder Bay National Marine Sanctuary, National Oceanic and Atmospheric Administration, http://thunderbay.noaa.gov/.

North of Mile Marker 284

"County Centennial Newspaper 1975," Otsego County Historical Society/ Otsego County Herald Times, Aug. 21, 1975, http://www.otsego.org/ ochs/county_centennial_paper/cent_paper_1975.htm.

North of Mile Marker 287

"All About Snow," National Snow and Ice Data Center, http://nsidc.org/ snow/faq.html.

"Institute of Snow Research," Michigan Technological University Keweenaw Research Center, http://www.mtukrc.org/snow.htm.

"Winter," The City of Houghton Preservation Committee, http://history .cityofhoughton.com/history/winter.html.

Exit 290

"Gaylord-to-Mackinaw City Rail-Trail," Rails-to-Trails Conservancy, http:// www.traillink.com/ViewTrail.aspx?AcctID=6016210.

North of Mile Marker 293

"Black Bear Golf Club," Black Bear Golf Club, http://www.golfblackbear.net/ home/index.php.

"Michigan Elk: Past and Present," Michigan Department of Natural Resources, http://www.michigan.gov/dnr/0,1607,7-153-10363_10856_10 893-28275--,00.html.

"Why Is Snow White?" Howstuffworks.com, http://www.howstuffworks. com/question524.htm.

Mile Marker 297

"DNR Develops New Strain of Brown Trout," press release, Michigan Department of Natural Resources, Oct. 4, 2007, http://www.michigan.gov/dnr/0, 1607,7-153-10366_46403-177994--,00.html.

Exit 301

Runk, David. "First Michigan Wolverine Spotted in 200 Years: Last confirmed sightings were by fur traders in early 1800s," Associated Press/MSNBC. com, http://www.msnbc.msn.com/id/4374309/.

Nolan, Jenny. "When Michigan Rode the Rails," Detroit News, http://info. detnews.com/history/story/index.cfm?id=203&category=business.

"Black Lake Sturgeon Spearing Season Application Period Begins Jan. 7," press release, Michigan Department of Natural Resources, December 17, 2007. http://michigan.gov/dnr/0,1607,7-153--182146--,00.html.

Mile Marker 304

"Michigan Fossils," Michigan Department of Environmental Quality, http:// www.deq.state.mi.us/documents/deq-ogs-gimdl-MFPFITB.Pdf.

"Pictured Rocks National Lakeshore," National Park Service, http://www2
.nature.nps.gov/geology/parks/piro/.

Mile Marker 305

Brain, Marshall. "How Power Grids Work," How Stuff Works, http://science
.howstuffworks.com/power3.htm.

Exit 310

"Blessed Kateri, Model Ecologist," Catholic Conservation Center, http://
conservation.catholic.org/kateri.htm.

Brown, Alan S. "William A. Burt and the Upper Peninsula," Michigan History,
May/June 1980, http://www.michiganhistorymagazine.com/extra/
surveying/burt.html.

"Burt Lake State Park," Michigan Department of Natural Resources, http://
www.michigandnr.com/parksandtrails/Details.aspx?id=439&type=SPRK.

"The National Shrine of the Cross in the Woods," The National Shrine of the
Cross in the Woods, http://www.crossinthewoods.com/.

Mile Marker 312

Historic Context Study: Decommissioning and excessing the USCGC
Mackinaw," U.S. Coast Guard, http://www.uscg.mil/systems/gse/FINAL_
MACKINAW.pdf.

"Icebreaker Mackinaw Among Sites to Receive Michigan Historical Markers,"
press release, State of Michigan, Dec. 11, 2007, http://www.michigan.gov/
som/0,1607,7-192-29938-181700--,00.html.

"Inland Waterway, Locks, Cheboygan, MI," Michigan Interactive, http://www
.fishweb.com/maps/cheboygan/cheboygan/river/locks/locks.html.

"Northern Michigan's Inland Waterway," Indian River Resort Region Chamber
of Commerce, http://www.irchamber.com/inlandwaterway.htm.

"WLBB 30 United States Coast Guard Cutter Mackinaw," MightyMac.org,
http://www.mightymac.org/newmackinaw.htm.

Exit 313

"Inland Lakes of Michigan—Top 20," Tip of the Mitt Watershed Council,
http://www.watershedcouncil.org/Michigan_InlandLakes_Top20.pdf.

Mile Marker 321

"University of Michigan Biological Station," University of Michigan, http://
www.lsa.umich.edu/umbs/.

Exit 322

ìHow Products are Made: How is propane made?î Answers.com, http://www
.answers.com/topic/propane?cat=health.

Mile Marker 325

"National Christmas Tree Association," National Christmas Tree Association, http://www.mcta.org/teachers.htm.

Nix, Steve. "Top Ten Christmas Trees Sold In North America," Answers.com, http://forestry.about.com/cs/christmastrees1/a/top10_xmastree.htm.

"Michigan Christmas Tree Association," Michigan Christmas Tree Association, http://www.mcta.org/.

Exit 326

"Bois Blanc Island," Cheboygan Area Chamber of Commerce, http://www.cheboygan.com/boisblanc.php.

"Great Lakes Piping Plover: An Endangered Species," brochure, U.S. Fish and Wildlife Service, April 1994.

Great Lakes Piping Plover Call, Great Lakes Piping Plover Research and Recovery Team of the University of Minnesota, Aug. 30, 2004, http://www.michigan.gov/documents/glppc_aug04_101048_7.pdf.

"Piping Plover," brochure, U.S. Fish and Wildlife Service, April 1994.

Nolan, Jenny. "How the Detroit River shaped lives and history," Detroit News, Feb. 11, 1997, http://info.detnews.com/history/story/index.cfm?id=186&category=locations.

"The Great Lakes Fur Trade," The Mitten, Michigan History, October 2004, http://www.michiganhistorymagazine.com/kids/pdfs/mittenoct04.pdf.

Mile Marker 327

Auleric, Richard. "Michigan's Fur Bearing Animal Industry," Michigan State University Department of Animal Science, http://web1.msue.msu.edu/imp/modsr/sr499201.html.

Cooley, Thomas, Stephen Schmitt, Paul Friedrich and Tim Reis. "River Otter Survey—2002–2003, Michigan Department of Natural Resources, July 2003, http://ww2.dnr.state.mi.us/publications/pdfs/HuntingWildlifeHabitat/Reports/WLD-library/3400-3499/3402.pdf.

Frawley, Brian. "2006 Michigan Furbearer Harvest Survey," Michigan Department of Natural Resources, http://www.michigan.gov/documents/dnr/3480_214909_7.pdf.

"The Beaver Fur Hat," White Oak Society Inc., http://www.whiteoak.org/learning/furhat.htm.

Mile Marker 333

"Adopt A Highway: About the Program," Michigan Department of Transportation, http://michigan.gov/mdot/0,1607,7-151-9621_11041_1 4408-29047--,00.html.

Mile Marker 335

"Welcome to the Mackinac Bridge Website!" Mackinac Bridge Authority, Michigan Department of Transportation, http://www.mackinac bridge.org/.

Exit 337

"About Us," Ho-Chunk Nation, http://www.ho-chunknation.com/About Us.aspx.

"Lighthouse Preservation, Department of State, State of Michigan, http://www.michigan.gov/sos/0, 1607,7-127-1585_1595_9026-23624--,00.html.

"Port Huron Museum," Port Huron Museum, http://www.phmuseum.org/ lighthouse.html.

Mile Markers 337–338

"Welcome to Green Generation," Consumers Energy, http://www.consumers energy.com/welcome.htm?/products/index-nomargin.asp?asid=672.

"Wind Turbine Generators," Village of Mackinaw City, http://www.mackinaw city.org/wind-turbines-42/.

Exit 338

"Historic Mill Creek History," Mackinac State Historic Parks, http://www .mackinacparks.com/parks/historic-mill-creek-history_195/.

Exit 339

"Colonial Michilimackinac History," Mackinac State Historic Parks, http:// www.mackinacparks.com/parks/colonial-michilimackinac-history_193/.

"Mackinac Island Ferry," Arnold Transit Co., http://www.arnoldline.com/ cruises.htm

"North Country Trail Association," North Country Trail Association," http:// www.northcountrytrail.org/.

"Shepler's Mackinac Island Ferry," Shepler's Ferry, http://www.sheplersferry. com/story/story.html.

Star Line Mackinac Island's Hydro-Jet Ferry," Star Line, http://www.mackinac ferry.com/.

Mackinac Bridge

"Dysentery," BBC News, http://news.bbc.co.uk/2/hi/health/medical_notes/ 4134539.stm.

"Grand Hotel," Grand Hotel, http://www.grandhotel.com/.

"History of Mackinac Island: High Cliffs," Mackinac.com, http://www.mackinac .com/content/general/history_highcliffes.html.

"In Memory of," Mackinaw Bridge Authority, Michigan Department of Transportation, http://www.mackinacbridge.org/in-memory-of-45/.

"Mackinac Island: Early Visitors," Mackinac Island Tourism Bureau, http://www.mackinacisland.org/history.html.

"History of the Bridge," Mackinaw Bridge Authority, Michigan Department of Transportation, http://www.mackinacbridge.org/history-of-the-bridge-14/.

Sellars, Richard. "Growth of the National Park Concept," Preserving Nature in the National Parks, http://www.nps.gov/history/history/online_books/sellars/chap1a.htm.

"St. Helena Island Light," West Michigan Tourist Association, http://www.wmta.org/st.-helena-island-light-92/.

"St. Ignace Spirit of the Straits," brochure, St. Ignace Area Chamber of Commerce, 1997.

Voss, Edward. "Observations on the Michigan Flora, IIP: The flora of Green Island (Mackinac County," https://kb.osu.edu/dspace/bitstream/1811/3764/1/V50N04_182.pdf.

Zacharias, Pat. "The Breathtaking Mackinac Bridge," Detroit News, June 6, 2000, http://info.detnews.com/redesign/history/story/historytemplate.cfm?id=156.

Exit 343

"Saint Ignace Welcome Center," Michigan Department of Transportation, http://www.michigan.gov/mdot/0,1607,7-151-9621_11041_21800_21802_22720-62690--,00.html.

Exit 344

"St. Ignace Spirit of the Straits," brochure, St. Ignace Area Chamber of Commerce, 1997.

"Tribal Gaming Q&A," Michigan Gaming Control Board, http://www.michigan.gov/mgcb/0,1607,7-120-1380_1414_43365---,00.html.

"North Country Trail Association," North Country Trail Association," http://www.northcountrytrail.org/.

"North Country Trail," informational sheet published by the U.S. Department of Agriculture Forest Service, Hiawatha National Forest, undated.

Mile Marker 347

Gould, Karen. "14 Handpicked Draft Horses Serve Island in Cold Months," Mackinac Island Town Crier, Dec. 9, 2006, http://www.mackinacislandnews.com/news/2006/1209/Front_Page/002.html.

"Mackinac Winters," E-Mackinac Ltd., http://www.mackinac.com/content/winters/gettinghere.html.

Exit 348

"Upper Michigan: Big Mac and More," North Country Trail Association, http://www.northcountrytrail.org/explore/ex_miup/miup.htm.

Mile Marker 348

Paquin, Ellen. "1920s Dance Hall Once Graced St. Ignace Waterfront Readers Share Memories of Birchwood Arbor," The St. Ignace News, http://www.stignacenews.com/news/2005/0818/Front_Page/007.html.

"Upper Michigan Geology/Hydrology," Department of Geosciences, Mississippi State University, http://www.msstate.edu/dept/geosciences/CT/TIG/WEBSITES/LOCAL/Spring2002/Michael_Marsicek/geology.htm.

Mile Marker 350

Carter, James L. *Superior: A State for the North Country*. Marquette, Mich.: The Pilot Press, 1980.

O'Brien, Bill. "Span opened up commerce in U.P.: Most Yoopers say bridge has been a boon," Traverse City Record-Eagle, July 1, 2007, http://archives.record-eagle.com/2007/jul/01mack-biz.htm.

Mile Marker 351

"Great Lakes Circle Tour: Background," Great Lakes Commission, http://www.glc.org/tourism/background.html.

Exit 352

"A History of Moran by William J. Luepnitz, Jr. (1873-1957)," MoranMichigan.org, http://www.moranmichigan.org/history.htm.

Great Lakes Pilot, Vol. 6, No. 2, 2000.

'Tahquamenon Falls State Park," Michigan Department of Natural Resources, http://www.michigan.gov/dnr/0,1607,7-153-10365_10887-124495--,00.html.

"Tahquamenon: Is it just a name or a glimpse into the past?" Michigan Department of Natural Resources, http://www.michigandnr.com/publications/pdfs/edopps/TFSPname.pdf.

Zyble, Lisa. "Looking Back," Mackinac Island Town Crier, Feb. 11, 2005, http://www.mackinacislandnews.com/news/2005/0211/Looking_Back/.

Mile Marker 356

"Hiawatha National Forest: Carp River Campground," U.S. Forest Service, http://www.fs.fed.us/r9/forests/hiawatha/recreation/camping/developed_campgrounds/carp-river-campground/index.php.

"Wild and Scenic Rivers by State," National Wild and Scenic Rivers System, http://www.rivers.gov/wildriverslist.html.

"Mackinac Trail/Carp River," Michigan Department of Transportation, http://www.michigan.gov/mdot/0,1607,7-151-9620_11154_11188-29689--,00.html.

Exit 359

"Drummond Island, Michigan: Hub of the Great Lakes Water Wonderland," brochure, Drummond Island Chamber of Commerce, undated.

"Great Lakes Monitoring: Shipwrecks," U.S. Environmental Protection Agency, http://www.epa.gov/glnpo/monitoring/great_minds_great_lakes/history/shipwrecks.html.

"Les Cheneaux Islands," brochure Les Cheneaux Chamber of Commerce, undated.

"Michigan Underwater Preserves—Sites," Michigan Department of Environmental Quality, http://www.michigan.gov/deq/0,1607,7-135-3313_3677_3701-14591--,00.html.

Nevill, John. "Monsignor B Had Busy Time in Early Days at DeTour," Sault Ste. Marie Evening News, June 24, 1954, http://207.75.94.2/bateski.html.

Polk, Amy. "Fine Arts Council to Rescue DeTour Church Hall From Disrepair," The St. Ignace News, Oct. 12, 2006, http://www.stignacenews.com/news/2006/1012/News/012.html.

"Sacred Heart, DeTour," Diocese of Marquette, http://www.dioceseofmarquette.org/parishhistory.asp?parishID=215.

"St. Stanislaus Kostka, Goetzville," Diocese of Marquette, http://www.dioceseofmarquette.org/parishhistory.asp?parishID=213.

Mile Marker 369

"Native Languages of the Americas: Chippewa (Ojibway, Anishinaabe, Ojibwa)," Native Languages of the Americas, http://www.native-languages.org/chippewa.htm.

Exit 373

"Burbot," Fish of the Great Lakes, Wisconsin Sea Grant, http://www.seagrant.wisc.edu/greatlakesfish/burbot.html.

Exit 378

"A Brief History of Kinross/Kincheloe Air Force Base," Kinross Charter Township, http://www.kinross.net/history.htm.

"Gray Wolf (Canis lupus):Recovery in Minnesota, Wisconsin, and Michigan," Midwest Region, U.S. Fish and Wildlife Service, http://www.fws.gov/midwest/wolf/recovery/r3wolfct.htm.

"Iven Carl Kincheloe, Jr., Captain, United States Air Force," Arlington National Cemetery, http://www.arlingtoncemetery.net/kinchel.htm.

Exit 386

Dobner, Jennifer and Glen Johnson. "Romney family tree has polygamy branch," Associated Press/The Boston Globe), http://www.boston.com/news/nation/articles/2007/02/24/romney_family_tree_has_polygamy_branch/.

Henslee, K.A. "2005 Seney National Wildlife Refuge Trumpeter Swan Monitoring Project," Midwest Region, U.S. Fish and Wildlife Service, www.fws.gov/Midwest/seney/documents/Tswans05.pdf.

"Iversons Snowshoe and Furniture," Iversons Snowshoe and Furniture," http://www.iversons-snowshoes.com/.

"Seney National Wildlife Refuge," Michigan Department of Natural Resources, http://www.dnr.state.mi.us/publications/pdfs/wildlife/viewingguide/up/29Seney/index.htm.

Mile Marker 387

"Lake Superior Circle Tour," MichiganHighways.org, http://www.michiganhighways.org/other/lsct.html.

"Lake Superior Circle Tour," Great Lakes Information Network, http://www.great-lakes.net/tourism/circletour/superior/#road.

"Lake Superior," Great Lakes Information Network, http://www.great-lakes.net/lakes/superior.html.

Mile Marker 389

"The Early Immersion of Étienne Brûlé," GreatCanadianLakes.com, http://www.greatcanadianlakes.com/ontario/lake_ontario/history-home.html.

"Étienne Brûlé," MSN Encarta, http://encarta.msn.com/encyclopedia_761554794/Etienne_Brule.html

Explorers and Discoverers of the World. Detroit: Gale Research, 1993.

"Étienne Brûlé (c. 1592-1633): The First Coureur de Bois," Canadiana.org, http://www.canadiana.org/hbc/person/brule_e.html.

Exit 392

"Cultural Division - Historical Preservation & Outreach - Sault Tribe History," The Sault Tribe of Chippewa Indians, http://www.saulttribe.com/index.php?option=com_content&task=view&id=29&Itemid=205.

Exit 394

"About Lake Superior State University," Lake Superior State University, http://www.lssu.edu/about/facts.php.

Arbic, Bernie, "Sault Ste. Marie: City of the Rapids," Michigan History, January/February 2004, http://www.michiganhistorymagazine.com/extra/soo/saulthht.pdf.

"Establishing a Fort," Lake Superior State University, http://www.lssu.edu/
  brady/history.html.
"Sault Visitor's Guide," booklet, Sault Convention and Visitors Bureau, 1994.

At the International Bridge

"About the Bridge: Welcome to the International Bridge," Michigan
  Department of Transportation," http://www.michigan.gov/mdot/0,1607,
  7-151-9618_11032-22039--,00.html.
"100th Anniversary: Hydroelectric Power Plant," Edison Sault Electric Co.,
  http://www.edisonsault.com/The%20HydroPlant/esehydro.htm.

INDEX

305

306